Praise for *The Woman's Hour*

"At the heart of democracy lies the ballot box, and Elaine Weiss's unforgettable book tells the story of the female leaders who—in the face of towering economic, racial, and political opposition—fought for and won American women's right to vote. Unfolding over six weeks in the summer of 1920, *The Woman's Hour* is both a page-turning drama and an inspiration for everyone, young and old, male and female, in these perilous times. So much could have gone wrong, but these American women would not take no for an answer: their triumph is our legacy to guard and emulate."

—Hillary Rodham Clinton

"Stirring, definitive, and engrossing . . . Weiss brings a lucid, lively, journalistic tone to the story. . . . *The Woman's Hour* is compulsory reading."

—NPR.org

"Weiss is a clear and genial guide with an ear for telling language. . . . She also shows a superb sense of detail, and it's the deliciousness of her details that suggests certain individuals warrant entire novels of their own. . . . Weiss's thoroughness is one of the book's great strengths. So vividly had she depicted events that by the climactic vote (spoiler alert: the amendment was ratified!), I got goose bumps."

—Curtis Sittenfeld, *The New York Times Book Review*

"With a skill reminiscent of Robert Caro, [Weiss] turns the potentially dry stuff of legislative give-and-take into a drama of courage and cowardice."

—Fergus Bordewich, *The Wall Street Journal*

"Anyone interested in the history of our country's ongoing fight to put its founding values into practice—as well as those seeking the roots of current political fault lines—would be well-served by picking up Elaine Weiss's *The Woman's Hour*. By focusing in on the final battle in the war to win women the right to vote, told from the point of view of its foot soldiers, Weiss humanizes both the women working in favor of the amendment and those working against it, exposing all their convictions, tactics, and flaws. She never shies away from the complicating issue of race; the frequent conflict and occasional sabotage that occurred between women's suffrage activists and the leaders of the nascent civil rights movement make for some of the most fascinating material in the book."

—Margot Lee Shetterly, author of the #1 *New York Times* bestseller *Hidden Figures*

"A genteel but bare-knuckled political thriller . . . The account reads like a reality show, impossible to predict. . . . Weiss's narrative is energetic and buoyant even at the most critical moments."   —*Ms. Magazine*

"Weiss tells the story in gripping detail. We all know, of course, how the vote ended, but most modern readers will be astonished to learn exactly how it all went down. . . . Weiss's narrative is an out-and-out nail-biter."

—*The Christian Science Monitor*

"Remarkably entertaining . . . A timely examination of a shining moment in the ongoing fight to achieve a more perfect union."

—*Publishers Weekly*, (starred and boxed review)

"[An] important tale . . . Weiss's reportage . . . enables her to add splashes of color [and] wonderful dimension."   —*USA Today*

"A nonfiction political thriller . . . Weiss zeroes in on the final campaign of the suffrage movement."   —Bustle.com

"Riveting . . . Weiss provides a multidimensional account of the political crusade. . . . The result is a vivid work of American history."

—*The National Book Review*

"Even the most informed feminists will learn a thing or two."

—*HelloGiggles*

"This timely exploration of the history of American gender politics reverberates during the present debate over female equality in all aspects of life and reminds us of how long and complex that struggle has been."

—*The Knoxville News-Sentinel*

"An intriguing, timely read. Ripe for book club discussion."
—*SouthCoast Today*

"A page-turner . . . The story here is told in all its ugliness."
—*New York Journal of Books*

"This well-researched and well-documented history reveals how pro-suffragists sometimes compromised racial equality to win white women's enfranchisement, and that, although the Nineteenth Amendment was ratified, there exists to this day an ongoing battle to effect universal, unrestricted suffrage."
—*Library Journal*

"Weiss does a wonderful job of laying out the background of the American women's suffrage movement. . . . A lively slice of history filled with political drama, Weiss's book captures a watershed moment for American women."
—*Book Page*

"Writing with the verve this story deserves, Elaine Weiss brings to life the women who rallied in Nashville to get the nineteenth amendment ratified. From the gracious Carrie Chapman Catt to the radical Sue White, they were fearless in battle and elated in a victory that changed history. Three cheers for Weiss for this spirited and inspiring account."
—Lynne Cheney, author of the *New York Times* bestseller *James Madison*

"Imaginatively conceived and vividly written, *The Woman's Hour* gives us a stirring history of women's long journey to suffrage and to political influence. Making bold connection with race and class, Weiss's splendid book is as much needed today as it was in 1940 when Eleanor Roosevelt noted that men hate women with power. As every victory since the Civil War faces the wrecker, *The Woman's Hour* is an inspiration in the continuing struggles for suffrage, and for race and gender justice, and for democracy."
—Blanche Wiesen Cook, author of the *New York Times* bestseller *Eleanor Roosevelt*

PENGUIN BOOKS

THE WOMAN'S HOUR

Elaine Weiss is an award-winning journalist and writer whose work has appeared in *The Atlantic, Harper's, The New York Times,* and *The Christian Science Monitor,* as well as in reports and documentaries for National Public Radio and Voice of America. A MacDowell Colony Fellow and Pushcart Prize Editor's Choice honoree, she is also the author of *Fruits of Victory: The Woman's Land Army in the Great War* (Potomac Books/University of Nebraska Press). She lives in Baltimore.

Look for the Penguin Readers Guide in the back of this book.
To access Penguin Readers Guides online, visit
penguinrandomhouse.com.

ALSO BY ELAINE WEISS

Fruits of Victory

The Woman's Hour

◆ ◆ ◆

THE GREAT FIGHT TO WIN
THE VOTE

◆ ◆ ◆

Elaine Weiss

Elaine Weiss

PENGUIN BOOKS

PENGUIN BOOKS
An imprint of Penguin Random House LLC
penguinrandomhouse.com

First published in the United States of America by Viking Penguin,
an imprint of Penguin Random House LLC, 2018
Published in Penguin Books 2019

CREDITS

First Insert, between pages 144 and 145
1: New York State Library; 2: (top) Library of Congress, (bottom) Wiki-Commons; 3: (top) New
York Public Library, (bottom) Library of Congress; 4: (top) Jackie Partin, Grundy County,
Tennesssee, (bottom) Library of Congress; 5: (top) University of Rochester Library, Rare Books and
Special Collections, (bottom) Tennessee State Library and Archives; 6: (top) Bryn Mawr College
Special Collections, (bottom) Tennessee State Museum; 7: (top) Tennessee State Library and
Archives, (bottom) Library of Congress; 8: (top) Nashville Public Library Special Collections,
(bottom) Library of Congress; 9: (top) New York Public Library, (bottom) Library of Congress; 10
(both): Library of Congress; 11 (both): Bryn Mawr College Special Collections; 12: (top) Library of
Virginia, (bottom) National Woman's Party; 13: (top) Library of Congress, (bottom) First Baptist
Church, Capitol Hill, Nashville; 14 (both): Tennessee State Library and Archives; 15 (both): Library
of Congress; 16: Tennessee State Library and Archives

Second Insert, between pages 304 and 305
1: (top) Library of Congress, (bottom) Nashville Public Library; 2: (top) Bryn Mawr College Special
Collections, (bottom) Library of Congress; 3: (top) National Woman's Party, (middle and bottom)
Tennessee State Library and Archives; 4: (top) Memphis Public Library, (bottom) Schlesinger Library,
Radcliffe Institute, Harvard University; 5 (both), 6 (top and middle): Tennessee State Library and
Archives; 6: (bottom) *Washington Herald,* August 15, 1920; 7, 8 (both), 9 (both): Tennessee State
Library and Archives; 10 (both): Calvin McClung Historical Collection, Knox County Public
Library; 11: (top) Bryn Mawr College Special Collections, (bottom) Library of Congress; 12: (top)
Library of Congress, (bottom) Bryn Mawr College Special Collections; 13: (top) Division of Political
History, National Museum of American History, Smithsonian Institution, (bottom) Tennessee State
Library and Archives; 14: Special Collections, University of California, Davis; 15: (top) Marchand
Archives, the History Project, University of California, Davis, (bottom) National Susan B. Anthony
Museum and House; 16: Alan LeQuire

ISBN 9780525429722 (hardcover)
ISBN 9780143128991 (paperback)
ISBN 9780698407831 (ebook)

Printed in the United States of America
7   9   10   8

Set in Adobe Garamond Pro
Designed by Francesca Belanger

In memory of my parents,
who took their little girl into the voting booth,
let her pull the magic curtain, and taught me
to treasure my right to vote

and my dear friend Natalie Moore Babbitt,
who taught me how to be a writer

The time has come to shout aloud in every city, village and hamlet, and in tones so clear and jubilant that they will reverberate from every mountain peak and echo from shore to shore: "The Woman's Hour has struck."

—Carrie Chapman Catt,
"The Crisis," Presidential Address to the National
American Woman Suffrage Association, September 1916

The right of citizens of the United States to vote shall not be denied or abridged by the United States or by any State on account of sex.

—Nineteenth Amendment of the U.S. Constitution

CONTENTS

The
Woman's Hour

Introduction

O N A SATURDAY EVENING in mid-July 1920, three women raced toward Nashville's Union Station on steam-powered trains. They each traveled alone, carrying a small suitcase, a handbag, a folder stuffed with documents. They were unremarkable in appearance, dressed in demure cotton dresses and summer hats; their fellow passengers could hardly imagine the dramatic purpose they shared: they had all been summoned to command forces in what would prove to be one of the pivotal political battles in American history.

This is the story of that battle, the furious campaign to secure the final state needed to ratify the Nineteenth Amendment to the U.S. Constitution, giving women the most fundamental right of democracy—the vote.

Carrie Catt, the president of the National American Woman Suffrage Association, the preeminent suffrage organization in the nation, was on a southbound train from New York City. Josephine Pearson, president of the Tennessee State Association Opposed to Woman Suffrage, traveled north from her family home in the Cumberland Mountains of Tennessee. Sue White, a young activist for the National Woman's Party, the "militant wing" of the suffrage movement, came fresh from a protest in the Midwest.

They converged on Nashville for the explosive climax of American women's seven-decade struggle for equal citizenship, and there was much at stake: thirty-six state approvals were required for ratification, and thirty-five were in hand. If the Tennessee legislature ratified the Nineteenth Amendment, woman suffrage would become the law of the land and twenty-seven million women would be able to vote, just in time for the fall presidential elections; if the legislature rejected it, the amendment might never be enacted. It all came down to Tennessee.

There were powerful forces opposing federal woman suffrage as it approached the legal finish line: political, corporate, and ideological adversaries intent upon stopping the Nineteenth Amendment. Some of the most vociferous foes of enfranchisement were the women "Antis" such as Josephine

Pearson, who feared that women's entrance into the polling booth would hasten the nation's moral collapse. The "Suffs" had reason to worry, as the amendment had already been rejected by nearly all the southern states, for the same blatantly racist reasons as put forth by Tennessee: if women got the vote, black women would also be entitled to the ballot. The presidential candidates were playing their own games, using woman suffrage as a pawn. This was the moment of reckoning, and both sides were willing to use every possible weapon to prevail.

Over the course of the next six weeks, the three campaign commanders were joined by more than a thousand women and men from around the state and across the country—Suffs, Antis, governors and senators, political operatives, corporate lobbyists, and beleaguered legislators—all pouring into Nashville to enter the fray. The conflict quickly devolved into a vicious face-off, brimming with dirty tricks and cutting betrayals, sexist rancor, racial bigotry, booze, and the Bible, with the ghosts of the Civil War hovering over the proceedings and jitters lingering from the Great War amplifying the tension. The outcome remained in doubt until the very last moment.

The intensity of this battle in Nashville, the strength and nature of the suffrage opposition—led by women!—the racial dimensions of the conflict, and the uncertainty of the outcome may seem surprising to us now, even shocking. It's too easy to imagine that the enfranchisement of American women simply arrived, like some evolutionary imperative, a natural step in the gradual march of progress. Or as a gift eventually bestowed by wise men on their grateful wives, daughters, and sisters. The women asked politely, staged a few picturesque marches, hoisted a few picket signs, and without much drama, "Votes for Women" was achieved. That's not how it happened.

The very idea that women should have the right to participate in a government "by and for the people" was long considered radical, even dangerous, in the United States. Despite Abigail Adams's exhortation in 1776 to her husband, John, to "remember the Ladies" when forming the new American democracy, our esteemed Founding Fathers had absolutely no intention of giving women a voice in public affairs. Throughout the nineteenth and early twentieth centuries, women were condemned from the pulpit and in the press for thinking about suffrage; they were spit upon and pelted with rotten eggs for speaking out about it; and they were jailed for demanding it.

The struggle for woman suffrage was a long, bitter fight. It was waged on street corners and atop soapboxes, in city halls, Grange Halls, and the halls of Congress; it was fought in parlors and kitchens and bedrooms, under statehouse domes, at the bench of the U.S. Supreme Court, and finally in the Capitol building in Nashville and the elegant lobby of the nearby Hotel Hermitage.

Winning the vote required seventy-two years of ceaseless agitation by three generations of dedicated, fearless suffragists, who sought to overturn centuries of law and millennia of tradition concerning gender roles. The women who launched the movement were dead by the time it was completed; the women who secured its final success weren't born when it began. It took more than nine hundred local, state, and national campaigns, involving tens of thousands of grassroots volunteers, financed by millions of dollars of mostly small (and a few large) donations by women across the country.

The movement developed great women orators, talented executives, and tenacious lobbyists. It nurtured feminist philosophers and astute politicians who—though they had no legal standing or governmental representation—learned to manipulate the levers of political power and pull the strings of public opinion. Women who had never had public lives were emboldened to speak out, to march in the streets, even to raise picket signs in public protest for the first time. Some were more strongly radicalized in their quest for civic equality and became willing to commit acts of civil disobedience and go to jail in pursuit of the franchise. Through the decades, "the Cause" changed the way women saw themselves and transformed society's view of women.

The controversy over ratification of the Nineteenth Amendment—and, more broadly, the long battle over woman suffrage—wasn't simply a political argument, it was also a social, cultural, and moral debate, a precursor to what we now call "culture wars," raising issues that were complex and divisive. Allowing women to vote had the potential to not only upend the electoral process and the political status quo, but also alter societal and personal relations and—according to suffrage's opponents—disturb the home and endanger the family. The political became the personal, and for many men, as well as some women, it was frightening.

That women might oppose enfranchising and empowering their own sex seems counterintuitive, even preposterous, but the stance of the females against suffrage, the Antis, opens a fascinating window on the role of social and religious conservatives in our public policy decisions. Like the key sociopolitical issues of today—from reproductive rights to same-sex marriage—attitudes toward woman suffrage divided communities, families, and friends, thrusting women into opposing camps.

While this book chronicles a great triumph—women mobilizing for their own political freedom—it also poses some uncomfortable questions about the sincerity of American democracy, questions as urgent today as they were in 1920. Our cherished national self-image is of a proud democratic republic, one where the citizen's right to vote is both a sacred trust and the cornerstone of our government by the people: but that image is only a partial reflection of reality. From the nation's founding, Americans have had—and continue to have—a deeply ambivalent attitude toward full participatory democracy and a conflicted stance toward universal suffrage.

Voting rights have been a contested issue from the very beginning of the American experiment. When the founders wrote "We the People," they really meant "We the White, Wealthy Men." Despite much lofty rhetoric, all men were not created equal, and women didn't count at all.

The rest of our national history can be seen as a continuing push toward—and reaction against—expanding the franchise to include those groups of citizens purposely left outside. Fear of the mob, fear of the other, and fear for the erosion of white political hegemony made for slow and hesitant progress, punctuated by contractions and reversals. Access to, or denial of, the ballot became an instrument for gaining political party advantage, a dynamic put to use in Nashville and one that remains prevalent today, as voting rights for minority groups continue to be jeopardized by intimidation and violated by suppression, all for partisan ends. The cry of "states' rights" and antipathy toward federal oversight of voting rights were voiced loudly in Nashville in the summer of 1920 and still echo in newspaper headlines today.

Holding the franchise, exercising the vote, is a form of power, so this book is—as suffrage leader Alice Paul once described her primary goal—about women claiming their rightful power of citizenship. And it is also about the forces that strenuously resisted that claim. "Power concedes nothing without a demand," insisted the great universal suffragist Frederick Douglass, and he taught this essential lesson to the early advocates of votes for women.

But this sort of power cannot be wrested simply through demand: it requires a huge societal shift, a slow change of public attitudes, eventually translated into public policy. Such change can be brought about only by decades of patient persuasion and persistent pressure, transforming an idea once considered unthinkable into something inevitable. Winning the franchise was a crucial milestone in American women's struggle to secure their legal, economic, and societal rights, claiming their place in the modern world; but that struggle continues.

As this is an American story, it is, inevitably, about race. The cause of woman suffrage was, from the very beginning, entwined with contemporary efforts to emancipate and enfranchise the nation's black citizens, but the relationship between the movements was often tense. When the Nineteenth Amendment reached its decisive hour in a southern city, the legacy of that historic alliance was tested, and prevailing racial bigotry played a dominant role. The long shadow of the Civil War and its violent aftermath also affect these events; the threat to southern traditions and institutions, the power of states' rights, and the emotional scars of the Confederacy's defeat all come into play in Nashville, fifty-five years after the war's last battle.

There is a heartening, even thrilling, lesson to be found here, too: ordinary women banding together to become activists, keeping faith through decades of humiliation and discouragement to challenge an oppressive system and force change. There is also a chastening lesson to be learned from the moral compromises these mostly white, middle-class suffragists make in pursuit of their own freedom, leaving their black sisters, and some of their own ideals, behind. And in the actions of the forces aligned against suffrage there is an instructive example of just how far some Americans were willing to go to protect their own careers, business interests, and entitlement by preventing others from obtaining their rights.

The crusade for woman suffrage stands as one of the defining civil rights movements in the history of our country, and its organizing strategies, lobbying techniques, and nonviolent protest actions became the model for the civil rights campaigns to follow in the twentieth and twenty-first centuries.

Although these events took place almost a century ago, the story's compelling themes—power and political will, race and gender equality, states' rights and voting rights, and corporate influence in politics—remain urgent, present-day concerns.

It all begins with three women on their way to Nashville.

Chapter 1

❖ ❖ ❖

To Nashville

CARRIE CHAPMAN CATT had spent a long night, day, and early evening on trains clattering over a thousand miles of track from New York City to Nashville. In the hours she wasn't reading field reports and legal documents, rimless eyeglasses perched on her nose, she read the newspapers and indulged in the guilty pleasure of a detective novel.

By the time the train pulled into Nashville in the dusky twilight, it was hard to make out the copper-and-bronze statue of the messenger god Mercury perched atop the Union Station tower, greeting travelers to the bustling capital city. Minerva, the warrior goddess, might have been a more fitting figure for the president of the National American Woman Suffrage Association, Susan B. Anthony's anointed heir, the supreme commander of its great suffrage army, the woman they called "the Chief." Carrie Catt had been summoned to lead her troops into the fray one last time. At least she dearly hoped this might be the last time.

She'd already devoted half of her life to the Cause, three decades of constant work and travel. Her hair was silver and wavy, and she wore it short and brushed close, parted in the center, easy to groom on the run. Her face, once angular and strikingly handsome, was fleshier now. Her heavy eyelids drooped a bit, and the line of her jaw had softened, but she retained the same sly, thin-lipped smile, piercing blue eyes, and arched eyebrows that made her look either surprised, amused, or annoyed depending upon how she deployed them. She was definitely not amused this evening; she was worried, and she wasn't sure she could take the strain much longer.

It was Catt's job—more precisely, her life's mission—to guide American women to the promised land of political freedom, securing for them the most basic right of democracy, the vote. For more than seventy years, since that first audacious meeting in Seneca Falls in 1848, generations of her suffrage sisters had faced public disdain, humiliation, rotten eggs, violent opposition, and prison as they petitioned, campaigned, lobbied, marched, and pleaded for their simple rights as citizens. Now the promise of the franchise, so long delayed, was within sight; the political emancipation of half of the United States' citizens was at stake. And here, of all places, where she'd never imagined it possible, in the South, in Nashville. Tennessee could become the elusive thirty-sixth state to ratify the federal woman suffrage amendment. Or it could end the quest in failure.

The Tennessee legislature would soon be called into special session to vote on ratifying the Nineteenth Amendment to the U.S. Constitution, popularly called "the Susan B. Anthony Amendment," one simple sentence stating that a citizen's right to vote could not be denied on account of sex. Nothing revolutionary, to Carrie Catt's mind. It was really just a clarification, an essential *correction,* of the Founding Fathers' damned shortsightedness.

Just over a year earlier, in June 1919, the amendment had finally been pushed through both houses of the U.S. Congress—after forty years of willful delay. Catt had kicked up her heels and broken into a wild dance when that news arrived. The amendment then moved to the states for ratification. She knew it would be a tough slog: suffragists had to convince at least thirty-six state legislatures—three-quarters of the forty-eight states in the Union—to accept the amendment, while those opposed needed just thirteen states to vote it down and kill it. The ratification campaign proved even slower and uglier than Catt expected; she had been sure it would be over by now, but it wasn't. By midsummer 1920, thirty-five states had ratified the amendment, eight had rejected, three were refusing to consider; North Carolina and Tennessee were still up in the air, but North Carolina was a sure bet to reject. That left only Tennessee as a possible thirty-sixth state.

If the Tennessee legislature could be persuaded, pressured, cajoled, and coerced (all these techniques would be needed, Catt was certain) to ratify the amendment, suffrage would become federal law, allowing every woman, in every state, to vote in all elections. Victory at last, hallelujah, and just in time for the upcoming presidential election.

But if Tennessee did not ratify, derailing the full enfranchisement of twenty-seven million women before the fall elections, all might be lost. The momentum was stalling after several state legislatures had voted down ratification this past spring and summer. Although the "No" votes in Georgia and Louisiana had surprised no one—nearly every southern state of the old Confederacy had rejected the amendment—the loss in more moderate, midAtlantic Delaware was a shock. A defeat in Tennessee, which enjoyed stronger suffrage sympathies and deeper organization than the other southern states, would allow the forces against suffrage to gain strength, new legal obstacles to be thrown into the path, men to forget what women had contributed to the Great War effort, women to lose heart. That crucial sense of inevitability, the public assumption that to support woman suffrage was simply to keep in step with the march of progress, was faltering. And that infuriating question—is America really ready for women to vote, to be equal citizens?—was bubbling up again. Adding to her agitation, the newspapers were filled with the sorts of stories that gave Americans good reason to be in a sour mood.

Even after seventeen million people had been killed in the so-called Great War, the world was still aflame. The Russian Bolsheviks were invading Poland and vowing to advance into Romania and Bulgaria, Latvia, and Lithuania; the Ottoman Turks were fighting the Greeks while continuing to massacre and deport Armenians; the Irish nationalist Sinn Féin was skirmishing with British troops. Mexico was spiraling into civil war again; factions were battling in China. The premise, trumpeted by so many posters and in so many parades, that American men had fought and died in the War to End All Wars looked to be a fake.

Even the peace seemed chimerical: the negotiations in Paris had dragged on for months, and the U.S. Senate had recently refused to accept the terms of the Treaty of Versailles, objecting to President Wilson's plan for a League of Nations to settle international disputes. Americans wanted nothing more to do with foreign entanglements. Catt thought the league was the only good thing to come out of the horrible war; she'd written and spoken in its favor and was disgusted by the backlash against it.

The war had brought neither the peace nor the prosperity the nation had been promised. As Catt's train sped toward Nashville, streetcar workers were striking in Chicago, coal miners were stuck in long, bloody lockouts in West Virginia, Kentucky, and Illinois, garment workers were threatening in New Jersey. There'd been nationwide steel mill, coal, railroad, and shipbuilding strikes in 1919—more than two thousand strikes around the country—while race riots had erupted in many cities. The postwar economic recession had now deepened into a full-blown depression. National Prohibition, which Catt had supported as a way to protect women and children from alcohol-fueled abuse, was only adding to the climate of violence, as federal agents pulled their enforcement shotguns on backwoods moonshiners and city bootleggers while mobsters jockeyed for turf with machine guns.

Anarchists were taking advantage of the turmoil, and accounts of exploding bombs in mail packages, in cars, and in offices and homes were a staple news item. The government was responding with raids, mass arrests, and deportations of suspected radicals (a pair of Italian anarchists, Nicola Sacco and Bartolomeo Vanzetti had recently been arrested in Massachusetts) authorized by Attorney General A. Mitchell Palmer, whose own home had been bombed the year before. The "Palmer Raids" were executed by his ambitious young assistant J. Edgar Hoover, who'd begun keeping secret files on those who questioned or criticized the government, anyone who wasn't a "Good American." Carrie Catt was also being watched.

And every day this summer there was another article about a cheeky fellow in Boston named Charles Ponzi, who had convinced thousands of people to give him their money with promises of too-good-to-be-true investment returns: double your money in ninety days. Ponzi's clever pyramid scheme was definitely too good to be true, and he would soon be under arrest. Even the national pastime, baseball, was under a cloud of suspicion: rumors were circulating that several Chicago White Sox players had deliberately made bad plays to throw the 1919 World Series in exchange for cash from gamblers. All this only added to the national dyspepsia; Americans felt as if they'd been fed too many lies, taken for chumps one too many times.

The newly minted presidential candidates had quickly picked up on the zeitgeist. Republican nominee Warren Harding was already talking about a return to "normalcy" and "America First," which Catt understood meant a retreat from progressive ideas and a slide back to comfortable, conservative policies. Democrat James Cox was carefully hedging his bets on everything. If the amendment didn't pass now, before the election, before the nation swung into an isolationist, reactionary frame of mind, it might never pass at all.

Miss Josephine Pearson was dusty from the soot flying into her train's open windows and a bit stiff from the hard wooden-slat seat, but she didn't mind the discomforts. Pearson had received a telegram earlier that Saturday at her home in Monteagle, a hamlet perched high on Tennessee's Cumberland Plateau.

It warned that Carrie Catt was coming. "Our forces are being notified to rally at once. Send orders—and come immediately." She was to take command in Nashville.

The summons thrilled her. As president of the Tennessee State Association Opposed to Woman Suffrage and also head of the state division of the Southern Women's League for the Rejection of the Susan B. Anthony Amendment, Josephine was the proud leader of the Tennessee Antis. Now the fight had come home to her Volunteer State. This would be Tennessee's time of trial and, she prayed, triumph. With God's help, it would meet the challenge of beating back the scourge of woman suffrage, holding fast against the feminist epidemic sweeping the nation and now threatening her home. This was her crusade and this was her moment.

She was fifty-two years old, and all of her training—college, graduate degrees, and her years as an educator—had prepared her for this mission. She knew she was doing God's will, fulfilling a sacred vow to her beloved mother, who had understood the dangers of female suffrage, how it mocked the plan of the Creator, undermined women's purity and the noble chivalry of men, and threatened the home and the family. The Bible said a woman's place was in the home, as loving wife and mother, not in the dirty realm of politics, not in the polling booth or in the jury box, where her delicate sensibilities could be assaulted, her morals sullied and even corrupted. Her men knew what was best for her, would protect and cherish her, make laws and decisions for her benefit. Pearson felt there was no need to question the wisdom of Tennessee men or Tennessee laws.

But the threat went beyond this. Woman suffrage could upend the supremacy of the white race and the southern way of life. After the brutal disruptions of the Civil War and the upheavals of Reconstruction—when black men were allowed to vote (and some were even elected to the legislature) but former Confederate soldiers were considered traitors and stripped of their voting rights—the southern states had finally achieved a degree of equilibrium, in terms of restoring racial and political relations, the Pearson family believed. Jim Crow laws kept blacks in their place. But if a federal amendment mandated suffrage for all women, that would mean black women, too. Then Washington could demand that black men be allowed to vote, and that was totally unacceptable.

Barely a week before Mother had died in the summer of 1915, in the library of their house on the Methodist Assembly grounds in Monteagle (Father was a retired Methodist minister), Amanda Pearson had grasped Josephine's hand and implored: "Daughter, when I'm gone—if the Susan B. Anthony Amendment issue reaches Tennessee—promise me, you will take up the opposition, in My Memory!" Josephine bent to kiss her mother's brow, to impress the vow upon her forehead, and answered: "Yes, God helping, I'll keep the faith, Mother!"

So when the telegram arrived late Saturday afternoon, it was with a sense of holy purpose that Josephine Pearson quickly packed her travel case, walked from her house to the Monteagle depot, and bought a one-way ticket for the late train to Nashville.

Even before Josephine made the vow to her mother, she had come to the conclusion that suffrage was a dangerous idea; she arrived at this judgment by what she considered empirical and scholarly investigation, as befitted a woman with higher education and intellectual accomplishments. Early in her career she served as a high school principal and went on to teach English and history at Nashville College for Young Ladies and Winthrop State Normal College for Women in South Carolina. In 1909, she assumed the position of dean and chair of philosophy at Christian College in Columbia, Missouri, at a time when Missourians were debating a woman suffrage measure.

She found she often fell into argument with her colleagues and students about woman suffrage and was frequently the sole naysayer at the faculty table. She began to feel isolated, shunned for her resistance against the popular political tide. She came to resent her faculty colleagues who snubbed her and used their positions to coerce their impressionable students with their terrible suffrage ideas. During semester breaks, Josephine undertook her own version of field research to determine whether women in those few western states where females already had the right to vote, such as Wyoming, were really better off for having the franchise. She collected her own data and conducted interviews and came to the conclusion that suffrage had exposed women to the filth of politics without improving their lives at all. She began to give lectures to antisuffrage audiences and found herself hailed as an Anti leader in the state.

Her academic career in Missouri was cut short in the spring of 1914 by the call to come home to care for her ailing mother, and she returned to Monteagle to nurse her mother and aged father. From her sickbed, Mother continued to write her diatribes against the evils of whiskey and suffrage, and after her death, honoring the vow, Josephine continued the work. She sat at her desk, writing deep into the night, sending her missives to the newspapers in Nashville and Memphis and Chattanooga. The publisher of the *Chattanooga Times,* Adolph Ochs, was especially welcoming to her antisuffrage proclamations; Ochs's editorial pages, in both his Chattanooga paper and its sister publication, *The New York Times,* were firmly in her Anti camp. Pearson's dedication was recognized and she was eventually tapped to become president of the Tennessee antisuffragists. And now, like the Confederate generals whose brave exploits had been extolled in her family's parlor, whose names and deeds she knew by heart, she would stand in defense of the South.

Sue Shelton White departed Columbus, Ohio, for Nashville on July 17, just as five hundred purple, white, and gold suffrage banners and two trunks of picket signs were being readied for action. Sue White and Alice Paul and a dozen other National Woman's Party leaders had gone to Ohio to confront the two men who wanted to be the next president of the United States. Both were from Ohio, which made logistics easier. Governor James Cox was the surprise compromise choice of the fractious Democrats; Warren G. Harding, senator from Ohio, emerged as the Republican candidate. Both seemed like spineless men, eager to please but probably unwilling to put any muscle behind completing the ratification of the Nineteenth Amendment. They'd need to be convinced.

Alice Paul had already announced to the newspapers that her Woman's Party "shock troops" were ready to descend, wave their banners, break out their picket signs, and spend the rest of the summer and fall camped outside Cox's office in Columbus and Harding's home in Marion. She had her eye on the vice presidential candidates, too: Franklin Roosevelt in New York and Calvin Coolidge in Massachusetts. Whichever party did not come through for the nation's women at this crucial juncture would be punished, she promised.

Sue White was by now, at age thirty-three, a veteran picketer. Two years before, she'd left Mrs. Catt's mainstream suffrage organization to join the more aggressive Woman's Party (which had itself splintered from Catt's NAWSA in a dispute over both strategy and tactics), and now White was one of Miss Paul's trusted deputies at headquarters in Washington, the party's research director, and chairwoman of the Woman's Party in her native Tennessee. A few weeks before, she was hoisting a picket sign in front of the Chicago Coliseum, where the Republican Party was in convention. A year earlier, she had been arrested and imprisoned for burning President Wilson in effigy at the gates of the White House. After serving her five days of incarceration, she signed up for the "Prison Special" railroad tour, joining twenty-five of her jailbird Woman's Party comrades, dressed in well-tailored facsimile prison outfits, on a nationwide lecture tour.

Pleading and quiet protestation no longer suited Sue White. She was no longer a genteel Tennessee suffrage lady, like those in Mrs. Catt's camp who abided by the motto "Graciousness is our watch-word" while waiting for men to do them the honor of giving them the vote. She was now one of those suffragists called a militant, a radical, a fanatic, a zealot—and she was proud of it.

White had once been a loyal and active member of Mrs. Catt's National Association, a follower of the moderate, plodding, polite approach to gaining suffrage. Being polite was an important social virtue in Tennessee, even if you were advocating for something as socially unacceptable as women entering the voting booth or taking a seat in a jury box. Sue White had an unfailingly sunny disposition and a quick, warm smile, but she had no patience for the empty niceties of the society set of Nashville or Memphis or Knoxville; she was not part of that world. She grew up poor, was orphaned while still a girl, had to support herself. She became a first-rate court reporter, and she built her own thriving stenography agency. She made her own way. She wanted to study law—it bothered her that she could not serve on the juries whose decisions she dutifully transcribed—but the lawyers at the courthouse laughed at the idea, told her she was being impractical. Nevertheless, she still hoped to become a lawyer someday.

Slim and lithe, her brunette hair cut in a fashionable bob, her dresses simple but stylish, her hat set at a jaunty angle, Sue looked the part of a modern career woman. Sweet but sassy, with a steely resolve behind soft brown eyes, she called herself a "practical idealist." Those who saw her in action called her "Lady Warrior." Everyone liked working with "Miss Sue," as she was affectionately called, men as well as women; they respected her intelligence, appreciated her sense of fairness, marveled at her energy, enjoyed her sense of humor. She had actually admired the NAWSA suffrage women she had worked with in Tennessee, finding them sincere and brave enough to confront the ridicule they faced in their churches, their clubs, and even their homes for their suffrage stance. But these women inhabited a different social world from the one in which Sue lived: they came from old southern families and old money, lived in fine houses, had husbands and servants, did not need to work to pay the rent for a flat.

Though she'd spent more than a decade working with these women within Mrs. Catt's National Association, White now felt more comfortable in Alice Paul's Woman's Party. Paul had rejected NAWSA's state-by-state approach to gaining suffrage; she insisted that all efforts be put toward a federal amendment and demanded that Congress and President Wilson put it through—or else. Paul vowed to make them the target of public spectacles and protests, the kind the nation had never before seen, and she followed through on the threat. Catt and NAWSA wouldn't tolerate this risky "militant" strategy; whether Paul and her rebellious cohort were expelled or voluntarily broke away from the mother organization in late 1913 makes little difference. The American movement split into two rival camps.

The Woman's Party staff was filled with ambitious, impatient, and mostly single young women who could no longer tolerate their second-class citizenship, refused to wait, and were willing to make a fuss. Sue White felt at home among them.

The telegrams and letters urging Carrie Catt to hurry to Tennessee had begun arriving while she was tending her summer flower garden at Juniper Ledge, her house in the town of Briarcliff Manor, about thirty miles north of New York City. It had been such a welcome, if brief, time at home, after more than a year of crisscrossing the country overseeing the state ratification drives. She had just returned from a trip to Geneva, Switzerland, where she presided over the conference of the International Woman Suffrage Alliance, of which she was also president, in its first meeting since the end of the war. It had been a humiliation: more than twenty nations had already granted the vote to women—including Germany! It was a national disgrace to have just fought a war to make the world safe for democracy and yet not allow half the citizens of America to participate in that democracy. As much as she disagreed, vehemently disagreed, with Alice Paul and the flamboyant tactics her Woman's Party had employed during the war, Catt had to admit some of the slogans on their picket signs rang true: "Democracy Begins at Home." Indeed.

Catt sailed home from Europe in the last days of June and was met at the dock with the news that Tennessee might come into play. She dispatched her young aide-de-camp, Marjorie Shuler, to Nashville to survey the situation. Marjorie helped with publicity efforts in the ratification states, was a quick study, and had learned to spot trouble. She'd been in Delaware in May, when the ratification fight took an unexpected bad turn after the Antis' corporate friends swooped into Wilmington with money and gifts and threats. What had seemed like a sure thing had turned into a disastrous disappointment, not only a victory for the Antis, but a dangerous shift in the ratification momentum. The suffragists couldn't allow that to happen again.

Scouting in Nashville, Marjorie met with the Tennessee suffrage leaders, talked to the politicians, read the newspapers, and listened to talk in the hotel lobbies. It was a hornet's nest. The Tennessee suffragists were fractious; the legislature had a well-deserved reputation for susceptibility to bribery; Governor Albert Roberts was embroiled in a nasty primary fight to hold on to his job, and getting tangled in the politics of the amendment's ratification was the last thing he wanted to do. He was being pressured by the White House and the national Democratic Party to call the legislature back into special session to deal with ratification, but he was holding up the amendment for political ransom: he would convene the legislature only after his primary and, presumably, only if he won.

All this dissension made organizing difficult and gave the Antis a ripe opportunity. Marjorie feared the same forces that had sunk the amendment in Delaware were poised to converge and torpedo ratification in Tennessee. "Advise Chief," Shuler wired to NAWSA headquarters in New York, "political situation exactly like Delaware only worse. Regard outlook hopeless under present conditions."

Catt had wanted nothing more than to stay at home at Juniper Ledge. She was tired, her deep-set blue eyes circled in dark, puffy rings. She was tormented by migraine headaches. She was sixty-one years old and had been fighting this battle for so long. She could still feel the sting of the very first time she had confronted the idea of woman suffrage (she hadn't yet known it was a "Cause") many years ago, sitting at her family's kitchen table. Carrie Lane was a pigtailed Iowa farm girl then, bookish and inquisitive, with the earnest self-confidence of a child who knows she is clever. She devoured historical tomes while perched high in a swaying tree bough, taught herself anatomy by pickling rodents' brains in her mother's canning jars, and loved riding her horse to the one-room schoolhouse down the road. Carrie was hungry to learn how the world worked and to be part of it.

Lively political discussions were a dinner table staple in the Lane family; Carrie read the newspapers, she liked to chime in. But on Election Day 1872, with incumbent Ulysses Grant facing off against crusading newspaper publisher Horace Greeley, thirteen-year-old Carrie watched as her father and the farm's hired men prepared to ride into town to vote, dressed in their Sunday best, while her smart, politically minded mother, an ardent Greeley supporter, remained in her house frock.

Shouldn't she be getting ready to go with the other grown-ups? Carrie asked her mother. Wasn't she going to vote for Greeley? Carrie's father, her older brother, and the hired hands erupted in peals of laughter; worst of all, even her mother laughed. She still remembered the bewilderment and embarrassment, the hot tears welling up. Women couldn't vote, only men, her father explained, didn't she realize that? It was too important a civic duty to be left to women. Carrie grew angry: her mother knew as much about the candidates and the issues as her father, maybe even more. Her smirking brother Charles was no smarter than she was. The guffawing farmhands couldn't even read! Carrie could hear the men still laughing in the wagon as they drove off toward town. She felt as if she'd been slapped.

She dedicated her life to changing the laws that barred women from voting. Now, here she was, a twice widowed woman, twice elected to the presidency of the National American Woman Suffrage Association. Her name was familiar in every American home and foreign capital, her comments appeared on the front pages of all the newspapers, and her notes to the White House were given prompt reply. She could demand audiences with kings, presidents, and senators, prime ministers, maharajas, and cigar-chomping mayors. She was the leader of a giant army: nearly two million women and men were members of the National Association's local affiliates, millions more were supporters and sympathizers, and in the International Woman Suffrage Alliance, the women of dozens of nations were organizing and agitating under her guidance. She led them with soaring oratory and nuts-and-bolts directives, with emotional exhortation and legalistic logic— always leavened with a sprinkle of dry humor.

During her years in the movement she'd seen slow—agonizingly slow— progress. On the wall of her office at NAWSA headquarters, as well as on the wall of Alice Paul's Woman's Party offices in Washington, hung a large "Suffrage Map" of the United States, with different colors and patterns marking the types of suffrage available to women in each state. (States hold the power to make their own election laws, unless superseded by federal law.) The map looked like a crazy quilt of dots, stripes, and crosshatches designating the states where women enjoyed full suffrage, able to vote in all elections and primaries, and where they could vote only in certain types of elections, such as school board or municipal or presidential. State politicians seemed more amenable to granting this kind of "limited" suffrage, as they could be confident that women would have no say in state policy decisions or patronage. Colored in black on the map were the states where there was still no franchise for women at all and little chance there ever would be. The federal amendment was the only way to equalize the map, paint it all in a radiant full-suffrage design.

She was a firm believer in evolution, in both biological and social realms; her faith in it kept her optimistic, confident of progress. Now it was her job to carry its glorious prospect to Tennessee. For Carrie Catt, woman suffrage was not simply a political goal; it was nothing less than the next logical step in the moral evolution of humankind.

Union Station was the pride of Nashville: a flying-buttressed, castle-grand monument to the capital city's energy and commerce; a gray limestone temple dedicated to the power of the railroad industry in Tennessee. But for Josephine Pearson, pulling into Union Station was like entering the large, very large, house of family friends; indeed, the man who envisioned and built the station, Major Eugene Castner Lewis, was something of a godfather to Josephine. The likeness of Louise Lewis, one of the major's four daughters (all of whom were Josephine's good friends), loomed above the whole station, emerging from the south wall in the form of a classically berobed, bas-relief figure of Miss Nashville.

Pearson was born just three years after the Confederacy's fall, in the fraught time of Reconstruction, when Tennesseans felt punished and humiliated. She was spoon-fed horror tales of the Civil War, laced with nostalgia for the Lost Cause: a potent combination that made a deep impression. This federal amendment, with its demand that Tennessee sacrifice its honor and traditions, submit once again to Washington's yoke, hearkened back to those times, stirring bitter memories. It must be repulsed. Tennesseans must not allow Nashville to be besieged by Yankees once again; it must not allow carpetbaggers from the North to further rend the South's social fabric. Mrs. Catt might come to Tennessee with her northern lady troops and her regalia and fancy weapons, but the Feminist Peril would be halted here. As Josephine Pearson saw it, this was a fight for the soul of Tennessee, it was a "Holy War."

Pearson was a patriot and a civic-minded woman, active in the Monteagle Ladies Club, her local Methodist church, and her chapter of the Woman's Christian Temperance Union. She did her bit for the Red Cross during the war and advocated for economic development through better roads as chairwoman of the Cumberland division of the Dixie Highway Association ladies' auxiliary. She believed in duty. And so Josephine Pearson suspended her teaching career to give all her time to antisuffrage work, mortgaging her property and taking boarders into the old house in Monteagle to make ends meet.

While her train approached the Nashville station, Sue White had time to reflect upon the meeting a day earlier in Columbus with the Democratic presidential candidate, Governor Cox. It had gone rather well, she thought. With the threat of Woman's Party picketers outside his door ready to pounce, he was most conciliatory, issuing a strong pro-suffrage statement to the press and promising to do all he could to line up Governor Roberts and all the Tennessee Democrats behind the ratification drive.

Satisfied for the moment with Cox's professed intentions, Alice Paul and her Ohio troops were now turning their fire toward the Republican candidate, Senator Harding, who expected to officially accept his party's nomination from the front porch of his home in Marion the following week. The Woman's Party would be there to greet him.

Now, however, Sue White was needed in Nashville to launch the party's campaign in Tennessee. She had already scoped out the situation and it did not present a pretty picture. She had given Miss Paul her candid assessment in a long letter: "The more I look into the Tennessee situation, the more I realize that we face a terrific fight," she told Paul. "The anti suffragists have already begun work, appealing, as they always do in Southern campaigns, to deeply seated prejudices and pouring vitriol into old wounds." Unless suffragists committed themselves fully and fought "relentlessly," she warned, Tennessee was in danger of being lost. And perhaps, with it, the amendment.

Now it was going to be Sue White's job to run that relentless campaign. She had never been fully in charge of a state campaign before, and it gave her a bit of a shiver to think of the challenges that lay ahead. She knew full well that the Woman's Party could not do it alone; in truth, there were not that many members of the Woman's Party in Tennessee. The state's mainstream suffrage leaders were appalled by the party's tactics, and the average

Tennessean still considered the party's picketing and protest actions during the war unpatriotic. To accomplish the all-important goal of ratification, Sue White understood that she was going to have to forge some sort of working relationship with her erstwhile state suffrage colleagues. It might be awkward, but White was willing to swallow a slice of humble pie for the sake of the Cause.

The train arrived and White mounted the steps from the platform into Union Station's glass-ceilinged main hall. On the far side of the hall was a bas-relief replica of the 1900 *Limited* train pulled by a Bully 108 locomotive, the pride of the L&N line, seeming to burst through the wall. On another wall was the grand station clock, guarded by the figures of Time and Progress, with Mr. Progress gripping a railroad wheel to his chest. All around her, draped over each of the station's archways, were the angels of Tennessee commerce, twenty carved winged maidens each holding an important state resource or product in her outstretched hands: a sheaf of barley, boll of cotton, lump of coal, ingot of ore, cornucopia of fruit, and flask of whiskey, good Tennessee bourbon, all the products the railroad carried to market to make the state great and prosperous. As she hurried through the station, Sue White must have realized she was surrounded by the symbolic renderings of the powerful interests—railroads, liquor, and manufacturing—that would soon be arrayed against her and her Cause.

Carrie Catt braced herself as her train pulled into the station at about half-past eight that Saturday evening. A comb would be a good idea, her hair was probably a fright, her careful center part off-kilter. There would certainly be reporters at the station, and she had better prepare something clever to say. She noticed that reporters these days enjoyed getting quotes from Alice Paul; she provided them with florid, perfectly sensational material, a far cry from Carrie's own carefully modulated statements. It galled Catt no end.

She had not modulated her own statements to her Tennessee suffrage leaders; during the past two weeks she'd mailed them stern, pointed letters of instruction and admonition. They were very fine and capable women, but she warned them: they had to set aside their silly rivalries and pull together, presenting an "absolute, united, optimistic front turned toward the enemy." And they had better get ready for an ugly fight: "The Anti-Suffs will flood Tennessee with the most outrageous literature it has ever been your lot to read," she told them, drawing from her experience in the other southern states. "It will contain outright lies, innuendoes, and near truths, which are more damaging than lies. It will be extremely harmful, and the 'nigger question' will be put forth in the ways to arouse the greatest possible prejudice." The race issue always reared its ugly head in the South.

"Whatever you do or whatever you think, allow me to urge you not to underestimate the power of the opposition which will be applied to the thirty-sixth state."

Catt shared her deep misgivings with Anne Dudley, the Nashville suffrage leader to whom she felt closest, in a chillingly candid evaluation of the situation, written just four days before she boarded the train for Nashville: "At this time, I do not believe that there is a ghost of a chance of ratification in Tennessee."

When Catt stepped off the train, Marjorie Shuler was there on the platform to greet her along with Catherine Kenny, a seasoned Nashville suffrage veteran who was shepherding the ratification effort for Catt's new League of Women Voters. They had a redcap take Mrs. Catt's little travel bag up the long flight of stairs from the platforms into the Union Station main hall, and as they made their way up the steps, they briefed Mrs. Catt on what awaited. The reporters were there, the press swarming Mrs. Catt as she entered the grand hall. "I've come to look over the situation," she pronounced rather breezily. She would be staying no longer than a few days.

"All the states consider Tennessee the queen of the Southern states and the leader in all progressive matters," Catt told the reporters. "Suffrage supporters feel certain that Tennessee will rise to the occasion and use its decisive vote for the women. The eyes of the country and the world are centered here at Nashville." Carrie Catt was demonstrating that confident, optimistic attitude that she'd urged the suffrage women of Tennessee to adopt. Whether she believed it or not.

The Hotel Hermitage in Nashville was a much grander place than Josephine Pearson might normally have chosen. When she registered at the desk she requested the cheapest room and, she added, a room far away from Mrs. Carrie Catt. Her room was stifling, and she was not accustomed to Nashville summer heat; it was nothing like the cool mountain night air in Monteagle. But she came up with an ingenious solution.

Miss Pearson sat naked in the bathtub, cold water trickling onto her toes, a candlestick telephone in her hands, and began her work. She gripped the telephone shaft and spoke into the daffodil-shaped mouthpiece: "Line me up with New York," she directed the switchboard operator. Upon completing one call, she went on to the next; she had a long list. "Put me through to Boston."

She had orders to relay. She had forces to mobilize, and so into the night she sat. "Connect me to Mobile." From the depths of her moist refuge, Josephine Pearson called her allies around the country, those who stood ready to provide the resources required for this fight to defend American civilization. Into the telephone she sounded the alarm: Mrs. Catt is here. Send help. We are under attack.

Chapter 2

• • •

Lay of the Land

I N THE MORNING, on the third floor of the Hotel Hermitage, Carrie Catt clipped her pince-nez eyeglasses onto her lacy blouse and prepared to survey the battleground terrain. It was a minefield, that was certain.

Nashville was one of the few American cities she'd not visited on a tour or campaign, but she had traveled to other parts of Tennessee. The first trip was with Susan Anthony in their 1895 swing (it might be better described as a trudge) through the southern states, trying to drum up interest in votes for women. They made their way through five states in four weeks, rallying, educating, and organizing clubs. They preached the suffrage gospel in cities and small towns, but the South was hard ground for sowing suffrage seeds, the social and political culture unyielding. To save money, they stayed in the homes of host suffragists, and Catt often had to share a bed with Aunt Susan, who was, thankfully, quite thin.

Catt returned to Memphis in 1900 as the featured speaker at the Tennessee Equal Rights Association state convention and again in 1916, as the newly reelected president of the National American Woman Suffrage Association, attempting to heal the rupture within the state's suffrage ranks. To her mind it was a stupid argument: the Memphis ladies didn't like the Nashville and Chattanooga ladies; their noses were out of joint because Memphis hadn't been chosen for the 1914 NAWSA convention. It wasn't about tactics or ideology or anything significant; it was a catfight, plain and simple.

Catt had naively thought she could breeze into town and broker a peace accord, but she failed. The warring Suffs kept at one another for several more years. At the same time, Catt had her own suffrage rift to deal with, the one with Alice Paul and her contingent, but that was about strategy and philosophy, she believed, not personality. The Tennessee women did manage to patch things up enough to put a limited suffrage bill through the legislature the previous year. But it was by all accounts a near thing.

They were splintered anew by this gubernatorial race. Suffragists opposed to Governor Roberts refused to work with Suffs who supported him. The governor refused to work with any suffragists who opposed him in the primary—or even women whose husbands opposed him—all those he considered his enemies. Republican Suffs were leery of working with Democratic Suffs, lest a Democratic state get credit for putting the amendment over the top. And then there were the Woman's Party people, going their own unpredictable, and to Catt's mind unhelpful, way; at least there weren't too many of them here. Competing ratification committees were being formed. Separate polls of the legislature were being taken. There was harping all around. Catt had no patience for this; it was embarrassing and dangerous.

She knew that if the political men of the state discovered such internal strife among the Suffs, they could easily dismiss the campaign for the amendment as a "woman's fight" and find plenty of excuses for declining to ratify. They'd unpack the old chestnuts: women were too emotional, too high-strung, for the rough-and-tumble of political life, too inclined to hair-pulling spats. Catt resented having to play referee in this sorority squabble; the issues were so petty, so parochial. For heaven's sake, she had just convinced the British, French, and Germans to peaceably work together.

Just a few weeks earlier, at the International Woman Suffrage Alliance meeting in Geneva, she'd had to walk gingerly through the grim emotional detritus of the recent war. As president of the alliance, Catt was thrust into the role of conciliator among women whose nations had been slaughtering one another for four years. Some of the European delegations initially refused to attend the conference if the German representatives were present; Belgium did not attend. If they couldn't agree to sit in the same room again, the alliance was doomed. Behind the scenes, Catt maneuvered the agenda to take resolutions of blame and retribution off the table. Then she initiated a teatime diplomacy, inviting the British, French, and German leaders to her room before the conference began. She fed them tea and sweets, got them talking, coaxed them to set aside their anger and grief, fix their sights on their common goal of helping women achieve political and economic equality. Over pastries, the head French delegate extended her hand to her German counterpart. The conference was saved. Catt had quietly, cunningly, defused an explosive situation. Somehow, Tennessee seemed more daunting.

Not that Catt was ever a woman to shrink from a challenge. She possessed a serene confidence and a steel-sheathed-in-velvet manner for getting her way. When her father had discouraged Carrie's plans to go to college (a girl didn't need that sort of education, and in any case, he couldn't afford to send her), she wasn't deterred; she simply found a job teaching school and saved enough money to put herself through Iowa Agricultural College, washing dishes and stamping library books to pay her board. When she joined the literary society and was told only the male students could give orations, she broke school tradition by insisting that female students also be allowed to speak publicly. Her male classmates had a debating society, so she formed a female debating counterpart. The men had compulsory military drills, so she petitioned that the coeds be offered the same kind of physical training. She graduated first in her class. In three years.

After Carrie decided to become a lawyer, but didn't have the funds for law school, she prepared by reading under a prominent attorney and working in his office to earn money. She was surprised one day to receive a telegram offering her a job and a salary she could hardly refuse: come to Mason City, Iowa, and become principal of the high school. She thought she was taking only temporary leave of her law books, but soon she found herself promoted to the post of superintendent of schools in Mason City, one of the first women in the nation to be appointed to such a position. There was considerable skepticism about this twenty-four-year-old woman's ability to tackle the district's administrative and morale problems: student discipline and truancy were at a point of crisis. The new superintendent needed to prove her mettle.

On her first day in office, Carrie Lane taught her high school classes in the morning and then began to make the rounds of the other district schools. In her handbag she carried a two-foot-long leather strap, which she had recently bought at a harness shop, a handle loop sewn on one end made to fit her hand. She walked into the first school, reviewed the list of recent truants and misbehaving boys, and called them out into the hall, one at a time, asking them to bring a chair with them. She instructed each boy to remove his coat and lean over the chair and proceeded to use her strap to teach him a painful lesson. She made her way through the other district schools, inflicting pain and tears. When she returned to her office she placed the strap conspicuously atop her desk, settling the matter of her resolve. It was a useful exercise for her future career in suffrage politics.

Superintendent Lane soon gained an admirer in town: Leo Chapman, the handsome publisher and editor of the Mason City newspaper, who was dazzled by the tall, dark-haired, silver-tongued Carrie. Leo brought Carrie into the newsroom to join him as coeditor and publisher. They were true partners. But barely eighteen months after their wedding day, Leo was dead, typhoid taking him at age twenty-nine. A stunned young widow, Mrs. Carrie Chapman demonstrated the sort of resilience that would become a hallmark of her character and her legend. This talent, for bouncing back and pushing forward, proved essential at every crossroads of her life. Carrie spent the next four years as a single working woman, scraping together a living writing freelance articles, editing newspapers, and giving public lectures on various topics. She suffered the kind of crude sexual harassment so common in the workplace: a businessman she was interviewing grabbed her and tried to force himself upon her, thinking any working woman must be a "loose" woman. She was horrified and began to understand what women faced when they ventured into a man's world.

Carrie also began earning money as a paid field organizer, first for the temperance society, then for the Iowa Woman Suffrage Association. While she'd always been a strong supporter of the suffrage movement, ever since that moment in her family's kitchen, she hadn't thought of it as a career. Veteran suffragists quickly recognized her potential. She was a brilliant speaker, brimming with what people called "magnetism," and she was an organizational dynamo. She soon gained notice in national suffrage circles. Susan Anthony kept a close eye on this up-and-coming Iowa Suff.

In 1890 she married again, giving her hand to George Catt, a civil engineer who was making a name for himself, and a very comfortable living, as a bridge builder on the West Coast. They became "a team to work for the Cause," as Carrie liked to put it. George gave her the economic freedom and the loving support to devote herself to suffrage work. "My husband used to say that he was as much a reformer as I," Carrie once explained, and his role was to "earn living enough for two . . . and I could reform for two. That was our bargain and we happily understood each other."

Carrie and George moved to New York City, where George had his own engineering business and Carrie worked with Susan Anthony as a national organizer of suffrage campaigns. She became one of "Aunt Susan's Girls," part of a coterie of young apprentices and acolytes—"nieces," as Anthony affectionately considered them. In 1900, Anthony chose Carrie to succeed her as president of the National American Woman Suffrage Association, believing she possessed the skill and the fire to carry the Cause into the twentieth century.

It was rumored that Carrie and George had long ago signed a nuptial contract guaranteeing her two months each spring and fall to travel, wherever she was called, for suffrage organizing. It's doubtful there was ever any such contract; that would be much too formal and legalistic a way to express the manner in which the couple worked together. They simply had a mutual, silent, agreement. They were a team, for the fifteen years of their marriage, until George's health began to deteriorate. Carrie resigned the presidency to take care of him, but he died soon after, at forty-five, in 1905.

Carrie was shattered; she lost interest in suffrage, her own health collapsed. She moved out of the comfortable Manhattan apartment she'd shared with George—the memories were too painful—moved into a hotel, and asked her suffrage lieutenant and friend Mary "Mollie" Garrett Hay to stay with her as her roommate. She couldn't bear to be alone. She and Mollie had been together ever since, living and working as a new team.

With Mollie's help, Carrie slowly recovered, submerging her grief (she lost George, her mother, her brother, and Susan Anthony all within the space of two years) in work. While she kept her hand in the affairs of the National Association as a vice president, she redirected her energies into building an international suffrage movement, cofounding the International Woman Suffrage Alliance with her friend Millicent Fawcett of England. She made an around-the-world trip to survey the condition of women—in China, the Philippines, Africa, and India—and to spark new suffrage groups. She came back to New York, home to Mollie, and they embarked upon a quest to win the vote for themselves.

With the federal amendment stalled in Congress, Carrie and Mollie set their sights on increasing political pressure by winning suffrage in a trophy state, the nation's most populous: New York. Carrie and Mollie combined their talents to wage a New York state referendum campaign in 1915, which failed, but they went right back to work and succeeded in 1917. The victory convinced more nervous politicians that suffrage was a winning proposition and is credited with providing leverage for the federal amendment. In the midst of their referenda work, Mollie also encouraged Carrie to accept the presidency of NAWSA once again in late 1915, convincing her that she was needed to steer the listing mother ship of suffrage, which seemed to have lost its way. Then they worked together to execute Catt's "Winning Plan" for the federal amendment and, over the previous year, to win ratification.

They were a formidable pair. Mollie liked the rough-and-tumble of backroom politics; some likened her to a Tammany Hall pol. Like Carrie, Mollie was a midwesterner, from Indiana; unlike Carrie, Mollie was very blunt, even abrasive. Many suffragists simply did not like her, and many were jealous of her close relationship with the Chief. They discussed politics as other couples might talk about the weather, as a natural phenomenon, subject to endless fascination. One friend said Carrie was a statesman, Mollie a politician, and together they were invincible. But it was hard for Carrie Catt to feel invincible this morning in Nashville.

Marjorie Shuler entered the room. She was tall and athletically trim, with lustrous dark hair, rosy cheeks, and full lips that usually broke into a ready smile. Today, however, poor Marjorie looked very haggard. She'd spent most of the past week chasing after the governor, his friends, and his many foes, all over the state. The reports she'd wired to headquarters could curl your hair. Catt at first assumed that Marjorie must be overreacting, being a bit melodramatic; she was young and impressionable. But now Catt sensed that Marjorie hadn't been exaggerating at all.

The newest set of complications was that Luke Lea, former U.S. senator, influential publisher of the *Nashville Tennessean,* and political rival of the governor, planned to print a cutting satire of Roberts in his paper. The parody would emphasize Roberts's political paranoia and his equivocating on the ratification issue, zeroing in on his insistence on a friends-only Ratification Committee. If this mockery hit the streets in the pages of the city's leading pro-suffrage newspaper, it would embarrass the governor: he might renege on his promise to call the legislature into special session to consider ratification. And, he had hinted darkly to Marjorie, possibly withdraw his shaky support for ratification altogether.

During the past few days, Marjorie had frantically tried to broker a compromise. She'd tracked down the governor somewhere on the campaign trail and convinced a Nashville Suff with a car to drive her there. She'd pressed him to agree to recognize the official League of Women Voters Ratification Committee, chaired by his "enemies" Abby Milton and Catherine Kenny, alongside his own hand-appointed committee, headed by his loyal supporter Kate Burch Warner. He refused. He wouldn't countenance Milton and Kenny; the most he would allow was appointment of a couple of neutral political women to his own Ratification Committee. Marjorie then motored all through the night, arriving back in Nashville at five in the morning, to present the compromise deal to Luke Lea. He rejected it.

"Newspaper attack on chief executive postponed only on condition of immediate arrival of our Chief," Marjorie wired in a panicky telegram to NAWSA headquarters in New York. Catt fumed, but she was on the train to Nashville less than forty-eight hours later.

Catherine Kenny moved briskly through the downtown streets toward the Hotel Hermitage. The city was quiet, slow to wake on this summer Sunday morning, groggy from the heat. The shops on Church Street stood locked under rolled-up awnings; it was the Sabbath. Nevertheless, this was going to be a very busy day.

More than a hundred of the city's most influential citizens would be coming to meet Mrs. Catt at the hotel. Kenny arranged it all, on very short notice, and was forced to handle all the social niceties and political intricacies of the occasion alone. Everyone was away just when she needed them. Anne Dudley, former Nashville and Tennessee state suffrage president and a vice president of NAWSA under Mrs. Catt, was still out west after the Democratic National Convention in San Francisco. Abby Milton, president of the new Tennessee League of Women Voters, who was also a delegate to the convention, was obviously taking the slow, scenic road home to Chattanooga. Kate Warner, the governor's pet suffragist and newly named chair of his official Ratification Committee, had the audacity to be vacationing in cool Michigan. Kenny would be away, too, if she had any choice; Nashville in deep summer, at the bottom of the Cumberland Basin's bowl, was not the most pleasant place to be.

Kenny booked Mrs. Catt into the Hermitage, the most elegant hotel in town. Mrs. Catt insisted she would stay in Nashville only two, at most three, days. She meant to set things on a proper course, then go home, as she'd done in other ratification states. In truth, Catt didn't believe Tennessee could pull itself together to act on ratification at all, so no use staying very long. But Kenny had a different plan: Mrs. Catt must remain in Nashville to the end, till they put ratification through. They needed her.

Outside Catt's hotel window, the Stars and Stripes flew above the Tennessee state flag atop the Capitol building. The state flag reflected an important truth: Tennessee had long been divided. With three bold white stars barely contained within a blue circle, floating in a sea of red, the flag offered a graphic depiction of the state's three Grand Divisions and the historic regional tensions between the mountainous East, the rolling hills of Middle, and the flat deltas of West Tennessee. The mountaineers of East Tennessee (where cotton plantations and slaves were few) resisted secession during the Civil War and remained loyal to the Union, fighting against their Johnny Reb Tennessee brothers; the scars remained. The East Tennessee unionists stuck with the Republicans during the bloody Reconstruction period and long after. In 1920, East Tennessee remained a Republican Party stronghold in an overwhelmingly Dixie Democrat state; one-third of the legislators in the Tennessee General Assembly were Republicans, and they had the power to tip a balance. The big cities of each region sometimes acted like squabbling siblings: Memphis in the West Division jealous of booming Nashville in the Middle; Knoxville and Chattanooga in the East Division envious of the others' wealth, swinging their allegiance for best advantage.

The Grand Divisions were also enshrined legally in the state constitution, specified in the judicial system and expressed culturally in distinct accents and even musical styles: Appalachian bluegrass in the East, gospel in Middle Tennessee, and Memphis blues in the West. These regional differences and animosities colored the general political landscape and certainly spilled over into the state's suffrage groups. It was just a fact of life, something you had to take into account as a Tennessee Suff. But it was hard to explain clan fights to an outsider. Kenny had tried to capture the sense of things for Mrs. Catt with a dash of her usual down-home humor:

"You know we Tennesseans and Kentuckians are rather strong on 'feuds,'" she'd told Mrs. Catt just the previous week. "Sorter drink it in with our mothers milk." That was a nice way of putting it.

Kenny wasn't convinced that the state's suffrage split, though silly, was so harmful: last year they all managed to work together to push the limited suffrage bill through the legislature, giving Tennessee women the vote in municipal and presidential elections. Kenny was in charge of the Suffs' publicity campaign, which appealed to Tennessee men's vaunted sense of chivalry, while also making veiled threats to the state's ego: "This [bill] will place our state among the progressive ones," the Suffs told the legislators, "and belie the present indication that it is reactionary and slow in taking up new and progressive ideas." They brought the Speaker of the state senate over to their side and even convinced a few of the red-handkerchief boys from rural East and West Tennessee to go along. Tennessee women's record of selfless work during the war certainly seemed to sway some votes.

And in a moment Kenny would never forget, on the day of the vote, the Speaker of the house, the handsome and ambitious Seth Walker, experienced a hallelujah conversion, just as in a revival meeting. It was so thrilling. Walker had been openly opposed to the suffrage bill, but suddenly, with no warning or explanation, he switched sides. Kenny and all the Tennessee Suffs were in the gallery of the lower house, mouths agape, as Walker stepped down from his high perch at the Speaker's desk, walked onto the floor of the chamber, and, like a man who'd been born again, announced that he was now converted to the cause of woman suffrage.

He declared that his former stand in opposition was wrong, and he was now convinced of the justice of enfranchising the women. He told his fellow legislators that suffrage had been granted to Negroes and that it should not be withheld from their own white women kin. What's more, Walker reminded his colleagues, the American colonies fought Great Britain over taxation without representation, and the same principle was at the heart of the suffrage issue: women pay taxes and must obey the law.

"I declare to you that this is not right," he boomed, "and that they should have a voice in our government." It would be a "crime and a shame," Walker insisted, "if women were not given this right." The chamber erupted into cheers. The Suffs never quite understood why the Speaker switched sides, but no one was going to look a gift horse in the mouth.

Walker's change of heart no doubt brought more delegates over to favor the limited suffrage bill, but the governor's people were still convinced it would go down in defeat and never reach his desk. Their head count was wrong: it narrowly passed. The governor was not pleased. The Suffs had to twist both his arms and legs, but he signed the bill in the last hour of the last day possible, as if he were waiting for the clock to run down and save him. He signed it, Kenny was sure, only because his advisers told him it would be declared unconstitutional. The Antis did try to get it tossed out by the courts (Kenny was told the governor was secretly supporting the Antis' lawsuits), but they failed: the Tennessee Supreme Court dismissed the case. Tennessee became the first state in the Deep South to give women such voting privileges, and Kenny was very proud of that. Tennessee women still had no say in choosing their state representatives or U.S. congressmen or senators—or their governor—but it was better than nothing.

Now it was going to take stronger muscle to get Governor Roberts to make good on ratifying the federal amendment. Of course, the Tennessee Suffs were also taking a risk in bringing Mrs. Catt here. The newspapers were full of her arrival, not only in the *Tennessean* and the *Banner*, but in the

Chattanooga News and *Memphis Commercial Appeal* and *Knoxville Journal,* and in the wire service dispatches in all the small-town publications. There were already whispers about "Yankee carpetbaggers" coming to town, and Mrs. Catt herself was sure to become a lightning rod. But they would simply have to take that chance.

Suffrage had been Catherine Kenny's ticket into Nashville women's society, Protestant society, where Catholic women like her were rarely admitted. It would be a stretch to say she was also admitted into Nashville's highest social circles; those were still off-limits to her. She was also an outsider, a native Chattanoogan from a large, very poor Irish family, which didn't help her social standing. Her father died in Chattanooga's yellow fever epidemic, leaving her mother to support six children under the age of ten. Young Catherine was considered very clever, began studies at a Catholic high school, but she could stay for only a single semester before starting work, at age sixteen, to help the family scrape by financially. She married an ambitious fellow from Nashville and moved to that city, and she moved up in the world.

As her husband's Coca-Cola bottling plant prospered, they were able to move out of the Irish section of Nashville and into the fashionable west side of town. Catherine could join the right civic organizations, the do-gooder leagues, where her can-do attitude was valued. She also climbed on the suffrage bandwagon and was welcomed into the Nashville Equal Suffrage League. The Catholic Church was no great friend of woman suffrage, it was true, she often had to explain to her WASP friends, but while many high-profile cardinals and bishops railed against suffrage, the church actually had no set dogma on the subject. Catherine Kenny chose to be a good Catholic suffragist.

And Catholic clergy were certainly not the only men of the cloth to castigate the idea of women's enfranchisement, she was quick to remind her friends. "When you hand her the ballot, you simply give her a club to knock her brains out," Reverend T. H. Harrison once proclaimed from the pulpit of Nashville's Adams Presbyterian Church. "When she takes the ballot box, you've given her a coffin in which to bury the dignities of womanhood."

Whatever your religion, it took some gumption to be a Suff in Tennessee; it wasn't a very respectable calling. You had to grow a thick skin, you had to laugh about what people, and the clergy, said about you and what most of the other women in town thought of you. Your husband and children had to be able to let the nasty words and queer looks roll off their backs, too. Kenny put herself on the line when she presided over the very first suffrage parade in the South, the great procession in Nashville in May 1914. She'd directed it all: the flower-decorated automobiles driving through downtown and the stunning suffrage tableau performed on the steps of the Parthenon in Centennial Park. Some said it wasn't "ladylike" to parade through the streets like that, but Kenny managed to make suffrage enticing, and fun, and the good publicity spurred the growth of local suffrage clubs around the state.

Mrs. John Kenny, forty-six years old, saw herself as a suffragist, a Catholic, and a Democrat, but most important, as a mother—of four children. It was motherhood that led her to suffrage, made her realize how important the vote would be for protecting her children and making their world safer and healthier. The abstractions, those greater goods of justice and democracy, were all fine, but it was the concrete things, such as better schools, safe milk, and decent hospitals, that drove women like her to want, and work for, the vote. Now all those years of work might be coming to fruition, right in her own backyard.

Kenny walked into the hotel through the ladies' entrance on Union Street (unless accompanied by a gentleman, that was the only proper way to enter), and the uniformed operator took her to the third floor. She needed to explain just who was expected to make an appearance today, how they fit into the political picture, how useful they might be, how trustworthy. And with whom they were aligned: that was crucial. Above all, Kenny needed to shine a positive light on the circumstances. The Suffs of Tennessee were determined to prove to the Chief that Volunteer State women could, as Kenny put it, "do something else besides fuss."

As Mrs. Catt had ordered, the Tennessee Suffs had put together a Men's Ratification Committee: "Get the biggest and most important men of the state," Catt insisted, "and do it quick before the opposition has made it impossible." They signed up almost two hundred men of all stripes, from the state's U.S. congressmen to city mayors and rural legislators, sympathetic clergymen and businessmen, Republicans and Democrats, all headed up by former governor Tom Rye. As Catt instructed, they'd printed all of the men's names on official letterhead stationery; they had to shrink the type very small to fit them all on the page.

Most auspicious, two very prominent men, the publishers of the rival newspapers in town—Luke Lea of the *Nashville Tennessean* and Edward

Stahlman of the *Nashville Banner*—men who couldn't agree on anything in the world, had both signed on to the Men's Ratification Committee. They detested each other, but they both joined, even contributed a bit of money, and said they would be coming by to greet Mrs. Catt this Sunday, at different times, of course. If these men both backed ratification in such a public way, it only proved how broad support for the amendment really was in Tennessee.

Even the delicate racial theme was moot in Tennessee, Kenny assured Mrs. Catt, who could only give her a sidelong look of skepticism. "I don't believe the 'nigger question' will be raised here," Kenny maintained, "since Negro women have voted now in the five largest cities of the state, and many of the towns, and in every instance have made good.

"The suffragists organized them and they voted with the best white women, thereby eliminating any political prejudice," Kenny explained with pride. In the 1919 municipal election, Kenny had worked with Nashville's leading black suffragists, whom she considered intelligent and very able women—mothers like herself—to register black women and get out the vote. It made her proud to be a Tennessean. It made Carrie Catt nervous. Unless Tennessee was different from every other southern state, and Catt doubted that, there was no resting easy about that particular issue.

In most respects, Catt admired Catherine Kenny's political instincts and clever footwork. She'd executed a beautiful maneuver a few weeks ago, in late June, when Governor Roberts was still balking at calling the special session. Kenny went straight to the top, to the White House.

"Our Governor says Woodrow is his Moses," she explained, "and he'll stand by him and follow him forever." So Mrs. Kenny deployed the Moses on Pennsylvania Avenue, the Virginian president who had publicly endorsed the Nineteenth Amendment, to soften the heart of the governor of Tennessee. "I conceived the idea of having the President wire him a loving message telling him to deliver the 36th state for the Democrats," she crowed. It was a brilliant ploy. The governor was sunk. He agreed to call a special session the next day.

Now Kenny presented Mrs. Catt with the results of the first poll of the legislature conducted by the Suffs in every district of the state. Catt studied the poll results, noticing that only about one-third of the members of each chamber had responded. Kenny explained that many delegates simply hadn't replied or had refused to commit just yet; there were also some influential men who leaned favorably toward ratification but weren't yet ready to be placed on the definite "Yes" list. Seth Walker, the Speaker of the house, for one.

Kenny described to Catt, in dramatic detail, Walker's surprise conversion to the Cause last year, how he'd helped swing votes for the limited suffrage bill. Walker hadn't yet committed publicly but was letting it be known that he would support ratification and possibly even introduce the ratification resolution in the house himself, giving it his imprimatur. That would be a great boon, Kenny told the Chief.

The first in a parade of visitors knocked on Mrs. Catt's door. Scores more followed: district chairwomen of the new Tennessee League of Women Voters (the league, launched by Catt in February 1920, was already established in states where women enjoyed some degree of suffrage); Democratic Party ward chairmen; local politicians who'd bravely stuck their necks out for woman suffrage long ago; and wary strivers watching to see how the political winds might blow. They lined up to shake the hand of the Chief, and Catt displayed her remarkable talent—a politician's talent—for making each of the visitors feel important. She looked them straight in the eye, asked them specific questions, cocked her head thoughtfully as she listened to their replies. They all sang a version of the same refrain: Tennessee could do it; it could definitely be the thirty-sixth state. If only she would lead them.

Mrs. Kenny noticed that Major E. B. Stahlman, publisher of the *Nashville Banner,* was not among the visitors. Personally, Kenny was relieved not to have to deal with Stahlman; he could be so unpleasant, so abrasive. But his absence was puzzling. Perhaps he didn't want to encounter Luke Lea, but not showing up at all was simply rude.

The stream of visitors continued into the afternoon, but the buzz of conversation abruptly stopped when Lea strode into the room. He was the sort of man who strode, never just walked and certainly never ambled. He was tall, six feet three, and broad-shouldered, youthfully handsome, with pale eyes, carefully combed hair, and full lips that curled into a slight smile. He was a sharp dresser and moved, always quickly, with an air of utmost confidence; some might call it a swagger.

He was the scion of a distinguished Tennessee family—his grandfather had been a mayor of Nashville—and he was raised on the thousand-acre ancestral estate, Lealand, just outside the city. After college he went north to Columbia University Law School in New York City, then came home to Nashville. He was an ardent "dry" man, not so much for moral reasons, but because he felt the liquor interests held too much sway in Tennessee politics, as did the railroads. He fancied himself a progressive reformer in the Theodore Roosevelt mold: he was for busting up the trusts, regulating the railroads and other corporations, and enacting Prohibition, and well before TR came over to the Suffs' side, Lea supported woman suffrage.

He decided the most efficient way to promote his worldview was to have his own megaphone, so when he was barely twenty-eight years old Lea founded the *Nashville Tennessean;* he was its owner, publisher, and editor. He gained influence with men who wanted his support, and in 1911 the Tennessee General Assembly selected him as the state's junior U.S. senator. (This was before direct popular election of senators, when state legislatures held that power.) He was the youngest senator ever sent to Washington, only thirty-one years old; they called him "the Baby Senator."

Carrie Catt knew Lea from his time in the U.S. Senate, where he was a steadfast friend of suffrage and, remarkable for a southern senator, a solid supporter of the federal amendment. The Suffs could always count on him, and he was a champion of other progressive legislation as well. But before Lea's first term was over, the Seventeenth Amendment took effect, state legislatures lost their ability to appoint senators, and Lea had to run in a popular election to retain his seat. The Democrats were splintered (it was a chronic condition), and he lost the primary election to Kenneth McKellar, the candidate of Memphis "Boss" Edward Crump. Soon after Lea returned home to Nashville, the nation went to war. Though he was almost forty years old by then, Lea recruited a brigade of Tennessee volunteers to fight as the "Old Hickory" artillery unit, and he took command. Colonel Lea grew a mustache, looked smashing in his high boots, and led his unit in some of the fiercest battles in France.

After the armistice, while Lea and his men sat in Luxembourg, bored, waiting to be shipped home, he had time to think about the war and the precarious peace. He decided it was simply not right for the German kaiser, the man responsible for so much misery around the world, to be sitting in luxurious asylum in a Dutch castle. The kaiser should be forced to go to Paris, where the terms of surrender were being drafted, and stand trial for his war crimes. Lea was a man of action and decided to take international matters into his own hands: he would kidnap Kaiser Wilhelm. He gathered up a few of his best men, got hold of some automobiles and fake passports, and took off with his little crew on what he told them was a secret mission.

It was so secret that Lea's superiors knew nothing about it. The party posed as journalists, bluffed their way through border crossings, found their way around a washed-out bridge over the Rhine, and talked their way into the moated and heavily guarded castle where the kaiser was kept. "We wanted to bring him to President Wilson as a Christmas present," Lea explained.

Lea and his men got within earshot of Kaiser Bill but were sent packing by armed guards. They climbed back into their autos and scooted back to base, returning without the president's Christmas gift. Lea came home a hero, marching with his men through the streets of Nashville and Chattanooga in the welcome-home parades in the spring of 1919. At the ceremonies, no one mentioned the little matter of Colonel Lea nearly being court-martialed for his kaiser adventure. Lea's bravado was part of his charm, personally and politically.

Lea looked much older, his face more lined, than Catt had remembered him in Washington just a few years ago. The war, of course. But also the news he'd received while on the transport ship coming home to the States and the welcome parades: his wife was dead. No warning—gone—leaving him with two young boys. He buried himself in work, cofounded the American Legion to give war veterans a voice. But the boys needed a mother. So now, just over a year later, he'd married his late wife's youngest sister. They were planning a new family. He was a very busy man.

Catt thanked Lea for his continued help and support, then got down to brass tacks. This parody of the governor he was planning to print. It was so dangerous to the ratification effort, it could cost Tennessee and, possibly, the amendment. She didn't exactly plead but issued more of a calm, cool-voiced order. Lea listened. He was a man who relished a fight, and Mrs. Catt was demanding that he stand down.

After a long pause, Colonel Luke Lea reluctantly but gallantly agreed not to publish the parody, but only if the governor would agree to acknowledge other ratification committees besides his own. Mind you, Lea emphasized, this agreement did not mean his paper would relent in its critical coverage of Roberts. Mrs. Catt agreed that the First Amendment could not be sacrificed for the Nineteenth. The matter concluded, the colonel strode out of the Chief's suite.

One down. Now the governor.

Chapter 3

The Feminist Peril

J OSEPHINE PEARSON'S NIGHT in the tub had been uncomfortable but her phone calls remarkably fruitful, yielding pledges of help and funding from national and regional antisuffrage coalitions. On Sunday morning, she was reading through the flurry of overnight telegrams delivered to her door when Mrs. George Washington and the Nashville delegation of the Tennessee State Association Opposed to Woman Suffrage arrived at the hotel to greet their president. They were horrified to find her in such a cramped, sweltering room and aghast to learn she'd spent the night in the tub; they whisked her to a much larger, airy, corner room with a pleasant view, never mind the cost. No reason to sacrifice comfort, they assured her, there will be money enough for this fight.

Meanwhile, their able ally Nashville attorney John Jacob Vertrees was at his desk in his summer house in Florida, on the phone with important friends and clients. Josephine considered John Vertrees her mentor and champion. She felt he'd "discovered" her, recognizing her skills and leadership potential, molding her into the proud Anti commander she'd become.

Before he even met her, it was Josephine's pungent antisuffrage essays, published in various Tennessee newspapers, that caught his attention. Vertrees was a respected attorney, former newspaper publisher, and state Democratic Party leader who represented liquor industry and railroad clients in his lucrative practice. Vertrees and his wife, Virginia, were both staunch opponents of woman suffrage, and they enjoyed reading Josephine's colorful public diatribes on its many dangers ("modern Eve asks for the forbidden fruit that may give out its essence of deadly poison in the possible disruption of home . . .") and admired her zealous defense of "the spirit of the woman of the Old South." The Vertreeses soon began to court her to take an active role in the state's fledgling antisuffrage movement.

Until 1913 or so, when the Tennessee Equal Franchise Association began to gain some traction, there was no need for an anti–woman suffrage movement in the state: almost everyone was safely against giving women the vote.

But when suffragists such as the socially prominent Anne Dudley began to make political and popular inroads, gaining some male friends in government, and when they dared to parade through the streets in yellow-flower-bedecked cars and make speeches from flag-festooned platforms, the Vertreeses woke up to the uncomfortable realization that woman suffrage was becoming socially acceptable, even in Tennessee. They vowed to stop it.

The Vertreeses organized the Tennessee State Association Opposed to Woman Suffrage, with Virginia as president and John heading the men's contingent, bringing his lawyer friends, Nashville businessmen, and Vanderbilt University faculty into the group, while also forging ties to the loose amalgam of antisuffrage societies already established around the country.

Vertrees held strong moral and legal objections to giving women the vote, which he pronounced in his 1916 manifesto, *To the Men of Tennessee on Female Suffrage*. With the publication of this pamphlet, Vertrees took on the role of philosopher of the state's Antis. He assembled all the hardy specimens of opposition: women were irrational and not intellectually equal to the responsibilities of suffrage; they were too emotional and sentimental to vote on policy matters; government was based upon force, so only those who must bear arms should be allowed to vote; and suffragists advocated free love and personified loose morals. Extending the reach of his biological claims, he reminded his readers that women's dual physical handicaps, pregnancy and menses, rendered them unfit for public duties: "A woman's life is one of frequent and regular periods marked by mental and nervous irritability, when sometimes even her mental equilibrium is disturbed."

He also added the characteristic southern twist to the standard Anti thesis: if handed the ballot, not only would Tennessee women be torn from hearth and home and plunged into the depravity of politics, but the social order would be irrevocably disrupted, as equal suffrage would nominally place black women on the same political plane as white women. He quoted the "zealous suffragette, Miss Helen Keller," who in her letter to the National Association for the Advancement of Colored People, urged all to "advance gladly towards our common heritage of life, liberty, and light, undivided by race or color or creed." Encouraging this kind of dangerous racial equality would undermine southern society, he thundered.

The region's social fabric had already been ripped apart fifty years before—first by the Civil War and then by Reconstruction; the racial rules had been shattered, societal relations disordered. Even by 1920, the South had not emotionally recovered from the trauma or reconciled itself to the concept of racial equality. For educated men such as Vertrees, who'd lived through the war and its convulsive aftermath, the threat of black women's enfranchisement—imposed by the federal government—seemed like a bitter reprise of the disruptions Washington had wrought decades ago.

Beyond all his other arguments, Vertrees framed the suffrage discussion with blunt simplicity: "I do not believe the women of Tennessee want the ballot, but even if they do . . . it is not a question of what women want, but what they *ought* to have, and . . . it is a question for men alone to determine."

Vertrees's attitude wasn't unusual, and it wasn't new. Men had always taken for themselves the prerogative to decide for women, unilaterally determining what women should do, prescribing what they must not do, announcing which rights women were "entitled" to have. Men decided what was "best" for women, without their consultation or consent, then wrote laws to codify this judgment. That was the way of the world, learned men liked to say, claiming God had bestowed upon them such authority: one half of humanity held dominion over the other half, by right of a certain shape of genitalia.

Just as American men had once taken it upon themselves to decide whether their wives were their property, now they were called upon to rule on whether it was "best" for women to be granted equal citizenship. In the future this awesome sense of male responsibility would take other forms, involving other issues. Future generations of American women would continue to chafe as men in positions of power presumed to control their bodies, the training of their minds, the choice of their professions, the pursuit of their livelihoods.

Mr. Vertrees kept his eye on Miss Pearson as her letters were printed in the state newspapers and she gained a reputation for feisty advocacy of the Anti point of view. When illness forced Virginia Vertrees to retire from the presidency of the Tennessee Anti organization in early 1917, Pearson was the obvious choice to replace her. The Vertreeses had to convince Pearson to accept the position, but once they did, she jumped into her new role with gusto, taking on the suffragists as the legislature debated a limited woman suffrage bill. Pearson became the public face of the Anti campaign to defeat the 1917 suffrage measure, but Mr. Vertrees was always close behind. "It seemed never necessary for our Anti-Suffrage women to even climb the capitol steps," Pearson recalled, and Vertrees did not want them to climb those steps, giving her strict instructions to keep the Anti women away from the statehouse. He would handle the lobbying. Josephine shared Vertrees's disapproval of women lowering themselves into the muck of politics, especially when the honor of Tennessee women was at stake.

The Antis won that fight, thanks in no small part to Mr. Vertrees's manifesto, which meshed so well with the thinking of many legislators. And they won despite William Jennings Bryan's big pro-suffrage speech in the Capitol building, which was high on florid oratory but didn't swing many votes. But by 1919, the situation had changed. John Vertrees was still smarting from that humiliating defeat last year, when the suffrage people bamboozled the Tennessee legislature into giving women some voting rights—not full rights, very limited, but even a little was too much as far as he was concerned. They claimed the time had come, the world had changed, the women had earned it by their war work, all such specious arguments. The legislature hadn't been manly enough to stand firm; the governor caved in and signed.

Vertrees flew into court, attempting to nullify the new law, have it ruled unconstitutional because it didn't provide for women voters to pay a poll tax, as men were required to do. The lower court sided with Vertrees, declaring the law unconstitutional because the state constitution did not provide for woman suffrage and the legislature didn't have the power to change that. But then the Tennessee Supreme Court slammed him down, reversing the lower court's decision, holding that the legislature did have the power to enact presidential and municipal suffrage. The suffrage law was amended to include a poll tax for women and was declared valid. Women were at the polls in last fall's city elections in Nashville; he saw them—white and black women. John Vertrees wasn't going to let that happen again.

So this Sunday morning he was on the phone with his colleagues in the American Constitutional League, the men's legal arm of the Antis, who were eager to help him fend off ratification in Tennessee. The Constitutional League lawyers were already contesting several of the completed state ratifications—in Ohio, West Virginia, and a few others—claiming the ratifications were illegitimate. Should the Tennessee legislature take up ratification, a contingent of league lawyers, armed with motions and maneuvers, was ready to take the train to Nashville as soon as Vertrees gave the signal.

Vertrees also rang up his longtime legal clients in the railroad and liquor industries. They had their own reasons for helping him fight suffrage. The whiskey boys were hoping that damned Eighteenth Amendment,

Prohibition, would not be enforced; that was certainly the plan in Tennessee. But if women were allowed to get mixed up in voting and politics, especially the strident "dry" ladies, they might insist on enforcement.

The textile manufacturers didn't want women having a say in government, especially those labor reform types; after labor reform, they'd move swiftly to child labor laws and wage and health protections for women workers: it could get expensive. And the railroads were dead set against women voting. The Louisville and Nashville and the other railroad lines had bought the Tennessee legislature long ago, keeping it in its pocket with free passes and cushy jobs, with the understanding that the legislature would be friendly to railroad interests and take a hands-off approach to railroad regulation. This comfortable equation could be easily upset by unpredictable women voters.

Anti activists such as Vertrees and Pearson would have to admit that their work had grown more difficult in the past few years. The swing toward public acceptance of women's right to vote, once so slow and hesitant, with successful surges punctuated by reversals, had lately speeded up. There were no public opinion polls to statistically chart the attitudinal shifts that create pressure for political change, but there'd been some signals: encouraging for the Suffs, dismaying for the Antis.

Since 1910, eleven states had granted women full suffrage, though the Antis had managed to temper those victories with a long string of suffrage campaign defeats. (Antis managed to thwart suffrage in Oregon five times before it passed in 1912.) But win or lose, the state referenda proved that millions of American men approved of granting women the vote. Also telling was that in some contests—notably Michigan in 1912—only outright electoral fraud had kept the suffragists from winning, a sure sign that their success was scaring the political powers and stimulating concerted opposition. Congress and other elected officials took notice. The Antis were also forced to take notice and began to seriously organize around 1911, after California had granted its women the vote. They kept suffrage at bay in New York in 1915, but it triumphed in 1917, a pivotal loss that spurred new levels of effort.

Since America's entry into the world war in 1917—when American women took on new, unorthodox roles—the pace of change had accelerated: between 1917 and 1920, eleven more states (including Tennessee) had given their women some type of voting rights, perhaps restricted but still significant. Yet the Antis were in no way discouraged: they'd scored impressive victories by halting ratification in eight states already, stymied legislative action in Vermont and Connecticut, and had several more rejections—North Carolina, Florida, and Tennessee—within sight. They were ready for the challenge in Nashville.

On the seventh floor of the Hermitage, Josephine Pearson and her Nashville Anti colleague, Queenie (Mrs. George) Washington were writing to-do lists. Pearson had already reserved the mezzanine and first-floor spaces for the Antis' headquarters and reception rooms. They must arrange rallies and receptions, dinners and teas—social functions were very important, Mrs. Washington insisted. The top officers of the National Association Opposed to Woman Suffrage would be coming to Nashville, as would the leaders of the Southern Women's Rejection League, bringing troops of volunteers. Every Anti in Tennessee must be mobilized. Orders must be placed for banners, Confederate flags, and the Anti emblem, red roses, from the best florists.

Two former NAWSA suffrage officers turned Antis, Kate Gordon and Laura Clay, promised to come, bringing their inside knowledge of Mrs. Catt and the suffragists' playbook, as well as their own powerful arguments against the federal amendment. They had proved so helpful in stopping ratification in the other southern states. Miss Charlotte Rowe, the Antis' national field secretary and fiery orator, was already on her way to Nashville. Pearson hoped that perhaps Ida Tarbell, the famous muckraking journalist who wrote wonderful essays opposing woman suffrage, might be persuaded to make a surprise appearance, too.

Pearson saw the looming fight in Nashville as a chance to display her leadership talents, show them what a true small-town daughter of Tennessee could do. The world was going to hell in a handbasket, Pearson believed, and she felt compelled to sound the alarm. The world war had changed things for women, and not for the better, she was convinced. Women had borne the traditional wartime burdens, as sorrowful mothers and bereft widows, and they'd rolled bandages and knitted socks for the boys over there, but in this last war they'd also been unsexed, thrust into the brutish man's world in the name of patriotism. They'd been called upon to take up men's work, in the coal mines, in the fields, in the munitions plants, in the streetcars and elevators. They'd donned men's clothes and been paid men's salaries, and the worst part of it was—the women seemed to enjoy it! Some of them wanted to stay, even now, after the war, after the men had come home. They'd rather toil in a truck or a factory than tend the hearth, and that's how feminism was going to destroy civilization, she was certain.

These "new women" and "modern women" weren't content with the sacred tasks of helpmate and motherhood; they lusted for things not meant for them, and it frightened her. Look at the suffragists right here in Nashville, especially the young ones, in short, clinging skirts, their legs almost bare, their corsets thrown away, flaunting their almost naked bodies on the street, their hair bobbed short and mannish, a cigarette in their painted fingers. It was disgusting and it was dangerous. The ranks of the suffragists were teeming with, as she liked to call them, "short-haired women and long-haired men," the kinds of moral degenerates who could hasten America's downfall. How much worse it would be if they were allowed to plunge into the muck of politics, too. Pearson was an educator of women; she'd devoted most of her life to shaping their minds and, teaching by example, their morals. When she was called to answer to her God, she wanted to be able to say that she'd done all in her power to prevent American women from tumbling down the road to disaster.

Huddled around a table in her Hermitage room, Pearson, Mrs. Washington, and the other planners all agreed on what to emphasize: the dangers the Nineteenth Amendment posed to the American family, white supremacy, states' rights, and cherished southern traditions. They would focus on making Mrs. Catt the living symbol of all that was alien and evil, ungodly and un-American, Bolshevik, and detestably Yankee.

Chapter 4

• • •

The Woman Question

MOTHER PEARSON WAS RIGHT about one thing: abolition and woman suffrage did sprout from the same root, nourished by the rich loam of early-nineteenth-century religious zeal and moral reform. She taught her daughter, Josephine, that the causes were intertwined, and both were dangerous.

The early advocates of legal rights for American women all began their activist careers as fervent abolitionists. They believed slavery was a grievous wrong and they were obliged to confront and stop it. But even as they devoted their intellect and energy to this urgent moral campaign, often placing themselves in physical danger to do so, they encountered a striking hypocrisy among their male colleagues so devoted to "universal liberty."

"Many a man who advocated equality most eloquently for a Southern plantation could not tolerate it at his own fireside," was the way they described it.

In the 1830s and 1840s, the South Carolinian Grimké sisters left their slaveholding home and risked their lives to speak out publicly against the evils of the slavery system, awakening the conscience of large audiences in the North with their tongues and their pens. As they drew greater numbers to their lectures, both women and men filling the seats, the Grimkés found themselves vilified by distinguished northern clergymen and other high-minded abolitionists—not for their antislavery sentiments, but for their willingness to defy church teachings and speak in public. The clergy denounced the sisters for trespassing out of "women's sphere" of home and hearth and spearheading these "promiscuous gatherings." The sisters gave sharp reply to the men of the cloth and kept on speaking out.

Lucretia Mott, a devout Quaker, bore eloquent witness against slavery in her Philadelphia meetinghouse and in the national American Anti-Slavery Society, where she became a leader of the movement beginning in the early 1830s. Susan B. Anthony began as a professional organizer for the American Anti-Slavery Society; the sweet-voiced Lucy Stone was in high demand as a gifted abolitionist speaker; and Elizabeth Cady, already sympathetic to the abolitionist cause, also married into the movement.

The willful, intellectual daughter of a prominent judge in upstate New York, Elizabeth was educated at the finest school open to women at that time—Miss Emma Willard's Troy Female Seminary—and was lured away from the polite parlor world of her social set by her cousin Gerrit Smith, a firebrand abolitionist. Smith's country manor was the scene of a perpetual house party for radical reformers and fugitive slaves (it was a station on the Underground Railroad), and Elizabeth was mesmerized by the dinner table debates over politics and religion. At cousin Gerrit's house she was introduced to a young seminary dropout, itinerant journalist, and antislavery agent, Henry Brewster Stanton. Elizabeth was charmed by Henry's persuasive oratory skills and his moral certainty; their honeymoon was a voyage to London to attend the 1840 World's Anti-Slavery Convention, where Henry was an American delegate. Elizabeth's wedding journey set in motion a long chain of events that would lead—almost precisely eight decades later—to Carrie Catt's trip to Nashville and Josephine Pearson's mission to confront her there.

The British Parliament had already abolished slavery throughout the empire in 1834, freeing almost a million subjects from bondage, so the focus of the London conclave was on strategies to eliminate slavery in other parts of the world, especially in the United States, where 2.5 million black people were enslaved. Among the approximately fifty American delegates at the London convention were seven women, chosen to represent their Pennsylvania and Massachusetts antislavery societies, groups that not only included women as full-fledged members, but placed them in leadership roles. The American abolitionist standard-bearers, William Lloyd Garrison and Wendell Phillips, insisted on this highly unusual gender equality in their American Anti-Slavery Society, and the women had become adept at organizing, raising funds, and speaking their minds at public forums.

Mott, a forty-seven-year-old mother of five, led this delegation of women to London. She and the six other American women delegates were rejected by the conference organizers: it was improper for women to participate in a public meeting; it went against biblical teachings on women's roles; and it was an affront to societal norms and sensibilities. Allowing women to participate would hold the meeting up to "ridicule" in the morning papers, the men maintained. (That these same rationales—biblical views and societal custom—were routinely employed to defend the institution of slavery itself was an irony not lost on the women.)

Lucretia Mott and Wendell Phillips demanded that the "woman question" be put to the full convention, setting off a bitter debate lasting an entire day, in which 350 men postured and pontificated about women's "proper sphere": how she was "constitutionally unfit for public or business meetings" and how God's law made Eve subordinate to Adam for good reason. Mott was indignant; Elizabeth Stanton was infuriated: "It was really pitiful to hear narrow-minded bigots, pretending to be teachers and leaders of men," Stanton recalled in her memoirs. "They would have been horrified at the idea of burning the flesh of the distinguished women present with red-hot irons, but the crucifixion of their pride and self-respect, the humiliation of the spirit, seemed to them a most trifling matter."

The convention voted overwhelmingly to deny the women delegates' credentials and ejected them from the convention floor, relegating them to an upstairs gallery behind a bar and a cloth curtain. When William Lloyd Garrison arrived, several days late, he refused to take his own seat, instead joining his countrywomen in the gallery: "After battling so many long years, for the liberties of African slaves, I can take no part in a convention that strikes down the most sacred rights of all women," he insisted.

Their treatment in London was a galvanizing moment, an unexpected pivot point that "stung many women into new thought and action," Stanton remembered. Mott and Stanton decided that once they returned home they must gather like-minded women to their own meeting, to discuss and demand more equitable treatment for women.

It would be eight years before Mott and Stanton managed to call together that women's meeting, delayed by distance, distraction, and the arrival of the first three of Stanton's seven children. They kept in touch by letter and met whenever they could at abolition conferences, keeping the vague idea of this women's conclave alive; but their notions took real shape over teacups one midsummer afternoon in 1848. Mrs. Mott was attending a Quaker Yearly Meeting in western New York, not far from where Stanton lived. Sitting around a mahogany table, pouring out their frustrations to one another, Stanton, Mott, and three other friends decided to finally do it: to call a convention to discuss women's rights.

The very phrase "women's rights" was an oxymoron, they all knew. American women possessed precious few rights under the law of the state or the nation. Elizabeth had learned this while still a girl, in her father's law office and courtroom, where she often curled up in a corner to read and watch. It was there that she listened to women beg Judge Cady to help protect them from a drunken, abusive husband (men were not punished for beating their wives) or offer counsel on how to obtain a divorce and still keep custody of her children (fathers retained rights of custody). They sought guidance on how to possibly manage on their own—as either a single woman, divorcée, or widow—with limited rights to their own money or property or even inheritance. Judge Cady would listen sympathetically, shake his head, and patiently explain that there was little he could do, that the law offered them little protection, redress, or even legal standing. (Women could neither bring legal suit nor testify in court.)

In one girlish fit of rage, Elizabeth decided to expunge the offending laws by taking a scissors and snipping them out of her father's law tomes. When he got wind of her silly plot, he explained that a scissors was not an effective way to change the law: when she grew up, she would simply have to convince the legislatures of men to change the laws. That must have seemed like safely far-fetched advice.

Elizabeth was now a married woman—albeit wedded to a progressive-minded man. Nevertheless, she was, in legal terms, Henry's possession: "civilly dead," as she summed up a married woman's legal status. She was chattel, not unlike a slave. Henry was very often away on business or abolitionist work, leaving her alone to contend with all the chores of a growing household. They had moved from Boston to a very small town, Seneca Falls, in the Finger Lakes district of New York State, and she was at once overwhelmed with domestic duties, restless, and bored. It was the perfect time to dream of rebellion: "My experience at the World's Antislavery Convention, all I had read of the legal status of women, and the oppression I saw everywhere, together swept across my soul, intensified now by many personal experiences," she recalled. "It seemed as if all the elements had conspired to impel me to some onward step. I could not see what to do or where to begin, my only thought was a public meeting for protest and discussion."

They swiftly created an announcement to be placed in the local papers the next day, calling for a Woman's Rights Convention "to discuss the social, civil and religious rights of woman" to be held at the Methodist Wesleyan Chapel in Seneca Falls.

The abolition and temperance meetings the women were used to attending always featured a "declaration" of some kind, a statement of principles and purposes, and then some resolutions to agree upon and adopt. The five women leafed through history books and abolitionist literature to find a model, but nothing seemed to work. Finally, Elizabeth picked up a copy of the most revolutionary document she knew, Mr. Jefferson's Declaration of Independence, and read it aloud. This was it; it had both the eloquence and the fury they needed. She took it apart, line by line, paraphrased and substituted, and came up with her own Declaration of Sentiments, a litany of affronts to the dignity and well-being of women. The cadence was familiar:

"When, in the course of human events, it becomes necessary for one portion of the family of man to assume among the people of the earth a position different from that they have hitherto occupied . . . We hold these truths to be self-evident: that all men and women are created equal . . ."

Mrs. Stanton's Declaration of Sentiments was every bit as outrageous in her time as Mr. Jefferson's had been. It brought up grievances ranging from inequitable divorce, custody and property laws to prohibitions on women's higher education and entry into fields of medicine, law, and the ministry— and her unequal pay. It castigated the "different code of morals for men and women" as well as a male society that degrades women and keeps her subordinate by "destroying her confidence and self-respect." But the very first set of grievances Mrs. Stanton listed was, in some ways, the most controversial:

"He has never permitted her to exercise her inalienable right to the elective franchise," and, "He has compelled her to submit to laws, in the formation of which she had no voice."

Elizabeth was assigned to formulate a list of resolutions, a list of remedies and demands to emerge from the convention. A few days before the convention was to open, she read the resolutions to her husband, Henry, and he readily approved of her efforts, until she got to resolution number nine:

"Resolved: That it is the duty of the women of this country to secure to themselves their sacred right to the elective franchise."

Henry was appalled. More equitable property rights, divorce laws, and access to education and the professions were one thing, but demanding the vote went too far. The vote meant making decisions for the nation, it meant power, and with all due respect to his wife, power was still the exclusive prerogative of men. If she went ahead with presenting that crazy franchise demand at the convention, Henry told Elizabeth, he would not attend. She refused to cut it; he did not show up.

Even more rattling to Elizabeth was Lucretia Mott's reaction to the franchise resolution: "Lizzie, Thee will make us ridiculous," the veteran reformer warned her protégée. "We must go slowly."

One of Elizabeth's only allies on resolution nine was a thirty-year-old black man who had recently moved to nearby Rochester to open an abolitionist newspaper. Frederick Douglass had escaped his own slavery just a decade before, but in that short time he had become the great spokesman and powerful symbol for emancipation: his autobiography was a best seller, his lectures were electrifying, his fame propelled the movement. Even more, he was, as he would describe it, an unabashed "Woman's Rights Man," as he saw slaves, free blacks, and women all shackled by American law and custom. Very early in his freedom he came to realize that many of the same arguments used to justify the enslavement of black people were employed to explain away women's subjugation. He'd already had long discussions about these parallels with Elizabeth Stanton, whom he'd come to know when both he and the Stantons lived in Boston during the mid-1840s.

Douglass admired the courage and sacrifice of the abolitionist women who stood on the ramparts with him (and financially supported him), and he decided to settle in Rochester precisely because it was the home of so many female antislavery activists. Douglass published the notice of the women's rights meeting in his newspaper, *North Star,* and he made the fifty-mile trip from Rochester to Seneca Falls to see it for himself.

The scene outside the Wesleyan Chapel was startling: in the hours before the meeting began, hundreds of people, both women and men, began arriving in farm wagons and buggies, on horseback and on foot; Stanton and the others had not expected this kind of turnout. The first day was intended to be a "women only" affair, but there were too many men at the door to turn away. More than three hundred people, including many young farm women, packed the chapel, listening eagerly to the spirited talks and participating in the debates, which stretched from morning till late night over the course of two days.

They heard Lucretia Mott give several "eloquent and powerful" talks and heard Elizabeth Stanton's first major speech. They heard Stanton read aloud the Declaration of Sentiments and then discussed each paragraph; the declaration was passed unanimously by the meeting, and sixty-eight women and thirty-two men stepped forward to affix their signatures to the document.

On the second day, the resolutions were put forward, and the first eight were easily adopted. Then came resolution nine. Mott urged Stanton to withdraw it. Stanton refused. The debate over the suffrage proposal was contentious. Many saw it as a dangerous distraction from the more urgent legal, social, and economic demands, and it looked as though the resolution would go down in defeat. Stanton looked to Frederick Douglass for support. "I knew Frederick, from personal experience, was just the man for the work."

Douglass asked for the floor, stepped forward. Woman, like the colored man, will never be taken by her brother and lifted to a position, he insisted. What she desires, she must fight for. The ballot was the guarantor of all other rights, the key to liberty, and women must be bold. His arguments, together with Stanton's, carried the day, if just barely: resolution nine was passed by a slim majority.

Not only did Douglass turn the tide for the suffrage resolution inside the chapel, he returned home to Rochester to publish a highly sympathetic report of the proceedings at Seneca Falls in his *North Star,* accompanied by an editorial voicing unequivocal support for this new "grand movement":

"In respect to political rights," he wrote, "we hold woman to be justly entitled to all we claim for man. . . . If that government only is just which governs by the free consent of the governed, there can be no reason in the world for denying to woman the exercise of the elective franchise, or a hand in making and administering the laws of the land." Douglass would attend almost every national women's rights convention for the next fifty years and was one of the staunchest friends of the movement.

Word of the meeting at Seneca Falls spread, producing a torrent of outrage and ridicule. Newspapers denounced it with headlines screaming INSURRECTION OF THE WOMEN and REIGN OF PETTICOATS. Ministers, Bible in hand, delivered angry homilies about woman stepping beyond her proper sphere; those who participated in the Seneca Falls Convention faced derision in their own communities. "So pronounced was the popular voice against us, in the parlor, the press, and the pulpit," Stanton remembered, "that most of the ladies who attended the convention and signed the Declaration, one by one, withdrew their names. . . . Our friends gave us the cold shoulder and felt themselves disgraced by the whole proceeding. If I had had the slightest premonition of all that was to follow that convention, I fear I should not have had the courage to risk it."

In truth, Elizabeth Cady Stanton was rather delighted by all the ink and vitriol spilled on the convention. "That is just what I wanted," she gleefully wrote to Lucretia. "It will start women thinking, and men too; and when men and women think about a new question, the first step in progress is taken."

Lucy Stone had just graduated from Oberlin College in Ohio, the first college in America to admit black students and women, and she was already sensitized to the inequalities women faced: as a teacher, she was paid half of what less experienced men earned; as a student, even at progressive Oberlin, she was denied the right to speak or debate in public. She defiantly decided to become a public orator: "I expect to plead not for the slave only, but for suffering humanity everywhere. Especially do I mean to labor for the elevation of my sex," she wrote to her mother, who did not think this a wise career choice.

Lucy quickly landed a job as a speaker and organizer for the Massachusetts Anti-Slavery Society, lacing her talks about emancipation with examples of women's oppression. Her abolitionist employers did not like her mixing the two causes, worrying that the combination would dilute their primary objective or, worse, alienate audiences. "I was a woman before I was an abolitionist," she replied tartly, but arranged to speak for the society on abolition on weekends while giving her women's rights lectures on weekdays.

She was a gifted orator, with great persuasive powers and a voice described as a "silver bell." She helped organize the first national women's rights conference in 1850, held in Worcester, Massachusetts, featuring a roster of illustrious abolition stars stepping up for the nascent women's rights cause, including William Lloyd Garrison, Wendell Phillips, Angelina Grimké, Lucretia Mott, Frederick Douglass, and a former slave who'd taken the name Sojourner Truth. Women's rights conventions began popping up all over the country, but abolition and temperance continued to be the prime focus of dedicated reformers.

Then in 1851, Mrs. Stanton was introduced to a thirty-year-old teacher turned Anti-Slavery Society organizer named Susan Anthony from Rochester. Susan Anthony was not particularly interested in the "woman question" yet, though she had, in fact, already confronted it: as a schoolteacher she'd been paid much less than her male colleagues, and when she stood up to protest this disparity at a state teachers' convention, she was booed down for having the temerity to speak. Anthony attended her first women's rights convention in May 1853. This conference marked her conversion to "the Cause" and the start of her life's work: "When she once got fairly started in the woman's rights agitation," a colleague noted, "she made up for lost time."

It also marked the beginning of one of the most extraordinary partnerships in American history, a collaboration that lasted for more than half a century and changed the lives of half the nation. They were a study in contrasts: Anthony tall and prim, highly disciplined, and abstemious; Stanton plump and jovial, gregarious, and indulgent. Anthony never married; Stanton enjoyed a long but difficult marriage and a large brood of children. Susan often came to live with the Stantons to babysit, giving Elizabeth a chance to write their polemics. Anthony always referred to her colleague as "Mrs. Stanton"; Elizabeth simply called her friend "Susan." They were collaborators and co-conspirators, confidantes and critics, clashing sisters. Stanton was "thought" and Anthony was "action."

"I forged the thunderbolts and she fired them," is how Stanton described their work together. Anthony would later teach Carrie Catt how to aim such missiles. In the 1850s, there was no official women's rights organization and no feeling among activists that such a structure was even necessary—it might be too rigid and cumbersome. This was a time for broaching formerly taboo topics, discussing them privately in parlors and openly at conventions, engaging in debate with doubters, wrestling with contradictions, and forging an ideology. It was the period—to borrow a term from a much later women's movement—of "consciousness raising." Over the decade the circle of women widened steadily, though it did not extend to the women of the southern states, where the culture did not allow for such questioning of social roles and relationships. At the center were Elizabeth Stanton, the new movement's philosopher; Lucretia Mott, its moral force; Lucy Stone, its voice; and Susan Anthony, its organizer.

But those who advocated women's rights were still just a small segment of the larger, organized, more urgent push to abolish slavery, and as the nation veered toward a cataclysmic confrontation, there could be no doubt about priorities. During the Civil War—in a decision that presaged the one Carrie Catt would make six decades later when America entered the Great War—those who considered themselves "feminist abolitionists" reluctantly suspended their work for women's rights and channeled their energies into the righteous crusade for emancipation and the preservation of the Union.

Many abolitionists, including Stanton and Mott, did not support

Abraham Lincoln's presidential candidacy in 1860, believing the Illinois senator was not sufficiently committed to the ideal of immediate emancipation for slaves; even after his election and the outbreak of war, ambivalence about Lincoln persisted. Abolitionists spent the Civil War years pressuring Lincoln to actually break the shackles of the slave. Even when he issued his Emancipation Proclamation, many abolition activists questioned the sincerity of his motives—was it truly an act of moral courage or just a wartime expediency to undermine Confederate morale?—and bemoaned the fact that the proclamation did not truly abolish slavery in America, only outlawed it in the rebellious states where it could hardly be enforced. What was needed was a surge of public pressure to push Lincoln and Congress to follow through with a comprehensive measure to abolish slavery completely and permanently by law, not just executive order. Better yet, by constitutional amendment. The abolitionists' ally in the Senate, Charles Sumner of Massachusetts, asked for help in turning up the heat under Congress: Bring me visible proof of the will of the people, he told the abolitionists.

"Here then is work for you, Susan," Henry Stanton wrote to his wife's collaborator, urging her to join this effort, "put on your armor and go forth!" Elizabeth and Susan strapped on their shields and put out a call "To the Loyal Women of the Republic," convening a meeting in May 1863 of the group called the Women's National Loyal League. The goal: to muster an army of women into a massive grassroots effort to push for a stronger emancipation policy. This was a different sort of war work from anything women had ever been asked to do, a far cry from nursing or knitting or fund-raising fairs on behalf of soldiers. This was political work, organized agitation for a governmental solution to slavery, utilizing the one legal tool women possessed—the petition. Women did not have bullets, Susan Anthony reminded them, and they certainly did not have the ballot; but the "sacred right" to petition the government for redress of grievances was enshrined in the Constitution's First Amendment, and it was not restricted to men. Now they aimed to use it, and on a larger scale than had ever been done before.

With Stanton and Anthony in charge, the Loyal League was infused with a strong feminist flavor, and at that first organizing meeting they inserted a controversial resolution: "There can never be true peace in this republic until the civil and political rights of all citizens of African descent and all Women are practically established." As usual, there was an outcry from some attendees; even William Lloyd Garrison protested Stanton and

Anthony's transformation of the inaugural Women's National Loyal League meeting into a "women's rights convention." One newspaper called the meeting a "witches sabbath." But the resolution was passed.

Stanton became president and Anthony secretary of the Women's National Loyal League and quickly built a structure and an elaborate outreach mechanism. League members wore breastpins bearing the image of a slave breaking out of his chains and the motto "In Emancipation Is National Unity." Anthony, with her superb organizing skills, recruited more than two thousand women to take women's emancipation petitions door-to-door, collecting the signatures of both women and men, white and black, and asking for a penny donation. Even children were encouraged to knock on doors to collect signatures and pennies and were rewarded with a badge. The petitions were forwarded to league headquarters in New York City, where they were recorded and tallied, the pages pasted together and rolled into giant scrolls (Elizabeth enlisted her children to help), packed into trunks, and mailed to Congress. There they became the star props in a grand bit of political theater.

On a February morning in 1864, two tall black men marched into the Senate chamber carrying sets of scrolls, the first installment of the league's petitions, one hundred thousand signatures strong. They strode across the room and handed the scrolls to Senator Sumner, who stood to accept them with a dramatic flourish. He pronounced the petitions "the prayer of one hundred thousand" and used them to bolster his drive for a constitutional amendment forever abolishing slavery. In an extraordinary logistic feat, the Women's National Loyal League would deliver Sumner a total of four hundred thousand signatures, which he presented in batches to Congress every few weeks over the next year. It was the largest petition drive in national history, an undeniable demonstration of public sentiment that is credited with helping to convince Lincoln and Congress to push through the Thirteenth Amendment.

Stanton and Anthony could take rightful pride in the role the Women's National Loyal League played in realizing emancipation, but the lessons they learned from the process were even more valuable: they had just built and run the very first national woman's political organization in the United States, a team of five thousand members working toward a single goal; and they had seen firsthand the power of organizing women for political action within a strong structure. They had demonstrated women's patriotism, shown proof of their political abilities, and engaged a new and wider cadre of activists. The Loyal League was an ideal training ground for a movement that would usher in a new era of what Elizabeth called "True Democracy" as soon as the war was over.

Little wonder that Josephine Pearson's Confederate family prayed that the "virus of Equal Rights"—for blacks or women—would not spread. They need not have worried. As the suffragists would sadly learn, the political will to enact True Democracy was feeble. Now, more than half a century later, the loyal Pearson daughter, Josephine, was confident that the political will for woman suffrage in Tennessee was still lacking—or, at the very least, could be stifled.

Chapter 5

◆ ◆ ◆

Democracy at Home

WHILE NASHVILLE'S HOTEL HERMITAGE buzzed with activity on Sunday, a few blocks away at the quieter Hotel Tulane, Sue White unfolded a large map of Tennessee, draping it over the bed like a stiff, crinkled coverlet. She stared at the long horizontal expanse of her state, pennant shaped, with the southeast corner ripped off, fringed edges on its sides where the Smoky Mountains on the east and Mississippi River on the west formed jagged borders.

The three Grand Divisions were spelled out geologically on the map: the steep Appalachians of East Tennessee dropping down into the highlands and gorges of the Cumberland Plateau, then rolling into Middle Tennessee's hills and valleys, and finally smoothing into the flat deltas of West Tennessee. The state was sliced into thirds by the Tennessee River as it took its long oxbow loop into, out of, and back into the territory; the Mississippi River flowed by Memphis, and the Cumberland River curved around Nashville. The rugged beauty of the state, the mountains and hidden hollers, the plunging valleys and lofty knobs, the rivers and creeks and caves—all were a big problem for Sue White right now.

The logistics were going to be tough. To cover ninety-seven counties—some with only dirt roads and no rail—and 132 members of the legislature, Sue estimated that a Woman's Party campaign would require fifteen organizers: two in each of the major cities—Chattanooga, Knoxville, Nashville, and Memphis—another to shuttle between Bristol and Johnson City in the northeast, and six more assigned to the rural counties, plus a press director at Nashville headquarters. There was no way the tiny Tennessee branch of the Woman's Party could afford such staffing. The National Woman's Party itself could barely afford her modest paycheck of $100 a month. Ratification campaigns in the states had been harder and more expensive than expected, the party had drained its bank account, and checks issued by headquarters were bouncing left and right.

Alice Paul seized upon White's discouraging analysis of Tennessee as an opportunity—Miss Paul was a wizard at that sort of alchemy—and turned the report into a fund-raising tool. She mailed copies to every Woman's Party member and possible friend around the country, distributed it to the press, and announced an emergency Tennessee campaign drive to raise $20,000 for the ratification fight. One dollar from twenty thousand women who wanted to secure political liberty for their sex could do it, or a nice fat check from the Woman's Party's fairy godmother, Alva Belmont, but Miss Paul had not yet managed to pry open Mrs. Belmont's purse. Paul followed up with urgent telegrams to her best donors:

"Beg you to give largest sum you can spare in this emergency. Opportunity to win this last state will not come back if we lose it now." White had no idea if enough dollar bills tucked into envelopes would roll in through the mail at headquarters to enable her to execute a proper campaign in Tennessee; she would just have to work with what she had. She was used to hardscrabble.

It wasn't just money that was scarce, it was woman power. The National Woman's Party, which had split off from the NAWSA in 1913 (it was called the Congressional Union for Woman Suffrage then) did not have a robust presence in the state. Lizzie Crozier French in Knoxville and Lulu Colyar Reese in Memphis were suffrage stalwarts who had crossed over the line to join the Woman's Party, but there weren't too many others. Back in April, Sue had tried to boost party membership with an impassioned call to arms addressed "To the Suffragists of Tennessee"—virtually all of whom were members of NAWSA—warning them that if they'd been "misled" by Mrs. Catt's organization into believing that ratification was secure, that it was time for a victory party and celebration, they were dead wrong.

"This is a time for work and not a time for rejoicing," she admonished, giving a jab to NAWSA's premature victory convention in Chicago several weeks before, when the thirty-fifth state had been gained and the thirty-sixth probably seemed imminent. "And if any of us have laid down our arms in the thick of battle for the purpose of rejoicing in a victory not yet won—or to partake in other work"—that was a poke at Mrs. Catt's new hobby-horse, the League of Women Voters—"in the name of High Heaven and the Pioneers, let us once more put on our armor and strive to hold the line against the concentrated attack of our ancient enemies." The Woman's Party was still fighting. She'd enclosed a membership card, asked for twenty-five cents dues and perhaps a small contribution. The response was underwhelming. The party had a bad reputation in Tennessee. White knew this only too well.

Everything about the National Woman's Party irritated southern sensibilities, even among ardent suffragists: its federal amendment doctrine, its fierce opposition to President Wilson and the Democrats, and especially its combative, distinctly unladylike style. These had also bothered White at first, and she'd publicly criticized the party's tactics. But then the war came and made everything more complicated.

When America entered the war in April 1917, Sue White dutifully followed the policy Mrs. Catt prescribed for all good suffragists, placing war work alongside suffrage work. She believed, as did Mrs. Catt, that suffragists could best prove to the public and to Congress their good citizenship, their patriotism, and how much they deserved the vote by pledging themselves to national service. White maintained her active role in the National Association's Tennessee branch while also joining the state chapter of the Woman's Committee of the Council of National Defense and used the organizational skills she'd learned in suffrage work to register fifty thousand Tennessee women—white and black women—for duties supporting the war.

Alice Paul and her Woman's Party, however, refused to support American involvement in the European conflict or participate in the home front war effort. For them there was only one issue: suffrage. They picketed the White House, confronting the government that sent sons to die for democracy in Europe while denying their mothers and sisters and wives the rights of democracy at home. In Tennessee, as in many parts of the country, Alice Paul and her protesting ladies were branded unpatriotic, even traitors.

White did not support the picketing, but she tried to understand the logic behind the tactic. "I see a determination—at any cost—to show the inconsistency of men and agencies who declare war for the right of Europeans to have a voice in their own governments, while turning a deaf ear to the right of American women to have voice in *their* own government," she reasoned. White continued her volunteer war work as well as her suffrage work, remaining in the fold of Catt's NAWSA, and was secure in her conviction that America was doing what was right in the war, defending democracy. Until the Woman's Party came to Tennessee and tested the bounds of democracy at home.

Maud Younger, a Woman's Party star speaker and organizer, arrived in Tennessee in November 1917 as part of a tour through the South to explain the party's position on the war and the role of the picketing protesters. The first stop on the tour was Memphis, but no public hall would allow Younger to speak, branding her "disloyal, pro-German, and un-American." White's sense of justice was aroused, and she went to Memphis to try to defuse the matter, defending Younger and the Woman's Party, calling the allegations against them "base political slander." Still, she could not convince any meeting hall in Memphis to allow Younger to speak. Sue was appalled: "I saw with my own eyes a situation which was enough to alarm any one who holds American ideals dear."

Those ideals were being compromised around the country, as the Wilson government stoked a shrill patriotic hysteria, useful for pumping up support for an unpopular war. Newspapers were shut down, pacifist professors fired from universities, war skeptics thrown into prison, and German Americans accused of disloyalty under enhanced alien and sedition laws. "I determined then that if the same thing occurred throughout the state," White explained, "I would have to join the pickets at the White House gates, not so much for equal suffrage as for freedom of speech."

In Jackson, where White lived and worked, antagonism toward the Woman's Party's picketing was so "hot and sharp," and threats of violence so loud, that the mayor threatened to call off Younger's lecture in the local schoolhouse. White called the mayor, called the chief of police, convinced them that the Woman's Party meeting must go on and the visitors given whatever protection necessary. Miss Sue's word was golden in Jackson, and the lecture went ahead, but the scene was tense, and two burly sheriff's deputies walked up and down the aisle of the auditorium, watching for trouble.

White continued on tour with Younger and the Woman's Party group for another five days, closing up her stenography office (her only source of income), using her political contacts to ease their way, acting as a sort of moral bodyguard. Even if you do not agree with their methods, she insisted, the Woman's Party had the right to speak. This was America, after all.

When White returned home to Jackson, she was stunned to find herself the target of a barrage of hostility from, of all people, her sister suffragists. Her attackers included Anne Dallas Dudley, her friend and fellow officer in the state suffrage association, who lambasted her for cozying up to the enemy in wartime: the enemy in this case being not Germany, but the Woman's Party. Dudley slammed White in the pages of the *Nashville Tennessean,* and an accompanying editorial took White to task; the Memphis papers reported similar denunciations. Words such as "disloyalty" and "un-American" were used to describe White. Dudley and other Tennessee suffragists were anxious that the antiwar actions of the Woman's Party (which they considered a renegade suffrage group) not tar the entire suffrage movement in the public mind. White's friends resented the slurs aimed at her, but she refused to be baited: "I prefer to presume that my loyalty to my country is above reproach."

Shortly after, White received a shocking message from the Chief herself, Mrs. Carrie Catt, all the way from New York. Catt had read an editorial in the Woman's Party organ, *The Suffragist,* about White's "cooperation" with the Woman's Party emissaries in Tennessee. Catt jumped to the conclusion that White may have done more than just smooth the way for their talks; she accused White of being a turncoat and possibly a spy, suspected of revealing NAWSA strategy secrets to the Alice Paul crowd.

Miss Sue was insulted by the accusations, but not angry; that was not her way. She wrote her own calmly reasoned letter to Mrs. Catt, explaining that she had assisted the Woman's Party on its tour in an effort to uphold democracy and free speech, something all suffragists should cherish. Growing bolder, White also expressed her frustration with the National Association's abandonment of Tennessee and the southern states in the "Winning Plan" strategy, Catt's dual-track effort to pressure Congress to pass the federal amendment by achieving suffrage victories in pivotal states—all of them northern states. The Woman's Party was at least trying to "wake up" and organize in the South, White noted; NAWSA seemed to have given up.

After six months of letters back and forth, Catt presented White with an ultimatum: "Take your stand, fair and square, one side or the other." White was torn, but this was not a time for sentimentality, it was a time for action: "In spite of every effort to curb my militant tendencies," White explained to Catt, "my mind continues to revert to the suggestion of Abigail Adams to her John more than a hundred years ago, that the ladies might be constrained to foment a rebellion. Is a hundred years behind the times conservative enough?" Sue White made her choice: she joined the Woman's Party.

Sue's relations with her former Tennessee suffrage colleagues were still raw and awkward. This sort of alienation played out everywhere suffragists traded the respectability of the NAWSA for the outlaw mystique of the Woman's Party, but the friction was even more intense in a place like

Tennessee, where the movement was already splintered and grudges were nursed, with pleasure, for a long time.

Both NAWSA and the Woman's Party set their sights on the same ratification goal, but they insisted on pursuing it in their own way: each conducted its own polling, lobbying, organizing, and publicity campaigns in every state. A very similar split had taken place in the British suffrage movement: followers of the confrontational Pankhursts adopted "militant" methods and broke from Millicent Fawcett's more conservative organization. The American split mirrored this, with Mrs. Pankhurst's students Alice Paul and Lucy Burns pulling away from Fawcett's friend Carrie Catt and her NAWSA. But unlike the Pankhursts, whose forces attacked shops and office windows with hammers, planted small bombs in postboxes, and set fire to government property, Alice Paul was a pacifist Quaker, and the Woman's Party was never violent and anything but "militant." Hoisting a picket sign, chaining wrists to a fence, and burning paper was as violent as the party's protests ever got.

This sort of strategic schism isn't uncommon in social and political movements, especially when the struggle is long and success seems far from reach. Abolitionists fractured over the use of tactical violence as practiced by John Brown, just as Carrie Nation's saloon-bashing hatchet divided temperance advocates. The labor movement was riven by the adoption by the Industrial Workers of the World—known as the Wobblies—of violent means and later, in the 1930s, by unions' use of sit-down strikes. The mid-twentieth-century civil rights movement would undergo its own splintering over the wisdom of violent resistance, with younger activists wrestling for power with the resolutely nonviolent Martin Luther King, Jr. Later in the century, the confrontational playbook of ACT UP would divide the gay rights community, while in the early twenty-first century, the controversial methods of some environmental and animal rights activists would shake those campaigns. There's always a tricky trade-off between the benefits of gaining attention from dramatic action and the risk of alienating the public and jeopardizing popular support. One thing seems certain: such painful rifts within protest movements appear to be essential components of the ecosystem of change.

That said, Sue White knew that competition could also have a nasty edge. White warned her party colleagues about Dudley, "who inclines to hydrophobia at the thought of the N.W.P.," she explained, likening the reaction to a dire symptom of rabies. "Guard against the cunning of our sister-in-arms," White cautioned, as Dudley "would do almost anything to discredit our efforts. These were the same women White would have to cooperate with in Nashville.

Sue White knew what needed to be done to win ratification in Tennessee; she had an instinctive feel for the political pulse of her state. She'd lived in Tennessee all her life, and her years of working in the courthouses and organizing for suffrage introduced her to many of the political players: she knew their backgrounds, their professional alliances, their historic rifts, their personal foibles, and their soft spots. She was a loyal Democrat, but she could get Republicans to confide in her. She considered herself a progressive but had a good rapport with the machine pols. White was from West Tennessee, but she could make the eastern mountain men in the legislature feel at ease. She had forged excellent relations with Tennessee's junior senator Kenneth McKellar, a firm suffrage friend, and maintained valuable contacts with the staff of the profoundly antisuffrage senior senator John Knight Shields, one of the two stubborn senators who'd held up passage of the federal amendment in Congress for so long.

During the past few weeks, she'd watched with some delight as Governor Roberts squirmed under pressure from the White House and the national Democrats, who forced him to finally call the special session. Even now, she didn't quite trust him to carry through on the promise. She'd already tried, and failed, to convince him to convene the session in early July, so that the federal amendment might be ratified in time for Tennessee women to vote in the state primary elections on August 5. A speedier ratification would also allow the women of eighteen other states holding primary elections during the summer to vote. Roberts refused. White knew Roberts feared women might deny him the nomination if they could vote in the primary. The national Democrats didn't push him on the date, as the politicos in those other states were also wary of unleashing the unpredictable "woman vote" in their primaries. So Roberts set the opening of the special session for August 9: after his primary and, there was no doubt, only if he won the primary. If he didn't win, all promises were off.

Roberts really didn't want women voting, she knew that. If given the chance, women voters might well drum him out of office in the general

election, even if he held on in the primary. The suffragists had a long memory of his years as an Anti, and even Anti women were hearing those whispers about his very pretty and highly paid private secretary.

His cronies, his "advisers," were dead set against woman suffrage, and
they were probably busy designing ways to kill ratification in the legislature
without leaving fingerprints—if it even reached the legislature. White reported to party headquarters that just before Roberts was forced to set the
date for convening the legislature, the governor's campaign manager was
asked when the special session might be called. He replied: "I hope never."

Both Democrats and Republicans—the presidential candidates, the
party people at their conventions—were talking a good game now, but the
truth of their campaign promises remained to be seen. White understood
the basis of all this sweet talk as election season drew close:

"So all the political leaders should be in a more or less amorous mood as
they face the inevitable influence of women upon their destinies," she'd
quipped to one of her party colleagues. That didn't mean that those men
wouldn't try their darnedest to postpone the inevitable as long as possible.

Some people seemed to think that just because the Tennessee legislature
had agreed to the limited (presidential and municipal) suffrage measure last
year, and the governor, very reluctantly, had signed it into law, the legislature
would merrily go along with ratification of the federal amendment. Mrs.
Catt's Suffs in Tennessee were touting this scenario, and to Sue's mind it was
nothing more than wishful, and risky, thinking. The limited suffrage measure passed the legislature by the skin of its teeth, even though it didn't face
any states' rights objections or fears of Washington oversight. The federal
amendment carried all that baggage, which would certainly cost votes. The
East Tennessee Republicans who had supported the partial suffrage bill were
probably not going to be so obliging this time around, lest ratification be
fashioned into a feather in the Democrats' cap for the fall elections. And
then there was the issue of the state constitution and the legality of the legislature ratifying: some legislators were moaning that they would be violating their oath of office if they took up ratification, no matter what the
Tennessee Supreme Court said. It was a convenient excuse to duck ratification altogether, but it might still be potent, and it might still hurt.

Chapter 6

• • •

The Governor's Quandary

I N THE GOVERNOR'S MANSION at the foot of Capitol Hill, Albert Houston Roberts punched his arm into his rumpled linen jacket and wrapped a too-short tie around his neck. He was expected at Mrs. Catt's room at the Hermitage; he did not have time for this. He'd come in on a late train last night, after delivering three sweat-soaked campaign speeches on Saturday, and awoke to face a fresh crisis. The firefighters in Memphis were on strike. Another strike.

The postwar labor unrest roiling the rest of the nation hit Tennessee, too. Though the unions and the Wobblies weren't as strong here as in other states, they still managed to cause trouble. Roberts had already faced a shoe-manufacturing strike in Nashville and a street railway workers' strike in Knoxville. He'd clamped down quickly—you couldn't let them think the governor was a weakling—calling up the Tennessee National Guard and creating a state police force to squelch strikers. He tried to swing public opinion against strikers, mobs, and all others who wanted to hurt the state's reputation and economy by encouraging citizen "Law and Order Leagues." The labor people were furious with him, denounced him for "setting the classes against the masses," and were out for revenge.

Now the firemen in Memphis had walked off the job, demanding better pay. Nashville and Knoxville sent some of their men to take up the hoses, but they were being met with a rash of arson fires, false alarms, and some violence. The Memphis mayor was in a panic, reporting that the situation in the city was "extremely grave," and he begged for more militia troops. Roberts was sending them in. And all these women could think about was their suffrage amendment.

Roberts hadn't had it easy since his term began just nineteen months before. No sooner had he taken his oath than the Spanish flu ripped through the state on a second swing. Then, with the war and its lucrative contracts ended, the war industry plants, such as the DuPont gunpowder plant in Nashville that at its peak employed twenty thousand men and women, closed down, throwing thousands of people out of work—just as inflation ramped up. The returning troops couldn't find jobs and resented the black men who had taken their jobs; and the black men who had served in the military returned expecting better jobs as a proper reward. It made for friction. Race riots tore through Knoxville in the summer of 1919: white mobs marauding through the black precincts, burning and looting, storming a jail to lynch a black man. Roberts called out the Tennessee National Guard, but they couldn't control the violence and sided with the white rioters, shooting machine guns into the black crowds; about forty people, mostly blacks, were killed. In the tense atmosphere, the Ku Klux Klan was finding eager new recruits and enjoying a resurgence.

Roberts's first act as governor was to certify Tennessee's ratification of the Eighteenth Amendment, Prohibition. It had gone into effect earlier in 1920, and the heavy-handed federal raids were riling up people. Tennessee had been officially "dry" since 1909, but it had its own ways of handling it, and everyone sort of understood the rules; Memphis and Nashville simply ignored them and remained happily, defiantly "wet." Roberts didn't like the federal agents snooping around, arresting and shooting people, but it was out of his hands.

Roberts was short, with a small paunch around his belly, big ears, bushy brows, and an unruly forelock curl that he attempted to plaster down each morning. He vaguely resembled the popular humorist Will Rogers, except he wasn't good at telling jokes and rarely cracked a smile in public. He was a serious, earnest man with a milquetoast personality: a teacher turned lawyer, a circuit-riding judge turned hapless politician. He had good intentions, but he couldn't execute his ideas smoothly or get people to understand. He did not seem to have a gift for politics. He did seem to have an uncanny gift for attracting political enemies.

Roberts thought of himself as a progressive politician, and he wanted Tennessee to make strides, lead the South. What the state needed was better education and better roads, paid for by fairer taxes. Everyone nodded in agreement, but no one wanted to pay. He set about overhauling the antiquated tax code and caught hell on all sides. He tried to push through road-building bills and earned the enmity of the railroad owners, who correctly saw automobiles as competition. Tennessee ranked toward the very bottom of the states when it came to literacy, and Roberts wanted to change that by extending mandatory schooling to the eighth grade and improving teacher training. He expected to win some applause for this, but the clapping wasn't loud enough to drown out the boos from the manufacturers who thought children should be working, not wasting time in school.

Roberts was unpopular, and his enemies smelled blood. He could accept the animosity of those who opposed the policy changes he'd made, but he got riled by the naked opportunism of those in his own party who wanted to derail his career for their personal advantage. Luke Lea wanted him out of contention down the road: that was the reason the *Tennessean* and Lea's people were pounding him. They put up a candidate to run against him in the primary, the former mayor of Chattanooga, Colonel William Crabtree, just for spite. And they began this despicable rumor campaign about his private secretary, about how she was "disreputable" just because she was pretty. She was very well qualified, and besides, it was none of their business. Albert Roberts was in a desperate fight to hold on to his job and perhaps his marriage.

On top of all this came the Nineteenth Amendment. Roberts had hoped the amendment circus would never roll into town. His dream to dodge the whole mess at first seemed a sure thing: the Tennessee Constitution prohibited a sitting legislature from acting on a federal constitutional amendment; the legislature had to be elected after the amendment was passed by Congress and brought to the states for ratification. This provision was to ensure that constituents would know where their legislators stood on that amendment and could take their stance into consideration in the next election. The provision was placed into the state constitution in 1870, after the Reconstruction legislature and a radical Republican governor had rammed through ratification of the Fourteenth Amendment—giving black men civil rights and due process while disenfranchising the sons of the Confederacy—over the objection of the people, the white people, of the state. Tennessee did not want a repeat of that.

So the present legislature, the Sixty-First General Assembly, elected in 1918, was legally prohibited from acting on the Nineteenth Amendment. Roberts was greatly relieved. As he'd told Mrs. Catt in June 1919, when the ratification process first began and she pressed him to act: Sorry, he simply couldn't call an extraordinary session to ratify, his hands were tied. Exactly a year later, he clung to the same excuse when a delegation of Tennessee suffragists marched into his office to convince him to call a special session.

Then the U.S. Supreme Court pulled the rug out from under him. On

June 1, 1920, the court ruled that the process for ratifying a federal constitutional amendment could not be impeded by any state law or action. Ohio law provided for a popular referendum after legislative ratification of any federal amendment, but the Supreme Court held that this could not stand: the ratification process was clearly spelled out in the federal Constitution, which said it was to be done by the state legislature. That took precedence over state law.

Roberts's careful avoidance of the Nineteenth Amendment ended abruptly, on June 23, with a telegram from the White House: "It would be a real service to the Party and to the nation if it is possible for you under the peculiar provisions of your State Constitution having in mind the recent decision of the Supreme Court in the Ohio case to call a special session of the legislature of Tennessee to consider the suffrage amendment. Allow me to urge this very earnestly. Woodrow Wilson."

Roberts was certain that his hero, fellow southerner Woodrow Wilson, would not have written this of his own accord; it must have been drafted under pressure from the suffragists, who were salivating at the notion that Tennessee might be in play for ratification. They'd managed to stick their hat pins into the president. Roberts was right about that.

To fortify his request, President Wilson also asked the U.S. Department of Justice for an opinion on the applicability of the Supreme Court ruling to Tennessee. Luckily, thought Roberts, Acting Attorney General William L. Frierson (holding down the fort while his boss, Attorney General A. Mitchell Palmer, was away in San Francisco trying to get himself nominated for president) was a good Tennessean who would surely respect the sanctity of his home state's constitution.

Frierson produced an opinion that did not please Governor Roberts: the Supreme Court ruling did indeed apply to Tennessee: "If the people of a State through their Constitution can delay action on an amendment until after an election, there is no reason why they cannot delay it until after two elections or five elections," Frierson held, and this ran counter to the federal Constitution's clear amending procedure. The current Tennessee legislature was free to vote on the ratification of the Nineteenth Amendment. Governor Roberts lost his good excuse.

Now Roberts was squeezed all around. The Tennessee suffragists screamed for him to immediately call a special session of the legislature. The

Democrats at their convention in San Francisco adopted a special platform plank—pointed right at him—demanding that he convene the legislature and achieve ratification quickly. He was pelted with telegrams and phone calls from all the party top brass, from all the prospective presidential candidates (there must have been two dozen of them), and, most painfully, from his own Tennessee delegation, men and women, at the convention.

The president, the man he'd once called his Moses, was urging him, very earnestly, to jump off a cliff. Roberts's advisers and friends counseled, just as earnestly: Don't do it. The federal amendment, they warned, is a hydra-headed monster capable of swallowing you and your career. People won't read the legal opinions, they'll just remember that Governor Roberts was willing to go along with the idea that the Tennessee Constitution plays second fiddle to Washington's Constitution. Don't mess with the Antis; many of whom were his friends and supporters. If he did call a special session, they threatened to undermine his bid for renomination in the primary, leave him stranded. So Roberts did the safest thing he could think of: he stalled. But he was undercut by the state attorney general's opinion, stating that the U.S. Supreme Court's ruling applied to Tennessee and there was no longer any legal barrier to calling a special session.

Feeling cornered, Roberts announced that he would agree to call an extraordinary session of the legislature, but he wouldn't say exactly when that session would meet. He was buying time, giving the matter his "grave consideration," but if he thought the maneuver would buy him any peace, he was fooling himself. The White House went public with its "disappointment" in Roberts's refusal to speedily call the special session, and the headline in the *Nashville Tennessean* read: ADMINISTRATION AGGRAVATED BY ROBERTS' STAND.

The Democrats, still tied in knots in San Francisco, seemed to delight in using him as a punching bag—perhaps the only thing they could agree upon—insisting that he name a firm date for the special session so they might announce it at the convention and take credit for rounding up the thirty-sixth state. The Democrats were trying to improve their party's image among potential women voters; Republicans had a much stronger record of supporting suffrage in Congress as well as in the states—Republican-led legislatures had delivered twenty-six of the thirty-five ratifications thus far. Many national suffrage leaders considered themselves Republican, as that party had championed progressive social and economic reforms. In the late nineteenth and early twentieth centuries, the Republican Party was considered the more liberal of the two major parties.

Both Democrats and Republicans had endorsed ratification of the Nineteenth Amendment at their conventions earlier that summer, and so had both state parties in Tennessee. All the gubernatorial candidates running in the state primary claimed to support the amendment, and Roberts's Democratic challenger, Colonel Crabtree, warned that Roberts's indecision was bad for the state: "Some Republican state will ratify and rob Tennessee of its chance for glory." The Tennessee suffragists of both parties squawked at him to convene the legislature at once, to get the amendment ratified in time for them, and the women of other states, to vote in the summer primaries.

But women were not good for him, his campaign advisers reminded him. If the women could vote, they might well defeat him. Giving them the ballot would be like handing them a shotgun and inviting them to shoot. They no doubt remembered he'd campaigned for governor as an Anti and had equivocated on the partial suffrage bill; and then there were those rumors about an "other woman." Keep them away from the primary and, ideally, away from the general election, his friends advised. Tennessee women could already vote for president and for mayors; they already had more than enough suffrage.

There were other reasons to be wary of giving women the vote in all elections, including state elections, his advisers warned: the state's major corporate interests didn't like the idea one bit. How could the railroads, just emerging from wartime federal control, successfully compete with the automobile and the truck, and recover all those state dollars being siphoned off into road building, if the legislators with whom they'd already curried favor were defeated by women voters who didn't understand how things worked?

And how could the once profitable liquor industry, reeling under the new Volstead Act enforcing the federal Prohibition law, survive? They'd managed to keep going for a decade under the lax, wink-wink implementation of Tennessee's own "dry" laws, but now federal agents were shooting to kill small-time moonshiners operating stills in the Tennessee hills. The big distillers had already moved out of state—Jack Daniel's was operating out of Alabama and Missouri—pinching tax revenues from a lucrative business. The only hope for the industry was to finance the election of wetter congressmen and state legislators who might be able to dial back, or even wipe out, the punitive Prohibition enforcement laws. The problem with women voters was that they tended to support temperance and probably would not cast ballots for the types of lawmakers the industry needed.

And the manufacturers, especially the state's cotton cloth mills and clothing makers, were also angry about woman suffrage. They were worried about reform-type women voters insisting upon labor laws that would limit the hours women could work, calling for equal pay and, worst of all, perhaps outlawing child labor. The entire cotton-manufacturing economy of the South was based upon the cheap labor of women and children: Was Governor Roberts willing to destroy it for the promise of a few women's votes? And oh yes, Roberts's advisers warned: all those Negro women who would suddenly be able to vote if Tennessee ratified the federal amendment—they were going to vote Republican!

Feeling cornered, on June 28 Roberts finally announced that the extraordinary session would convene on August 9, safely after his primary. The suffragists howled but had to accept it. He reminded them, not too subtly, that if he did not win renomination, the special session might not take place at all, in what would be his lame-duck misery. His friends in the legislature could hardly be expected to support ratification if he was defeated. To shield himself, he would name his own Ratification Committee, headed by a suffrage woman he could trust, Mrs. Kate Burch Warner, not the League of Women Voters leaders, Mrs. Kenny and Mrs. Milton, who were his active antagonists. Mrs. Kenny was Luke Lea's little protégée, and Mrs. Milton's husband, George, gleefully ripped Roberts apart in the pages of his *Chattanooga News*. He would not entrust the dangerous ratification campaign to his enemies.

Roberts was still on the road when Mrs. Catt arrived and was in no mood to placate the suffragists today; they were causing him nothing but headaches. He pulled on his jacket. The time had come to meet with Mrs. Catt. He knew what she wanted.

It was a short walk from the Governor's Mansion to the Hotel Hermitage, and Governor Roberts intended to make it a very short visit. He had an early campaign whistle-stop scheduled in the morning. The guests were gone and Catherine Kenny had carefully excused herself to return home and avoid bumping into the governor. Carrie greeted Roberts at the door to her suite, cordially, with a smile and rather friendly manner, but she made it clear this was no sweet-tea social occasion. They adjourned to the little office set up next to her bedroom, to speak privately. She looked almost grandmotherly, with her smoothed and carefully pinned gray hair, but her eyes were intense, her mouth firm, like no grandmother he knew.

They were, in fact, two politicians making a deal. Governor Roberts wasn't accustomed to negotiating political deals with ladies, it made him uncomfortable. And more malleable. Look, he told Mrs. Catt, as he had already written to her last week, how can you expect me to allow my political enemies to steer an official Ratification Committee: that is tantamount to suicide for me and defeat for you, he insisted. The Nineteenth Amendment cannot be ratified without the support of my political friends to steer it through the legislature, and they will not abide Mrs. Milton and her husband, and Mrs. Kenny and her friend Luke Lea, all of whom have been maliciously attacking me. Why not have them all simply work under the committee I created, under Mrs. Warner?

Kenny and Milton had already told her they would not work under Warner, they didn't trust her political judgment or skill—it was the feuds again—so that solution was not going to fly. And Catt, as NAWSA president, could not let her Tennessee affiliate be snubbed and superseded.

Well then, Mrs. Catt offered, why not have several ratification committees, lots of committees, the more the merrier? All working toward the same goal, but not necessarily together. A Governor's Committee, a Men's Committee, a League of Women Voters Committee, a Democratic Committee, a Republican Committee. Greater involvement, less friction. Though coordinating them all would be a bear, she knew.

Politics was a game of fear and favors, and Catt decided this was the moment to spring both upon the governor: he could not afford to alienate his president, his party, and his Tennessee women any longer with this sort of procrastination and manipulation, she insisted. His rival in the primary, and the general election, would be able to take good advantage of it. His party, and his own career, would certainly suffer in the fall. And then she held out her most valuable piece of currency: she had done him a great favor today, she could tell him. She had convinced Luke Lea to quash the rabid satire piece in the *Nashville Tennessean*. But the deal would hold only if Roberts agreed to remove the satire's tempting target and accept the legitimacy of other ratification committees beyond his own. She had rescued the governor's exposed hide, not to mention his fragile ego, from the fire. Now he owed her.

The additional ratification committees were suddenly acceptable to Governor Roberts. He bade Mrs. Catt good-bye and hurried out to catch his train.

Catt had seen clearly today that the Tennessee Suffs simply did not have the tactical know-how or breadth of experience to face a fortified opposition on multiple fronts. And she couldn't allow Alice Paul and her Woman's Party people—who would no doubt be coming into the state—to take any credit for winning Tennessee, should the Suffs somehow manage to pull it off. The Chief called the hotel switchboard to send a night telegram to NAWSA headquarters in New York:

Tennessee promising. Must stay indefinitely. Address Hermitage Hotel, Suite 309.

Chapter 7

◆ ◆ ◆

The Blessing

WOODROW WILSON AWOKE agitated from another bad night of nightmares. In his bedroom, in the second-floor private quarters of the White House, his valet, Brooks, and his wife, Edith, helped him to dress, pulling a starched white shirt over his listless left arm.

Washington, like Nashville, was gripped by a heat wave and the air was already sultry, but Edith draped a shawl over her husband's left side, so the visitors would not be able to see that he was paralyzed. She'd managed to keep the extent of his stroke secret for months, and there was no good reason for the men calling on him this morning to learn any more than they needed to know. She wheeled the president of the United States onto the south veranda.

Several blocks away, Democratic presidential and vice presidential nominees James Cox and Franklin Roosevelt tied Windsor knots onto their collars, determined to look their best even in this wilting weather when they met with President Wilson at the White House. They were seeking his blessing.

Woodrow Wilson wasn't at all sure he wanted to bestow that blessing, even if it was just a formality, the patriarch of the Democratic Party laying hands upon his hopeful successors. Wilson didn't want successors; he wanted a third term, and he'd even tried to get himself renominated at the party convention in San Francisco a few weeks before. Wilson's doctor, his closest aides, and his wife knew this was delusional, that he was neither physically nor mentally capable of handling another campaign, much less another term, but they dared not confront him lest he plunge into an even deeper depression. The president who had just led his country through a world-shattering war was a very fragile man.

The strain of conducting the war was compounded by the stress of negotiating the peace at Paris, then intensified by the frustrations of trying to sell the Treaty of Versailles and his League of Nations concept to the American public, over the heads of what he called "the little group of willful men" in the Senate who stood in his way. He'd been confident that if the American people could be made to understand that joining the league would not relinquish the nation's autonomy, but build the foundation for lasting peace, they would demand that Congress accept the treaty. Wilson insisted on going out on the road to convince the public himself, a grueling, monthlong cross-country rail tour with dozens of rallies and speeches. His doctor believed such a tour might kill him; Wilson was already suffering from fatigue, severe asthma, and occasional "cerebral incidents." But Wilson insisted: as commander in chief he'd sent American doughboys into the trenches of Europe, promising them it was the War to End All Wars. He felt he must make good on his end of the bargain, make whatever sacrifice was necessary, even his health, to secure the treaty and prevent the world from sliding into war again.

In early September 1919, Wilson and his wife set off on the presidential railroad car, the *Mayflower,* on their own mission to sell the treaty to America. Wilson tipped his straw boater hat in parades, gave speeches defending the league in armories, coliseums, and fairgrounds across the nation. Between stops he spoke to cheering crowds from the back of the *Mayflower*'s bunting-festooned caboose. But Wilson suffered blinding headaches and breathing attacks almost every night; he was trembling and coughing. His physician, Dr. Cary Grayson, also on board, grew alarmed.

Three weeks out, in late September, as the tour steered east, steaming through Colorado on its homeward journey, the president seemed confused: tripping on a step, pausing in the middle of his speech, jumbling his words. The pain in his head worsened in the night, en route to Wichita, and by morning his left leg and arm had gone numb. Dr. Grayson finally intervened: the rest of the tour must be canceled. The *Mayflower* rushed back to Washington.

Three nights later Wilson suffered a second, more severe, cerebral embolism in the White House, where Edith found him unconscious on the bathroom floor. He was carried to the Lincoln bed, where "he looked dead," recalled one close aide. The doctors were not sure he could pull through. He was paralyzed on his left side, with that side of his face drooping, and his vision and swallowing were impaired. He could still speak, though indistinctly, more like a mumble. His mental functions were not permanently injured, but his psychological state became unsteady, his moods volatile.

Since that night in early October 1919, the president of the United States had remained an invalid, but Edith Wilson had taken unprecedented—and possibly unconstitutional—steps to keep that reality a secret. Wilson's own vice president and cabinet secretaries were kept in the dark about his condition. Press inquiries were rebuffed; Congress was left uninformed. Wild rumors spread, fanned by the White House's obsessive secrecy. The president was simply recovering from "nervous exhaustion," according to Dr. Grayson's evasive bulletins.

The consulting doctors had told Edith Wilson that any mental strain, any of the usual hard decisions required of a president, would be like "turning a knife in an open wound" in her husband's weakened condition, undermining any chance for recovery. Her husband's recovery was her singular concern, so she devised a system to keep the White House functioning under her command, or "stewardship," as she later dubbed it.

Edith, together with Wilson's private secretary, Joseph Tumulty, and Dr. Grayson, became the president's guardians and gatekeepers, and Edith, married to Wilson for only four years, became his surrogate. She read every official report, document, and item of correspondence—foreign, domestic, even top secret—and decided whether her husband should be bothered with it or not. If she deemed the matter worthy of his attention, she presented her own précis of it to him, reading her summary out loud and interpreting his response. She devised a set of form letters to notify governmental officials of the president's desired outcomes. Edith was not a complete novice in this sort of sensitive work: during the war she had helped decipher coded military communiqués for her husband, and he confided in her on many policy matters. But as she filtered the world for the president, protecting and isolating him, she assumed what some have called "the bedside presidency."

Edith knew that Woodrow was still depressed about losing out to James Cox for the presidential nomination earlier in July, and there was great trepidation in the White House this morning about how the president would react to Cox's visit.

Democratic candidate James Cox had dashed to Washington directly from his conference with Sue White and Alice Paul in Ohio. He took the midnight train from Columbus and was very pleased upon his arrival in D.C. to read the extensive newspaper coverage of that meeting in the morning papers. As an old newspaperman himself (he'd been a reporter, editor, and publisher), he was impressed by the Woman's Party's ability to generate press attention: COX PROMISES TO HELP OBTAIN EQUAL SUFFRAGE and COX PROMISES AID TO SUFFS, the headlines announced.

"I give to you without any reservation the assurance that my time, my strength, and my influence will be dedicated to your cause," the papers reported his telling the suffragists, "with a view to procuring a favorable result in Tennessee." He promised to do "everything in my power" to see the federal amendment through.

Perhaps he'd been a bit effusive—"I find nothing in Holy Writ or elsewhere which shows the Almighty ever gave man the right to say that he could vote and women could not"—and gone a bit far in promising to appoint more women to high government positions. But he had a decent record on suffrage in Ohio, even if he stuck to a middle ground, leaning toward the Suffs when it suited him while able to make the Antis think he had an open mind. But many suffragists were still wary of him: there were rumors of corruption, a nasty divorce, and he was "thoroughly wet," making Suffs fear that he was in thrall to the liquor interests who were bankrolling the skirmishes against ratification in the states. Cox's enthusiastic response to Paul's delegation was his attempt to allay those fears.

He certainly wasn't exaggerating his desire for a Democratic state such as Tennessee to clinch ratification, allowing him to take credit for it during the upcoming campaign. He knew he'd need women's votes as he struggled to overcome Woodrow Wilson's, and the Democratic Party's, disfavor with the war-weary, and even peace-wary, American public.

Even Carrie Catt was sending encouraging signals to him as she branded Warren Harding's refusal to push the Republican governors of Vermont and Connecticut to call special sessions unacceptable.

"It is true that the Republican party has a record of nearly five times as many ratifications as the Democratic," Catt told reporters, "but without the 36th state that record is like a great tail without a kite. Apparently it is the Democrats who must supply the kite."

Cox knew that Tennessee offered him a shining opportunity to provide that kite and a chance to reset the national map of ratification, giving Democrats a boost. He didn't like poking his nose into another governor's business, and Governor Roberts was certainly in a sticky spot, but he would try his best to gently nudge the governor and the Democratic legislature to sew up ratification of the amendment. Get all those women on board for

November, thankful to Democrats. This was Cox's presidential moment, his time to lead the party—and, with luck, to lead the nation—and he didn't want anything to spoil it.

The Democrats tapped the brash young assistant secretary of the navy, Franklin Delano Roosevelt, to be Cox's running mate. Roosevelt brought attractive attributes to the ticket that Cox lacked: a famous name, Ivy League connections, buoyant energy, and—in anticipation of at least some women voting in the presidential election, whether or not the federal amendment was ratified in time to give all women the ballot—good looks and gregarious charm. He sure beat the Republican VP candidate, Calvin Coolidge, in that department, the Democratic power brokers chortled.

Democrats also hoped he would appeal to woman suffragists, who counted FDR as a dependable friend. He liked to claim that he'd been converted to the Cause in 1911, when he was a novice New York state senator and the sultry suffrage activist Inez Milholland came to his office to lobby him in support of a proposed suffrage amendment to the state constitution. Roosevelt had been ducking the suffrage question, claiming his conservative Hudson Valley district wasn't much for it, so he couldn't commit. The way Roosevelt liked to tell it, Milholland, the suffrage movement's most glamorous crusader, a brilliant Vassar grad with a law degree who was soon to become famous for leading suffrage parades astride a white horse, sat on his desk and "dazzled him" with her legal and moral arguments for suffrage. She convinced him that suffrage was "the only chivalric position for a decent man to hold."

Whether or not that was the true or whole story (and his wife, Eleanor, did not like that version of events, disputing the singular persuasive power of "that memorable visit"), FDR came out for woman suffrage and his wife was flabbergasted by his new stance. "I was shocked," she would later confess, "as I had never given the question serious thought, for I took it for granted that men were superior creatures and knew more about politics than women did." Eleanor wasn't "violently opposed" to woman suffrage, as some biographers have inferred, she'd simply absorbed the women's proper sphere rationales still prevalent in her family and social set. And as the wife of an up-and-coming politician, she didn't think she should have political opinions of her own. Even after New York women won suffrage in 1917, Eleanor did not exercise her franchise, declining to accompany Franklin to the polls at Hyde Park in the fall 1918 elections.

Edith Wilson also didn't approve of enfranchising women and made no bones about it. Her hostility toward the idea of woman suffrage had only hardened as she watched zealous women make spectacles of themselves in the streets, trying to intimidate—to humiliate—her husband. She despised those picketers.

A stance in favor of women's political equality did not come naturally to Woodrow Wilson, either, a Presbyterian minister's son with a conservative Virginian upbringing. Wilson was raised with reverence for the southern traditions of True Womanhood, and he placed his mother, wife (both first and second), and three daughters on proper pedestals. He adored the women in his life and needed them to adore and coddle him. But his women were meant to be comforters and confidantes, not colleagues, and not fellow citizens participating in the life of the nation.

Wilson was a scholar of American democracy and a hands-on practitioner of the American political system. He served as president of Princeton University and governor of New Jersey at a time when woman suffrage was being hotly debated in intellectual circles and fiercely contested in many state campaigns. But for most of his public career, Woodrow Wilson tried to avoid the issue of women's equal suffrage as best he could. When pressed, he admitted: "I must say very frankly that my personal judgment is strongly against it. I believe that the social changes it would involve would not justify the gains that would be accomplished by it."

As Wilson eyed a run for the White House in 1912, knowing he needed to attract a broader constituency—including the women of nine western states who already enjoyed the franchise and could vote in both state and federal elections—he modified his suffrage stance somewhat. Even as Teddy Roosevelt's third-party Progressives beat the drum for woman suffrage in the 1912 presidential campaign, Wilson managed to sidestep the issue, saying it wasn't a national matter, but purely a state decision and not within the purview of a presidential candidate. This placed him in a safe zone with the base of his party, the southern "states' rights" Democrats who feared a coercive federal amendment.

Wilson was confronted by the suffrage question even before he could take his oath of office. If he'd managed to duck the issue in the campaign, Alice Paul, the new director of NAWSA's lobbying department, the Congressional Committee, made sure he could ignore it no longer. To draw attention to the issue, Paul organized a huge suffrage parade through

Washington on the day before Wilson's inauguration, March 3, 1913. More than five thousand marchers from every state—led by Inez Milholland on her white horse—stepped down Pennsylvania Avenue, accompanied by bands and elaborate floats. Carrie Catt and Anna Howard Shaw marched, too. Eleanor Roosevelt, in Washington to join the inauguration festivities (her husband had just won a Wilson political appointment), watched the parade go by: "The suffrage parade was too funny," she wrote to a friend, "and nice fat ladies with bare legs and feet posed in tableaux on the Treasury steps!"

Washington had never seen anything like it, and some spectators definitely didn't like it. The marchers were attacked by mobs of irate men and boys, outraged by the sight of women demanding their rights in so public a fashion. Women were grabbed off floats, thrown to the ground, their banners pulled from their hands and smashed, their clothes ripped. The police stood by and didn't intervene, leaving the marchers unprotected. Federal troops from a nearby base had to be called in to restore order. The march, and the melee, made headlines around the country on the day Woodrow Wilson put his hand on the Bible.

Within the next months Wilson was bombarded with pleas, petitions, processions, automobile caravans, and other novel types of agitation— organized by the very insistent Miss Paul—to convince him of the popular demand for woman suffrage and the need for a federal amendment. He responded with a confusing mix of evasion and equivocation. Ever the astute politician, even while he dissembled, Wilson kept track of the shifting political winds and the changing popular attitudes on the woman suffrage question. Even when state suffrage referenda were defeated, the number of aye ballots cast by men was growing larger. The number of senators and representatives sent to Washington by suffrage states, and so answerable to both men and women voters, made up a small but not insignificant proportion of the Congress. The number of women whose states allowed them presidential suffrage—who could vote for, or *against,* him in the 1916 election—was nothing to sneeze at. But still he waffled.

Wilson believed that suffrage for women would be a disaster for the American home, and he was determined to defend men's castles. His own home was mostly a happy one; his first wife, the sweet and selfless Ellen, doted on her husband. She was a southern social conservative who saw no need for women to tromp into a polling booth to vote for her husband or anyone else. The Wilsons allowed their daughters to go off to college, though the girls had to convince their mother that higher education would not make them "unfeminine."

When Ellen died in the middle of Woodrow's first term, he was bereft and despondent. But just six months after Ellen's death, he became smitten with a beautiful and vivacious widow, Edith Bolling Galt. He proposed to her within weeks of first setting eyes on her. His aides worried that the public would think it unseemly for him to marry so soon after Ellen's death, and voters (especially those western women who had the vote) might punish him when he ran for reelection. Wilson announced his engagement to Edith in early October 1915 and on the very same day declared his intention to travel home to Princeton to cast his ballot in favor of woman suffrage in the New Jersey referendum later that month. "I believe that the time has come to extend that privilege and responsibility to the women of the State," he declared, emphasizing that he was voting not as the leader of his party, or as the leader of the nation, but as a private citizen who believed that woman suffrage was a matter to be decided by each state, not foisted on them by Congress.

Wilson knew the New Jersey referendum was safely doomed, but the move was symbolic, part of his reelection strategy to win back disaffected progressive voters who'd been alienated by some of his first-term decisions (including imposing racial segregation in the federal civil service) while mollifying those western women voters and winning points with eastern suffragists. And this new suffrage stance might even protect him from any negative fallout from his remarriage.

Carrie Catt, then leader of the Empire State campaign to win the franchise for New York women in the same 1915 election, immediately sent a telegram of thanks to the president: "On behalf of a million women in NYS who have declared they want the ballot, please accept my gratitude for your announcement that you will vote for the woman suff amend in NJ." She hoped Wilson's coattails might extend across the Hudson and help her win the New York referendum. His coattails were threadbare; the male voters of both states, as well as those in Massachusetts and Pennsylvania, voted woman suffrage down.

Alice Paul, now leader of a breakaway suffrage organization, the Congressional Union for Woman Suffrage (which would later be renamed the National Woman's Party), was much less impressed with the president's intentions. With his pledge to vote in New Jersey, he also repudiated the federal amendment in favor of a doomed state-by-state approach. Paul intended to hold Wilson and all Democrats responsible for the failure of the federal suffrage amendment to progress one inch in Congress during his first term. She announced the Congressional Union would actively campaign against Wilson's reelection in the western suffrage states and against the reelection of all Democratic congressmen and senators, whether or not they supported woman suffrage. Paul and her followers would punish the party in power, just as her mentor Mrs. Pankhurst had done in England; it was a promise she intended to keep.

With the White House announcement that the president was remarrying *and* voting for woman suffrage, the press took the coincidence of the two statements as evidence that the soon-to-be new Mrs. Wilson had transformed the president into a Suff. "The joke is that she's against it," Cary Grayson reported to a friend, "but she's too good a diplomat to say anything on the subject these days."

Edith Bolling Galt was certainly no Suff. Like Woodrow, she was a proud Virginian, claiming to be a direct descendant of Pocahontas; her grandparents owned slaves. She was clever and opinionated, though she admitted she'd paid no attention to national or political affairs until she met Woodrow. A stickler for propriety, the tall, blue-eyed widow had definite ideas about a woman's proper role (it was to cherish and support her husband), but she had no problem assuming control of her late husband's lucrative jewelry business and no qualms about showing off her independence and driving prowess as the first woman to hold a driver's license in the District of Columbia, zipping around town in her own open-top electric car.

Wilson married Edith on December 18, 1915, in a private ceremony at her Washington town house. Just blocks away at the Willard Hotel, the suffragists of the National American Woman Suffrage Association were celebrating the election of Carrie Catt as their new president, drafted (she might say dragooned) into leadership once again at a time of crisis for the movement. The day after the wedding, as the president and his bride embarked on their honeymoon, two of their wedding guests, the president's daughter Margaret and his cousin Helen Woodrow Bones (who had stepped in as official White House hostess when Ellen died), sat on the stage with Carrie Catt, in places of honor, at the National Association's convention rally.

And in a basement office on F Street, Alice Paul, Lucy Burns, and the officers of the Congressional Union—their split with NAWSA having been made final during that week's convention—sketched their plans to go their separate way: maneuver around Carrie Catt and the suffrage establishment and defeat Woodrow Wilson.

Along with an expensive trousseau, Edith brought her antipathy toward woman suffrage to the White House, so it was painful for her to sit through her husband's effort to woo the women of NAWSA during his reelection campaign in the summer of 1916. While Alice Paul and her followers were campaigning against Wilson, Carrie Catt saw Wilson as a potential, persuadable, ally. She invited the president to address a special National Association conference in Atlantic City. The president was escorted to the podium by his wife on one side and Carrie Catt on the other, walking through an honor guard of besashed Suffs from every state, purposely selected for their beauty. (Among them was Tennessee suffragist Anne Dudley.) Edith sat on the podium, "a lovely being to look at," as one attendee described her, "and as remote, as detached, from that scene as if she had come from another world. As she sat there, her small feet crossed, an invisible line seemed to separate her from all these women. They knew without her having said it that she did not sympathize with them."

Edith's distaste for suffrage grew only deeper as Alice Paul's followers, now organized into the National Woman's Party, intensified their attacks on her "Precious One," making them more personal and bitter. When they began picketing the White House in January 1917, with placards imploring "Mr. President, How Long Must We Wait for Liberty," Edith began calling them "disgusting creatures." During the war, when those placards lambasted her husband as "Kaiser Wilson," she railed against "those detestable suffragists."

When the picketers were arrested for obstructing the sidewalk and thrown into jail, abused, and force-fed, Edith dismissed them as "those demons in the workhouse." She questioned her husband's decision to pardon suffrage prisoners in July 1917, a move intended to get the news of their illtreatment off the front page. Edith wanted the suffrage protesters who'd taunted and embarrassed her husband to serve their time in jail, be taught a proper lesson.

But Edith also witnessed, at close hand, from her favorite window seat in the southwest corner of the White House, how the war altered the national landscape in so many ways: changed circumstances, changed minds. Eventually changed her husband into an advocate for the federal amendment.

During the war, as Wilson slowly, hesitantly, made that swing to embrace
the amendment, Edith could sense the political forces pressing upon him,
the attitudinal shifts he was forced to accommodate. America had a new role
in the world, as both the beacon and the guardian of democracy. And Edith
also recognized that an element of his change of mind was the debt Woodrow owed to Mrs. Catt, a debt he was honor-bound to repay.

Mrs. Catt had not sent her National Association women to picket the
White House, nor did she intervene on behalf of Paul when the young zealot
called herself a political prisoner. Most important, Mrs. Catt had helped
Woodrow to wage and win the war, bringing the women of America, even
the suffragists, to his side.

That had been the most wrenching, and most controversial, decision of
her entire life. Carrie Catt, the confirmed pacifist, founding member of the
Woman's Peace Party, had come around to accepting America's entry into
the war, and even more significant, she had pledged the loyalty and assistance of the two million women affiliated with NAWSA for whatever war
work was needed. It was the gamble of an astute, if agonized, suffrage politician. She'd watched her International Woman Suffrage Alliance comrades
go through the same torment. When the United Kingdom went to war three
years before, all the British suffragists—mainstream and militant, even the
Pankhursts—had put aside their demands for the vote to devote themselves
to war work: "What's the use of having a vote if there's no country to vote
in," Emmeline Pankhurst famously explained.

Catt called an emergency meeting of NAWSA's executive council, and
after tearful debate they approved her suggested policy, calling for suffragists
to work simultaneously for the war and for the vote, allowing members to
do their war work under the NAWSA banner and prove suffragists' patriotism. Catt paid a steep personal price for her decision. She was booted out
of the Woman's Peace Party and shunned by her fellow pacifists, who felt she
had deserted them. She'd made a Faustian bargain with Woodrow Wilson,
they complained; she had bartered her principles for uncertain political gain.
She had become a patsy for the warmongers and profiteers. She took the
blows silently but vowed that once suffrage was won, she would devote herself to peace and disarmament work for the rest of her life.

But when Woodrow Wilson helped to round up the last votes needed for
the amendment's passage in the House of Representatives in January 1918,
Carrie Catt could, and did, take credit for patiently, skillfully, bringing the

president around. Just as she'd calculated, American women, by their loyalty and deeds, had earned the vote in the eyes of the president. Alice Paul would insist that credit for the turnaround belonged to her brave, defiant picketers and prisoners, who'd shamed Congress and the president into acknowledging that democracy needed to begin at home. They were both right.

From that time on, Woodrow Wilson never refused Carrie Catt's appeals for help. "My Dear Mrs. Catt," was his salutation in his notes to her. Even if he could not manage (or, as some said, did not try hard enough) to fulfill her requests, twist the right arms, translate his pledges into action, he always promised her he would try. And when the amendment remained stuck in the Senate in September 1918, Catt prevailed upon Wilson to make a direct appeal in the Senate chamber.

Wilson made the argument that woman suffrage was a "spiritual instrument" he needed, "vital to the winning of the war." Women deserved the franchise, there was no longer any question: "We have made partners of the women in this war; shall we admit them only to a partnership of suffering and sacrifice and toil and not to a partnership of privilege and right?"

The senators took huffy offense—no president had ever made a personal appearance in their chamber to push for legislation—and they ignored Wilson's entreaties. The very next day, the Senate humiliated him by rejecting the amendment again, two Democratic votes shy of passage.

President Wilson fell ill just when Carrie Catt needed him most. She'd been counting on his help during the fall of 1919 to secure ratification of the amendment in states where governors or legislatures were being stubborn or slow, where a note or call from the White House might do the trick. Like the rest of the country, she didn't know how sick the president really was, nor did she realize that her pleas for help were probably being routed through Mrs. Wilson. She was saved by White House secretary Joseph Tumulty, a suffragist, who did his best to take Catt's missives directly to the president when he could, sidestepping Mrs. Wilson or even handling the matter himself, as he assumed the task of writing many of the president's more routine statements and letters. So Catt's requests for presidential letters were faithfully dispatched, and that telegram urging Governor Roberts to convene a special session in Tennessee was put through promptly. But if President Wilson considered the ratification of the Nineteenth Amendment and the enfranchisement of American women to be a significant part of his legacy, it was not part of the discussion with his political heirs.

...

After their hour with the president, Cox and Roosevelt walked to the executive wing of the White House, where Cox put his newspaperman's skills to good use, quickly jotting down a statement for release to the press. "From every viewpoint the meeting was delightful," Cox scribbled. "I found the President in splendid shape and I was most agreeably surprised by his condition," he lied to the sixty journalists gathered for an impromptu press conference. After lunch with the candidates and Edith, Tumulty, and Grayson, Wilson dictated his own press statement to his stenographer: "Governor Cox and I were absolutely at one on the great issue of the League of Nations."

Unity was the theme of the day. There was no mention of enfranchisement, nothing about ratification, nor was there any strategic discussion of the prospect of twenty-seven million women headed to the polls in November. Or not. Carrie Catt feared she knew why. There were what she called "sinister forces" at work. There might be no tail and no kite.

Chapter 8

• • •

On Account of Sex

CARRIE CATT DID NOT bring her sapphire-blue battlefield uniform, her ratification dress, to Nashville. It was the dress she'd ordered to celebrate passage of the federal suffrage amendment in the U.S. House of Representatives in early 1918. That blue dress was Catt's sartorial symbol of the amendment, her shout of confidence in the ultimate—however maddeningly delayed—triumph of the Cause.

In one of those odd quirks of fate, the federal amendment began to be forged on the very day that young Carrie had awakened to the woman suffrage issue. On Election Day morning 1872, when Carrie first felt the slap of political exclusion in her mother's kitchen, she didn't know that at that very moment hundreds of other women were also pounding on the closed doors of the American polling place.

That same morning in Rochester, New York, Susan Anthony calmly walked into her local polling place and broke the law by dropping a paper ballot into a wooden box. She brought along her three sisters and about a dozen of her local suffrage club friends; the election registrars weren't sure what to do. She convinced them that voting was women's legal right as citizens. The women were permitted to cast their ballots.

"Well I have been & gone & done it," Anthony gleefully wrote to her suffrage collaborator Elizabeth Cady Stanton. "Positively voted the Republican ticket—strait this a.m. at 7 Oclock—& swore my vote in at that."

Anthony was experimenting with a new legal strategy to win the vote, a concept called the New Departure, which relied on a novel reading of the Fourteenth Amendment and a nervy bid to test the interpretation. If that amendment, enshrined as law in the U.S. Constitution four years before, defined all native-born or naturalized persons as American citizens and accorded those citizens "privileges and immunities" that could not be denied by the states, then women—who were persons, who were citizens—must enjoy those same privileges, including the franchise. It was simple: American women already possessed the right to vote, it was there in the Constitution, and women simply needed to exercise that right. A group of 170 New Jersey suffragists had tried the ploy in 1868; their ballots were placed in a separate box and not counted.

The plan, coordinated by Anthony and Stanton's infant organization, the National Woman Suffrage Association, was to get suffragists all over the country to attempt to vote in the presidential election of 1872. If the women were refused at the polls, lawsuits would be filed against the local election board and, hopefully, the cases would be carried all the way to the U.S. Supreme Court. Like many civil rights activists to follow, they were provoking a legal test case.

So on the first Tuesday of November 1872, more than 150 women around the country, including Susan Anthony, her sisters, and her friends, did attempt to vote. In St. Louis, Missouri, a suffrage worker named Virginia Minor had tried to register to vote, but the election clerk refused her; she and her husband filed suit against the registrar. And in Battle Creek, Michigan, a former slave and political activist known as Sojourner Truth went to her local polling station to vote, but she was turned away.

Truth was a veteran of the abolition and suffrage meeting circuits, mesmerizing audiences with her powerful testimonies to the indignities she suffered being both black and female. It is reported that at an 1851 women's rights meeting in Akron she famously challenged her white audience— "Ar'n't I a Woman?"—a question that would haunt the suffrage movement for years to come. For Truth, and all the other women who took part in this action of mass civil disobedience, the consequences they faced, including heavy fines, public rebuke, and possibly prison, paled in comparison with the thrill of demanding a ballot and taking the law into their own hands.

Susan Anthony and her cohorts were arrested by a deputy U.S. marshal and charged with "illegal voting" in a federal election, a criminal offense. As the most celebrated of the electoral scofflaws, Anthony was made an example by nervous government officials eager to quash this voting nonsense. She asked to be handcuffed and refused to post the $500 bail; she wanted to go to jail, all the better for publicity and legal maneuvering to a higher court. One of her lawyers, over her protests, paid her bail out of his own pocket. While awaiting trial, she set off on a headline-grabbing tour through every district in her home county, attracting large and sympathetic audiences to her fiery presentation, asking, "Is It a Crime for a U.S. Citizen to Vote?" When prosecutors noticed that Anthony's performances might influence potential jurors, they moved her trial to another county. Undaunted, Anthony took to the platforms there; she made fifty speeches in all. Her trial, in U.S. district court, was a sensation, covered daily by the national press, just as she'd hoped.

Judge Ward Hunt, soon to take a seat on the U.S. Supreme Court, would not allow Anthony to testify on her own behalf, and when the arguments of the prosecutors and defense lawyers concluded, Hunt pulled his written opinion from his pocket, obviously drafted before hearing any of the evidence of the case. He directed the men of the jury to bring in a verdict of guilty and refused to poll them on their decision; when Anthony's attorney protested, Judge Hunt discharged the jury. Before sentencing her, Judge Hunt asked if "the prisoner" had anything to say. He got an earful:

"Yes, your honor, I have many things to say," Anthony blasted, "for in your ordered verdict of guilty, you have trampled under foot every vital principle of our government. My natural rights, my civil rights, my political rights, my judicial rights, are all alike ignored. Robbed of the fundamental privilege of citizenship, I am degraded from the status of a citizen to that of a subject; and not only myself individually, but all of my sex, are, by your honor's verdict, doomed to political subjection under this so-called republican form of government."

"The Court orders the prisoner to sit down," Judge Hunt snapped. She refused and continued. "It will not allow another word," the judge bellowed. Exasperated, he finally imposed the sentence: a fine of $100, plus court costs, or face imprisonment, though authorities had second thoughts about allowing her to become a jailed, noisy martyr. She wasn't jailed, never paid the fine, and there was no attempt to collect it. Anthony was unable to pursue her case to the U.S. Supreme Court, but Virginia Minor did.

Minor's husband, Francis, a lawyer, filed a suit on her behalf (because women couldn't initiate lawsuits) against the election registrar, maintaining that Missouri's laws prohibiting women from voting were unconstitutional under the Fourteenth Amendment. Rebuffed in the lower courts, the Minors appealed to the U.S. Supreme Court, and Francis Minor pleaded the case to the justices himself. The court ruled against them, saying that women were a special category of nonvoting citizens—"members of the state," was the term used. The high court held that despite the Fourteenth Amendment's privileges and immunities clause, a state can prohibit women from voting. The ruling dashed any hopes that suffrage could be won through the courts, and by allowing a state to withhold the franchise from a whole class of citizens, the decision would lay the foundation for Jim Crow voter exclusions for nearly another century.

The failed voting experiments of 1872, coupled with the U.S. Supreme Court defeat, forced Anthony and Stanton to reevaluate their strategies. Trying to change voting laws in every state, one by one, would take forever. So they renewed the idea of their own amendment to the federal Constitution, one that would correct the omissions of the post–Civil War Fourteenth and Fifteenth Amendments, when women were left out of the extension of the franchise to black men. It would supplant that malevolent phrase "male citizen" sneaked into the Fourteenth and add those three vital little letters "s-e-x" into the Fifteenth's list of reasons why an American citizen could not be denied the right to vote. A Sixteenth Amendment, an explicit woman suffrage amendment, became the primary goal of their new National Woman Suffrage Association, while its rival, Lucy Stone and Henry Blackwell's American Woman Suffrage Association, chose to pursue change state by state.

Anthony and Stanton drafted and refined the wording of this new amendment, boiling it down to a single sentence, using the template of the Fifteenth Amendment, and leaving no room for legal ambiguity: "The right of citizens of the United States to vote shall not be denied or abridged by the United States or by any State on account of sex."

They found their champion in Congress in Senator Aaron Augustus Sargent of California. Anthony had befriended the Sargent family on a train stranded in snowdrifts in the Rockies, and in the long hours trapped in the railroad car, she and the Sargents shared food and talked suffrage. Sargent became a trusted friend and advocate, withstanding the ridicule of his colleagues, and introduced the amendment into the Senate on January 10, 1878. It was referred to the Senate Committee on Privileges and Elections for consideration.

It sat in Congress for the next forty years.

The amendment was reintroduced into every succeeding Congress, only to promptly disappear into the dark recesses of various committee file cabinets. It was allowed to surface briefly from time to time for hearings, where Stanton, Anthony, and other suffrage stateswomen were allowed to make their carefully reasoned arguments, only to be subjected to crass ridicule by the lawmakers. Stanton reported that during her testimony at one such hearing, the presiding senator clipped his fingernails, sharpened his pencils, and read the newspaper rather than pay attention; she said she had to restrain herself from throwing her manuscript at his head. Then the amendment would be tabled for another year.

Carrie was in college when the amendment was introduced into Congress, and it had confronted its first Senate vote, a two-to-one defeat, in 1887, just as she joined the suffrage movement as a field organizer in Iowa. It had been stuck in Congress for a dozen years when she caught the eye of Susan Anthony, always on the lookout for young talent, at the 1890 National American Suffrage Association convention.

The amendment had already been tabled by Senate and House committees ten times at the opening of the 1892 NAWSA convention in Washington, when Susan Anthony invited Catt to join the suffragists' annual trek to Congress. Anthony assigned her to be the first to testify for the amendment—obviously a test—and Catt had to think fast and speak off-the-cuff. It was her congressional debut, but only the first of scores of futile, infuriating trips to the Hill.

There was little progress during the latter 1890s while Catt became one of Aunt Susan's apprentices. With the amendment trapped in Congress, Anthony led her "Girls" into a series of punishing state campaigns, to alter constitutions or put the question of woman suffrage to popular referenda, in which, of course, only men had a say. There were a few victories—Colorado in 1893, Utah in 1896—and many more bitter defeats.

The amendment had been marooned in Congress for a generation, twenty-two years, when an aged Susan Anthony brought Catt onto the stage of the 1900 NAWSA convention and introduced her as her successor, confident that Catt had the skill and the passion to lead the movement. Catt also had the financial security of a prosperous and supportive husband—something many of the other contenders, including Anna Shaw, did not enjoy—enabling her to take on the unsalaried presidency. Catt tried to both shake up and shore up the National Association, emphasizing solid organizational structure and more centralized control, while also shifting the image of suffragism from radical to respectable by recruiting more professional and society women into the ranks. Now it was Carrie Catt leading the annual delegations to the Hill on behalf of the amendment, but Congress did not even consider the amendment during her first four-year administration.

After she stepped down from the presidency in 1905, and Anna Shaw stepped up, neither the Senate nor the House reported on the amendment in committee or considered it on the floor for almost another full decade, a maddening period some called the Doldrums. Shaw was a great evangelist but a poor administrator, and she lost control of the National Association. Into this void stepped Alice Paul, a twenty-eight-year-old Quaker woman from New Jersey with a PhD from the University of Pennsylvania and several years' experience with Emmeline Pankhurst's corps in England, willing to undertake violent protests and suffer prison to make their point. The amendment had been gathering dust for thirty-five years when Paul and her fellow Pankhurst veteran Lucy Burns returned to the United States and took charge of the National Association's congressional lobbying office, with plans to blast it out of its lethargy. That they did, but in the process they almost blasted the American suffrage movement apart, too. Or propelled it forward, depending upon one's point of view.

By 1915, with Paul making headlines for her provocative actions and siphoning off some of the most talented Suffs to her breakaway faction, the officers of NAWSA were desperate for Anna Shaw to retire and for Carrie Catt to retake the helm. Catt reluctantly assumed the presidency again just as the world war posed both a great human catastrophe and a great political opportunity for the movement. Everyone was forced to make sacrifices: women gave their husbands, sons, and brothers; Alice Paul gave her body, tortured in jail; Carrie Catt gave her soul, joining the war effort she detested.

Almost a year after America entered the world war, on January 10, 1918, both Carrie Catt and Alice Paul sat anxiously in the House galleries as the chamber voted on the amendment. Just the day before, Woodrow Wilson had finally announced his support for the amendment and urged Democratic congressmen to vote for it; whether Wilson was influenced more by Paul's castigating or Catt's cajoling remains a matter of debate.

Everyone knew the vote would be close. One congressman, a suffrage supporter, was wheeled in on a gurney, defying his doctor's orders to remain in the hospital; another took his seat with a broken shoulder, refusing to have it set despite the pain, lest the anesthetic make him dopey. It brought tears to the eyes of the Suffs in the House gallery to see Representative Frederick Hicks of New York appear on the floor, ashen-faced, having left his wife's deathbed, at her insistence, to vote for the amendment. He returned home for her funeral. The drama on the House floor was surpassed only by the harrowing tension of the roll call: the amendment passed the two-thirds majority threshold by a single vote. Catt and her suffrage sisters left the Capitol building crying and singing hymns of joy.

Despite the dangerously thin cushion, Carrie was certain that congressional victory, after forty exasperating years, was near. The Senate would surely speed its consideration and approval of the amendment, and the elaborate plans she'd drawn for the ratification campaigns in every state could be launched before spring 1918. The Great War was still raging, austerity was the byword, but Catt, in a burst of girlish enthusiasm, ordered her ratification dress to wear as she stumped in the states. Her friend Helen Gardener, one of the National Association's chief lobbyists in Washington, warned her—"You can't hustle the Senate"—but Carrie went ahead and had the dress fashioned in her favorite color.

The ratification dress hung in Carrie's closet for a full year and a half as the Senate dithered and filibustered and twice more voted down the amendment. When the Senate finally passed the amendment in early June 1919, Catt was not even in the Senate gallery. She refused to suffer through the torment of watching stubborn men make a mockery of justice any longer and remained in New York. Mollie Hay was there, keeping tallies with Marjorie Shuler and NAWSA's lobbying team. They had to sit through the last, vituperative gasps of opposition: one senator bloviated for five hours about the downfall of the nation. Other die-hard senators introduced insidious amendments to the amendment, including one to allow the states to enforce the law as they saw fit, another inserting the word "white" to define the women citizens entitled to vote.

When the amendment finally squeaked through, with a margin of votes you could count on one hand, Hay ran out of the chamber, commandeered a telephone, and called Catt at home. Catt listened quietly, placed the earpiece back in its cradle, and broke into a wild dance, stomping all over the house, whooping and singing. Then she calmed herself, settled down to her desk, and wrote telegrams to the governors of every state, asking them to convene their legislatures—in special session, if necessary—to ratify the amendment. She quickly dispatched another batch of wires to all the National Association's state presidents: Put your ratification plans into motion. Immediately.

It was finally time to put on the blue dress, but before she could, it needed to be remodeled and shortened by a seamstress, as fashion styles had changed so rapidly in the meantime. It became a joke among her colleagues, a rare political miscalculation, a flight of wishful thinking by the master pragmatist. The dress was a good reminder to not count chickens until hatched, to not count votes till cast, to distrust talk of promises. It might be a good dress to wear in Tennessee, if it weren't so darn hot.

Though the dress had hung in her closet for an infuriating eighteen months, Catt eventually put it to good use as she blazed through the states, chasing the thirty-six required legislative ratifications. The Anti senators, in their spiteful wisdom, had delayed passage, knowing that sending the amendment out to the states in a year when most legislatures weren't in session would make it much more difficult to complete ratification with any speed. Most legislatures did not meet every year, and the governors of thirty states would have to be convinced to call their legislatures back for extraordinary sessions, which, many of them complained, involved too much bother, risk, and expense.

The amendment faced an uphill climb in the states where the legislature, or the male voters, had rejected woman suffrage time and again over the years, the states that had remained solidly black on the suffrage map. These states, most in the South and Northeast, would need to undergo quick conversions—or exorcisms—if they were to approve the amendment. Even the states that were white or polka-dotted on the map, those that had already enacted some form of suffrage for their women, might need to be cajoled into action. Catt knew ratification would be no cakewalk, but she believed that with strenuous work it could be accomplished by the end of 1919. She was wrong.

The first votes rolled in effortlessly. In the first week following submission of the amendment to the states, Illinois vied with Michigan and Wisconsin for the honor of being the first legislature to ratify. (Wisconsin rushed its certificate of ratification to Washington on a fast train, delivering it by hand to the secretary of state.) New York whisked its ratification through both houses in Albany in less than three hours, in a late night special session. Minnesota's legislators stood and sang "The Battle Hymn of the Republic" in celebration of their ratification. Members of the Pennsylvania House of Representatives in Harrisburg also burst into patriotic song when the amendment passed in their chamber. Utah, where women had enjoyed the vote since 1896, approved the amendment unanimously, with an assemblywoman presiding over the quick, decisive roll call in the lower house. Ohio suffragists celebrated their legislature's ratification at a saloon—toasting their success with lemonade—but even as they quaffed their Prohibition-compliant libations, Antis were already busy circulating petitions to recall the ratification.

After that initial burst of activity—within the first three months, seventeen states were in the ratification "Yes" column—the pace slowed and the trouble began. Some governors used the excuse that it was too expensive to call a special session. Both Catt and Alice Paul encouraged suffragists in those states to ask their legislators to accept a bare-bones per diem; the legislators of a few states actually agreed to pay their own way back to the capital city. Suffs also volunteered to serve as secretaries, pages, and stenographers for the special sessions, to minimize state expense. A few governors expressed broader fears, nervous that calling a special session exposed them to danger: revisited budgets, reconsidered bills, and hostile legislation slipped into the agenda. At least two governors worried that they might be impeached by their legislatures.

Governor Ruffin Pleasant of Louisiana tried to organize a bloc of thirteen southern governors to pledge to defy calls for special sessions and, failing that, to do their best to defeat ratification in their legislatures. That would have killed the amendment for the foreseeable future, possibly for good, right then and there. He wasn't able to get his fractious fellow chief executives to go along, but Governor Pleasant and his wife made pilgrimages to many of the southern states to personally convince legislators to stand against ratification. Catt heard that Mrs. Pleasant was on her way to Nashville.

Even in the few instances where Suffs were victorious in the border states of the old Confederacy, as in Arkansas, they still had to endure the rabid rants of defiant legislators: "I'd rather see my daughter in a coffin than at the polls," one doting father exclaimed during floor debate in Little Rock. When Texas suffragists finally prevailed in the knockdown ratification brawl in Austin, the Antis vowed to rescind legislative approval as soon as possible. But there was one statehouse melodrama below the Mason-Dixon Line that the suffragists enjoyed: West Virginia state senator Jesse Bloch's wild cross-country dash home from California, on special express trains, arriving at the Capitol in Charleston just in time to vote and break the tie in the state senate, clinching ratification.

One Oklahoma Suff died fighting for ratification. Miss Aloysius

Larch-Miller, though seriously ill with the Spanish influenza, ignored her doctor's instructions to stay in bed and insisted upon speaking at a ratification rally. She summoned her strength to make an impassioned plea for a special session, stirred her audience to action, went home, and died two days later. The Oklahoma legislature made ratification of the amendment her memorial.

Both NAWSA and the Woman's Party headquarters dispatched teams of organizers to help augment state efforts and stir up popular demand for ratification. Alice Paul showed up in the statehouses where legislatures were still in session in early June 1919, even before the amendment documents were delivered from Washington. In the next months she sent her best organizers, including Sue White, to all the states where action on ratification was tardy or in jeopardy. In parallel but uncoordinated tactical moves, Carrie Catt sent Marjorie Shuler and other trusted deputies to the most troublesome states. When she sent Marjorie to reluctant New Hampshire, Catt told her, only half-joking: "You thought you had a real job in Vermont—that was only a pleasure trip. This is a job. Come through with your shield or upon it." The Spartan imagery was apt because by the fall of 1919, the fight had grown grimmer, the opposition stiffer. Catt marched into the field herself.

She put her dress to work again on her "Wake Up America" tour through the western states in the late fall of 1919, a trip to rally those states that had already accorded full suffrage to women but somehow were taking a very lazy—to her mind, selfish—approach to extending suffrage to the rest of the nation's women. The governors there were balking and the state suffragists were too passive: their women could vote, why bother with ratification? By fall of 1919, only five of the fifteen full-suffrage states had ratified.

Catt packed her ratification dress and jumped on a train. It was like one of her old barnstorming campaigns from the early days: fourteen conferences in thirteen states in a whirlwind eight weeks. She gave pep talks, she administered scoldings, she negotiated with governors and legislators. Four thousand people packed the Mormon Tabernacle in Salt Lake City to hear her speak. It was nostalgic and gratifying, if also exhausting. She encountered women she'd worked with in her very first campaigns, in the horse-and-buggy days when some of these western states were still territories. The women were old and stooped but still fighting, still working for change, and they traveled long miles to greet Catt tenderly, like old soldiers remembering their wars together. A high school beau from Iowa showed up at one of the rallies and proposed marriage to her. She smiled, thanked him, and pushed on to the next event.

She wrapped up her "Wake Up America" tour with pledges from every governor she visited: yes, they would call special sessions. Some continued to drag their feet, but, prodded by newly energized Suffs in their states, they eventually came through. Still, by the end of 1919 only twenty-two states had ratified; by spring of 1920, the count had finally risen to thirty-five—one vote away from victory. But since March there'd been only rejections.

In May 1920, Catt rallied a suffrage Emergency Corps of representative women from all forty-eight states, to descend upon Connecticut in a massive lobby. The goal was to convince, or shame, stubborn Governor Marcus Holcomb to call the Connecticut legislature back into session to act on the amendment. The Emergency Corps was an impressive gathering of women doctors and lawyers, professors, scientists, and other professionals prominent in their fields. They held rallies in all the major cities and towns, gave rousing speeches (Catt herself spoke in New Haven, with the mayor at her side), and presented petitions and resolutions from tens of thousands of citizens, demanding the session. Connecticut could have been the thirty-sixth state prize—all the polls indicated the legislature was willing to ratify—but the governor would not budge. Now, in July, he was still adamant. Voting women would not be good for the political health of Governor Holcomb or for his friend Senator Frank Brandegee, both Republicans up for reelection in the fall, both rabid antisuffragists. Now Governor Holcomb dared not set foot beyond the boundaries of his state because his lieutenant governor vowed to convene the legislature to ratify in his absence. But presidential candidate Warren Harding simply refused to intervene.

Catt made an appearance in Richmond's Capitol to urge Virginia's ratification (the legislature still rejected the amendment) and addressed the General Assembly in Dover—and was so sure that Delaware would become the thirty-sixth state. She left for Geneva, optimistic that the final state would be won while she was away and she could return home to bask in glory, indulge in rest, putter in her garden at Juniper Ledge. Retire the ratification dress. It didn't turn out that way. Which was why she was forced to be in Tennessee.

"It looks as though you will be lashed to the mast until after the special session, according to your wires," Clara Hyde, Catt's personal secretary at NAWSA headquarters in New York, teased her boss. But news of Catt's intention to stay in Nashville for the duration made Sue White a bit nervous: "Things are interesting here," White joked in a note to Woman's Party headquarters. "I'm playing a four hand—Mrs. Catt in town."

While Catt established her base camp in Nashville, she also widened her field of view. She had to look at the big picture, look beyond Tennessee, to Ohio, where the leaders of both the Democratic and Republican Parties were gathering with their presidential candidates. It was where Cox's men in Columbus and Harding's men in Marion were making decisions about the upcoming campaigns, hatching plans, setting priorities, striking deals. It was where, she feared, political men were making their gentleman's agreement. Just as they had in the Congress.

During the agonizing Senate delays of 1918 and 1919, she and other suffragists frequently noticed a curious scene unfold during debate in the chamber. The small, obdurate band of Republican and Democratic suffrage opponents—Henry Cabot Lodge of Massachusetts, James Wadsworth of New York, Frank Brandegee of Connecticut, Oscar Underwood of Alabama, John Shields of Tennessee—what Catt called the Unholy Alliance, enjoyed the bonhomie of smug collusion. The Suffs watched these senators from opposite sides of the aisle, who were "as divided as the Kaiser and the King of England" on most policy issues, wrap their arms around one another's shoulders, slap backs, and laugh in jubilation, and Catt knew the amendment would be knocked down for another round. That's all it took: an understanding. That's what she feared was going on now in Ohio.

Catt's suspicions weren't paranoid, they were practical: Why else would there be no report of Cox and President Wilson discussing ratification at their meeting? Because they were afraid of upsetting the Democratic base in the South? Why would Harding and the Republican leaders sit on their hands and make no real attempt to push the Vermont and Connecticut governors to grab the golden ring for the party, bring in the thirty-sixth state, get credit for securing the woman vote?

"Knowing men pretty well, I am very certain that these Republican governors would never have taken this action had they not been convinced that no Democratic state would enter the lists as the much wanted 36th," Catt told a suffrage colleague. "They are confident no Democratic state can be secured. They are too clever and crafty not to have some reason for that attitude."

The reason, she was hearing from her political informants, was that a mutual agreement was being forged between the parties to stop the ratification count at thirty-five states, both parties doing their part to quietly block the amendment from going into force before Election Day. "We are now so convinced that the opponents have sewed us all up in a bag and will prevent ratification before the Presidential election," she fretted to another suffrage colleague. It was easier this way, relieving both parties' anxiety about millions more unpredictable women voters flooding into the polls, upsetting apple carts. And, conveniently, neither party would get credit, or blame, for giving all women the vote. It would also protect vulnerable congressmen and senators who feared being punished by women voters for their long stands against suffrage. It made perfect sense.

And if that weren't enough reason to stall ratification, the Antis were already making good on their promise to throw injunctions and lawsuits in the path of state ratifications, and now they were also threatening to contest the presidential election itself, if ratification was completed in time and all women could vote in the fall. The chaos of a disputed White House contest was spooking both parties.

Catt also heard that the Antis were busy talking to the big party donors, painting a lurid picture of potential November madness, and convincing them to make their campaign donations contingent upon a pledge that the party would put the brakes on ratification, hold it where it stood, at a useless thirty-five. After the election, well, who knew if the amendment would reach the thirty-six-state threshold or if some of the Antis' legal challenges to the completed ratifications would keep things in limbo for years longer.

Catt felt that the women of America should not stand for it. She made her first move, sending a telegram to Esther Ogden, an officer of NAWSA and a Democratic Party insider who served as Catt's personal envoy to the party leadership. Ogden was in Columbus awaiting the arrival of Cox, Roosevelt, and the Democratic National Committee (DNC) for their campaign-planning powwow. Ogden was poised to pounce.

Her demands were polite but had a distinct edge: the party had the opportunity to "render an act of supreme justice to the women of America," she told them. The amendment was on the verge of success, "but the 35 ratifications it has to its credit make a lifeless record without the 36th to vitalize them." She insisted the DNC assume responsibility for securing ratification in Tennessee, "and rest satisfied with nothing short of that achievement." The message Catt wanted to convey was between the lines but perfectly legible: Enough of your resolutions and promises. We want action.

"Get some kind exclusive statement Cox and Harding," Catt wired to Ogden. "Put in newspapers and wire to me so I can give it publicity here."

Ogden, who also wore the hat of president of the National Woman Suffrage Publishing Company, knew what the Chief meant by "exclusive": grabbing the press spotlight from Alice Paul, who'd commanded so many inches of newspaper space in the past week with her meetings with Cox and threat of confrontation with Harding. After presenting Catt's demands to the DNC, Ogden, together with a few other Democratic women, dined with Governor Cox and Catt got her statement, vague but useful.

Catt also sent a delegation of Republican women to Marion to wrangle a statement on Tennessee from Warren Harding. Harding was a sleek specimen of that genus of politician Catt found most odious: the white-plumed dissembler, the golden-throated waffler. She'd seen his kind before. For weeks he had been privately promising both NAWSA and Woman's Party Suffs that he would soon announce the "good news" of his efforts to convince the Vermont or Connecticut governors to call their special sessions. Republicans assured Catt: Soon, soon. Nothing happened; the governors only dug their heels in deeper. "Nothing can give us that state except the death of the governor," an exasperated Catt said of Vermont, "and we haven't come to murder yet."

The question now was: Would Harding commit to influencing the Republican legislators in Tennessee to ratify? Ogden and the NAWSA delegation paraded into his office, unannounced, just as he was stepping out to dinner. Their meeting lasted just a couple of minutes; whether Senator Harding was eager to improve his image among Suffs or simply eager to eat isn't clear, but the women quickly left with their trophy in the form of a telegram to Mrs. Catt:

"I am exceedingly glad to learn that you are in Tennessee seeking to consummate the ratification of the equal suffrage amendment," Harding said. "If any of the Republican members of the Tennessee Assembly should ask my opinion as to their course, I would cordially recommend an immediate favorable action."

Harding's statement, such as it was, went out to the newspapers, and Catt took some small pleasure in the press's mention that Harding's statement to her "stole a march" on the Woman's Party's plans to confront him at his notification ceremony the next day. Stealth always trumped screaming, Catt believed. But the oddly passive tone of the statement only confirmed Catt's suspicions about Harding. While on the surface the message seemed positive, it clearly revealed his reluctance to lift a finger for ratification in Tennessee or anywhere else. "If they should ask me" and "cordially recommend" were rather pathetic commands from the man who wanted to be commander in chief.

As to his exceeding gladness that she was in Nashville, Catt realized it probably meant that Harding was simply relieved that she was not camped on his doorstep in Marion, ready to make a scene. But Alice Paul and Sue White were.

Chapter 9

♦ ♦ ♦

Front Porch

WARREN GAMALIEL HARDING had a very fine front porch. It sat on a limestone block base surmounted by a handsome white balustrade with pairs of Ionic-capitaled columns rising up, giving it that classical-revival look. It was all-American, midwestern solid, forthright, strong. From that porch Warren Harding intended to catapult himself into the White House.

He had no plans to go out on the stump, wear himself down crisscrossing the nation, plead for votes from sooty train cabooses and rickety platforms. He could just stay at home, sleep in his own bed every night, let the voters come to him. They'd see him in his comfortable, natural habitat, his own hometown of Marion, Ohio, and understand and admire him all the more. A Front Porch campaign. It had worked for those other Ohio Republican presidential candidates, James Garfield in 1880 and William McKinley in 1896, and Harding was sure it would work for him. It lent an aura of "above the fray" statesmanship and calm electoral confidence. It also protected him from unwelcome scrutiny. The nation would come to Marion—to his porch.

This Thursday, July 22, was the official start of the campaign, Notification Day, when the Republican Party came to its chosen candidate's home to complete the nomination process. A fixture of nineteenth- and early-twentieth-century presidential campaigns, Notification Day was a strange mixture of political wedding, coronation, homecoming parade, and Fourth of July celebration.

Marion had never experienced anything quite like this, but it was thrilled. A Marion Civic Association was hastily formed to prep the town for its moment in the spotlight. Every store—almost every store—downtown was dressed up in red, white, and blue bunting. Every house had a photo of Harding in the front window. Hundreds of local men and women were deputized as official greeters and hostesses. Enough food to provide two meals for all the visitors was on hand, with restaurant pantries bulging and thirty quarters of beef roasting on spits on the high school playing field.

Dozens of special chartered trains were headed to the Marion station, loaded with Republican legislators and dignitaries; thousands more spectators would pour in on trains and in automobiles. Between fifty and one hundred thousand visitors were expected in Marion for Notification Day. Among those expected, with some degree of dread, was Alice Paul and a troop of her Woman's Party "militants."

Republicans enjoyed the picketers when they were protesting against Wilson and the Democrats these past years but were horrified when the women turned fire on their party convention in June. Convention delegates complained of being unable to enter the Chicago Coliseum without passing a gauntlet of stubborn suffragettes, who assaulted them with signs and slogans and accusatory glares. The "militants" had unfurled a banner over the balcony of the convention center reading: "Why Does the Republican Woman's Party Block Suffrage? We Do Not Want Planks. We Demand the 36th State." Woman's Party picketers were not welcome in Marion, certainly not at this grand celebration of Warren Harding, native son. But Harding's advisers knew that Paul must be handled carefully or things could get ugly.

Alice Paul and her women had come chasing after Harding as soon as he won the nomination, cornering him in Washington when he was having his first meetings with campaign officials. That's when he told them that he would not attempt to force any state to ratify the federal suffrage amendment, and he would not push the Connecticut or Vermont Republican governors. "I could not with propriety attempt to force any chief executive to hasten action in violation of his own sense of duty," he told the women come to plead with him.

"It's the same old bunk," sputtered one Woman's Party member from Texas, who considered herself a good Republican, after the meeting with Harding. Another accused Republicans of "chicanery, false promises, and dilatory tactics" and warned that women were getting so fed up with both parties that a third party, a real woman's political party, was not an idle threat. Harding further antagonized the suffragists when, under pressure from his party, he began making some half-hearted, perhaps duplicitous, efforts to bring the Connecticut and Vermont governors into line. He kept promising the Suffs that he'd soon have "good news" to report about special sessions in those states, but the good news never came. Republican operatives reassured the suffragists that the delay was really just a publicity ploy to make it seem as though Harding were negotiating furiously, solving a difficult diplomatic problem—being very presidential—but success was definite. Then, just a few days before Notification Day, a Hartford newspaper asked Harding if he would advise Connecticut governor Marcus Holcomb to call a special session: "I answer no," Harding replied. Alice Paul loudly announced that there would be pickets in Marion on Notification Day. And they would stay all summer if necessary.

The last thing Republicans wanted was a wire service photo showing suffrage women being forcibly turned away from the launch of the presidential campaign. Negotiations began: Harding's handlers offered the Woman's Party delegation a handshake and photo opportunity with the candidate; Alice Paul rejected that. Harding's staff then suggested that the suffragists join the parade marching by the front porch, but no chanting or hostile demonstrations. Paul said no again and gave the signal for the picket signs to be assembled. Finally a compromise was struck: two party representatives would be allowed to address short statements to Harding on the front porch, but only if Paul called off the picketing. Somewhat reluctantly, Paul agreed.

Warren and Florence Harding had been married in the parlor of the green-shingled, Queen Anne–style beauty he built on Mt. Vernon Avenue for his bride in 1891. He was only twenty-six years old, but already a successful newspaper publisher. He grew up nearby, in the small town of Caledonia, went to a local college, and at age nineteen chipped in with two buddies to buy a bankrupt newspaper, the *Marion Pebble*. He signaled his intentions to make the paper something larger, and more profitable, by renaming it the *Marion Star*. Florence Kling was thirty, daughter of the richest man in Marion, who also owned the town's rival newspaper. She was a gifted pianist and had a good head for business, better than Warren's, and she became the *Star*'s business manager, boosting circulation and profits. Warren was happiest in the press room, setting type and composing pages with the printers, or at lunch at the Commercial Club, making the *Star*, and himself, a pillar of the community. Florence was ambitious for her husband and was not at all displeased when he entered politics: first state senator, then lieutenant governor, than a failed bid to be governor of Ohio in 1910, but a successful run for the U.S. Senate in 1914. Florence helped Warren with his speeches, his press releases, his political maneuvers, his wardrobe. Warren didn't make much of an impression in the Senate; he missed almost half of the roll call votes and ducked out when many of the most controversial issues were being debated. But by lying low, he didn't make enemies and did make friends; he was always well liked, if not enormously respected. He watched how the political winds blew and sailed with them. When the Nineteenth Amendment seemed inevitable, he voted for it, which pleased Florence, as she was a keen suffragist.

The ceremonies began as soon as the sun came up, with the Harding Marching Band, composed of neighbors, friends, and town boosters, noisily arriving at the Harding home for a flag raising. Harding came onto the porch to greet the early morning revelers, climbed down the steps, and pulled on the ropes of the flagpole to raise the Stars and Stripes, and for the next seven hours the happy, noisy outpouring continued: bands and glee clubs; Republican groups from around the country, wearing top hats, capes, and costumes; brigades of scouts and soldiers, farmers and printers (the *Marion Star* gave its staff a half holiday). Harding was most delighted by the musical greeting of his old bandmates from Caledonia, with whom he'd played the trombone long ago; the men made a valiant effort to fit into their old uniforms and coax melodies from their ancient instruments in his honor.

In the doorway of the house leading to the porch, Albert Lasker watched the festivities. This was the opening act in his plan to shape and sell Warren Harding to the American people. Lasker was an accomplished Chicago advertising man, known for his clever campaigns for canned pork and beans, California oranges, and Quaker puffed cereal ("Shot from Guns"). Now his product was a middle-aged marshmallow of a man from small-town America—you had to work with what you were given—who needed to project strength, calm, and security, with a dash of pizzazz. This front porch was a brilliant stage, and Lasker was lining up a cavalcade of high-wattage celebrities to visit, and endorse, Harding here: movie stars, sports legends, Broadway and vaudeville luminaries—Al Jolson was writing a Harding song and would sing it on the porch. The press were going to love it. Lasker was going to give Americans the president they wanted, and he'd tell them why they wanted Harding.

A few blocks away, Sue White slipped a purple, white, and gold sash over her white dress. She'd just begun launching the Nashville campaign when she received a telegram from Miss Paul, asking her to return to Ohio to take part in the Harding deputation. She was reluctant at first—she had a thousand details to attend to in Nashville—but when Miss Paul gave a command, or even a request, there was no refusing.

White's train from Nashville had arrived in Columbus on Wednesday, just in time for her to dash to the afternoon meeting of the Executive Committee of the Republican National Committee (RNC) at the Deshler Hotel, where she made the case for a concerted Republican Party effort to get every Tennessee Republican legislator on board for ratification.

Early the next morning, White, along with Woman's Party staff organizer Anita Pollitzer and board member Louisine Havemeyer of New York, made the sixty-mile trip straight north from Columbus to Marion for Notification Day. It was like old times. Pollitzer was White's close friend, a fellow southerner (from South Carolina), and a seasoned field worker who'd worked shoulder to shoulder with her in many of the toughest ratification skirmishes. They had an easy understanding, a sisterly bond, an unspoken trust; they could make each other laugh. White was very glad that Pollitzer would soon be joining her in Tennessee.

Miss Paul was already in Marion, micromanaging, as usual, every detail of the event. Her tiny body was in constant motion, her dark eyes intense. She never raised her voice but gave firm, precise, some thought imperious, commands; her authority was unquestioned among her followers. Her power was the quiet, ferocious force of moral certainty. Miss Paul never asked her Woman's Party troops to do anything she would not be willing to do herself. She was no armchair general who sent her soldiers into peril while she directed from safety behind the lines. Paul was a true leader, White often marveled, always with her women, in the front line of every assault. And, more than any of them, suffering the consequences.

It was hard, even for Sue White and the other party activists, to understand how this slight, pale, shy, and seemingly frail woman could not only mount the barricades, but endure the torture she'd been subjected to by the authorities, the police, and the White House. Physical and mental torture. The many imprisonments, the solitary confinement, the hunger strikes and forced feedings: strapped to a table, tubes rammed down her nose, lacerating her throat. And then the ultimate degradation, the attempt to undermine her leadership: the claim that she was insane. They sent psychiatrists to examine Paul and threatened to commit her to St. Elizabeths mental hospital. She was perfectly sane, of course, and the doctors had to admit they could find nothing at all wrong with her mind. She emerged with her spirit unbroken, but the imprisonments had had an effect. Everyone at headquarters could see Miss Paul was, even now, a few years later, still prone to periods of illness, pain, depression, and exhaustion. But she was unwilling to slow down. Certainly not now.

Miss Paul was darting among the two hundred Woman's Party marchers, women from fifteen states lining up for the parade. The trunks of regalia, filled with sashes and flags and banners, were unlocked and thrown open. Tall, polished wood poles were fitted with the party's purple, white, and gold fabric gonfalons.

The women, all dressed in white, donned their tricolored sashes, hoisted the poles, stretched out the banners, and stepped to the beat of the brass band assigned to lead them. They marched in a long single line through the streets of Marion, with every state's name held high on a vertical cloth pennant striped in the Woman's Party colors. Leading the processional was a giant banner, stretching almost the entire width of the street, carried on each end by distinguished suffrage veterans, including Lizzie Crozier French of Knoxville, who managed to be a member in good standing of both NAWSA and the Woman's Party. It was a rather wordy pronouncement to carry around, it certainly could have been punchier, but it managed to get its message across:

> The Republican platform endorses ratification of suffrage. The first test of the platform will come when the Tennessee legislature meets in August. Will the Republicans carry out their platform by giving a unanimous Republican vote in Tennessee for suffrage?

When the first line of suffragists reached the edge of the front porch, those behind fanned out to form a semicircle, many rows deep, facing the Hardings. They set down the base of their poles onto the lawn but held them upright, so the banners were still aloft and very visible. The Woman's Party representatives walked up the porch steps to be introduced to Senator and Mrs. Harding. Alice Paul had chosen her two speakers for the occasion with care: women who could speak cogently, colorfully, and loudly. Sue White would represent Tennessee and the aspirations to make it the thirty-sixth state; Louisine Havemeyer, of New York, would speak for the women who already had the vote and intended to use it against Warren Harding if he didn't shape up.

Miss Paul had begged Havemeyer to travel to Marion for this event, even though she knew the overnight trip in a bumpy sleeper train car would be uncomfortable and tiring for the plucky, sixty-five-year-old grandmother. Havemeyer was the Woman's Party's most popular speaker—vivid, funny, disarming—she charmed audiences and had a big, booming voice that could carry in the open air. She knew how to make a sharp point, embellished by erudite asides and curlicues of wit. She was the extremely wealthy widow of Henry Osborne Havemeyer, the "Sugar King," whose family owned the American Sugar Refining Company, which controlled virtually all sugar supplies in the nation. She and Harry had enjoyed collecting art, and with the advice of Louisine's close friend Mary Cassatt, the American painter, they assembled one of the world's great collections. They commissioned Louis Comfort Tiffany to design the furniture and stained glass windows for their Fifth Avenue mansion. Harry Havemeyer was a resolute suffrage supporter, encouraging his wife to sign petitions and get involved. When Harry died in 1907, Louisine plunged more deeply into suffrage activities, displaying a taste for the more radical strain of the movement. She joined, and helped bankroll, the short-lived Women's Political Union of Harriot Stanton Blatch, Elizabeth Cady Stanton's daughter, which tried to recruit more working-class women into the movement. When Blatch joined forces with Alice Paul's Congressional Union, and then the National Woman's Party, Havemeyer threw her allegiance, and her checkbook, there.

Havemeyer and Blatch were partners in the bruising 1915 New York state suffrage referendum contest, working parallel to Carrie Catt and Mollie Hay's campaign apparatus, and Havemeyer overcame her fear of public speaking to deliver dozens of impassioned speeches from the back of her landaulet touring car. Havemeyer also raised money for the campaign by selling tickets to a gallery exhibit of her art collection, convincing Mary Cassatt to contribute a few paintings to be auctioned. Blatch and Havemeyer also concocted some of the great suffrage publicity stunts and wonderfully wacky props that drew crowds and newsreel coverage: the traveling Suffrage Torch and the electrified Ship of State.

So it was Havemeyer who appeared in those newsreels, wearing her "Votes for Women" sash, overcoming seasickness to balance on the deck of a ship bobbing in the middle of the Hudson River, leaning over the rail to hand her Suffrage Torch to New Jersey suffrage comrades in another boat. And it was Havemeyer holding aloft her Ship of State, a *Mayflower*-like model she designed, decorated by tiny light bulbs, which she would flick on dramatically at a pivotal moment in her speech. (Men and boys were particularly fascinated by this electric wonder, and since men were the ones voting in the suffrage referendum, they were an important audience to hold.) And it was Havemeyer who famously appeared in nighttime suffrage parades wearing light bulbs strung on her body, a battery strapped onto her back, the walking embodiment of a woman-piloted Ship of State.

Sue White knew Havemeyer as a fellow traveler, literally: they had been arrested and imprisoned together, then spent a month traveling cross-country together on the "Prison Special" railroad tour in the winter of 1919. Slammed together in a "Black Maria" patrol wagon, held together in the cold, smelly, rat- and cockroach-infested jailhouse, and then living together in the cramped quarters of a Pullman train affords a certain sense of intimacy and camaraderie. Mrs. Havemeyer was a trouper, and as different as they were—the small-town Tennessee girl and the Fifth Avenue doyenne—White was heartened to have Mrs. Havemeyer by her side again.

White and Havemeyer climbed the porch steps; White spoke first. She made it short, sweet, direct: My home, Tennessee, provides the opportunity for both political parties to help secure a thirty-sixth state. We look to you, Mr. Harding, to get all the state's Republican legislators on board for ratification. White left the rhetorical flights of fancy to Mrs. Havemeyer; Havemeyer took off.

"We need a thirty-sixth state, and it seems as if it were as impossible for us to attain it as it was for the children of Israel to enter the promised land," Havemeyer said, pausing a beat to emphasize her first punch line. "We know Moses was slow, but when it comes to suffrage, I believe he would have to give the Republican Party time allowance. I have often wondered what would have happened if there had been picketers in Egypt. We know Pharaoh was visited by every plague under the sun, but history doesn't relate whether picketers were among them."

She voiced a "deep-throated protest" against her "unenfranchised sisters being used as fodder for any political machine" and suggested that any woman not allowed to vote should refuse to pay her taxes. This was not a new concept; Susan Anthony advocated it, and Anna Howard Shaw actually practiced it—Shaw's car was impounded for her tax protest—but coming from a woman of Mrs. Havemeyer's tax bracket, it carried a punch. And if casually suggesting a tax revolt did not get the assembled Republicans' attention, she knew what could: invoking the sacred name of the most venerated of all Republicans, Abraham Lincoln.

"The great Lincoln would have said to you, 'Men, these women have already thirty-five states to the good. Stop and think what a majority that is to be up against. Are you not foolish to resist the will of thirty-five states, instead of yielding the thirty-sixth one?'" She was warming up, finding her rhythm; the feathers on her hat bobbed and swayed.

"Fifty-six years ago Abraham Lincoln also wished to pass an amendment. He, too, needed a thirty-sixth state. Did he say, 'I have done enough' or 'I will request someone' or 'I will urge' or 'Ladies, don't bother me, I have done all I could.' No! He said, 'I need another state and I am going to make one,' and he did, and his amendment was ratified—and think of it, gentlemen, the Union lived on stronger and better for the brave act of a brave, just man."

Some of her listeners may have noticed that Mrs. Havemeyer jumbled the chronology of President Lincoln's efforts to abolish slavery with the Thirteenth Amendment. While he did everything in his power, including overt bribery, to win passage of that amendment in the reluctant House of Representatives, he was dead by the time a final state was needed for ratification, in December 1865 (with thirty-six states in the Union at the time, only twenty-seven states were needed to ratify). But historical details were not the point of Mrs. Havemeyer's performance: it was the spirit, the soul, of the story that mattered.

"Senator Harding. will you not urge the men of the Republican Party to do as much for us today and get us that thirty-sixth state?" she implored, glancing at him, her voice rising, her arms outstretched.

Harding leaned against a porch pillar and focused his gaze intently upon White and then Havemeyer as they spoke. He was always a good listener, one of his best political skills. He folded his arms, cocked his head slightly, appeared to be concentrating on every word. He was a distinguished-looking man, still considered very handsome. He had a fine aquiline nose, large expressive eyes, smooth skin, and perfectly clipped gray hair. He was a very attractive candidate, his advisers agreed; he looked presidential.

Watching this scene from behind, in the deep recesses of the covered porch, was Will Hays, chairman of the Republican National Committee. Hays, an expert political tactician, was working for a new boss now, the new presidential candidate, and what he'd learned in the past month was that Senator Harding had a different type of "woman problem" than just mollifying the suffragists. Harding seemed to have trouble keeping his pants fly buttoned. And Hays had to deal with it.

Hays had already expended a fair amount of energy making sure the press did not get wind of his candidate's very messy extramarital entanglements, which would certainly not go over well with any new women voters. When Harding was asked by the Republican leadership at the Chicago convention if there were any embarrassing skeletons in his closet that might pose problems in a presidential campaign, he thought about it for a few minutes, then answered, "No." That proved to be quite untruthful. There was the baby, and there was the blackmail.

The baby was safely tucked away, with her mother, in a small apartment in Chicago. The mother was Nan Britton, who as a Marion schoolgirl developed an inexplicable but unshakable crush on Harding. When she was twenty and he fifty-one, she became his "bride" in a Manhattan hotel room. Their daughter was now nine months old, though Harding had not yet bothered to see her.

At the same time, Harding was being blackmailed by his longtime paramour, Carrie Fulton Phillips. They'd been carrying on a torrid affair for fifteen years. Carrie and Jim Phillips, who owned a big department store in downtown Marion, were neighbors and good friends of the Hardings. Carrie Phillips was beautiful and vivacious, and when she and Warren weren't together they carried on a steamy correspondence; he wrote erotic love poems to her. Florence knew all about it. She'd opened one of their letters back in 1911. She'd considered divorce but decided to simply stand pat and hold it over Warren's head when necessary: a rising politician needed to display a stable home life. Florence had invested in Warren, and she wanted a return on that investment.

So Warren and Carrie Phillips carried on. But when Carrie learned about Nan Britton (there were other women, too, including his Senate secretary), she felt betrayed, and in the spring of 1920 she threatened to expose their affair unless he made it worth her while not to squeal. Harding offered to pay her $5,000 a year, but she wanted much more. He tried to convince her that the only way he could pay her more was to be nominated for president, opening new doors of economic opportunity. She wasn't impressed and planned to sell his love letters to the highest bidder. Only after Harding won the nomination did he fess up to the Republican leadership and reveal his dangerous predicament.

Will Hays had to clean up the mess. Hays brought both Carrie and Jim Phillips (she'd told her husband everything) to Washington and struck a deal: the Republican National Committee would pay the couple $25,000 to go to Japan and China—to the other side of the world, beyond the reach of the press—during the presidential campaign and also give them $2,000 each month to guarantee their silence. Mr. and Mrs. Phillips packed their bags and were now safely absent from Marion. But alone among the town's buildings, only the Uhler-Phillips department store was unadorned by celebratory bunting.

As Mrs. Havemeyer concluded her speech, Harding stepped forward to face the audience. He could see that a parade traffic jam had developed on the far reaches of the lawn, with impatient bands and marchers eager to make their way to the porch but blocked by the stationary suffragists. Time to move the Suffs on, which was just fine with him.

"To what these ladies have said I wish to reply, very briefly, that the consideration of suffrage and woman's participation in politics contemplates her taking her part equally and fully with the men of this Republic," he intoned as the sashed women surrounding the porch leaned in, eager to hear his response over the din of the bands. But there was no real response. He gave them their first taste of the reason Harding would forever be linked to the word "bloviate."

"Therefore, since I am speaking to all the citizenship of America in a formal manner this afternoon, if I may be allowed to state to America, and to you, and to all citizens quite alike, my position on the questions you have asked me, that, I promise you I will do." Wait till my official acceptance speech this afternoon, he told them. They waited.

At two o'clock that afternoon, the notification ceremony began, staged at Garfield Park on the edge of town, in the open-walled Chautauqua pavilion, which could hold two thousand people under its crossbeam roof. That wasn't enough room for this big event, so two thousand more chairs were crammed in. It's estimated that another thirty thousand people listened from the grounds outside.

Harding wrote the speech in longhand, in pencil, and even made the galley corrections for the printed edition himself, sitting down to a linotype machine in the offices of the *Star*. The crowd in the pavilion stood on their chairs, cheering wildly, waving Harding flags, as the candidate was escorted to the stage by Senator Henry Cabot Lodge of Massachusetts, who would officiate at the ceremonies. Lodge, whose antipathy toward woman suffrage and the federal amendment was surpassed only by his enmity for Woodrow Wilson's League of Nations—and he had managed to block both in the Senate chamber for long stretches—made the official "notification" to Harding of his nomination.

Harding then accepted, in what was for him a relatively short and shapely speech. He already had a reputation for platitudinous orations, light on substance and specifics ("wet sponges," in the inimitable words of journalist H. L. Mencken). Harding's speech that afternoon did have a sort of windy grandeur to it, as he urged a "return to normalcy" in national life and an isolationist "America first" posture in the world. He delivered it in the slow, ponderous cadences he preferred, conferring a synthetic gravitas to his words. Toward the end, as his collar grew damp with sweat in the sweltering pavilion, Harding finally came to his comments on woman suffrage.

"The womanhood of America, always its glory, its inspiration and the potent, uplifting force in its social and spiritual development, is about to be enfranchised. . . . By party edict, by my recorded vote, by personal conviction, I am committed to this measure of justice. It is my earnest hope, my sincere desire, that the one needed State vote be quickly recorded in the affirmative of the right of equal suffrage and that the vote of every citizen shall be cast and counted in the approaching election."

Always eager to please, and not offend, Harding even tried to soothe the nation's Antis: "And to the great number of noble women who have opposed in conviction this tremendous change in the ancient relation of the sexes as applied to government, I venture to plead that they will accept the full responsibility of enlarged citizenship and give to the best in the Republic their suffrage and support."

It sounded fine, it sounded sincere, but it said nothing about any firm commitment to securing that "one needed State."

Alice Paul made her displeasure known quickly to reporters: "If Sen. Harding refuses to live up to the suffrage plank and contents himself merely with 'earnestly hoping' and 'sincerely desiring,' how can he expect the country to take seriously the other planks in his platform?

"If Sen. Harding will use his full power, as a leader of his party, in behalf of enfranchisement of women, he can secure such a Republican vote in favor of ratification in Tennessee. Only by action and not by the expression of polite interest will women be satisfied."

Paul threatened to follow Harding wherever he went during the campaign, should he ever venture off his front porch, pressing the suffragists' demands. When a reporter asked whether picketing against Harding would be "indulged in" at Marion or elsewhere, the reply was: "That remains to be seen."

The Antis, now assembling in Nashville, saw only glad tidings in the hesitant words of Senator Harding. They had good reason to believe Harding would do nothing to displease them.

Chapter 10

◆ ◆ ◆

Home and Heaven

CHARLOTTE ROWE, field secretary of the National Association Opposed to Woman Suffrage, swept into Tennessee during this third week of July, making her customary loud entrance.

"They call us the Home, Heaven and Mother crowd in derision," she trumpeted to reporters in Chattanooga, alluding to the suffragists' favorite depiction of the Antis' bedrock rationales. "But we are determined to prevent women from descending to the political level of men, which if accomplished, will cheapen women and draw them into the mire of politics."

Miss Rowe herself was a highly skilled and well-paid political operative, working deep in the "mire" for over a decade, though she seemed none the worse for the toxic exposure. She was very fashionably dressed, with a knot of auburn hair tied low onto her neck, a broad-brimmed hat framing her narrow, thin-lipped face. She was a New Yorker in her late thirties with a quick wit, agile mind, and exceedingly sharp tongue. Rowe was the Antis' most astute and aggressive speaker, a roving pugilist itching to verbally box with the best of the Suffs, anytime, anywhere.

The Suffs despised her but also had to give her a grudging degree of respect. If she weren't so hideously misguided, they thought, she might have been an excellent advocate for the Cause. Rowe was their most talented and tenacious adversary; they had been dueling with her publicly for years. They first encountered her around 1911 in New York, in dazzling speeches, legislative hearing testimony, and debates all around the city and state. She was only in her twenties then, and the antisuffragists had just begun organizing, but she relished tangling with the veteran and venerated Suffs, daring them to debate her.

When the federal amendment moved out of its long dormancy in Congress in 1913, Rowe was there in Washington to testify against the amendment in committee hearings; and in the final, protracted stages in the House and Senate, she moved to the nation's capital to be at the center of the action. As soon as the amendment was passed by Congress, Rowe set off on an investigative tour of all the major southern cities, meeting with local Anti groups and sympathetic legislators, gauging their appetite for a furious fight against ratification. During the past year she seemed to be everywhere, in all the most contentious ratification states. Since spring she'd scored an impressive string of victories, and now she displayed a gunslinger's steely confidence. "Miss Rowe earned her spurs in Delaware," was the way one admiring Tennessee newspaper reporter described her, and she'd recently put another pair of notches on her ratification-slayer belt in Georgia and Louisiana. Now she was taking aim at Tennessee.

Rowe was in Chattanooga en route to Nashville, in the vanguard of national Anti leaders riding into Tennessee like the cavalry—no, like the American Expeditionary Forces—to defend a besieged strategic outpost, bringing fresh supplies and firepower to beat back an enemy assault. Since the war, Rowe and her Anti compatriots had adopted many military metaphors and allusions, to stir emotion. They postured themselves as the brave defenders of liberty and morality fighting the despotic Suffs, who, not unlike the Huns, were intent on destroying the foundations of American civilization. They likened their campaign to halt ratification of the federal amendment to the bloody, yearlong Battle of Verdun on the western front, in which almost a million men were killed contesting a patch of French soil. The Antis took as their campaign motto the Verdun rallying cry of the French staring down the German advance: "They Shall Not Pass!"

The Antis themselves were an odd coalition held together by the centripetal force of fear: fear of the political, economic, and social disruptions that equal suffrage might bring, not just at the polls and in the halls of government, but in the factory, the kitchen, and the bedroom. Standing under the Anti umbrella were men of the cloth and women of the club, corporate titans and black and immigrant workingmen, political bosses and university professors, united only by their dread of yet another element of upheaval. The nation had experienced many convulsive changes in the past fifty years, and woman suffrage threatened one more undesirable upset. Charlotte Rowe knew how to appeal to every constituency.

Though Rowe was an oppressively familiar figure to the Suffs, she remained a fascinating, infuriating enigma to them. She wasn't cut from the usual Anti cloth; she wasn't the daughter or wife of a conservative minister, rich banker, lawyer, or industrialist, as were so many who joined the antisuffrage movement. Nor was she a wealthy, cosseted, bridge-playing lady of leisure, as the Suffs liked to portray Antis, who cared more about preserving the privileges of her class than taking on the responsibilities of full citizenship. (To be fair, many Anti women were active in social reform and philanthropic projects, which they considered apolitical and acceptable.)

Rowe also wasn't a religious zealot, who feared eternal damnation if she set foot in a polling booth. She wasn't even a mother, though she waxed sentimental about the sacred role of motherhood and home as "the altar of human affection and the shrine of man's desire" placed in jeopardy by woman suffrage. With the advent of suffrage, Rowe warned, women were going to tear off their aprons, jump into the polling booth—and the working world—and never come back.

Rowe styled herself, very cleverly, as the realization of an ideal: a modern, single working woman (as neither a wife nor mother, she was free to assume this role) whose femininity was never in doubt. She dressed the part, favoring sleek-fitting business dresses with modestly plunging V-neck collars, hemlines swinging midway between her ankles and her knees, and the latest slim, pointy leather pumps. She was the modern woman who didn't need, or want, the vote. She lived out of a suitcase, traveling from city to city, clubhouse to statehouse, a professional politico striking deals, exerting pressure, and lobbying for the right of other women to stay at home.

Giving a modern spin to the trusty "women's proper sphere" arguments, Rowe often belittled Mrs. Catt and other suffragists for asserting that the work of twentieth-century women had moved out of the home into the factory and office. "Some women have indeed permitted their work to go out of the home," Rowe retorted, "as our foundling asylums, our reformatories, and our prisons testify."

Rowe took the suffragists' jocular, condescending "Home, Heaven, and Mother crowd" depiction of socially conservative Antis and flipped it to her advantage. Even though she wasn't a homemaker, wasn't a mother, and wasn't a pious churchgoer, she embraced the epithet, wearing it like a badge of honor. "In spite of this aspersion; in spite of this contempt; in spite of this everlasting ridicule to which we are subjected, I am not ashamed . . . ," she proclaimed proudly. "We have been called the enemies of womanhood; they say we are opposing woman's development. They say: you are trying to crush them in the four walls called home. . . .

"But if you everlastingly preach this doctrine that home is a small, narrow place," she scolded, "if you say to your women in your homes: 'Do not be satisfied with this existence of your grandmother; do not be content to be a woman with four or five children; come on out and be free; come out and have a pay envelope, come on out and be independent economically, politically, and socially'—and that is what the feminists are demanding—if you do this thing, you will prostitute your civilization, you are a vandal, and you have stripped from life its most beautiful thing. . . ." Rowe's guilt-tripping harangue seems timeless; every modern working mother has heard a version.

Keeping women at home was more vital to national security than any battleship, the Antis believed. A dramatic course correction was needed, lest the next generation be lost: "If working girls and women in colleges would study cooking and sewing and domestic science and hygiene," Rowe insisted, "and the fine and beautiful art of home making, it would be much better for them and better for the country than if they spend their time parading up the avenue of a crowded city and praying that they may some day, somehow, become policemen or boiler makers side by side with men."

It was folly for women to aspire to the world of men, the Antis preached, and it was not women's minds or muscles that needed cultivation, but her heart and her spiritual attributes; this was what made women special. This was a trusty rationale often used by men to keep women in their place, but Anti women were willing to employ it, too. American and European women confronted this attitude in the late nineteenth and early twentieth centuries as they attempted to enter the halls of higher education. They had to beat back the accepted medical wisdom that strenuous thinking harmed a woman's reproductive organs, draining the lifeblood from her ovaries to her brain, endangering not just civilization, but the human species.

The Antis' "biology is destiny" trope wasn't new in 1920, but it took on a different ring in the aftermath of the recent world war, when women had been forced—or had the opportunity—to assume such profoundly different, hitherto masculine, working roles. To some, the Antis' warnings sounded dated, but to sympathizers they seemed timely, even prescient, anticipating the arrival of shattering social change: the possible advent of not only the career woman, but the sex-crazed kid sister of the suffragist, the Flapper Girl.

Rowe's résumé claimed to include a stint as a newspaper writer, and she was sometimes identified as a lawyer, but the paper evidence of these professions was thin. In the first years of her Anti career, she led a group called Wage Earning Women Opposed to Suffrage, allowing her to fashion arguments that the vote, and other "feminist socialist" ideas such as a minimum wage, health insurance, and an eight-hour day, would be detrimental to working women. She still stood by that position: working women "are neither whiners nor whimperers," she'd insisted just a year ago, in spring 1919, in opposing labor reform legislation advocated by Mary Garrett Hay and New York State suffragists.

Suffragists howled, pointing out that Rowe's wage earning was derived exclusively from her Anti staff positions, and she had no right to speak for the factory or sweatshop women who needed labor protections. She sounded more like the voice of exploitive manufacturers than a representative of working women, the Suffs protested, and they thought they knew who was paying for her supper but could never prove it. The financial backing of the Antis was always hard to trace. No matter: once the vote was "forced" upon New York women in the 1917 referendum, Rowe changed her affiliation to the oddly oxymoronic Women Voters Anti-Suffrage Party, whose mission was to use the unwanted vote to punish pro-suffrage politicians at the polls.

But Rowe really was, in many respects, the model of modern American womanhood: independent, self-supporting, opinionated, accomplished. She was out in the world making a very public career, not sitting at home making and caring for babies. She spoke her mind, without false modesty or apology, to both rapt audiences and raucous crowds, to governors and legislators, and to any reporter within earshot. She was famous for sarcastically cutting to ribbons those who disagreed with her. Suffragists likened her tongue to a rasp. She delighted in calling them moral degenerates, and she ridiculed male suffrage supporters as emasculated, effeminate "Gwendolyns" or "Mabels." Real men and women, she insisted, would have no patience with equal suffrage, that precursor to a perverse mix-up of gender identities and roles. Suffrage would bring about a "sex war" between husbands and wives as traditional roles were distorted and arguments about politics tore couples apart.

Rowe was what could fairly be called an Anti militant, wielding incendiary words and lobbing explosive accusations into the public square. Like Mrs. Pankhurst, and more than Alice Paul, she relished the power of shock to mold public opinion. Even though public opinion had slowly, in the last few years, swung against her, with more Americans accepting woman suffrage as either right or inevitable, her apocalyptic visions of civilization on the brink of collapse—should the federal amendment be forced upon the nation—still sold well in certain circles. Especially in these postwar days, when anarchy seemed to be in triumphant ascent around the world.

This was Rowe's timely message: Woman suffrage was an insidious front for feminism and socialism, the door through which bolshevism could invade America: "The ultimate aim of suffrage is feminism," she insisted. "Feminism is intimately and inextricably allied with Socialism and belongs to the same distorted school of thought, the same ungodly dream of irresponsible power. Feminism is not an imaginary evil; it is a definite and logical doctrine, promulgated by the enemies of Christian civilization." The popular Anti theme of "the Red Behind the Yellow," bolshevism lurking under the skirts of suffragism, was echoed in all of Rowe's talks and writings. The letterhead of the national Anti association's stationery, and the masthead of their journal, *The Woman Patriot,* which Rowe coedited, spelled out their civil creed: "For Home and National Defense, Against Woman Suffrage, Feminism and Socialism."

Anarchists' bombs were exploding in the streets of American cities, in the home of U.S. Attorney General Palmer, and in the mailboxes of mayors, bankers, and judges. Was it a coincidence that such appalling events were occurring just as more states capitulated to the suffragists and the federal amendment reared its ugly head? No, it was not! Rowe insisted. Or that Great Britain, having succumbed to its suffragists' shrill demands, was now in a state of economic ruin, social turmoil, and national spiritual depression? (Never mind the ravages of the war.) Or that the first thing the Bolsheviks did when they came to power in Russia was to give their women the vote? No, it was not simple coincidence! Rowe claimed. And there was frightening historical precedent as well: "Unless America prevents itself from getting on the [suffrage] band wagon," she warned, "we will surely pay the bitter price of destruction which befell feminist-ridden Rome and feminist-ridden Greece."

If Rowe's reasoning often skipped a logical beat, she was so adept at spinning such spellbinding scenarios that for her eager audiences, all such quibbles melted away. Suffragists refused to debate her; Carrie Catt and, before her, Anna Shaw ignored her challenges. They didn't want to give Rowe an elevated platform on which to perform her sleight-of-hand reasoning, and they didn't want to give her any more publicity; it was enough that they had to contend with her at legislative hearings and joust with her in the press. Shaw used to snidely say that the Antis and their arguments, particularly

Rowe's, were like jellyfish: no head, no heart, just a quivering mass of emotion, fears, and prejudices. Squishy, hard to handle, and venomous.

Rowe was proud to consider herself a kindred spirit of the famous muckraking journalist Ida Tarbell, whose open antagonism toward women's enfranchisement seemed so paradoxical and yet all the more potent for the contradiction. Tarbell was the epitome of the educated, independent career woman: reared in a liberal home where woman suffrage pioneers were welcome dinner guests; a college-educated woman who'd lived in Paris, studied at the Sorbonne, and made her own living as a correspondent for the top magazines. She was a forceful writer and fearless investigator who made her name by exposing the machinations of John D. Rockefeller's Standard Oil monopoly in a blistering series of articles for *McClure's* magazine. Along with Lincoln Steffens and Upton Sinclair, she practiced a new type of deeply probing and powerful investigative journalism, and her pen could bring captains of industry to their knees. Her pen could also bring Suffs to their wits' end, so incongruent seemed Tarbell's writings about women's societal role with the spirit of her own life.

In articles, speeches, and books, such as *The Business of Being a Woman* and *The Ways of Woman,* Tarbell railed against the feminist worldview of equality: "The idea that there is a kind of inequality for a woman in minding her own business and letting man do the same, comes from our confused and rather stupid notion of the meaning of equality," she maintained. "Insisting that women do the same things that men do, may make the two exteriorly more alike—it does not make them more equal. Men and women are widely apart in functions and in possibilities. They cannot be made equal by exterior devices like trousers, ballots, the study of Greek."

Here was a woman who'd proven her intellect and nerve, risen to the highest levels of the male-dominated profession of journalism, and won the admiration of men such as Theodore Roosevelt, advising other women that they couldn't—or shouldn't—make their way into the wider world. Stay at home, she warned them, for your own happiness and for the sake of society. It was the old "woman's sphere" concept, the backbone of the Anti stand, spoken by one of the most famous and respected journalists in America.

"Women have a business assigned by nature and society which is of more importance than public life," she told her readers and audiences. That natural assignment was to find a mate, build a nest, nurture a family: all the things Ida Minerva Tarbell had not done in her life. Was she simply being a hypocrite, or did she so regret her life choices that she felt it her duty to warn other women away from that path?

Suffragists shook their heads. Anna Shaw and Carrie Catt made many attempts to convince Tarbell to use her prodigious talents for the good of her American sisters, for the suffrage cause; she repeatedly refused. It became rather awkward when Tarbell, Catt, and Shaw were all appointed by President Wilson to the Woman's Committee of the Council of National Defense during the war; sitting around a conference table in Washington, discussing women's enhanced wartime roles, was painful for Tarbell. Jane Addams expressed her disgust with Tarbell's stance: "There is some limitation to Ida Tarbell's mind." The Antis simply rejoiced; they took Tarbell at her word and welcomed her into their fold.

Charlotte Rowe was also delighted to frequently share the stage at Anti events with another unlikely ally, the women's education champion Annie Nathan Meyer. As a young woman in the 1880s, Meyer wanted a college education and was frustrated by the only option available to her in New York City, the "collegiate course for women" at Columbia University, a watered-down curriculum intended to produce clever wives for the city's elite men. Meyer hopped on her bicycle—she was one of the first women in New York to dare to cycle in public—knocking on the doors of wealthy women and influential men to sell her idea of building a woman's college in the city, a sister college to Columbia, with equally rigorous standards. In little more than two years, she'd raised the funds and steered the proposition through the very reluctant Columbia Board of Trustees, and Barnard College was established; Meyer was just twenty-two years old.

Meyer was known as an advocate for training and cultivating women's minds, allowing them to enter the professions, business, arts, and all other aspects of worldly accomplishment. In addition to her constant fund-raising for Barnard, she began publishing essays, novels, and plays. She was ahead of her time in her exploration of racial issues in her works of fiction and in her promotion of racial equality. Wife of a prominent and supportive physician, she wasn't of the Home, Heaven, and Mother crowd at all. But Meyer possessed an analytic, unsparing eye; she could spot hypocrisy and opportunistic inconsistencies, and she felt the suffrage movement was guilty of both.

Meyer didn't subscribe to the Antis' usual screed about women being defiled by their entry into a voting booth or sullied by political activity. But neither did she buy the Suffs' claim that women's entrance into the political world would purify politics, that women's finer instincts would lift politics out of the realm of self-interest, greed, ego, and corruption. Or that they would make governmental bodies more accountable and more humane. She certainly did not share Carrie Catt's faith in enfranchised women's ability to bring about world peace. All those suffragist promises of some sort of highly moral, pink political heaven were utter nonsense, Meyer insisted.

And in line with other reform-inclined Antis, those who were involved in municipal improvement and social betterment projects, Meyer also believed that by accepting the franchise, women would compromise their "soft power" of persuasion, their ability to influence male decision making and legislation free from the taint of political favor. This above-the-fray moral suasion was more powerful than any ballot, she claimed. Meyer delighted in the role of squinty suffrage skeptic and embraced the duties of an Anti leader, debating Carrie Catt in the pages of *The New York Times* and clashing publicly with her own sister, the civic reformer Maud Nathan, who was an ardent Suff. The sisters did not speak to each other.

Charlotte Rowe used Meyer's and Tarbell's arguments to good advantage, while adjusting her arsenal of antisuffrage weapons to changing circumstances. Since the war, Rowe had added a new arrow to her quiver, claiming that the suffragists, led by pacifists the likes of Carrie Catt, Jane Addams, and Alice Paul, were unpatriotic and even treasonous.

Rowe contended that at the outset of the war in Europe, Catt and Addams had tried to appease the kaiser with their Woman's Peace Party, then covered their traitorous tracks by taking on high-level women's war work committee assignments, all the while continuing their selfish suffrage work. Paul had called the president of the United States "Kaiser Wilson," burned him in effigy, and proclaimed that America was no democracy, while American boys were dying overseas to save democracy. That's what happens when women enter politics, Rowe asserted. Even this spring, Mrs. Catt went abroad to summon her international cabal of suffragists and socialists in Geneva, blaspheming the good name of America with her accusations that liberty was being withheld from American women by sinister forces. It was all baloney to Charlotte Rowe; it was bolshevism knocking at the door.

Rowe and the national Antis altered their strategy as the specter of the Nineteenth Amendment loomed closer. They toned down their opposition to state-granted woman suffrage (though they still didn't approve of it) and focused their objections on the tyranny of the federal amendment (the "Sex Amendment to the Constitution," as they liked to call it) forcing suffrage upon the states, whether they wanted it or not. Almost 20 percent of all the state legislatures had already rejected the amendment—with more on the way, the Antis predicted—and quite a few more had only narrowly approved it. Let New York and California and Illinois and Wyoming and all the other misguided states have their woman suffrage, the Antis now argued, but leave be all those states that didn't wish to force the vote upon their good women. States' rights became the Antis' new rallying cry, and it resonated especially loudly in the South, where it appealed to not only those fundamentally opposed to woman suffrage, but also to men and women who supported women's rights but cherished states' rights even more.

The Antis' core belief that women were inevitably disturbed and degraded by political endeavors had taken shape before Rowe's own eyes this summer when she watched how the Democratic Party suffrage women acted at the San Francisco convention. Celebrating their successful maneuver to place a pro-ratification plank into the party platform, they jumped upon desks, permitted men to hoist them onto their shoulders, screamed war whoops, and did a mock Indian dance in front of the Speaker's stand. She found it disgusting. It was enough to convince anyone that woman suffrage was a menace to true womanhood, she told the Chattanooga reporters.

Rowe settled into the whites-only section of her train car bound for Nashville, looking forward to a historic offensive. Being on the offense suited her natural, but still feminine, inclinations. When she reached Nashville she'd assess the situation, align her strategies with the local culture, and adopt the native Tennessee political dialect. She expected to be quickly fluent in that particular patois.

The first Anti fusillade was already under way. The plan was for a coordinated bombardment, launched from different platforms, aimed at Nashville but also hitting prime targets in Ohio: Marion and Columbus, Harding and Cox. It began with threatening letters to Governor Roberts from the legal lights of the American Constitutional League. First from the league's president, Everett P. Wheeler, a luminary of the New York State Bar Association, explaining all the legal reasons the amendment should not be taken up by the Tennessee legislature. This week the governor opened the envelope of a follow-up diatribe from Baltimore attorney William Marbury, who'd led the successful effort to defeat ratification of the federal amendment in the Maryland legislature, warning that Tennessee must think twice before imposing harm on other states.

"It seems monstrous to us here in Maryland, especially those of us who are Democrats, that the legislature of Tennessee should vote to ratify an amendment which would take away for us the right to determine this question for ourselves," Marbury scolded. Adoption of the amendment would harm Marylanders even more seriously than Tennesseans, Marbury told Roberts, adding sixty to seventy thousand Negro women voters to the electorate. And while the Negro women would be eager to exercise their new franchise on Election Day, white women would be reluctant to go to the polls, due to "the conditions which would exist" in the state.

Those conditions were tacitly understood by the two southern men: white women would not want to vote at a polling station where black women were also present; this public mixing would be abhorrent to any proper woman and keep her from setting foot in an integrated polling place. Democratic white women would stay home, while black women (who were expected to vote Republican, the historic party of Lincoln) eagerly took up their new franchise. The Democratic Party was putting itself at risk of losing the white southern male voter as well, Marbury warned, jeopardizing the "solid South" that was the party's power base. The Democrats, heavily dependent upon working-class and immigrant voters in the North, brewers and liquor industry men in the Midwest, and states' rights and Jim Crow preservationists in the South—all of whom felt threatened by women's enfranchisement—typically opposed woman suffrage more strenuously than their Republican counterparts. Governor Roberts was courting the wrath of them all, Marbury cautioned.

Soon after Governor Roberts received Marbury's letter, chastising him for endangering the Democratic Party, presidential nominee James Cox received an even sharper note from Nina Pinckard, president general of the Southern Women's Rejection League, just arrived in Nashville, furious at Cox's cooperation with the suffragists.

"The home loving women of the South, who do not picket, card-index or blackmail candidates, appeal to you as the leader of the Democratic Party to grant us a hearing," Mrs. Pinckard wrote in greeting. Cox and the Democrats had ignored and insulted the Antis while they kowtowed to the militant suffragists; southern Antis would stand for it no more. "The very safety of Southern civilization, the purity of Anglo-Saxon blood, is involved in this Amendment," Pinckard told Cox. "Why should the South support the Democratic Party if Democratic Party candidates, in time of peace, intend to crucify us on a Federal cross with the same nails used by our Republican conquerers after a bloody war?" The bloody war was understood not to be the recent European conflict.

Balancing their assault, the Antis simultaneously turned their fire on Senator Harding. Like the Suffs, they too were annoyed by his flip-flopping and vague assurances. The Antis watched as Harding squirmed in discomfort, caught in the dual pincers of the Suffs, forced to utter allegiance to ratification. The Antis then methodically increased his pain by reminding him of his equally sincere pledges to them. And made those pledges public.

Harding had been most courteous to the delegation of Antis that met with him just before he clinched the nomination in Chicago, a meeting arranged by their mutual friends Senators Lodge, Penrose, Wadsworth, and Brandegee. All the Antis asked of Harding was that he not interfere in states considering ratification of the federal amendment, not push the Vermont and Connecticut Republican governors, not poke his nose into Tennessee. During the first part of July, he seemed to be keeping that promise quite nicely; Vermont and Connecticut were securely stalled. But recently he'd begun dissembling about his "earnest hopes" and "sincere desires" for ratification, and he sent those little love notes to Mrs. Catt and entertained the Alice Paul picketers on his porch. The Antis demanded he explain such double-talk. They released to the press the letter Harding had written to them less than a fortnight before:

"I have ever an ear for any one who may ask to be heard," he'd written to the chairwoman of the Republican section of the national Anti association. "I should quite as readily give a hearing to those who are opposed to woman suffrage. I do not mean to be a candidate who is the partisan of any particular group in our American activities." Harding's trusted private secretary, George Christian, had sent another message to the Antis, reassuring them: Harding had no desire to "wield a club" over the states or the governors to satisfy the suffragists. The Antis released that statement to the press, too.

Now, in this third week of July, feeling more secure about Harding—as secure as possible when dealing with such a prevaricator—the Antis were calm as they watched Harding contort himself into knots. He was attempting to placate the Alice Paul women who didn't like what he'd said in his

Notification Day acceptance speech, while still sweet-talking Mrs. Catt, all the while avoiding the wrath of his manipulative sponsor Senator Henry Cabot Lodge. He was caught between the devil and the deep blue sea, as the newspapers said. It was quite a scene.

Just hours after Alice Paul rejected his acceptance speech comments on suffrage as inadequate, Harding's managers scrambled to repair the damage. They hastily arranged for John Houk, a Tennessee state senator and Republican committeeman who was attending the notification festivities in Marion, to send a telegram to the nominee, asking what advice he'd give to his party's Tennessee legislators facing a decision on ratification. The query was trumped up, everyone knew it was a plant, but it allowed Harding to once again play both sides of the fence.

"It is my earnest hope that the Republicans in the Tennessee legislature, acting upon solemn conviction, can see their way clear to give their support to this amendment," he wrote to the pro-suffrage Houk. "I believe in suffrage; our party has indorsed it in our national platform; twenty-nine Republican states have ratified the amendment, but one more state is needed to enfranchise every loyal American woman and it would be gratifying to me personally if the Republican members of the Tennessee legislature accomplished that enfranchisement."

The carefully phrased message enabled Harding to sound sincere and strong but contained enough airy ambiguities to make it soft at its center. It begged the question of what legislators' "solemn convictions" really were and seemed to give weight to the idea that there was a valid question about the legality and morality of voting for the amendment. And it allowed Harding to maintain his promise of not interfering with state deliberations on ratification, offering advice only when specifically asked. It was the perfect, weaseling pronouncement.

Before packing her bag for her trip to Nashville, national Anti association president Mary Kilbreth warned both presidential candidates to beware suffragist manipulations. And in a display of notable bipartisanship, the Women Voters Anti-Suffrage Party announced that its members would work "against all enemies" and "tools of feminism" of both parties in the fall elections. "The politicians have figured on the Antis refraining from active opposition," explained Mrs. Morton, the organization's president. Blacklists would be issued carrying the names of all those targeted for slaughter at the polls, the organization promised, and Anti women were urged to vote against any candidate who has been "prominent in efforts to inflict suffrage on the country."

As this aerial barrage intensified, the Antis moved ground forces into Tennessee.

Josephine Pearson welcomed the first of her distinguished guests to Nashville with gracious southern hospitality and American Beauty roses. She announced their arrival to the press as visiting dignitaries: The brilliant orator Charlotte Rowe, star of so many Anti statehouse victories. And Mrs. James S. Pinckard of Montgomery, Alabama, the president general of the Southern League for the Rejection of the Susan B. Anthony Amendment. Pearson made sure to emphasize Mrs. Pinckard's southern bona fides. The blood of the old aristocratic South ran through her delicate veins: she was the grandniece of John C. Calhoun, who served his country as U.S. senator from South Carolina, vice president, and secretary of state and who promoted slavery as a "positive good" rather than just a "necessary evil." He developed the ideological foundations for states' rights and nullification upon which the Confederacy and southern secession were based. Nina Pinckard kept her uncle's political concepts alive in her fight against ratification.

It made Miss Pearson proud: southern women defending southern womanhood. She was almost giddy with delight; the idea that these important women, including several wives of southern state governors, were coming to her own home and she was their hostess. She couldn't pretend to be on their social level, but they shared an essential outlook, a basic bond.

She was also pleased that this time around it would be women leading the fight for the Antis, not just men. From the beginning, Mr. Vertrees had instructed her how to use his arguments in her antisuffrage messages: he would supply "the idea and the bone-work" of the statements, but she should rewrite his communiqués and "put those frills and pleasant[ries] on it which you ladies usually do." In the campaigns against state suffrage initiatives in 1917 and 1919, Mr. Vertrees had been adamant that no Tennessee Anti woman—not even Miss Pearson, the president—set foot in the statehouse to lobby legislators or testify. This time the women were going to be out in front.

Just as southern women had bravely defended their homes and virtue during the War of Northern Aggression, Pearson was confident that they would now rally to defend southern principles endangered by the amendment. Her pleas rang true with those white southerners alarmed by the louder, bolder demands black people were making in 1920, as they chafed against the tightening grip of Jim Crow laws. Black men's service in the war and black women's work on the home front had emboldened their calls for equality, and white southerners were reacting with alarm. Blacks were clamoring for better jobs and better pay, trying to push themselves into better houses and neighborhoods, agitating for improved schools and public facilities, organizing themselves into the National Association for the Advancement of Colored People; in the eyes of many white southerners, black citizens were getting too assertive. The revival of the Ku Klux Klan—it was experiencing a vigorous resurgence in Tennessee as well as in the other southern and border states—and a surge in lynchings were accepted by some as the most efficient way to teach black people to stay in their place.

Of course, many blacks were leaving the South, following the train tracks north in the first waves of the Great Migration. The exodus had begun in 1916 as America prepared to enter the war and factories in the North were hungry for workers. Now, even with the war over and white men demanding their jobs back, black families were steadily leaving the South, willing to brave the cold and the tenements for the promise of higher wages and the prospect of less demeaning segregation laws.

But the recent arrival of tens of thousands of black southerners to industrial cities such as Chicago, Detroit, Cleveland, and Pittsburgh had enflamed racial tensions there and made northerners nervous about this influx of black men able to vote and make policy decisions. It also made northern politicians wary of increasing this black influence by giving black women the vote in their precincts. Somewhat ironically, this made Josephine Pearson's racist rationales for quashing the Nineteenth Amendment—so carefully calibrated to southern sensibilities—much more palatable and powerful in certain sections of the North.

Pearson wasn't concerned with sympathetic northerners; she concentrated on rousing her sister and brother Tennesseans. She'd already sent out a letter to sympathetic Tennessee women around the state, appealing for their "active moral backing" to fight the "deadly principles" embedded in the Nineteenth Amendment: surrender of state sovereignty, Negro woman suffrage, and race equality. And she'd taken the lead with a mailing to every

Tennessee Anti, man and woman, urging them to insist that their state legislators uphold their oath of office, and the honor of Tennessee, by rejecting ratification.

"The fate of white civilization in the South may hang on a few votes either way, and YOUR action may be the deciding influence with YOUR representatives," Pearson wrote with her customary fondness for capital-letter emphasis, "so please let your neighbors and your representatives know WHERE YOU stand in this great battle for State Rights, Honor, and the safety of Southern civilization."

Chapter 11

♦ ♦ ♦

The Woman's Hour

A
s soon as she arrived in Nashville, President General Nina Pinckard
of the Southern Women's Rejection League sent her calling card to
Carrie Catt. It took the form of an open letter, addressed to Catt,
printed on the editorial page of the *Chattanooga Times,* and laced with a
potent strain of political venom.

"Southern women abhor political combat for their sex," Pinckard opened.
"That is one of the reasons they deeply oppose the campaign of your organization to plunge women into perpetual political turmoil. We have no desire to make your campaign unpleasant," she continued, and then proceeded
to make it as unpleasant as possible.

"You are quoted in a morning newspaper as saying: 'There is nothing in
the past quarter of a century that would be so indicative of the traditions of
the old South as would the ratification of this amendment,'" Pinckard
wrote, referring to Catt's attempt to compliment the region's historic sense
of honor. Mrs. Pinckard of Alabama was not accepting the compliment.

"In view of this remarkable statement I must ask you what your association meant when it passed a formal resolution, printed in *The Crisis,* official
Negro organ, 'That all American men or women, white or black, shall share
equally in the privileges of democracy.'"

Mrs. Pinckard was just warming up: "Again, what did you mean when
in a signed article in the same issue of that official organ, you wrote: 'Suffrage democracy knows no bias of race, color, creed or sex'?" Such statements
obviously had no place in the traditions of the old or new South, Pinckard
made quite clear. "In Tennessee, as you know," she continued, "ratification
cannot be accomplished without the violation of legislators' solemn oath. Do
you dare intimate, however indirectly, that the commission of perjury by
public officers is indicative of the traditions of the old South?"

Mrs. Catt read on: "We intend to be as courteous to you as possible in
any political campaign, but we must demand that the truth, whole truth,
nothing but the truth be stated in this matter of life or death to our beloved

Southland." The *Times* framed Pinckard's letter with its own editorial commentary, warning that Catt was summoning "a formidable lobby of Amazonian fighters" to Tennessee "who know the game."

Catt finished Pinckard's diatribe. "Pure buncombe" was what she thought of it, but she would have to respond, she couldn't let it pass. She didn't mind the personal tone or the insinuations; she was accustomed to serving as the Antis' punching bag. The oath matter was an Anti canard, but she knew it would need to be vigorously refuted. The mental vision of her very proper, well-corseted Suff matrons as spear-brandishing, one-bare-breasted Amazon warriors was deliciously ridiculous. But she always winced when that certain other issue made its debut.

Anyone could have seen it coming. Catt knew the Antis would play what in future political confrontations would be called "the race card." She'd warned the Tennessee Suffs at the outset, before she'd even set foot in Nashville: "The 'nigger question' will be put forth in ways to arouse the greatest possible prejudice," she'd told them. Race had always been part of the picture; it bedeviled the suffrage movement much as it haunted so many aspects of American social and political life. The two civil rights movements born, as siblings, out of abolitionism—one dedicated to achieving full equality for black citizens, the other for women—had a tense, ambivalent relationship.

At the close of the Civil War, Elizabeth Stanton, Susan Anthony, Lucy Stone, and their fellow suffragists believed that universal suffrage, for black men and for all women, was just around the corner. In retrospect, they were naive in thinking that women's war work—in the Sanitary Commission, in the hospitals, in the Loyal League—would be rewarded with the franchise. Whether Abraham Lincoln would have ever supported a move as radical as giving women the ballot is doubtful and became a moot question after his assassination. His successor, the Tennessee Democrat Andrew Johnson (who had been a slaveholder but remained loyal to the Union), certainly had no such inclinations. And the suffragists' Republican friends in Congress had more pressing problems after the war's end.

Republican leaders complained that President Andrew Johnson was revealing his southern sympathies with his lenient approach to reconstructing the rebellious states and pardoning their confederate leaders, and this was undermining the spirit and letter of emancipation. Before the close of 1865, the Tennessee legislature was deliberating "Black Codes" to restrict the freedom and movement of the freed slaves, reducing the Negro to a kind of serfdom; other southern states would soon follow with their own Black Codes. Violence against freed blacks was spreading, and in Tennessee a new paramilitary group sprang up composed of ex-Confederate soldiers who dressed in white robes and hoods, riding under the banner of the Ku Klux Klan. Spasms of white mob violence erupted in Memphis and New Orleans, with scores of black citizens killed. Alarmed by the deteriorating situation, abolitionists urged their Republican allies in Congress to do something to offer protective rights for the black population as quickly as possible, enforced on the federal level. Drafts of a new constitutional amendment, the Fourteenth, began to circulate, one meant to secure equal protection, due process, and civil and voting rights to "all persons."

But not exactly all persons. For the very first time, in Section 2 of the proposed amendment (the part dealing with representation in Congress and penalties for infringing upon voting rights), the phrase "male citizen" appeared, where no such gender designation had ever before been made in the U.S. Constitution. The right of "male citizens" to vote. Elizabeth Stanton, Susan Anthony, and Lucy Stone screamed loudly, in furious pronouncements to the press, in protest petitions to Congress, in biting letters to their abolitionist brothers whom they felt, after so many years of toiling together, had betrayed them.

And their allies did abandon them, for a combination of practical and political reasons. For the abolitionists, this was the historic moment consecrated in the blood of war for transforming slaves into citizens once and for all. Yes, Frederick Douglass and William Lloyd Garrison and Wendell Phillips agreed, women should also get the vote, but the nation could not swallow two immense reforms at once, and the black man's very life depended upon his ability to protect himself with the vote. The terrible War Between the States had not, after all, been waged for women's right to vote. This was "the Negro's Hour"; "the Woman's Hour" would come, eventually, Douglass promised, but its time had not arrived.

While Stanton and Anthony protested, Lucy Stone slowly acknowledged the political reality: if the wording could not be changed, better to adopt a flawed amendment to protect endangered black men's civil rights than nothing at all. But Stanton could not accept such a compromise: "If that word male be inserted it will take us at least a century to get it out," she moaned.

"I will cut off this right arm of mine before I will ever work for or demand the ballot for the Negro and not for the woman," Susan Anthony declared.

The old abolitionist coalition tried to hold together under the banner of the American Equal Rights Association, dedicated to securing suffrage and political rights for all Americans "irrespective of race, color or sex." Frederick Douglass signed on as a vice president, and Garrison, Phillips, Stanton, Anthony, Mott, and Stone were all on the organization's masthead, but the alliance was a troubled one, riven by the question of whether "manhood suffrage" must take precedence over "universal suffrage." To Stanton and Anthony it was a false choice and a tragic lost opportunity: this was the nation's hour and a chance to perfect democracy. She urged women to "press in through that constitutional door the moment it is opened for the admission of Sambo." The Negro male must not "march to liberty over woman's prostrate form," Stanton and Anthony insisted.

"It is with us a matter of life and death," Frederick Douglass shot back, "and therefore can not be postponed." Women were not despised by society as black people were, said Douglass, framing the disparity in stark, heartbreaking terms:

> When women, because they are women, are hunted down through the cities of New York and New Orleans; when they are dragged from their houses and hung upon lamp-posts; when their children are torn from their arms, and their brains dashed out upon the pavement; when they are objects of insult and outrage at every turn; when they are in danger of having their homes burnt down over their heads, when their children are not allowed to enter schools; then they will have an urgency to obtain the ballot equal to our own.

Douglass was asked if this awful predicament was not also true for black women. "Yes, yes, yes; it is true of the black woman," he replied, "but not because she is a woman, but because she is black."

The feminist-abolitionist alliance continued to weaken as the Fourteenth Amendment wended its way toward ratification in the states and disintegrated completely when the Fifteenth Amendment was introduced in order to clarify and strengthen the voting rights provisions of the previous amendment: The right of citizens to vote cannot be denied or abridged on account of "race, color, or previous condition of servitude."

Why not include one more word, Stanton asked, why not just add the word "sex" to the protected status, and with those three letters enfranchise all citizens? No, that was impossible, she was told. We should all walk through the door to the Kingdom together, insisted Stanton and Anthony, and if women were not allowed to walk through that enchanted door to the franchise, they were prepared to block entry for the black man as well. They would fight against ratification of the Fifteenth Amendment with a vengeance.

Stanton and Anthony descended into depths of vile racist rhetoric, going so far as to warn against the "horrible outrages" against white women that were sure to follow the black man's enfranchisement and elevation in society. In a cynical ploy to appeal to southern states—which otherwise had little sympathy for woman suffrage—they argued that white women's enfranchisement would provide an electoral bulwark against "Negro rule" in the South. In other states they broadened their attack, vilifying the increasing number of immigrant men who were entitled to vote: "Think of Patrick and Sambo and Hans and Yung Tung," Stanton snarled, "who do not know the difference between a monarchy and a republic, never read the Declaration of Independence or Webster's spelling book," making decisions for educated and cultured white women.

Lucy Stone was horrified by the pair's unhinged diatribes, and Wendell Phillips cut off financial support from abolition funds, isolating Stanton and Anthony from the movement and making them susceptible to a brief alliance with George Francis Train, an eccentric, flamboyant businessman with an appetite for unpopular causes and an unsavory reputation for unbridled racist sentiments. Lucy Stone called Train a "raving lunatic" and denounced her longtime colleagues. Stanton brushed off the criticism: "If the Devil steps forward ready to help, I shall say good fellow come on," she insisted. In the end, the Fifteenth Amendment was ratified, while the abolition and women's rights coalition Elizabeth and Susan had nurtured for the past twenty years was torn asunder.

Stanton, Anthony, and their supporters formed the National Woman Suffrage Association, with the goal of advocating for a Sixteenth Amendment providing the franchise to women, but also agitating for equal pay, an eight-hour workday, more equitable divorce laws, and other social reforms. Lucy Stone, together with her husband, Henry Blackwell, Julia Ward Howe, and other more moderate feminists, formed the American Woman Suffrage Association, based in Boston, focusing on getting individual states to grant the vote to women (as states have authority over their own election laws, provided those laws agree with federal law) but steering clear of more radical issues. There was bad blood, both political and personal, between the two groups, and the split would not be healed for another quarter century.

Meanwhile, the rift between Frederick Douglass and the woman suffragists, even Stanton and Anthony, was overcome more quickly. By 1873 the leaders of the suffrage movement began to make peace overtures to Douglass, and by 1876 he was once again an honored guest at their suffrage conventions. Stanton and Anthony welcomed him, realizing they needed Douglass's star power in their continuing campaign. Douglass was still a true believer in woman suffrage, and his magnanimous spirit allowed him to forgive, if not quite forget, the slurs suffragists had hurled at black men. He was still "willing to be part of the bridge over which women should march to the full enjoyment of their rights." And Douglass was still proud of standing with Elizabeth Stanton in her demand for suffrage at Seneca Falls:

"There are few facts in my humble history to which I look back with more satisfaction than . . . that I was sufficiently enlightened at that early day, when only a few years from slavery, to support your resolution for woman suffrage," he told a women's convention in 1888. "When I ran away from slavery, it was for myself; when I advocated emancipation, it was for my people; but when I stood up for the rights of women, self was out of the question, and I found a little nobility in the act."

The suffragists tended to be less noble. When NAWSA held its first convention in a southern city, Atlanta, in 1895, Anthony personally asked Douglass to stay away, fearing his presence would antagonize white southern suffragists whom the movement needed to attract and appease. "I did not want to subject him to humiliation," Anthony explained to a young black colleague, the civil rights activist Ida B. Wells, "and I did not want anything to get in the way of bringing the Southern white women into our suffrage association now that their interest had been awakened." Douglass realized his old friend was making a naked political calculation; she was protecting her cause at the expense of his. This type of accounting would be repeated many times in the future.

Despite the difficulties the Suffs faced in their quest for equality—upending centuries of law and millennia of cultural tradition—all these paled in comparison with the challenges black citizens faced in securing their basic rights. It would always be safer and easier for the women to lay their claim, precisely because they were the close kin of the men in power: they were not "other" or alien, they were the wives and mothers, sisters and daughters, of the men of the white ruling class. They might not have the vote, but they had familial ties, social standing, and elite educations and connections. Most important, unlike the black man and woman petitioning for fundamental dignity and rights, the Suffs were not despised for their skin color or dismissed as lesser beings; they did not bear the perpetual scars of slavery.

Nevertheless, Frederick Douglass remained a steadfast "Woman's Rights Man" until the day he died in February 1895, just two weeks after that Atlanta convention and just hours after participating in another women's rights convention in Washington, D.C. When Susan Anthony received the news of his death, she rushed from the convention to Douglass's home in Anacostia, across the Potomac River from Washington, to console Douglass's widow. She sat grieving with Helen Douglass for the next days, helping to arrange the funeral services, staying in the guest bedroom the Douglasses reserved for her visits; her framed portrait hung above the hearth. In Douglass's own study, a large oil portrait of Elizabeth Stanton had pride of place on the wall, adjacent to a painting of Abraham Lincoln.

Anthony eulogized her friend at the Washington ceremonies, with senators, congressmen, and Supreme Court judges in the pews of Metropolitan AME Church, while thousands of mourners thronged the surrounding streets. The son of Douglass's last slave master sent a floral tribute. Reverend Dr. Anna Howard Shaw, who along with Carrie Catt was one of Aunt Susan's girls, used her preaching gifts to offer a stirring benediction. And Anthony read a tribute from Elizabeth Stanton, too infirm to attend, expressing her grief at Douglass's passing and her appreciation of his sustaining moral power:

Frederick Douglass is not dead! His grand character will long be an object lesson in our national history; his lofty sentiments of liberty, justice, and equality, echoed on every platform over our broad land, must influence and inspire many coming generations.

Carrie Catt was in that next generation, and when she read the press accounts of Douglass's funeral, the accolades offered by Anthony, Stanton, and Shaw—she was dismayed: "The relation of our leaders to the colored question at the Douglass funeral has completely taken the wind out of our sails," Catt complained to a fellow Suff. "You should see some of the clippings I have from the Southern press and some of the letters. They were a little suspicious of us all along, but now they know we are abolitionists in disguise, with no other thought than to set the negro in dominance over them." Carrie Catt had already become a suffrage politician.

Over the following decades, as Catt became the movement's preeminent politician, she was forced to grapple with the race issue again and again. Voting rights and race were inexorably bound together, as they would be for the rest of the twentieth century, as they continue to be now. It seemed to come down to a cruel, damnable choice, as if one group of citizens needed to win and another must lose, at each step of progress. There was no entering into the gates of the Kingdom together. When forced to choose between truly equal rights and women's rights, between insisting on justice for all or accepting injustice to protect their own cause, the Suffs almost invariably chose the easier, less noble, path.

In 1903, when racist southern suffragists steered NAWSA toward a "southern strategy" allowing each state association to handle the suffrage issue in harmony with its local customs—which, in the South, meant winning the vote for white women but not black and ignoring the federal amendment—Catt, in her first term as president, acquiesced. She also tolerated the use of a jaundiced rationale: to assuage the fears of southern legislators in Congress and in statehouses, suffragists often made the argument that giving the vote to women would not threaten "white supremacy" but actually amplify it. It was a matter of simple mathematics: there were more white women in the southern states than black women and men combined (even if blacks were actually allowed to vote) and more native-born women than immigrants in the northern cities. She allowed census statistics to be brandished as proof in hearing testimony, even in the pages of *The Woman Citizen:* white hegemony was safe.

Alice Paul made similar cynical calculations. When Ida B. Wells, the fearless black journalist and activist who chronicled the epidemic of lynchings of black men (and was forced to flee Memphis when her office was firebombed and her life threatened), wanted to join Alice Paul's suffrage march in Washington in March 1913, she hit the wall of convenient suffrage racism. Wells understood how essential it was for black women to gain the ballot to protect their families, and she founded Chicago's Alpha Suffrage Club, the city's first club for black women devoted to suffrage. But Paul refused to allow her to march with the delegation of Illinois suffragists, as an integrated contingent might upset white southern participants. Wells was told to march at the back of the parade with the black Suffs; she would not be intimidated and refused to march at the rear. As the Illinois contingent passed by, Wells stepped from the sidewalk into the procession, defiantly marching shoulder to shoulder with her white comrades.

Both Paul and Catt recognized that the federal amendment needed the support of white, southern, conservative women if suffrage ever hoped to make inroads in the region, and needed the votes of similarly inclined southern men if it was to ever succeed in Congress and in the statehouses for ratification. They tried to avoid antagonizing southerners with talk of full equal rights, black and white.

"Negro men cannot vote in South Carolina and therefore negro women could not if women were to vote in the nation," Alice Paul told a reporter in early 1919, to ease the federal amendment fears of southerners. "We are organizing white women in the South." When the NAACP asked Paul's Woman's Party to repudiate such statements, it refused.

Black suffragists such as Wells, NAACP cofounder Mary Church Terrell (who considered Catt a personal friend and insisted she was completely free of race prejudice), and W. E. B. Du Bois of the NAACP had every reason to be skeptical of—and at times dismayed by—the equivocations of white suffragists who spoke of justice but, more often, acted in their own self-interest. Dr. Du Bois was a steadfast universal suffragist, in the mold of Douglass, and while he spoke at many suffrage conventions and dedicated many pages in the NAACP's journal, *The Crisis,* to the topic of woman suffrage—for all women—he did not flinch from calling out Anna Shaw and Carrie Catt and Alice Paul for their lapses into hypocrisy.

Catt deliberately put on blinders as needed. Though she was an unabashed "dry," she distanced herself—and NAWSA—from any official ties to the temperance movement and its apotheosis, Prohibition, as the historically close links between the two movements had created too many enemies for suffrage. Catt refused to endorse Margaret Sanger's Birth Control League, though Sanger frequently and ardently asked for her support. Catt appreciated how important women's control of their bodies could be in achieving full social and economic freedom, but alliance with what was still an illegal enterprise—distributing contraceptives and providing abortions—was just too dangerous for the National Association. (She was also enough of a Victorian to find the public discussion of sexual matters distasteful.) When it came to war and peace, she made, what was for her, the most painful compromise, aligning herself and NAWSA behind the war machine for political advantage.

Personally, Catt was offended by Jim Crow segregation and appalled by lynchings, but even after the war, after black men had proven themselves in the military and black women distinguished themselves on the home front, Catt resisted the request of a consortium of black women's clubs to become cooperative members of NAWSA, knowing that the group intended to force the National Association to take a stand on African American women's voting rights. This was in the winter of 1919, when the U.S. Senate was still stalling on the federal amendment, several southern senators still digging in their heels. Catt feared the repercussions if NAWSA welcomed the black suffrage clubs. She asked them to withdraw their application for membership until the federal amendment was law, until suffrage for white women was safe.

So it was in keeping with Catt's willingness to make morally suspect compromise and capitulation that she determined Mrs. Pinckard's public accusations could not be allowed to go unanswered. Not in Nashville, not at this critical juncture. She called in her stenographer. "You ask if I will amplify my meaning when I wrote: 'Suffrage democracy knows no bias of race, color, creed, or sex,'" she dictated as the stenographer penciled curly symbols on a pad of paper. "I do not know that I ever wrote it or in what context it stood if I did."

Through her hotel window, Catt could see the state Capitol, just two blocks away. The statehouse was built of huge blocks of local gray Bigsby limestone and enormous columns of East Tennessee marble that had been quarried and cut, transported and hauled, in the 1840s and 1850s, by prisoners and black slaves, under the supervision of stonemasons and the occasional overseer's whip. It was a handsome building, at once imposing and delicate, graced with a tall cupola topped by a decorative finial. The Capitol building had been the despised Yankee headquarters through three years of Union occupation during the Civil War, fortified by a circle of cannons aimed at the restive city below. It was ironic that the Woman's Hour might finally toll inside a building built by the sweat of slaves, occupied by Mr. Lincoln's troops, where the marble railings were still pocked with bullet holes from the gunfight that erupted when the Tennessee legislature argued over the ratification of the Fourteenth Amendment, state sovereignty, and the rights of citizens to vote.

Chapter 12

◆ ◆ ◆

Cranking the Machine

I HAVE COME to help you win the 36th state," Carrie Catt announced to her Tennessee troops with the crisp inflection of a command. Under the circumstances it was a supremely optimistic notion, but Catt always liked to view her glass as half full. She'd learned it was the only sane way to approach the seemingly impossible.

Everything the Cause had accomplished—every state won, every piece of legislation, every change of heart and shift in policy—was once considered utterly impossible. Until it wasn't. The trick was to create a positive atmosphere, she believed, conjure your own climate of success, set an ambitious goal, and then build your own highway to reach it. "Roll up your sleeves, set your mind to making history, and wage such a fight for liberty that the whole world will respect our sex," she'd exhorted again and again.

Make success seem natural, inexorable, she always told her suffrage workers. People, especially men, especially politicians, liked to be on the winning side. So hers was the "Winning Plan," not just the "Workable Plan"; the Victory Convention, not simply the 1920 convention. Some called this premature boasting, others viewed it as hubris, but Catt considered it straightforward optimism. Optimism plus a plan—always a detailed plan—augmented by elbow grease would yield results.

Now was that time, to crank her political pressure machine—a multitiered engine designed to exert force downward from the White House, the presidential candidates, and national parties and upward from the people of Tennessee—all energies focused on squeezing the governor and men of the statehouse. She'd begun the action at the top, with Woodrow Wilson, Cox, and Harding; now she'd start the agitation from below and engage essential gears in the middle. The Chief took command and issued her first set of marching orders to the Tennessee League of Women Voters, sending them out into the field.

Mrs. Kenny's poll of the legislature had too many gaps. Too many legislators had not responded or refused to reveal their inclinations.

"That unheard from number can and may defeat the ratification," she told the league women, who were all veterans of NAWSA. Those secretive solons needed to be tracked down and pinned down. Go find them, go knock on their doors, she ordered.

Gather a group of local women to visit each legislator, Catt instructed—the larger the deputation, the more impressed the delegate will be—and demand he sign the pledge to support ratification. Be prepared to confront negative responses: the Antis were already busy, they were on the ground trying to convince legislators to pledge against ratification, Catt warned her tender troopers. "They will lie, misrepresent and appeal to all the sordid motives they may find. . . . Please hasten now and report as fast as you can," she implored. "We must 'Trust in God, but keep our powder dry.'" Even the devoted pacifist had taken up military lingo.

State suffrage leaders Kate Warner and Abby Milton had finally returned from their travels, and Catt summoned them, as well as Catherine Kenny, to her room for briefings. They agreed that Tennessee's friends of suffrage needed to be shaken awake from their summer stupor with a series of revival meetings across the state, starring the Chief. And Catt also needed to speak to the men, to the commercial-civic elite, that crucial middle layer of political influence. Abby Milton offered to escort Catt on the trip; Marjorie would join them. Those events were being arranged, and while Catt knew it was the absolute best way to spark enthusiasm and garner publicity, she wasn't looking forward to ten days on the road in this roasting heat.

Too many legislators were holding back, as if they were waiting for orders, or blandishments, before committing. The pledges already in hand were being carefully card-indexed by Catherine Kenny and her league workers, using NAWSA's proven system. At New York headquarters, file cabinets bulged with folders for every congressman and senator (they'd been compiled at Suffrage House in Washington over the years) as well as governors and key state legislators, detailing their political and personal lives. The cards recorded his background, character, and temperament; data on his political, business, social, and religious affiliations; a record of his votes and stands on woman suffrage and other public issues. There was also a confidential memo on any known scandals or indiscretions in his closet, his friends and enemies, his vulnerable spots. The Woman's Party maintained an even more detailed dossier system at their headquarters. The Antis railed against the indexing system, claiming it was, variously, an invasion of privacy, a diabolical blackmailing scheme, or, given its efficiency, an un-American tool inspired by Germany. Catt took their denunciations as proof that the system worked.

Esther Ogden arrived in Nashville, hand-delivering Governor Cox's message of support to Catt. Ogden was a shrewd, detail-oriented Suff, whom Catt had put in charge of the Woman Suffrage Publishing Company, which pumped out tens of thousands of pieces of informational literature a year (including the ever-changing versions of the Suffrage Map), published *The Woman Citizen,* and was readying the final volumes of the *History of Woman Suffrage.* Now Ogden offered Catt an unvarnished report from the temporary center of the political universe—Ohio. Cox was earnest, Ogden assured Catt; whether he could be effective was a different question.

Carrie Catt believed that evolution drives an upward arc. In her own lifetime she'd witnessed the progress of societal attitudes toward woman suffrage, the large cultural shifts that provided an opening for distinct victories, the accumulation of those small victories making change seem more natural.

Aunt Susan used to say that she could sense those shifts, mark suffrage's social and political progress, by what types of objects were thrown at her when she spoke on a stage or soapbox. The rotten eggs of the early days evolved into simply raw eggs, a big improvement. The rotten tomatoes transformed into more benign vegetal projectiles, the verbal assaults grew less vulgar, the physical threats less ominous. And then there was Aunt Susan's favorite liminal moment, when Buffalo Bill Cody saluted her—and, by extension, the Cause—on horseback at his Wild West show.

It was at the 1893 Chicago World's Fair where a grand Woman's Building showcased the accomplishments of women around the globe and the World's Congress of Representative Women of All Lands brought together five hundred delegates from twenty-seven countries to discuss a wide range of topics; suffrage was definitely on the agenda. The weeklong congress drew almost 150,000 spectators, and Anthony and Stanton gave speeches to very large, enthusiastic audiences. "We did a whizzing business," Catt noted with pleasure as the Suffs handed out reams of literature.

Anthony was so fascinated by the magnificent White City, and so delighted by public response to suffrage talks, that she stayed the whole summer. She gave more speeches, but just her presence on the grounds was a walking advertisement for the Cause; her face had become the

The Woman's Hour has Struck

WOMAN
SUFFRAGE
is
COMING

FOUCHER

3314N3

National Woman Suffrage Publishing Company, Inc., 171 Madison Avenue, N. Y.

PREVIOUS PAGE:
This poster was used confidently in the successful 1917 New York woman suffrage referendum campaign.

Susan B. Anthony and Elizabeth Cady Stanton worked together for fifty years to win the vote for women. "I forged the thunderbolts and she fired them," said Stanton about their collaboration.

Frederick Douglass supported Elizabeth Stanton's controversial call for women's enfranchisement at the Seneca Falls convention, and remained a steadfast "woman's rights man" all his life.

Carrie Chapman Catt, president of the National American Woman Suffrage Association, was both an idealist and a savvy politician. She came to Nashville reluctantly to lead the ratification effort.

Sue Shelton White, a young Tennessee suffragist, grew impatient with the slow, polite approach toward winning the vote. She joined the more militant National Woman's Party and led its ratification campaign in her native state.

A young Josephine Anderson Pearson, posing with a book and a rose. Honoring a vow to her mother, she would lead the local Antis in Tennessee in opposition to the federal amendment.

After an apprenticeship in direct-action tactics in Britain, Alice Paul returned home to launch more aggressive demands for a federal amendment, precipitating a split in the American suffrage movement.

As a young suffrage field organizer, Catt caught the eye of Susan Anthony, who recognized her management talents. Catt became one of "Aunt Susan's Girls" and was chosen by Anthony to succeed her as president of the NAWSA.

Anne Dallas Dudley was a socially prominent Nashvillian who made the cause of woman suffrage respectable in Tennessee. This image of beauty and maternal bliss was circulated to refute the stereotype of suffragists as ugly, unsexed "she-men."

Abby Crawford Milton of Chattanooga broadened and strengthened the state suffrage organization and served as the first president of the Tennessee League of Women Voters.

Catherine Talty Kenny organized Nashville's first suffrage parade, encouraging women to brave societal scorn to win their rights. A talented strategist, she led the Tennessee League of Women Voters' ratification committee.

Albert Houston Roberts tried to avoid calling the Tennessee legislature into special session to consider ratification of the Nineteenth Amendment, as the controversial move would complicate his reelection campaign.

Luke Lea, former U.S. senator and publisher of the *Nashville Tennessean*, was a strong supporter of woman suffrage. His newspaper advocated for ratification.

Edward Stahlman, a former railroad industry executive and publisher of the conservative *Nashville Banner*, signed on to the Men's Ratification Committee supporting adoption of the Nineteenth Amendment.

President Woodrow Wilson was an invalid in 1920, and his wife, Edith, assumed many gate-keeping and decision-making powers in the White House. Edith was an ardent antisuffragist.

Ida B. Wells, journalist and fearless civil rights activist, fought for racial justice and woman suffrage. She founded the Alpha Suffrage Club for black women in Chicago.

Protesting Congress's failure to act on the federal suffrage amendment, Alice Paul's National Woman's Party tried to punish the party in power by working against President Wilson and all Democrats in the 1916 elections.

Democratic presidential candidates James Cox of Ohio and Franklin Roosevelt of New York visited the White House in late July 1920 to secure President Wilson's blessing. The possibility of 27 million women voting in the fall was not discussed.

In early 1917, with America on the brink of war, Alice Paul's Woman's Party began picketing the White House. The picketers were vilified as unpatriotic, and hundreds of women were arrested, imprisoned, and mistreated.

Miriam Follin Leslie, a wealthy New York magazine publisher, bequeathed her fortune and jewels to Carrie Catt to benefit the cause of woman suffrage. Her money financed NAWSA's ratification campaign.

Carrie Catt and her partner Mary Garrett Hay spearheaded the New York state campaign to win suffrage by referendum. Here Catt and Hay cast the first ballots of their lives in the 1918 state elections.

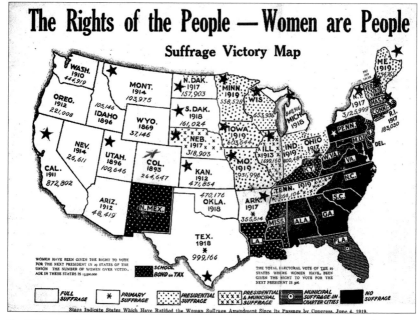

The Rights of the People — Women are People

Suffrage Victory Map

By 1920 the official suffrage map was a crazy quilt of designs representing the status of women's voting rights in the states.

Betty Gram left a promising Broadway career to join the Woman's Party; she was arrested and imprisoned for picketing the White House. She used her theatrical talents in the Tennessee ratification fight.

Anita Pollitzer, a twenty-five-year-old artist, was a national organizer for the Woman's Party. Here she consults with a Tennessee politician.

Juno Frankie Pierce, a Nashville civic leader, led efforts to gain suffrage for black women and register them to vote. In May 1920, she addressed the first meeting of the Tennesse League of Women Voters in the statehouse.

Uncle Sam struggles to secure the last button—the final state—needed for ratification of the Nineteenth Amendment as a frustrated woman complains: "It's that thirty-sixth button, Samuel—"

Antisuffragists used images like this—depicting a father returning home from work to find his children abandoned by their suffragist mother—as a warning that voting women posed threats to the home and family.

Warren G. Harding was the 1920 Republican presidential candidate, and his prosuffrage wife, Florence, took a leading role in his campaign and his career. But suffragists, with good reason, did not trust him.

The National Woman's Party demonstrates at Harding's Notification Day ceremonies in Marion, Ohio, in late July 1920, trying to push Harding toward a more active role in Tennessee's ratification fight.

"PLEASE!"

"Please!" a woman pleads with a courtly Tennessee gentleman as she begs for a special session of the General Assembly to consider ratification of the Nineteenth Amendment.

personification of the movement. Crowds gathered around and cheered her on the pathways; audiences applauded her; even if she wasn't speaking, they wanted her to stand up and take a bow. She was a celebrity. After so many years of ridicule and rebuke, she enjoyed it mightily. And the ideas of woman suffrage seemed to have emerged from the realm of freakish and frightening into popular conversation.

Buffalo Bill's show, starring that amazing lady sharpshooter Annie Oakley, was the entertainment hit of the fair, and Cody invited Anthony to be his guest in a ringside box. Cody made his entrance astride his horse, racing full tilt around the sawdust arena, waving his hat as the band played; he galloped straight for Anthony, wearing her trademark red silk shawl, clapping in the front row. He pulled up the reins, whipped off his cowboy hat, and gave her a grand salute. The crowd cheered and gave her an ovation; she stood, bowed, and waved her handkerchief in thanks.

It was one of those moments when Anthony felt that things changed, attitudes shifted. It wasn't just the respect and affection shown to her at the Wild West show, it was the audiences at the fair, the way they listened respectfully and didn't jeer. It was the way the press suddenly treated her differently. Catt noticed the change, too: "The cartoonists had pictured Miss Anthony for years with a dress hanging in uneven scallops and carrying a large umbrella," she explained. "Other suffragists were made to look like escapers from the insane asylums. Anti-suffragists were good-looking, fashionably dressed, highly respectable women. Now the cartoonists changed their clothes. Miss Anthony never carried her umbrella in a cartoon after 1893."

"Failure is impossible," was Anthony's parting exhortation to her followers, and Carrie Catt accepted this as not simply an upbeat motto, but a working philosophy. There would be many failures, but failures must be transformed into valuable lessons.

From the time of their first bitter referendum defeat in Kansas in 1867 to this moment in Nashville in 1920, the suffragists undertook 480 petition and lobbying drives to get state legislatures to submit suffrage amendments to voters; 277 campaigns to get state party conventions to include woman suffrage planks in their platforms; and 56 state referendum campaigns, trying to convince male voters to grant them the vote. Most of these campaigns were unsuccessful, and nineteen sessions of Congress rebuffed their efforts for a federal amendment. But always, the Suffs tried again.

When Catt lost the first suffrage referendum in New York in 1915 (after orchestrating 10,300 rallies, distributing 7.5 million leaflets, parading down Fifth Avenue with forty thousand marchers before more than a million spectators), she and Mollie watched the returns from headquarters, saw the tears in the eyes of their faithful workers. "How long will it delay your fight, Carrie?" Anna Shaw had asked her that night. "Only until we can get a little sleep. Our campaign will be on again tomorrow morning," Catt replied. Suffrage had not been defeated, she insisted, only postponed. They learned from their mistakes and tried again: "Victory in '17!" was their new motto. On election night 1917, Carrie and Mollie watched as the building that housed *The New York Times*—whose editorial pages opposed suffrage with every pica inch of type it could muster—flashed its rooftop white spotlight to signal that the referendum had passed, New York women had won the vote. It was another of those moments when Catt could feel the shift, in both popular opinion and political consequence. Winning New York, the nation's most populous state, caught the attention of every politician, from President Wilson on down, and turned the tide for the federal amendment.

If things looked iffy in Tennessee, Catt would never admit it in public. She would be resolutely, defiantly, optimistic. Hope was a powerful motivational tool. But privately, she was worried.

All around Tennessee, suffragists were roaming the countryside, hunting down the legislators who'd not yet responded, many of whom lived in remote areas of the state. Some deputations traveled by train to tiny depots to find the village home of their delegates; others were carried in wagons as far as the road would go, finishing the journey to an isolated farmstead on foot, their dresses trailing in the dust or mud. Still others set off on the state's rutted mountain roads to confront their reluctant representatives. They were drenched by rainstorms, chased by watchdogs, and stranded by flat tires, but they found their men.

On the second floor of the Commercial Club of Nashville, in the handsomely draped dining room, the Kiwanis Club held its luncheon meetings, and the guest speaker at this hastily called special event on Friday, July 23, was Mrs. Catt. She entered the inner sanctum of Nashville's business world with the brisk air of an experienced executive. This was her debut public performance in the Tennessee campaign, and she needed to make a strong impression.

The Kiwanis Club men were the friends and colleagues, partners and clients, fishing buddies and poker chums, of the men who made decisions in this town and in the statehouse. She had to convince them that it was in their interest to support ratification of the federal amendment. It was the perfect place to try out her approach: the lines of logic, the persuasive arguments, the bits of color she'd use on the stump around Tennessee.

Her primary goal was to refute the contention, being circulated by the Antis, that any legislator who voted for ratification would be abrogating the state constitution and violating his oath of office to protect that constitution, no matter what the U.S. Supreme Court ruled. She needed to smash that specious argument with the solid hammer of legal reasoning before it became accepted as fact.

Earlier in the week, the Tennessee Bar Association muddied the waters by deciding that they would not recommend that the governor include ratification of the federal amendment in his agenda for the special session, as they thought that a ratification vote would be of questionable legality. Catt fumed: Can't they read the law? She'd telephoned NAWSA's legal counsel, former U.S. Supreme Court justice Charles Evans Hughes, in despair. He chuckled. Most lawyers don't know how to read the U.S. Constitution, he told her. Sometimes it was convenient to be ignorant.

After a flattering introduction, Catt rose to take the lectern. It was an hour past noon and the thermometer had already passed the ninety-degree mark. The ceiling fan paddles spun fast, making a low whirring sound, circulating the sweet, musky scent of tobacco smoke around the room. Reporters from the *Tennessean* and the *Banner* opened their notebooks and poised their pens. Seated at a table in the audience, Major Edward Bushrod Stahlman, publisher of the *Banner,* turned in his chair to listen.

Stahlman had limped into the dining room to take his seat, announcing his arrival with the thump of his ornate walking stick. He was a true self-made man: he'd arrived as a ten-year-old immigrant boy from Germany, begun work as a cart driver for the Baltimore and Ohio Railroad, and made his way up to vice president of the Louisville and Nashville Railroad and then to commissioner of the Southern Railway and Steamship Association. Railroads built the city of Nashville, and he was a railroad man. He became a highly persuasive lobbyist for L&N interests in statehouses around the South; some hinted that his persuasive powers were enhanced by an open wallet.

When the L&N was threatened by unfavorable legislation in the

Tennessee General Assembly, Stahlman bought a newspaper to serve as a platform for pro-industry opinions. He pumped new life into the *Nashville Banner,* and it prospered as he enjoyed broadening the paper's political opinions and his own clout. He left the railroad to become a full-time publisher and helped to establish the Associated Press news syndicate. He was still a good friend of the L&N, and railroad interests continued to wield clout in the halls of the Tennessee legislature.

Though he'd never served in the military—"Major" was just an honorific—Stahlman was a proud American, despite what his enemies said, and a dedicated Nashville citizen: he served a term as an alderman, took a seat on the Tennessee State Board of Education, cared about his adopted city. He was a man who valued loyalty: he was loyal to his friends and employees and equally devoted to crushing his enemies. He didn't mind having enemies; all important men made enemies, it was a mark of power. He counted mayors, governors, and senators among those who did not like him or did not like his newspaper, which was one and the same. He was the *Banner.* He could make or break a Tennessee candidate or cause with his little finger.

His feud with Luke Lea began years ago as a friendly rivalry between competing newspapers. But when the *Tennessean* took to attacking the railroads, especially the L&N, claiming they, together with the liquor industry, owned the legislature and effectively ran the state, a sharp edge entered the relationship. Then Lea carried this crusade with him to Washington, where he initiated Senate hearings to investigate the railroad "trusts" with the aim of regulating them more stringently.

Stahlman used the *Banner* to lash back at Lea and used his political leverage to help oust Lea from his Senate seat. For the first time, thanks to the Seventeenth Amendment, the people would elect their U.S. senators in the 1914 elections, and Stahlman backed a congressman from Memphis, Kenneth McKellar, to run against Lea in the Democratic primary. McKellar won, Lea was booted out. And then the feud turned ugly.

Stahlman was an unapologetic "wet" man, which put him on another collision course with the ultra-"dry" Lea over Prohibition laws. Stahlman also refused to jump on the war bandwagon and used the *Banner's* editorial pages to argue against entry into the European conflict. For this he paid a terrible price. The *Tennessean* launched a witch hunt against Stahlman, calling him "a Hun by birth, a Hun at heart, a Hun with all his evil and devilish characteristics."

Lea used his Washington contacts to spur a Justice Department investigation of Stahlman's citizenship and loyalty while the *Tennessean* beat the drum for Stahlman to be classified as an enemy alien under the Wilson administration's draconian alien, sedition, and espionage laws, punishing anyone who disparaged, or even questioned, the war. Stahlman defended himself by switching the *Banner*'s editorial page toward supporting America in the war, and he became a leader in selling Liberty War Bonds. Meanwhile, the *Tennessean* continued to publish editorial cartoons portraying Stahlman in a German uniform.

The war was over now, but Stahlman could neither forget nor forgive Lea for this vicious vendetta, and the *Banner*'s editorial pages reflected the continuing animosity. The publishers were at loggerheads about the gubernatorial primary at the moment, Stahlman supporting Roberts and Lea working against him, though they were stiffly aligned, at least on paper, in the Men's Ratification Committee. The political was always personal for Edward Stahlman. The feud lived on.

At the lectern, Carrie Catt didn't pussyfoot around. She launched right into her main themes, in terms the Kiwanians could readily understand: It would be bad for Tennessee's business image and Nashville's future to delay or deny ratification of the amendment. Moreover, it would be downright embarrassing. "Tennessee will be made ridiculous in the eyes of all citizens of this country who know the U.S. Constitution if she refuses to ratify on the grounds of unconstitutionality," Catt told them flatly. The Supreme Court had spoken decisively, she insisted, and the Tennessee Constitution's prohibitions on a sitting legislature voting on ratification of a federal amendment had been ruled null and void.

She tackled headlong the rumors about legislators violating their oath of office by voting on ratification. Every legislator takes an oath of loyalty to both the state and the federal constitutions, she reminded her audience, and the federal Constitution takes precedence, as it is the supreme law of the land. Always the schoolteacher, Catt urged everyone to go to a bookstore, buy a copy of the U.S. Constitution, and read Article VI, Sections 2 and 3, on the oath of office, so they could approach a wavering legislator on the issue and set him right.

Having dispatched the legal arguments, she moved on to the political. Both major political parties and both presidential candidates were urging ratification (not urging it quite strongly enough, she thought, but did not let that slip from her lips), and it would not be wise for Tennessee to disappoint. There were many ways the state could be punished, she didn't have to elaborate on that, everyone in the room understood.

She ended on an emotional patriotic note: "We have just emerged from the greatest war known, which was fought for liberty and democracy," she told the Kiwanians, and more than a hundred thousand American men gave their lives in service to that cause. Democracy was ascendant in Europe, and European women—even German and Russian women—were voting. Where was democracy for American women? she asked incredulously, making suffrage a matter of national pride. In closing, she made a rousing exhortation for Tennessee to come forward and take its place within the glorious movement toward world democracy. There was loud applause.

Major Stahlman approached Mrs. Catt and the suffragists surrounding her after her speech, his cane rapping toward them. Even at seventy-seven years he was a powerful presence, with strong features, a head of snowy hair, and an energy, perhaps best described as barely contained ferocity, that expressed itself in an abrupt manner. He introduced himself. He assured them of his support for Governor Roberts and for ratification. They could count on him.

Catt wanted to set off on her road tour with a strong tailwind of positive publicity. By Saturday, with pledge results from the roving league deputations trickling in, Catt decided that the legislative poll was complete enough, and positive enough, to announce that Tennessee was certain to ratify. It was a stretch, she knew. The poll was still incomplete, and still unstable, but she was willing to make the leap. Going public with the poll might make it harder for legislators to slink out of their pledges later, might encourage hesitant ones to jump off the fence and join the winning side. It was blue-sky optimism, and she was an optimist. Catt and Marjorie Shuler quickly sketched out a press release declaring that a majority vote for ratification was clinched.

"Suffrage is all the rage now," Catt asserted with confident élan. Politicians gravitate toward success, she knew. Her analysis was mostly anecdotal, of course, based upon scattered intelligence from those with their ears to the ground or their shoes in the mud of the districts, chasing their lawmakers. But it was also based upon assurances from knowledgeable Tennessee political men, such as Congressman Cordell Hull, who consulted with Catt over the weekend. Catt wanted to make it seem as though a tipping point had already been reached and ratification was sliding smoothly downhill to victory.

Catt was also cheered by the arrival of Anne Dallas Dudley, back home from the Democratic convention. Dudley had long been the beautiful face and charming ambassador of the movement in Tennessee, a silky secret weapon. Bringing her wealth, social prominence, and southern bona fides to the side of the Cause, she'd made suffrage respectable in Nashville. She'd founded the Nashville Equal Suffrage League and had served as head of the Tennessee Suffrage League. Even more important, she was the Suffs' best answer to the usual Anti depiction of suffragists as ugly and masculine "she-men," unhinged and unsexed. Soft-focus photographs of Dudley reading to her adorable young children, the perfect maternal scene, were published and circulated by the Tennessee Suffs—even long after Dudley's children grew out of the nursery—as an antidote to the Anti disparagements. Even Dudley's businessman husband was a good suffragist, always in the forefront of any "men for woman suffrage" activity; now he was on the Men's Ratification Committee. Catt felt better knowing that Anne Dudley would be holding down the fort in Nashville while she was away.

On Sunday night, July 25, Catt, Abby Milton, and Marjorie Shuler departed Union Station on the overnight train to Memphis. Before they left, the press release announcing an assured victory in Tennessee went out to the local and national newspapers and all the wire services. It would appear in the Monday papers.

"More than a majority of both Tennessee Senate and House are pledged to the ratification of the federal suffrage amendment," the statement read. NAWSA was able to announce the completion of the poll so early owing to the "splendid performance of our Tennessee members," Carrie Catt proclaimed.

"We are rejoicing over the results of our work so far," Abby Milton, state president of the League of Women Voters, was quoted as saying, "but we intend to continue just as strenuously during the two weeks intervening before the special session because we want the vote for ratification to be as nearly unanimous as possible."

As the three suffrage missionaries lay in their Pullman berths, rocked by the rhythm of pistons turning wheels, there were many matters to trouble their minds and disturb their sleep. Among these was the article Marjorie had clipped from the front section of the Sunday morning *Banner*, headlined: ASKS MRS. CATT TO EXPLAIN STATEMENT. It was the *Banner's* publication of Mrs. Pinckard's attack letter, a strange way for Major Stahlman's paper to express support for the amendment.

Nevertheless, Mrs. Catt's words of sanguine certainty on ratification were rolling through printing presses around the country as she hurtled through the night on the Nashville–Memphis express.

Chapter 13

• • •

Prison Pin

I T'S ALL BLUFF, Sue White fumed on Monday morning. She'd just scanned the *Nashville Tennessean* and found Mrs. Catt's press release. It was preposterous, impossible that a majority had pledged favorably, certainly not yet. She was conducting the Woman's Party's own poll of the legislature and finding that getting straight answers, much less positive pledges, was akin to pulling teeth from a bear. And now there were the thirteen new wild cards, the candidates running to fill vacancies in the legislature in the special election on primary day, August 5. They could swing the ratification count one way or the other, and that cohort was still a mystery. Catt was dreaming. Or playing some fibbing game. Or both.

White was running on adrenaline, her nerves jangled and her mind racing, since she'd returned to Nashville late on Friday night, July 23. During the previous ten days she'd traveled more than sixteen hundred miles, back and forth and again to Ohio, the pulsing hiss of locomotive steam still ringing in her ears. Those ten days were a high-speed blur, a whirl of presidential candidates, handlers, boosters, and banners. Now her tough work was beginning.

Over the weekend she found a storefront to serve as Woman's Party campaign headquarters: a good spot, in the heart of downtown, with big windows facing busy Sixth Street. It was just half a block from the Hotel Hermitage and a quick walk to the Capitol building. A storefront headquarters was so much better than a hidden hotel suite: it made a big, bold statement that the Woman's Party was a distinct and substantial force in the ratification campaign and not shy about saying so. People could look in, walk in, see that the Alice Paul Suffs weren't two-headed clawed monsters, just intelligent, civic-minded women.

In the past few days, White had also designed her ground game, or at least the first phase of it, determining her officers' placement in the field. She could count them on one hand, certainly not the fifteen staffers she'd initially requested, but they were the best, no amateurs. White's team was composed of the party's national organizers, its special operations squad, seasoned campaign operatives who'd worked in all the hot ratification states. White was placing Anita Pollitzer in the Republican stronghold of East Tennessee; Betty Gram would go to Memphis and the West Division; Catherine Flanagan would target the candidates running for seats in the special election, making a base in the northeast corner of the state. Each would have to cover a lot of ground, talk to the men who counted, and convince the men who pulled the strings. This was where Miss Sue's deep knowledge of her home state would be invaluable.

Sue White had traveled far in the past two years, farther than she could ever have imagined, from the life she'd expected to live in Tennessee. Enlisting in the party had taken her around the country, placed her in the vanguard of a great national crusade, and deposited her into the bosom of an eclectic community of idealistic and adventurous—fearless—women from every part of the nation. These past two years had changed her, not in a fundamental way, she was still sunny Miss Sue, but in a profound way nevertheless. Opened her eyes and opened the world.

Her roots were still in Tennessee, but for now it was just her place of assignment, her duty post, where Miss Paul had sent her on a mission. She couldn't think, or plan, beyond that. As soon as ratification was completed—if it was completed—the party, and Sue White, would have to make some major decisions about the future.

The issues were already being debated among the staff: When woman suffrage was finally secured, should the party disband, its work done? Should it transform itself into a political party of women, advocating for issues important to women, promoting women for elected office, fielding its own candidates? Or should it turn its energies toward winning equal rights for women in other societal matters, like equal pay and economic independence, access to education and professions, divorce and custody rights? White wanted to be part of that discussion, wanted to help make those decisions, but first she had to win Tennessee.

Now Governor Roberts's enemies were whispering to her that he had no intention of actually calling the special session, that he was stalling until it would be too late. According to these informants, his Anti advisers now had the upper hand and had convinced him his election prospects hinged on keeping women out. He'd announced the special election to fill vacancies, but not the special session: very suspicious. White wrote directly to

Governor Roberts, reporting that uncomfortable questions about his intentions were circulating around the capital, and the only way to quell them was to confirm his commitment to ratification in the special session. She stopped short of openly demanding he quit dawdling and officially announce the session, but that message was clear between the lines.

When White dressed that morning in her room at the Tulane, she pushed the sharp point of a pin through the fabric of her blouse, just at the vee where the lapels crossed. The small silver rectangle was her most treasured possession.

She had earned the pin on a Sunday afternoon in early February 1919, at the front gates of the White House. The war was over, and after more than a year of stalling, the Senate was going to vote on the federal amendment the next day. The amendment was expected to go down in defeat, one vote short. President Wilson was in Paris negotiating the peace treaty, making flowery pronouncements about democracy, assuring a delegation of Frenchwomen (who wanted woman suffrage to be included in the peace terms) that he favored women's enfranchisement around the world. But Wilson wasn't doing much to prove it at home, the Woman's Party complained, and wasn't working hard enough to wrangle that last recalcitrant Democratic senator needed to pass the amendment before the Sixty-Fifth Congress adjourned. Wilson seemed willing to let the amendment die again.

Since New Year's Day 1919, the Woman's Party had been using a new publicity tactic: lighting "Watchfires of Freedom" in Lafayette Park across from the White House, small bonfires contained in Grecian-style urns in which the president's lofty words about democracy and freedom were ceremonially burned. All through January and early February the watch fires burned night and day, guarded by shifts of suffragists, fed with replenishments of wood, paper, and the words of Woodrow Wilson relayed from Paris. Rowdy men and boys repeatedly tipped the urns and spilled the fires, policemen tried to extinguish them, but the women promptly rekindled the flames. The women were arrested on spurious charges, such as lighting fires in a public place after sunset. Upon refusing to pay a fine, they were sent to jail; insisting they were political prisoners, not common criminals, they launched hunger strikes in the jailhouse. After being released, many of the women went right back to their posts guarding the watch fires and soon returned to jail.

The spectacle of scores of women being hauled off in paddy wagons while the president was in Paris negotiating world peace was embarrassing, and the Democratically controlled Senate finally agreed to bring the amendment to the floor on February 10. But it was clear that the last Democratic vote needed could not be shaken loose. Woodrow Wilson was not negotiating hard enough to win that vote from within his own party, Alice Paul insisted, and so, on the eve of the Senate vote, she turned up the watch fire's heat.

Paul called for delegations from around the country to gather in Washington for a special demonstration and told them to be prepared to go to jail. She asked Sue White to play the leading role in the ceremony: burning President Wilson in effigy. Not just his words, but a likeness of him. This had never been done before in any suffrage protest; it was a step beyond, a highly provocative move. White's suffrage mentor in Memphis, civic reformer Lulu Colyar Reese, who was in sympathy with the Woman's Party methods of direct action, was nervous about this drastic ploy and pleaded with White not to participate. Reese feared not only for White's safety, but for the backlash she'd surely face in Tennessee and consequent damage to the suffrage cause in the state.

It was "the most difficult thing I was ever asked to do," Miss Sue admitted, "the greatest sacrifice I have ever made, and nothing but the deepest conviction could have moved me to do it." It was an initiation rite, she understood that, Miss Paul's test of her loyalty and commitment. White deliberated and fretted but finally decided to answer Paul's summons. She arrived in Washington a few days before the demonstration to rehearse the ritual she was expected to perform.

At four thirty in the afternoon, with dusk nearing, a silent procession of seventy-five women from twenty-two states marched out the door of party headquarters and headed across Lafayette Square toward the White House. Leading the parade was Louisine Havemeyer, holding high the American flag, followed by the Woman's Party colors, and then a column of picketers holding banners with such sentiments as "The President is responsible for the betrayal of American Womanhood" and "President Wilson is deceiving the world." Following these were a pair of women carrying an earthenware urn between them and then a brigade carrying kerosene-soaked wooden logs and kindling in their arms.

They placed the urn on the sidewalk in front of the White House gates with an honor guard surrounding it. An estimated two thousand spectators were gathered on Pennsylvania Avenue to watch this "little drama of democracy," along with a hundred policemen, a phalanx of fire extinguishers, and a troop of Boy Scouts assigned to help keep order.

Mrs. Havemeyer planted her flag and began her speech. This was Havemeyer's first, and only, experience in a picketing demonstration. She'd always told Miss Paul, "No picketing and no prison for me. I don't like the thought of either one." But when Paul asked her to join this special protest, she couldn't refuse. Bring your valise, Paul advised Havemeyer, packed with a warm cloak and a bottle of disinfectant. Mrs. Havemeyer carried her bag out of her Fifth Avenue mansion, telling her family she was just visiting friends in Washington for a few days.

Havemeyer's heart was beating fast and she had to struggle to retain her poise as the party protesters assembled inside headquarters, but once she stepped out with the flag, she "instantly felt as placid and calm as if I were going out to play croquet on a summer afternoon." At the White House gates, her booming voice rose above the crowd:

"Every Anglo-Saxon Government in the world has enfranchised its women. In Russia, in Hungary, in Austria, in Germany itself, the women are completely enfranchised, and thirty-four are now sitting in the Reichstag," she said as a red-faced police captain, his uniform adorned with gold braids and buttons, stared at her. "We women of America are assembled here today to voice our deep indignation that, while such efforts are being made to establish democracy in Europe, American women are still deprived of a voice in their government here at home."

While Havemeyer was speaking, the urn was lit and the flames rose high. Sue White stepped up to the burning caldron, holding the president's effigy. The newspapers described the effigy as "a huge doll stuffed with straw, slightly over two feet in height," but it was no such thing. This effigy was not the traditional stuffed dummy, but a paper doll with the figure of Wilson drawn in black ink, depicting him delivering one of his empty "freedom" speeches with a woman's head chained to his belt. White nodded to Havemeyer, then dropped the paper doll into the flames. There was a flash. The police rushed toward White, wielding their extinguishers, trying to rescue the effigy, but it was quickly consumed.

Before the police could reach her, White began reciting her statement of purpose: "We burn not the effigy of the President of a free people, but the leader of an autocratic party organization whose tyrannical power holds millions of women in political slavery," she shouted as the police doused the urn and grabbed her arm. "I have long been what is known as a 'Southern Democrat' and the traditions of the democracy of Jefferson and Jackson are still strong in my heart," she yelled as burly men in blue coats hustled her to one of the many waiting Black Maria patrol wagons. "The stronger because I feel that it is what we are fighting for now.

"Mr. Wilson as the leader of his party, has forgotten, or else he never knew, the spirit of true democracy," White screamed over the din of the commotion. "We feel that there is need of a determined protest of this sort; a protest which will shock Mr. Wilson and his followers into putting into action the principle that those who submit to authority shall have a voice in their government." The last words were inaudible as Sue White was pushed into the patrol wagon.

The scene turned chaotic, with policemen surging forward, spraying the women with the fire extinguishers, arresting as many of the protesters as they could capture, assisted in the chase by the loyal Boy Scouts. In the midst of the melee, Mrs. Havemeyer was assigned another task, one designed to get her arrested. Lucy Burns, in charge of the afternoon's demonstration, handed Havemeyer bundles of paper to light with a match and throw into the urn.

"Please, Miss Burns," the police captain begged, "don't let her do it. You know we don't want to take her. Please don't. . . ." The police felt queasy dragging off a grandmotherly protester. Havemeyer knew she must qualify for the "Prison Special" railroad tour by actually going to prison, so she kept throwing the bundles into the fire. Still the captain hesitated. "I believe I will have to kick him to keep in the game," Havemeyer whispered to Burns, but finally the policeman placed a hand on Havemeyer's shoulder, looped his arm through hers, and guided her to the Black Maria. In a caravan of patrol wagons and commandeered cars, Mrs. Havemeyer, Sue White, Lucy Burns, and thirty-six other party women were driven to the station house.

The police seemed nervous about the mass arrest; the commander telephoned the White House and spoke to Joseph Tumulty, the president's secretary. The women were held overnight in the police dormitory and arraigned the next afternoon. The charges were strange: for lighting a fire, for carrying wood to a fire, for incitement. Since burning the president in effigy wasn't actually a crime, Sue White was charged with lighting combustibles on White House grounds; Havemeyer was found guilty of striking a match.

The judge gave each woman a choice: a five-dollar fine or five days in jail. "Of course, no one thought of paying the fine," Mrs. Havemeyer recalled proudly. The women were sentenced just at the hour the Senate was voting down the amendment.

The Occoquan Workhouse was a decrepit, foul-smelling, vermin-infested jail, closed down a decade before as unfit to hold humans. The women entered dark, damp cells, each equipped with what Havemeyer described as "a disgusting closet, an iron support for a straw bed, one chair, and no light." The bed straw was dirty, the sewage vapors nauseating, the cells bitter cold. Rats and cockroaches scurried on every surface. The women, hunger striking, didn't touch the tins of soup or wormy bread set before them. Still, the conditions were better, and the sentences much shorter, than the six- and seven-month ordeals, often in solitary confinement, suffered by Alice Paul and other party women.

Mrs. Havemeyer's family in New York was horrified by the news that she was in jail, and they insisted she pay her fine, leave her comrades, and return home immediately. She resisted at first. They told her that the grandchildren were crying for her and her sister was deathly ill, how could she be so cruel? She sent word to Miss Paul, who gave her permission to pay her fine and leave; she still qualified for the "Prison Special."

When Sue White and the others were released after their five-day sentence and hunger strike, she returned, weak and wobbly, to party headquarters on Lafayette Square and was confined to bed. It was a brief convalescence. The next day she was on her feet to receive her prison pin in a little ceremony. Every woman who was "jailed for freedom"—there were almost 150 of them by then—was decorated with a distinguished service pin by Miss Paul. She'd been awarded one by Mrs. Pankhurst in England, after she'd endured her first imprisonment for suffrage activities there, and she carried on the tradition in the Woman's Party. The pin was a miniature of a jail door, modeled on the doors of Holloway Prison in London, gridded by little silver bars, draped with a chain of tiny links, secured by a diminutive heart-shaped lock. It was so precise a replica that even the door's hinges and bolts, the lock's keyhole, and the narrow slit in the bars for passing food to the prisoner were distinct. No diamond could ever mean more to Sue White.

The pin marked Sue's total break with the moderate Tennessee suffragists. Condemnation of the effigy burning was swift and ferocious. Speaking for NAWSA, Mollie Hay slammed the Woman's Party stunt, saying it "makes us question whether they want the success of the amendment or publicity for the organization," and she denounced the party as "the I.W.W. of the suffrage movement," tarring it with the brush of the radical, violent, and mostly despised Industrial Workers of the World.

Carrie Catt also lashed out: "If the women of America are betrayed, it will not be by the president. A vote for the amendment is a vote for what the president wants. A vote against the amendment is a vote for what the Woman's Party wants."

More punishing still was the contempt of White's Tennessee suffrage colleagues: joining the Alice Paul group was one thing; symbolically incinerating the president—a southerner, a Democrat—was quite another. It was unpatriotic and perhaps even treasonous. And with a bill to win partial suffrage for Tennessee women pending in the legislature in the winter of 1919, the mainstream Tennessee Suffs deeply resented the damage that Miss Sue's inflammatory indulgences might inflict on their campaign.

A few weeks later, when that suffrage bill was being debated in the statehouse, Sue White's name and her notorious act were invoked time and again by those opposed to woman suffrage. Legislators advocating the bill on the floor took pains to note that White did not in any way represent the sentiment of Tennessee suffragists. She became the symbol of hysterical suffrage zealotry. She didn't care.

White believed she was a true daughter of Susan B. Anthony, who had understood the power of direct action to bring attention to injustice. When Miss Anthony cast her defiant ballot in the election of 1872, and when she disrupted the official Fourth of July ceremonies at the 1876 Centennial Exhibition in Philadelphia by barging up to the podium and presenting her "Declaration of Rights of the Women of the United States"—she knew she wasn't being polite. When she climbed onto that bandstand in front of Independence Hall and read the angry declaration and its list of grievances aloud to a startled audience, Miss Anthony was most definitely defying the rules of ladylike society. The Woman's Party was heir to Anthony's indomitable spirit, Sue White was convinced; it kept the flame of her honorable, nonviolent militancy burning bright.

And there was that other Susan, her namesake, her aunt, who had also taught her to take a stand, even if it was not a public stand, if it was only an act of principle. Her own aunt Susan had broken the law, defied society and her father, by secretly teaching the family's slaves to read. Aunt Susan had been a clandestine abolitionist, Sue learned years later, when her elderly relative confessed it all to her. And her aunt also admitted she'd always admired Susan Anthony for her outspoken support for abolition. Her aunt's revelation was all slightly shocking to young Sue, but galvanizing. It was a small action, a private defiance, but it made a deep impression on Sue and guided her in moments of decision.

She knew it was a risk to wear her prison pin in Tennessee, but she would wear it, brazenly, proudly, every day.

Anita Pollitzer was only twenty-five years old, but she was already a seasoned veteran of the suffrage wars. She could drop into a new territory, scan the terrain quickly, and map its political contours effortlessly, much the way a quick-sketch artist can draw the basic shapes and lines of a scene, capturing the essence of the whole. Pollitzer's powers of political observation were enhanced by her own artistic training.

Pollitzer was an artist who'd traded her brushes and charcoals for the picket poles and train tickets of a Woman's Party crusader. Unlike many women who joined the movement, Pollitzer enjoyed the support of her family, who encouraged her work; she was no rebel to them. She was the adored youngest daughter of a prosperous Charleston cotton merchant family, pillars of the city's thriving Jewish community. The Pollitzers' parlor on fashionable Pitt Street was filled with music and art, and very often it was also filled with meetings on progressive social and political themes, especially women's rights. Anita's two older sisters were both active suffragists. Anita grew up assuming that working for the Cause was a natural thing for a proper young woman to do.

Anita went north to Teachers College of Columbia University in New York City to study art and education. She took painting classes at the Art Students League and became good friends with a moody but talented classmate named Georgia O'Keeffe. They were very different personalities— Pollitzer optimistic and ebullient, O'Keeffe sullen and self-absorbed—but they shared a love of art and a thirst for all things modern and bold. They hung out at photographer Alfred Stieglitz's gallery at 291 Fifth Avenue, where they had their first exposure to the paintings of Pablo Picasso, Georges Braque, and John Marin. When O'Keeffe left New York for a succession of unsatisfying teaching jobs, Pollitzer kept her connected to the New York City art world with long newsy letters, art magazines, and poems for inspiration. O'Keeffe replied with introspective notes and packages of her latest drawings and paintings. When Pollitzer opened her college mailbox in early 1916 to find a particularly striking set of O'Keeffe charcoal drawings, she disobeyed her friend's instructions to keep them private and went downtown to show them to Stieglitz, and he was impressed. "At last, a woman on paper," he famously exclaimed, and began displaying O'Keeffe's work in his gallery and promoting her talent; Stieglitz and O'Keeffe would later marry. Pollitzer changed the course of O'Keeffe's life and career, but she chose a totally different path for herself.

At home in Charleston on her summer vacations, Pollitzer joined her sisters in suffrage work, helping to proselytize and organize. She did everything from drawing recruitment posters to selling lemonade to debating Antis on the street. In New York, she wore a cap and gown to march with the collegiate contingent in the great October 1915 suffrage parade down Fifth Avenue, writing excitedly to O'Keeffe about the "tremendous affair" with tens of thousands of participants. When her sisters grew frustrated with NAWSA's slow pace of suffrage progress in the South, they signed on with the Woman's Party and its more aggressive agenda, and Anita joined them in that camp. Soon after Pollitzer graduated from college in 1916, she moved to Washington to work for the party.

She was a "Silent Sentinel" on the steps of the U.S. Capitol in the fall of 1918, holding a banner protesting the Senate's refusal to act on the federal amendment: "America Enters the Peace Conference with Unclean Hands for Democracy Is Denied to Her People." She and her fellow picketers were treated roughly by the police: knocked down, shaken, dragged down the Senate steps. It only stiffened her resolve. Though she'd been arrested, she never served time, so she didn't own a prison pin.

When the ratification campaign began, Miss Paul frequently sent Pollitzer to Capitol Hill to convince a reluctant congressman or senator to apply pressure on his state's governor or legislature to ratify. She did her homework before approaching her assigned prey; she sweetly asked pointed questions. She was a good listener and had a brilliant smile. But she learned not to trust any politician's promise of aid: she stood over his shoulder while he telephoned or wired his colleagues back home, making sure the task was accomplished in her presence. The petite Pollitzer might appear an ingenue, but gullibility was not one of her traits, and gumption was.

Alice Paul recognized her potential and dispatched her to organize and lobby in the states—Wyoming, Florida, Virginia, and more—where she mastered the art of persistent persuasion. Pollitzer loved the work: it was like being a soldier, spy, and agitator all rolled into one. Her job was to find things out and shake things up. She often worked in a team with Sue White, Betty Gram, or Catherine Flanagan, and she was tickled to think they'd now be reunited for the big push in Tennessee. She was ready.

Her first stop was Chattanooga, where she was to meet with former U.S. senator Newell Sanders, a loyal suffragist whose confidence Pollitzer was eager to gain. Sanders was a courtly gentleman, seventy years old, with soft, droopy eyes, who might be taken for a kindly country minister. He was actually a shrewd businessman and canny politician, respected throughout the state. He sat Pollitzer down at his kitchen table, his wife puttering nearby, and spent the entire afternoon giving his guest a crash course in Tennessee Republican politics. He explained the different factions, the splits, the feuds, the issues, the bosses, and who gave orders to whom. She listened attentively, fixing her gray eyes upon him, scribbling in a notebook on her lap.

Pollitzer had a knack for getting powerful men to talk freely. The startling combination of a vivacious brunette who could knowledgeably talk shop with an old pol, and seemed delighted to do so for hours at a time, enchanted more than a few flinty backroom characters, turning them into valuable informants. And when she was working in the southern states, it certainly didn't hurt that Pollitzer spoke with the honeyed accent of a Charleston girl.

Sanders briefed her on which Republicans she needed to reach, which men might try to dodge her, which might cause trouble. The first man to tackle was Jesse Littleton, Sanders told her, the former mayor of Chattanooga, now running for the Republican gubernatorial nomination. Littleton was a "wet," an attorney representing liquor interests, and he had power over a significant Republican faction; he was a kingpin. A few hours later, Pollitzer was facing Jesse Littleton in his Chattanooga office. Pollitzer took an instant dislike to Littleton. "He is a slick, Cox-like politician, only he wears white and weighs 300 lbs!" she reported to Paul. "He appears to be friendly," Pollitzer concluded, "but his face does such queer things when I pin him down."

Pollitzer was now on a train from Chattanooga to Athens, chugging along the ridges of the Appalachian foothills, to find Tennessee Senate

Republican floor leader Herschel Candler, who'd voted "No" on limited woman suffrage last year. "We must make effort to get Candler, as he leads men," she wrote to Alice Paul. "He will hurt us unless he can be convinced." First she was going to see Candler's friends in his hometown of Athens; then, if possible, Candler himself; then Candler's protégé, Harry Burn, a Republican representative from the town of Niota. Down the political food chain. It was the only way.

As her train approached Athens, Pollitzer dashed off the last of her letter to Paul and, like Sue White, complained about Carrie Catt's claims of a ratification majority, scribbling her own expression of outrage: "The papers are full of Mrs. Catt," she wrote. "Today she comes out saying we have 'more than majority pledged in both houses'—and I had, before I took train, to see my men to explain we *haven't*—and they had to work."

Mrs. Catt was pouring cold water on the fire Anita Pollitzer was trying so hard to kindle under the East Tennessee Republicans, giving them too easy an excuse to sit back and twiddle their thumbs. Catt was a menace, Pollitzer was convinced, complicating an already difficult mission. "The Republicans are not going to be easy," she wrote to Miss Paul, underlining the words 'not' and 'easy' in bold strokes.

Pollitzer's colleague Hayden Rector, who was handling the Woman's Party's negotiations with both the Cox and the Harding camps in Ohio, was also livid when she saw the front-page headlines heralding Catt's claim of victory in Tennessee. "We must not have all our work and efforts brought to nothing like this," Rector told Alice Paul, excoriating Catt. "Her determination to end the fight in people's minds is simply satanic."

Chapter 14

◆ ◆ ◆

Fieldwork

THE DOG DAYS of summer, when July melts into August, was, in any normal Tennessee year, a quiet and restful time, when the pace of life slowed. But this was no ordinary summer. An abnormally hot-weather frenzy gripped the state as the intersecting trajectories of multiple political campaigns and suffrage missions etched zigzagging, crisscrossing, overlapping, and parallel trails across the map.

Carrie Catt was traveling eastward from Memphis to Knoxville to Chattanooga. Sue White was spiraling around Nashville, making quick trips into nearby towns to snag important legislators. Josephine Pearson was shuttling between the Hotel Hermitage and various planning meetings around Nashville, while Nina Pinckard zipped into the offices of prominent Tennessee attorneys, and Charlotte Rowe ventured to other cities to stoke Anti sentiment. Governor Roberts and his rivals (there were at least five other gubernatorial hopefuls) and their surrogates were snaking through every county. Dozens of candidates running for vacant seats in the legislature were campaigning in their districts, accompanied by their supporters. The League of Women Voters members were still combing the countryside, climbing up hills and plunging down into hollers to pledge laggard legislators. Woman's Party organizers were embedded in all three Grand Divisions, chasing after the regions' legislators and politicians. With just ten days until the state primary, which might determine the fate of ratification in Tennessee, everyone was in motion.

This was the fieldwork of democracy, the tough, sweaty, unglamorous enterprise of retail politics. Before the advent of radio or television broadcasting, this was how candidates won elections. But it was also how, over the years, the suffragists had slowly, methodically, built a constituency for change: selling their radical concept, door-to-door, town-to-town. Pageants and parades were fun, they caught public attention and energized the troops, but the real work was always accomplished on the ground: canvasses and petition campaigns, small meetings and personal pleas, knocking on doors.

Only after that sort of cultivation had been accomplished, only when the constituency for woman suffrage had expanded from a few women around a tea table to millions around the country, reached critical mass, and attained a robust voice, could the suffrage argument be advanced: carried into politicians' offices, subsequently hoisted onto legislative dockets, and finally presented as a fundamental alteration to the national Constitution. Women had done all that, over the span of decades, but now it was back into the field for the final stage, with both Suffs and Antis scrambling for advantage, with the clock ticking. Such was the natural physiology of change within a democracy, and the process was now being put to a stress test in the fields of Tennessee.

Mr. Crump wanted women to vote, he wanted the amendment ratified, and Mr. Crump gave the orders in Memphis. Carrie Catt was very pleased; it made her work in the city much easier.

Edward Hull Crump ran the Democratic Party machine in Shelby County, which includes Memphis. He was forty-five years old, with cup-handle ears that sprang out from his head, wavy red hair, a deeply cleft chin, and bushy eyebrows over intense eyes. "Scrappy" was the word that best described him. He grew up poor, married well, used his native smarts to make money and climb the political ladder quickly; he was elected mayor of Memphis, Tennessee's largest city, in 1909 when he was just thirty-five years old. He ran the city like a business, with an efficient administration and customer service approach, keeping a tight budget while improving public services. But when Crump repeatedly refused to enforce the state's prohibition laws, knowing the liquor ban would harm his city's lucrative industry of saloons, gambling parlors, and music joints, the temperance-inclined governor and legislature passed a special "Ouster Law" kicking him out of office. His removal didn't diminish his political influence; he simply shifted his center of power to Shelby County and ruled the city from there.

Crump was a political boss with progressive leanings, or at least he embraced those progressive measures that could enhance his power. Crump couldn't give a speech to save his life, but he had a genius for organization and an ability to work with different constituencies: give something, get something, everybody wins.

Memphis was home to the largest black community in the state, and Crump considered this group a valuable—and voting—constituency with whom he forged alliances. He was a traditional segregationist, but when the black community requested a city park of their own (they were forbidden to enter the other, grander parks in town under Jim Crow statutes), Crump listened and obliged. In return he expected, or demanded, black men's support at the polls. He made it easy: his organization paid the poll taxes for many black men and got them to the voting booths; they voted the Crump organization ticket; he, in turn, improved their neighborhoods. Black community leaders such as businessman Robert Church, Jr. (brother of suffragist and civil rights activist Mary Church Terrell), often found Crump a helpful ally. It was, as later politicians would describe it, a win-win transaction. A large new bloc of voters, white women and black women, was enticing to Crump. It didn't hurt that Mrs. Crump was a strong suffragist, too.

Was the arm-twisting, horse-trading, brutal, and bruising political world of Boss Crump the paradigm of democracy Carrie Catt had promised to American women? No. But it was the real world of politics. Women's entry might sanitize, elevate, and improve it—might—but women must at least take part. And, as she'd learned through many a campaign, especially dealing with Tammany Hall in New York: if the local political machine could be harnessed for your good, if it could help carry women toward enfranchisement, be willing to take the ride. When Carrie Catt arrived in Memphis, she was happy for Boss Crump's support.

Catt enjoyed a warm welcome to the city when her train arrived in the early morning. At a noontime Chamber of Commerce luncheon, more than 150 women and men, leaders of the city's suffrage establishment, as well as members of the political and civic elite, gave her a long, glassware-rattling ovation. Even more significant, the local politicians were lining up solidly behind ratification, with no apparent qualms or equivocations. She'd barely had to nudge; they were already on her side. It was remarkable. It was due to Mr. Crump.

To the suffragists' delight, Crump was taking strong measures to guarantee that the Shelby County Democrats would not only vote as a bloc, but also take the lead in promoting ratification in the legislature. He'd persuaded Thomas Riddick, a respected Memphis attorney, to run for one of the vacant legislative seats to serve in the special session. Political observers were shocked: "Million Dollar" Riddick (he had a very lucrative private practice) had often been mentioned as a candidate for governor, congressman, or U.S. senator, but not for a lowly seat in the Tennessee House of

Representatives. But when it was revealed that Boss Crump would serve as Riddick's campaign manager, it all made sense. Crump was placing Riddick in the special session to be his surrogate, keep the Memphis/Shelby delegation in line, and guide ratification efforts. For the Suffs, it was a happy prospect.

While Carrie Catt was in Memphis, Josephine Pearson was in a state of ecstatic anticipation. Fulfilling the dreams of her parents, she was marshaling the forces of good to defend southern and Christian civilization against the barbarians at the gates, against Gog and Magog, against . . . Mrs. Catt and the suffragists. It was a divine mission that suited her perfectly.

First, Pearson blew the trumpet, sending out a call for sympathetic helpers to join the Anti effort. She and her colleagues made a broad and clever appeal: Whether you oppose woman suffrage on principle, or approve of suffrage but oppose the federal amendment and Washington trampling on states' rights, we welcome you. If you support ratification of the federal amendment but believe Tennessee legislators would be violating their oaths of office if they voted on ratification in the special session, join us. Building a bigger tent for a wider coalition was a smart move, and the response was enthusiastic. Volunteers quickly formed committees to attend to every task: letters typed and copied, literature printed and distributed, envelopes stuffed and licked, the headquarters staffed and decorated, teas and receptions prepared. The cream of Nashville society, women from all the best families, were Pearson's eager recruits, working selflessly in shifts through the day and evening, under her command.

Pearson and the other executive officers of the Tennessee division of the Southern Women's Rejection League, together with Nina Pinckard and Charlotte Rowe, also devised a robust political program. Rowe would venture out to various Tennessee cities to stoke Anti sentiment in public speeches and private meetings. Pinckard would continue to hammer at the presidential candidates and Governor Roberts. Every Tennessee legislator would be contacted, made painfully aware of his legal and moral obligations to defeat ratification. Dozens of distinguished women from the states that had already rejected the amendment were invited to Nashville, as well as national leaders of the Anti movement. And a delegation of Tennessee women, led by Pearson's colleague Queenie Washington, was prepared to leave for a meeting with James Cox in Dayton the minute he signaled for them to come. He'd

said that a meeting would, of course, be granted, but no specific date had yet
been set. Josephine Pearson was delighted to give the full measure of her
bountiful intellectual and spiritual gifts to these efforts. She took to wearing
a little bouquet of three red silk roses on her bosom, signifying her leadership
status.

Anita Pollitzer continued her manhunt through the Appalachian foothills
of East Tennessee, Republican politicos in her sights. Unless she could bring
these "big men" around, the pledges she wrangled from their legislative un-
derlings wouldn't be worth much. She kept a list of important men to see in
each town, adding to it every day as those men suggested others. She compiled two notebooks filled with names and notes on "who could get to
whom" as she stalked the local movers and shakers and pounced on them in
their lairs.

When she'd stepped off the train in Athens, the McMinn County seat,
she'd headed for the courthouse, the political nerve center of the region.
McMinn was Republican territory, as during the War of Secession the
county had voted, narrowly, to remain in the Union. (Families and friends
were torn apart as the county sent twelve units of its men to fight for the
Union and eight units to defend the Confederacy.) Pollitzer visited the Republican county chairman, who sketched for her the personal and professional ties among the party men of McMinn, directing her to see some of
the more pivotal players. She compiled a checklist—see Luther, Boyer, Burn,
and Candler—and went after them, one by one. Senator Herschel Candler
was the most essential, antisuffrage and influential, a bad combination, but
she learned he was out of town. She hired a car to take her into the hills to
see Emerson Luther, the Republican house floor leader, and came away with
his pledge. She was told that delegate C. Fulton Boyer was not only too old
and stubborn and Anti to argue with, but also untrustworthy. "That is polite
for scoundrel," she explained to Paul, and decided not to bother finding him.
That left Harry Burn.

At twenty-four years old, freshman representative Harry Burn was the
youngest member of the legislature. He was, according to everyone Pollitzer
spoke to, earnest and hardworking, well liked by his constituents and his
colleagues in the statehouse. He lived on his family's land in the hill town
of Niota, north and a little west of Athens, supporting his widowed mother
and two younger siblings. He was a hometown boy making good. He was

holding down jobs as a Southern Railway agent and at a local bank while reading law at night under the tutelage of a senior attorney; everyone said he had the potential to go far. At this stage he had little clout in the legislature, and he was up for reelection in the fall, but Miss Paul thought he was worth pursuing. He'd voted for presidential suffrage last year, but he hadn't yet revealed his stand on ratification.

But getting to Burn was not going to be easy. Niota was a tiny town— population 467—nestled between wooded ridges. It was less than ten miles from Athens, and the local train did stop there, but the timetable wouldn't allow Pollitzer to get there in a timely fashion, and the Burn place was a long climb from the depot. She couldn't afford to hire another car and driver; it wasn't going to work. Pollitzer did the next best thing: she asked the helpful Republican county chairman to telephone Burn. Anyhow, the party chief would wield more clout with the young legislator.

Oh sure, Harry will be with you, the party chairman assured Pollitzer. Then why was he still claiming to be "uncommitted" in all the legislative polls? she asked. Oh well, Harry's up for reelection, you know, he's got to be careful. He needs to play things close to the vest. Pollitzer pressed the chairman to place the call. When the operator at central put him through, Harry came to the phone.

Lady here wants to know if you'll be voting to ratify, Harry—the chairman spoke into the cup of the phone's mouthpiece. There were muffled words coming from Burn into the chairman's earpiece, but Pollitzer couldn't make them out. The conversation was brief. The chairman returned the elongated bell of the receiver into its cradle. Harry will be all right, he told her.

Harry T. Burn was marked as pledged to ratify, and Pollitzer moved on to Knoxville.

Carrie Catt barely had time to swallow some dinner before delivering another speech at the suffrage rally in Memphis's Court Avenue Presbyterian Church. She was a talented speaker, able to combine cold logic and warm humor, mixing idealism with how-to practicality. But in truth, the woman renowned around the world for her oratory gifts was, even after decades on the podium, in agony whenever she spoke. She habitually calmed her nerves by clasping and unclasping her hands behind her back, twiddling her fingers, gnashing her thumbs. Only those sitting behind could ever see; her audiences never knew. Still, Catt was always happiest on the stump, out and doing, revving up the faithful, converting the doubtful, and she felt buoyed by this reception in Memphis. The church was packed.

In conjunction with Catt's tour, mass meetings, rallies, and petition drives were also being launched by the League of Women Voters in the state's smaller centers—Tullahoma, Murfreesboro, Mountain City—to bring public pressure to bear upon the legislature. The goal was to make it impossible for any member of the General Assembly to elude the suffragists' grasp as the time of decision neared. In the hours between her speeches, in every city and town on her tour, Catt met privately with the district chair-women of the local branch of the League of Women Voters to scrutinize the legislative polling data they'd collected. During these meetings with her suffrage fieldworkers, Catt probed beyond the bare numbers to ask blunt questions. In every meeting she asked, "Are there any known bribable legis-lators from your district?"

There was rarely a response of complete silence. Often the entire group shouted out a name in unison, as the shady reputation of a certain legislator was so well-known. Catt posed the same question to the local political lead-ers, the men behind the scenes, with whom she met privately in each city. The men usually reacted to the query with a startled look of suspicion, which they quickly masked with a blank expression, followed by what Catt called a "canny determination" not to reveal any names. Catt didn't let them off the hook: "Further discussion usually secured the names."

Using secret marks on the polling list, Catt corroborated the legislator's name with other reliable people. These suspect lawmakers were not counted in Catt's private tally of likely votes for ratification, even if they'd signed a pledge to do so. They were liable to fall under the sway of a generous Anti lobbyist. Catt kept two sets of books, so to speak: the accounting she gave to the press, which assumed every pledge was sound, and the real one, which took a more jaundiced, realistic view of lawmakers' promises.

As Catt and her entourage moved from city to city, she was alarmed to notice more secret marks accumulating next to various delegates' names and the numbers on the Suffs' pledge tallies softening. In consulting with the local suffragists and party politicians, she noticed a common theme emerg-ing: the "violation of oath" issue had taken hold, despite all the legal and practical arguments to the contrary. The opinions of former U.S. Supreme Court justice Charles Evans Hughes, the U.S. and Tennessee attorney generals, and all the other big legal names didn't seem to make much of a dent in the opposition. If anything, more Tennessee legislators seemed to be getting spooked by the oath issue.

This violation of oath business was simply a smoke screen being used by those who oppose ratification at heart, Catt kept insisting to her audiences and to the press. It was a subterfuge, an excuse. To counter the spreading oath menace, Catt sent orders to Nashville to launch a broader effort to refute the Anti claims. Squads of suffrage friends, both women and men, visited the law offices of respected attorneys in their districts, urging them to endorse the favorable legal opinions already in hand or write one of their own. The Suffs built a healthy roster of notable attorneys supporting ratification; but the Antis were recruiting their own all-star team of lawyers to take their side.

Nina Pinckard and Charlotte Rowe were ushered into the plush offices of some of Nashville's finest law firms, escorted by a staff member of the American Constitutional League. They carried introductions not only from prominent local attorneys such as John Vertrees and several Vanderbilt University law professors, but also from Charles S. Fairchild and Everett Pepperrell Wheeler at Constitutional League headquarters in New York. Both Fairchild and Wheeler were prominent corporate lawyers and veterans of the male antisuffrage movement. Both men had impressive résumés and were highly respected in legal circles: Wheeler a leader of the civil service reform movement and a founder of the American Bar Association; Fairchild known for his successful work for banking and railroad clients. They brought their legal skills into the suffrage fight through the Constitutional League, which they'd launched after the Antis' embarrassing defeat in the 1917 New York suffrage referendum. They both possessed nimble legal minds, which they devoted to developing novel attacks on the federal amendment and now on maneuvers to prevent, or even reverse, ratification.

The Antis' legal assault was assisted by a new ally: on the very day that Mrs. Catt began her speaking tour, the *Chattanooga Times* published the opinion of Foster V. Brown, one of that city's most distinguished lawyers—a former U.S. congressman and attorney general—contending that sitting Tennessee legislators would indeed be violating their oath of office by voting on ratification in the special session. That Brown was known as a champion of woman suffrage and supporter of the federal amendment made the opinion all the more potent and, for the Suffs, more damaging. The Antis quickly printed leaflets featuring Brown's statement and circulated them around the state, handy ammunition for the Anti delegation visiting Nashville's top lawyers. The Anti ambassadors were able to sway enough of those lawyers that within days, a Tennessee Constitutional League was formed. The Nashville lawyers and businessmen organizing the Constitutional League—several of whose wives were active Antis—then enlarged the organization by contacting their colleagues in other cities and distributing enrollment blanks around the state. The Tennessee Constitutional League, comprising both Democrats and Republicans, with John Vertrees heading the board of directors, vowed to protect "the letter and spirit of our constitution from the attacks of its enemies."

Betty Gram slipped into Memphis with no entourage and no welcoming delegation to greet her, but she made her entry with a certain theatrical flair that the press couldn't resist:

110 Pounds of Femininity to Hit Legislators for Vote
Young Militant Arrives to Make Canvas
IS HUNGER STRIKER
Miss Gram "Did Time" for Suffrage Cause

Betty Gram wasn't shy about being a "militant" and not coy about why she'd come to Memphis. She wore her prison pin and she made her intentions clear. The reporters got the hint.

"Here's just a little inside tip for Shelby county legislators," the Memphis newspaper article advised. "There's a real militant suffragist in town for the purpose of calling on each one of you and securing your written pledge to ratify the suffrage amendment. You'd better sign up, because she means business. And she has a record to back up her determination. She's been in jail three times and hunger-struck for ten days. Lest timorous legislators might suddenly feel the necessity of leaving town." Fear not, the news article continued, this militant was not what a legislator might expect: "She's young and she's pretty, and to add to the triumvirate of femininity, she's stylish."

Betty Gram was all of those things, but not only those things. She was also clever, wily, intrepid, and fiercely dedicated to her cause. The photograph of Gram accompanying the article (she provided the photo) proved the reporter's point: it was a close-up studio portrait, the kind movie stars used, Gram's lovely face framed by a stylish feather cloche hat. She enjoyed the role of ingenue agitator, and if unsuspecting legislators simply saw a pretty face, then woe be to them. Gram excelled in the arts of direct action.

Gram had aspired to become an actress and singer but abandoned her stage career for a part in the suffrage movement. Raised in Portland, Oregon, she discovered the Cause at college, then moved to New York City to further her theatrical career. She had just landed a part on Broadway when she answered Alice Paul's call for volunteers to join the "Silent Sentinels" picketing the White House in November 1917. Gram and her younger sister Alice took the train down to Washington, arriving at party headquarters just as the picketing crew was setting off. Drawn into the excitement, Betty and Alice Gram grabbed the last two picket poles and joined the protest. They soon found themselves in a Black Maria and carted off to jail.

The sisters were sentenced to thirty days in the infamous Occoquan Workhouse and, claiming they were political prisoners, joined in a suffragist hunger strike. They watched their comrades beaten by prison guards, thrown into isolation cells, forbidden to speak, read, or write; pens and pencils were confiscated. The squalor and starvation weakened them but also stiffened their resolve and strengthened their loyalty to Miss Paul. The intensity of the experience convinced them both to devote themselves to the Woman's Party. Alice joined the headquarters press staff, and Betty became a fixture on the picket line. She was imprisoned two more times, deepening her pride in her prison pin and earning a berth on the "Prison Special."

She met Sue White on that trip, and they struck up a fast friendship. That month of traveling together in the railroad car, packed into little sleeping berths, emerging in each city dressed in their prison outfits to lead a parade, speak on street corners, or conduct a big rally, was an experience they'd always share. Miss Paul dispatched Gram to eleven states during the ratification campaign; Gram was in New Jersey for that uncomfortably close decision and in Delaware for that disaster. She and Sue were side by side in the losing battle in Alabama and picketed together at the Republican National Convention in Chicago earlier in the summer. Now they were reunited in Tennessee.

Gram unpacked her bag in Memphis. She had her list of men to see; she began her calls. "Sentiment in favor of ratification is running high and everyone seems to think we will win," she wrote in her first report to Alice Paul, "but so did they in Delaware, and sentiment doesn't get votes."

Like an impatient fisherman, Sue White wanted to reel in Seth Walker quickly. He was the slippery sort, but he was an essential catch. As Speaker of the house, he had enormous visibility; legislators would be watching his movements and signs on the question of ratification. His position also endowed him with all sorts of parliamentary powers that he could use to ease, or obstruct, the passage of the amendment through the General Assembly.

Walker was a Roberts man; he sided with the governor on most policies and dutifully pushed through the administration's legislative agenda. He'd made that forceful speech on the lower house floor in favor of limited woman suffrage last year, and he'd given every indication that he would support ratification. But now that it was time to actually sign a pledge form, he was balking. He said he needed more time to investigate the "constitutionality" of the present legislature acting on ratification. White feared Walker had swallowed the Antis' bait.

She'd sent Betty Gram into Walker's district in Lebanon, about twenty-five miles east of Nashville, to talk to his political friends and associates. Gram had stopped in Nashville for a few days en route to Memphis and was a great help. White was stretched so thin: running the headquarters office, juggling orders from Miss Paul in Washington, maintaining close contact with the party's lobbyists in Ohio, sending detailed instructions to her field deputies around the state, all while coordinating the legislative canvass, keeping an eye on Anti activities, and getting her own assigned men pledged. White had never before been in charge of a state campaign all by herself, as the senior officer on the ground as well as the local political expert. And this was shaping up to be a campaign like no other; she was nervous about making a mistake. She tried not to feel overwhelmed, but she was anxious for Miss Paul to finally come to Nashville and take charge. In the meantime, it was up to her.

Seth Walker was tall and strapping, with the trim physique of the college athlete he'd once been. He was only twenty-eight years old, still something of a neophyte in the legislature, but his reputation as a clever lawyer, together with his canny political instincts and his loyalty to the governor, quickly boosted him into the Speaker's chair. He was a solid family man, married with kids; he was unapologetically ambitious. His career was well launched, as in addition to his law office and legislative post, he served as an attorney for the Nashville, Chattanooga, and St. Louis Railway. Gram found Walker in his district office in Lebanon; he was polite but abrupt. If he could convince himself that there were no legal obstructions to ratifying, he promised her, he could then see clear to support the amendment; he was looking into it. Gram reported all this to Sue White: Walker was still at large.

Anne Dallas Dudley, the savvy doyenne of Nashville Suffs who was helping Catherine Kenny keep some semblance of order at the League of Women Voters ratification headquarters, was also angling for Seth Walker. He'd been one of the unexpected heroes during the partial suffrage debate in the legislature last year—such a thrilling surprise—and she had high hopes for his ratification support now. He was a man whom others followed. But he hadn't responded to the poll, he hadn't sent in his pledge, he wasn't answering her messages. Dudley consulted with Mrs. Catt and they hatched a plan: Get Governor Cox, the new captain of the Democratic ship, to bring Seth Walker on board. Dudley wired to NAWSA's liaisons to the candidate in Ohio, asking them to deliver a message to Cox: Please urge Seth Walker to be your personal representative in the Tennessee legislature, ask him to lead the fight for ratification in the house. Action is urgent.

Sue White took a different tack in her pursuit of Walker: badgering him, appearing in his office, flooding him with legal opinions on the validity of ratifying. Finally, in the very last days of July, he informed White that he'd decided that there were no constitutional barriers to acting on ratification and he would support the amendment. White was elated: she wired the news to Alice Paul and called Anita Pollitzer in Knoxville, whooping with delight. She issued an announcement to the press. SPEAKER WALKER TO SUPPORT RATIFICATION, the headlines read. MISS SUE WHITE WAS CREDITED WITH THE CONVERSION.

With Walker secured, the Suffs could move to the next step. There is a formal choreography to amending the U.S. Constitution, an elaborate little dance set in motion as soon as both houses of Congress pass a joint resolution proposing a new article for inclusion. It must be signed by the Speaker of the House and the president of the Senate, then sent by the secretary of state to the governors of each state. The governor presents the proposed amendment to the presiding officers of the state legislature, convened in regular or extraordinary session, and these officers introduce it into their respective houses for consideration and ratification. This dance can be tripped or stalled at any of several key steps: by a governor who chooses not to convene his legislature, by legislative officers employing parliamentary maneuvers to block forward motion, or by a few hostile lawmakers intent on throwing the proceedings off balance.

The Tennessee suffragists couldn't afford to allow any such missteps, and even if they still had some doubts about whether Governor Roberts would keep his promise and play his part, they needed to secure their next set of necessary partners, the Speakers of the General Assembly. They chose Anne Dudley to fill the dance card. With a formal flourish, she, on behalf of the four official ratification committees—the Tennessee League of Women Voters, Democratic women, Republican women, and the Men's Ratification Committee (but not the Woman's Party)—invited senate Speaker Andrew Todd and house Speaker Seth Walker to introduce the federal amendment into their respective houses of the legislature. Both Speakers accepted Mrs. Dudley's invitation. Seth Walker confidently predicted that the legislature would ratify swiftly.

Meanwhile, Anita Pollitzer moved on to Knoxville, where she made her base at the Farragut Hotel and made herself a charming pest around town. She bantered with the fellows hanging around the courthouse; she cracked wise with the newspaper guys; she wangled appointments with the district party leaders; she found out which politicians were dining together, who was talking to whom.

She found a crucial ally in state senator Erastus Eugene Patton, who offered Pollitzer advice, assistance, and useful warnings: See this man, avoid that one, make sure these businessmen are with you. Patton also insisted: You must reach Herschel Candler. Candler was admired in the senate and respected as a man of strong, forcefully articulated convictions. But Candler had already made his stance pretty clear: "I will not perjure myself to open violation of the constitution of the state of Tennessee," he'd announced. "I unalterably oppose suffrage and shall vote against the bill." While Candler was already well-known to have Anti inclinations, sowing legality doubts among his colleagues made him even more destructive.

As she circulated through the environs of Knoxville, Pollitzer found that the legislators she approached seemed more and more skittish: those who'd not yet pledged tried strenuously to dodge; those who had already pledged favorably now hedged. "I fear the Republicans are holding back," Pollitzer wrote to Alice Paul.

Her suspicions were confirmed when the Harding-Coolidge Republican League, a Washington-based campaign group, conducted a telegraphic poll of Republicans in the Tennessee legislature during the first days of August and reported to state and national party leaders: "It does not look good." Republican legislators were claiming constitutional objections, "which is obviously only an excuse," the Harding-Coolidge Leaguers said bluntly, and the national party was just sitting on its hands. "Suggest that you put all forces in motion for ratification," the telegram continued. "If Tennessee fails to ratify the women will certainly blame the Republicans. . . ."

The Harding-Coolidge boosters sent an even more dismal assessment directly to their candidate: "Situation in Tennessee Legislature seems worse from Republican viewpoint," they reported to Harding. "We now know that majority Republican members are definitely against suffrage amendment although five of those men voted for suffrage last year. It is possible that women all over the country are now beginning to believe that Republican opposition in Nashville will be responsible for defeat of the Amendment." They begged him to take a more active role: "Suggest that a personal telegram from you to each Republican member of legislature will undoubtedly result in all voting for the amendment. Do not believe that anything else will result in solid Republican support."

But the Harding-Coolidge men were sorely disappointed by the tepid response they received from their candidate: "You can understand why I cannot consistently urge Tennessee legislators to vote for ratification without knowing their reasons for such commitment as they have made," Harding dissembled. "The situation is being reported to national headquarters where it will be given attention at once."

The Harding-Coolidge League was so frustrated by Harding's response that they leaked the correspondence; Woman's Party headquarters in Washington got hold of it and released the exchange of telegrams to the press. Tepid Harding was in hot water again.

Facing less resistance than Anita Pollitzer was encountering in East Tennessee did not mean that Betty Gram could take it easy. "Tired unto death," she reported to Paul. "Arose 6:30, motored 75 miles." In her travels to pledge the area's state legislators, Gram came across a thin, dapperly dressed, thirty-year-old Memphis delegate named Joseph Hanover, who not only eagerly signed his pledge to ratify, but was willing to make significant sacrifices to help achieve ratification.

Once Gram ventured beyond the protected precincts of Crump's Shelby County into the surrounding Mississippi River delta towns, things looked grimmer: "At present I am truly apprehensive," Gram wrote to Paul in the first days of August, "because these southern Democrats are concerned that their allegiance is just to the state constitution" and they'd break their oath of office by voting to ratify. "So many who voted for presidential suffrage will NOT vote for SBA this session," Gram reported, using the Woman's Party favored name for the federal amendment, honoring their patron saint, Susan B. Anthony. Gram's early optimism was fading; Tennessee was in danger of slipping away, she feared.

The Woman's Party sent Catherine Flanagan to Johnson City, in the northeast region of the state, near the tip of the pointing-finger section that poked toward North Carolina. Her assignment was to extract pledges from the candidates running for vacant legislative seats, get them on record: If elected, I will vote to ratify the federal suffrage amendment. It was just the kind of advanced pledge the Antis were railing about.

Flanagan was a slight woman, thirty-one years old, with auburn hair, a pale complexion, and a broad, toothy smile. When she wasn't on the road as a Woman's Party organizer—or in prison—she lived with her widowed mother in Hartford, Connecticut. She'd worked as a stenographer and had been secretary of the Connecticut chapter of NAWSA until the time, in the summer of 1917, that she decided to use her vacation to serve on the Woman's Party picket line at the gates of the White House. To those who knew Flanagan well, this wasn't so surprising: her father had been active in the Ireland home rule movement of the late nineteenth century, forced to flee to America as a political exile. The Irish Easter uprising of spring 1916 was still fresh in Catherine's mind in August 1917 when she decided to cast her lot with the suffrage group willing to fight, and be imprisoned, for women's freedom. Her father would have been proud.

She was arrested for obstructing traffic and sentenced to thirty days in the fetid Occoquan Workhouse. Her picketing actions were condemned by many of her colleagues in the Connecticut branch of the National Association but applauded by others, including Katharine Houghton Hepburn, president of the state suffrage organization. Flanagan's imprisonment split Connecticut's suffragists, and following her release, Flanagan joined Hepburn in forming a Connecticut unit of the Woman's Party. She went out to Montana to work on Jeannette Rankin's campaign for reelection to the Congress in 1918, and then Miss Paul dispatched her to the tough ratification states: West Virginia, Delaware, Vermont, and her own impossibly frustrating Connecticut. Now she was in Tennessee, sporting her prison pin.

She set out to find her men. "Today I drove over 30 miles in a jitney from Johnson City" to visit two uncommitted legislators, she reported to Miss Paul. One of them had no telephone and lived many miles down a badly rutted road; two miles from the lawmaker's house she had to abandon the jitney and walk, as the road was impassable. She was drenched by thunderstorms but finally made it to his door. He wanted to vote for ratification, he told her, but was afraid he'd be violating his oath. He refused to pledge but promised to deliberate on the matter. Flanagan came away encouraged. "I am sure we're going to win him over." The Antis were equally sure she would not.

About a hundred miles from where Flanagan was stationed, Anita Pollitzer kept up a punishing pace. She was managing a sprawling workshop of East Tennessee Republicans, working from their office desks or kitchen tables, telephoning, writing, and wiring their friends on behalf of ratification. She circulated among them: prodding them into action, keeping them on task. If they dillydallied on their assignments, delayed contacting someone they'd promised to approach, Pollitzer was over their shoulder in a flash. She had little patience for slackers.

When one high-level politician, a U.S. congressman, promised her he'd try to get hold of Herschel Candler—whom Pollitzer had still not managed to locate—and then failed to do so, she was in no mood to accept the congressman's feeble excuse: he'd tried to call Candler in Athens, but no luck. Pollitzer took hold of the congressman's telephone. She rang up Knoxville central and asked for the Athens town operator. There were clicks and rings as the Athens operator came on the line.

"This is a matter of life and death," Pollitzer told the operator, trying to sound breathless and urgent. "Congressman Taylor must speak with Senator Candler. I have been in Athens myself and I know it is such a tiny place that you have only to look out of the door to know where Senator Candler is. You must find him for me." Within minutes Herschel Candler came to the telephone.

"Cannot see my way clear to vote for amendment. Period," Candler defiantly told his own state party chairman, who was pressing him to get on board for ratification. "My oath of office would not permit." Candler repeated much the same thing to Pollitzer on the phone. Candler was hopeless.

Back in Nashville, Josephine Pearson and the officers of the Southern Women's Rejection League announced an ingenious new project of cultural, historical, and political importance: a museum exhibit. It was to be the centerpiece of their new headquarters space in the Hotel Hermitage, made possible by Nina Pinckard's superb curatorial skills.

"We have been able to secure, with great difficulty, the original United States Senate copies of the three Force Bills introduced in the last congress to enforce the 14th, 15th, and 19th amendments, if the latter is ratified," she explained to reporters. Any reference to force bills was poison in the southern states, Pinckard knew quite well, dredging up traumatic memories of federal enforcement of civil rights laws during Reconstruction, which southerners considered an insulting encroachment into their state affairs. The current force bills introduced into Congress by northern Republican pro-suffrage legislators sought to apply to the Nineteenth Amendment the second section of the Fourteenth Amendment, which stipulated that any state that abridged the voting rights of its eligible citizens could have its representation in Congress reduced by the proportion of those so denied. If the federal suffrage amendment was ratified, a state that refused to allow black women, or men, to vote could be punished.

"These Force Bills would rob the southern states of no less than seventy seats in Congress," Pinckard claimed, acknowledging that it was a matter of policy in the southern states to deny black citizens the vote. The infamous "Grandfather Clause" stipulating that only those men whose grandfathers had been eligible to vote could participate in current elections—eliminating virtually all black southern men, whose grandfathers had been slaves—had been struck down by the U.S. Supreme Court in 1915, but there were many other ways to prevent black men from voting. Exorbitant poll taxes and property requirements, arcane registration requirements, outrageous literacy and "knowledge" questions ("Recite the state constitution" was a favorite), threat of job loss, and brute physical intimidation did the trick just fine.

Southern states despised any mention of force bills, with their dual threat of federal election oversight and diminished congressional power, even though neither oversight nor the threat of reduced representation had ever been carried out. Defending against Washington's prying eyes peeking into the polling place remained a priority for the southern states throughout the twentieth century and into the twenty-first.

The menacing force bills were only one provocative element of the Antis' museum plans, as Mrs. Pinckard promised even more titillating artifacts: photographs of Susan B. Anthony's black friends, for instance, plus "photographs and documentary evidence of the true originators of the 14th, 15th, and 19th amendments, proving their common origin," Pinckard boasted. It was no secret that Frederick Douglass would appear in this section of the display. Another highlight of the exhibit, Pinckard revealed, would be a copy of the blasphemous *Woman's Bible*, written by Elizabeth Cady Stanton and edited and approved by Carrie Chapman Catt, proof of the suffragists' contempt for religion in general and Christian values in particular. This anti-ratification exhibit was going to be a blockbuster, Pinckard assured the press.

As Carrie Catt and her entourage moved eastward toward Knoxville, the murmurs they'd been hearing about various plots to stymie ratification grew louder. All of them were frighteningly plausible; some were actually true. The rosy prospect of a quick, favorable legislative majority faded, and Catt's mood grew darker.

She heard whispers that Governor Roberts, frightened by all the legal complications surrounding ratification, would, even if he won renomination, simply abandon plans for the special session, preserving the electoral status quo for himself in the fall. (Angry Tennessee Suffs couldn't vote against him because they wouldn't have the vote in gubernatorial elections.) Another version of this scenario, from very reliable sources, was that the governor would allow the session to convene, but his advisers, working with his loyal men in the legislature, were going to "ditch" the amendment, bury it in committee, until the twenty-day life span of the special session expired.

There were tales that three men, purporting to represent the Republican National Committee, were circulating among legislators, convincing them to stonewall ratification so Democrats could be denied the capstone of suffrage victory. In addition, the Rejection League was said to be teaming up with the Constitutional League to urge delegates to attend the special session but refuse to vote on ratification, as a matter of honor, citing their "oath of office" qualms. There was even a report that one high-level Tennessee

Republican leader was acting as a double agent, professing to work for ratification while actually doing his best to undermine it. Catt took these rumors of shenanigans very seriously and fired off a panic-tinged telegram to Republican National Committee chairman Will Hays: "Report 3 Republicans here representing national Republican committee, opposing ratification."

Hays's reply did little to assuage her fears: "Report is of course absolutely false," Hays insisted. The RNC had passed many unanimous resolutions favoring ratification "and is now doing all it can properly do" to support the amendment, he explained. The RNC might deny any knowledge of this ruse in Tennessee, Catt believed, but that didn't mean it wasn't happening. Even if it was not officially sanctioned, even if it was a rogue operation, these men, whoever they were, were making a plausible enough pitch to be effective with jittery Republicans. Catt was fed up with both parties' empty resolutions and pale excuses of "doing all it can properly do."

The latest news accounts were also alarming. Reporters, sniffing around Nashville and digging in Washington and Ohio, were filing stories with headlines such as TENNESSEE DOUBTFUL, POLITICIANS RELIEVED: NEWS THAT SUFFRAGE MAY NOT PASS LIFTS BURDEN FROM CANDIDATES and GOP LEADERS FEAR SUFFRAGE and SUFFS LOSING TENNESSEE, HARDING WON'T HELP.

Anita Pollitzer recognized the danger of this leadership vacuum and fumed as several of her East Tennessee legislators withdrew their ratification pledges on "constitutional grounds."

"I believe liquor influence making great headway under pretense constitutionality," she reported. "Situation extremely critical."

The Republicans were equivocating, but so were the Democrats. "Organizers report no signs of work being done by national leaders of either party in Tennessee," Alice Paul complained. Actually, Democratic National Committee chairman George White had secretly wired every Democrat in the Tennessee legislature, urging them to commit to ratify in time for James Cox to announce an assured majority in his official nomination acceptance speech on August 7. But the pledges were not coming in, and some of the responses the DNC did receive from Tennessee Democrats were certainly not positive:

"As to supporting proposed 19th Amendment," replied L. M. Whitaker, representing three counties in the south-central part of the state, "to do so I will have to violate my oath to support the constitution of Tennessee. Will have to lower the standard of Southern Womanhood. Will have to grossly offend sister states by enforcing an obnoxious measure on them. Will have to surrender the cordial principle of American government of states rights. It will be a long step [toward] degrading American homes. Will double the Negro purchasable vote of South. Will sacrifice settled social and domestic ethics and customs for a supposed political expediency. There can be but one answer."

Sue White was witnessing the Democratic resistance firsthand. Governor Roberts's men were not lining up to support ratification, she confided to Anita Pollitzer. By the latest Woman's Party count, the Suffs were ten votes short in the house, six in the senate, and some of the pledges White did have in hand were too iffy to be secure. Miss Sue was, she confessed, "worn out." She was scared. When are you coming to Nashville? she begged Alice Paul.

As all the Suffs, Antis, and politicos sprinted around the state, they warily watched the calendar and eyed the clock. The state primary was just a few days away; the fate of the governor and the future of the amendment were riding on that election. The special session, if it happened at all, was to convene in less than a week.

The suffragists' seven-decade quest for the vote was being squeezed into a mad dash; the Antis' cherished goal of protecting American civilization was being condensed into a tight time frame. And despite all the frenetic activity, ratification remained totally unpredictable; as the days passed, the uncertainties seemed only to multiply.

By Monday, August 2, Catt was in Knoxville, giving speeches, meeting with local suffragists, and making the rounds of politicians. After another long, draining day, Catt finally retired to her hotel room, but exhaustion, anxiety, and the oppressively heavy air made sleeping difficult. Sometime in the night, Abby Milton was awakened by loud, insistent knocking on her door. She opened it to find Marjorie Shuler, wrapped in a robe, breathless, frantic: "Mrs. Catt has suffered a heart attack."

It wasn't actually a heart attack, but Abby and Marjorie didn't know that in those first terrifying moments. All they knew was that their Chief was stricken, wounded in the field, just as the decisive battle was nearing.

Chapter 15

• • •

A Real and Threatening Danger

CATT HAD WHAT people called a "bad ticker." Her heart occasionally fluttered or skipped or squeezed painfully in her chest, took her breath away. The doctors told her to take it easy; less stress, less strain, more rest, was their usual prescription. She never obeyed those orders. Marjorie and Abby Milton found Catt dizzy, pale, and perspiring but sitting upright and alert. She was fine, she protested. It was just one of her little spells. It would go away.

Catt had not actually suffered a heart attack: it was most likely an episode of angina, a recurring symptom of her chronic heart ailment; it was unlikely to be fatal, even if it was very frightening. Catt had learned to live with it. Catt hated being ill, as if it revealed some embarrassing personal weakness or confirmed the silly stereotype of women as the "weaker sex." Yet she'd had her share of health problems over the years, and her tendency to overwork to the point of exhaustion triggered numerous collapses. Even an iron will could not always compensate for a more fragile body.

Catt spent the next day recuperating at the comfortable Milton home in Chattanooga, enjoying the quiet, a bit of pampering, and the three young Milton daughters, who were already veterans of many a suffrage parade. While Catt was cocooned in the pleasant hush of the Miltons' house and garden, the ratification fracas grew hotter and louder.

As news spread of Senator Harding's latest refusal to intervene with Republican Tennessee legislators, Harding also received a letter from the Tennessee Constitutional League—whether the notes crossed in the mail or one precipitated the other isn't clear—demanding that Harding keep "hands off" in Tennessee. It assured Harding that he'd made a wise decision in holding back. The Constitutional League guardians sent an identical letter to Cox and composed another set of sharp warnings to every Tennessee lawmaker.

"We ask you, as a sworn officer of our State Government, to stand with us . . . for the upholding of the honor of Tennessee and the rights of our people as guaranteed in our Constitution," the letter to the legislators read. The letter was strong but not strident, no histrionics, just very lawyerly; it conveyed a man-to-man ease and just the right tone of arrogance. "We feel justified in saying that you have not the right to . . . foreclose your freedom of action by any promise, express or implied. Your own obligation to obey the constitution rises above any party or personal consideration."

In other words, any written or verbal pledges to vote for ratification should be—and must be— considered null and void, the Constitutional League claimed. And on the other side of the equation, any ill-advised pledges made by the presidential candidates to assist in passing ratification should also be repudiated.

Carrie Catt, supposedly resting in Chattanooga but still receiving up-to-the-hour reports by telephone, recognized that this was the ticking bomb with which the Antis planned to blow up the supporting structure of the Suffs' campaign. She could sense the menace of this clever explosive device even as she sat in the cool shade of the Milton house. It must be defused—or preemptively detonated. Never mind her heart.

From the Miltons' parlor, Catt dictated a set of stinging telegrams to Cox and Harding: "There is a very real and threatening danger" to ratification of the federal amendment by the Tennessee legislature, she told them, resulting from "the tremendous effort being made by outsiders to persuade the legislators not to act on the amendment at all, under the pretense that it would be a violation of their oath." What's more, "these outsiders are inspiring messages to you," she told the candidates, taking direct aim at the Constitutional League, "signed by Tennessee names, asking you to keep hands off." Keeping hands *on*, Catt insisted, with a tight and forceful grip, was the only option if they honestly wanted to salvage the amendment. "We renew our appeal to you for the aid we so greatly need in this last battle for women's political liberty."

Catt's wires to the candidates, to Harding in particular, set off a cascade of sparks. Harding's patience for the whole ratification matter was fraying, as he was being harassed from all sides: the different camps of Suffs, the many varieties of Antis, the lawyers, the press, the Tennessee Republicans, and Will Hays at the RNC. The national election was only thirteen weeks away; Harding must focus, avoid mistakes, appear presidential. If he could hold on, allow Cox to make the unforced errors, and sidestep any controversial comments, he could win the White House. Harding sent Catt a quick, if hollow, reply: "Your telegram received. No discouragement is voiced from here. On the contrary we are continuing to encourage the Republicans of the Tennessee General Assembly to join cordially in the effort to consummate ratification." He really just wanted them off his back. And off his porch.

The reaction of the Woman's Party to Harding's newest evasions was precisely as he feared: they were already climbing his front porch steps. As soon as Alice Paul had gotten hold of Harding's equivocal response to the Harding-Coolidge League, she dispatched Abby Baker to confront him on his porch in Marion. Baker carried her own weapon into the meeting—if not a stick, perhaps the equivalent of a dainty, pearl-handled derringer: "I impressed upon him that, unless the Tennessee legislature acted favorably, the ratification question was likely to become an incubus on the back of the Republican Party," Baker recounted to reporters. And should Tennessee fail the women of America, the Woman's Party would have no choice but to assign blame and punish the offending national political party in the fall. She was threatening to unleash the "woman's vote"—a potent weapon, if it really existed.

"What will the Negro woman do with the vote?" Mrs. Juno Frankie Pierce asked her audience of several hundred white women at the inaugural convention of the Tennessee League of Women Voters, held in the statehouse in May. Pierce, a founder of the Nashville Federation of Colored Women's Clubs and an active suffragist, answered that rhetorical question with an air of calm authority:

"Yes, we will stand by the white women," Pierce explained. Nashville's black suffrage clubs had coordinated closely with Catherine Kenny and the city's white suffrage organization to get out the vote in the 1919 municipal elections, the first open to Tennessee women. "We are optimistic because we have faith in the best white women of the country, of Nashville. We are going to make you proud of us, because we are going to help you help us and yourselves."

It was an extraordinary moment. Hearing the voice of a black woman, the daughter of a slave, inside the house chamber of the Tennessee Capitol, was astonishing. Kenny, with Abby Milton's approval, had invited Pierce to address this founding meeting of the league, in a taboo-breaking experiment in political cooperation.

"We are interested in the same moral uplift of the community in which we live as you are," Pierce explained. "We are asking only one thing—a square deal."

Pierce was pledging the help of the black women of Tennessee to the white women of the state—proposing a working partnership to achieve their shared goals of social betterment. But Pierce's demand for a square deal wasn't just a vague, lofty notion, it wasn't just a promise to follow white women's instructions, it was solid and specific: "We want recognition in all forms of this government," Pierce said. "We want a state vocational school, and a child welfare department of the state, and more room in state schools."

The black and white suffragists of Tennessee had worked separately for many years—black Suffs weren't allowed to join the white mainstream clubs—so this event was an exciting departure, an ambitious way to launch the new Tennessee League of Women Voters, which was the successor to the state's national suffrage affiliate. (With the granting of limited suffrage, Tennessee became eligible to join the LWV.) Abby Milton and Catherine Kenny were elected to leadership positions of the league, and there was something thrilling to them about Pierce's idea of women forging political deals—joining forces, white and black—for their community's good. This was, they believed, perhaps naively, what woman suffrage in its purest, most idealistic form was all about; it was an example of what women's participation in government might accomplish.

But Pierce was posing another question, urgent but unspoken, to her audience that morning: Will you, the white suffragists of Tennessee, stand by the black women of the state who want, who need, to vote? Will you stand up for us when black women, like black men, are threatened and assaulted at the polls? Will you allow us to use the vote that we, like you, have been fighting for so long? Those questions remained unanswered.

Now, in the first days of August, the Tennessee League of Women Voters was only ten weeks old, but it was being forced to mature quickly. No woman attending the inaugural convention could foresee that Tennessee might be the thirty-sixth state or that their league would be thrust into the national spotlight while still in its wobbly infancy. Abby Milton, as the league's first president, accepted the challenge.

Milton saw her role in guiding the young league as her civic duty, and she took such obligations very seriously. Both George and Abby Milton felt strongly about public affairs, good government, and progressive policies.

George was the publisher and editor of the *Chattanooga News,* a careful and fair-minded man; a "dry," a Suff, and a progressive Democrat. He frequently locked editorial horns with his morning newspaper rival, Adolph Ochs's *Chattanooga Times,* and with Edward Stahlman's *Nashville Banner.* Abby's quick mind and organizational talents enabled her to rise quickly in suffrage circles, first in Chattanooga and then to the presidency of the state suffrage organization, where she played a leading role in pushing through the limited suffrage bill in the legislature. Abby believed God had a plan for the world, and woman's equality was just a neccessary amendment to that plan; she felt called to do her part.

While Carrie Catt was dictating her telegrams to Cox and Harding into the Miltons' telephone, Abby was off in Johnson City, substituting for Mrs. Catt on the stage of a suffrage rally: an intimidating position for anyone. She summoned her courage and walked alone to the podium. When she returned home to Chattanooga, she found Carrie Catt directing the Tennessee campaign from the parlor couch. It was obvious that after barely one day of rest, Catt was going to jump back into the ruckus; there was no restraining her. Catt wouldn't hear of canceling her speech to the Chattanooga Chamber of Commerce, scheduled for the next day. She would go on as planned.

At noon on Wednesday, August 4, in the ballroom of the Hotel Patten, Catt was introduced by the mayor of the city, and among the audience of about two hundred men and women were many political notables. Abby Milton and Marjorie Shuler sat at the head table, which was festooned with suffrage-yellow flowers, their eyes anxiously fixed on Mrs. Catt as she rose to speak, but their worries about her health and stamina dissolved as she launched into her address. Catt spoke with an unfiltered fury that even Marjorie had never heard before.

"Here in Tennessee the suffrage battle is being fought by those who do not live in Tennessee," Catt declared. She was referring not to herself, but to the men of the Constitutional League. "Their way is to put a few publicity-seeking women in the limelight, while they themselves work in stealth." Catt presented her evidence, spinning her narrative like a detective story, turning her magnifying glass on the Constitutional League.

"Some weeks ago from New York came emissaries of this group, to organize a men's Constitutional League in Tennessee, and they seem to be finding men willing to play into their hands," she charged. "They do not appear to be behind the opposition, but when they send to Cox and Harding messages to 'leave Tennessee alone' you may know it is this little band of determined New York reactionaries who are behind it." Reporters covering the event scribbled furiously in their notebooks, smiling to themselves as they recorded Catt's colorful castigations.

"These are the same New York people who call women 'skirts' and cry loudly that 'woman's place is in the home,'" Catt fumed. "The opponents of suffrage are trying to fool the people of Tennessee about the state constitution," she contended. "All the Antis are getting behind the 'constitutional objection.'" Catt was speaking without notes, taking off from her usual stump speech, inserting little rhetorical firecrackers, and she was getting a bit carried away.

"You can fool the people of Tennessee, but you can't fool posterity," she insisted. "If you won't consider the suffrage amendment, the action of the legislature will pass into history as a testimonial to the stupidity of Tennessee." Marjorie and Abby Milton could only wince at this insulting swipe, so out of character for the diplomatic Catt. "You may think you are right, but posterity will laugh." It was as if all the tension and anger Catt had felt during the past several weeks, the bitter frustration she'd kept bottled up, were now bubbling out.

"Go to see your representatives and senators, and set them right!" she exhorted. "Let them understand that if they want to claim that their oaths prevent their considering suffrage, they do so in response to the wish and will of reactionaries, woman haters, who hope to keep women disenfranchised forever!"

The Antis in Nashville were both outraged and elated by Mrs. Catt's remarks. They resented her gibes about "outsiders" and "New York reactionaries" invading and manipulating Tennessee—who was she, a New Yorker herself, to point a finger?—but they took Catt's febrile rants as proof that the Suffs felt themselves slipping, losing their grip. They were not wrong in this assessment.

Josephine Pearson took special delight in Mrs. Catt's tirade and used the nib of her fountain pen to puncture it. She had the fine hand of a teacher, her penmanship curvy and clear, her turns of phrase vivid, and her punctuation florid. Pearson was partial to exclamation points: they expressed her emphatic belief in the verities, her unshakable confidence in the absolute truths, in the Word of God, and in the great philosophers of man.

"Can anything more <u>outside</u> in its influences than Mrs. Catt—an alien in blood and in sentiment to every Southern instinct and inheritance—have ever come to Tennessee?" she asked Cox incredulously. The Anti leaders and Constitutional League lawyers from New York and other places were not outsiders, she protested, they were invited, honored guests: "That we, opposing Ratification in Tennessee, have and may employ every available ability, both state and national, to defeat the Federal Amendment that bears the name Susan B. Anthony—who was an organizer and propagator of Abolition—out of which Female suffrage is an unmistakable historical child—we do not deny but proclaim!"

Woman suffrage was an "infectious germ" foreign to the South, Pearson told Cox, and "Federal control of Southern elections" was a Republican plot originating with the likes of Thaddeus Stevens and Frederick Douglass. No self-respecting Democrat should have any part in such a ploy, Pearson insisted, not if he hoped to win southern votes. She advised Cox to ignore Mrs. Catt's "hysterical" pleas for his help and to take Catt's SOS calls as proof that public sentiment in Tennessee was opposed to the amendment, and ratification would naturally fail without his intervention. Though Pearson might be exaggerating the strength of popular opposition to ratification, she had a salient point: the Suffs were obviously fearful that ratification in Tennessee was impossible without strong, coercive pressure from both national parties; they couldn't trust the strength of their own forces to achieve victory. "Why then," she asked Cox, "should a distinguished Democratic candidate lend his efforts to pulling burnt suffrage chestnuts out of a Southern fire?"

While Pearson penned her letter to Cox at the Hermitage, two blocks away at Woman's Party headquarters Sue White wrote asking for help. Handling the entire state campaign with only three organizers was too much. White expected Miss Paul to arrive in Nashville within the next few days, but in the meantime, Paul promised reinforcements. She was sending two staffers from headquarters to handle publicity and another to raise money.

"The situation in Tennessee is serious but the situation of our treasury is more serious still," Emma Wold, Paul's secretary at party headquarters, wrote to a member that same week. "Miss Paul asks me to write you to see if you can not raise some money. . . ."

Running on empty was certainly not a new condition for the Woman's Party—it was chronically short on funds—but the expenses of the long ratification campaign had sucked the party deep into the red. All the while she was supervising the Tennessee campaign from Washington, Paul continued begging for money. "Need for money for Tennessee suffrage campaign urgent. Asking every state to contrib $100. Can you raise $100 in your state?" Paul wired to all her state chairwomen. She made special appeals to her wealthiest donors, going back to the wells she'd tapped countless times before; Mrs. Havemeyer sent a $400 check. Paul pleaded with her well-heeled supporters to solicit funds from their neighbors at the posh summer colonies. She even asked Sue White, Anita Pollitzer, and Betty Gram to hustle money while they canvassed in Tennessee. By the early days of August, the Woman's Party treasury was down to $10 and the bills were pouring in.

Paul was a brazen and guileless fund-raiser; she was known to ask anyone, at any time, for money. She didn't enjoy doing it, but she felt that, like going to prison, begging for money was a necessary discomfort for the Cause. She didn't wheedle, she didn't demand, she just asked directly, with the single-minded intensity with which she pursued all of her goals. She was hard to refuse; donors often gave more than they intended, simply because in her sincerity she made them believe or made them feel guilty. No one was safe in an elevator, or in a taxi, or even in a private box at Carnegie Hall, if Alice Paul had you alone and in her fund-raising sights. How she kept the party afloat at all was miraculous. There were the small donors—the elderly woman sending a dollar bill or two, the nurse sending five dollars of her salary, the child mailing a dime—and the more substantial checks from wealthier patrons. And then there was Mrs. Belmont.

Alva Erskine Vanderbilt Belmont was perhaps the American suffrage movement's most flamboyant benefactor. Born on the Erskine family's cotton plantation in Mobile, Alabama, she married into high New York and Newport society when she took the hand of a Vanderbilt scion; years later, her divorce became one of the great tabloid stories of the Gilded Age. Her settlement made her a very wealthy divorcée. She quickly remarried into another society family, the Belmonts, but when she was widowed in 1908 she decided to devote herself, and her money, to the woman suffrage cause.

Although she bankrolled NAWSA at first, providing the money for their New York headquarters office, and she funded Harriot Stanton Blatch's Women's Political Union to draw more working-class women into the movement, Belmont found the pace of progress too slow. She came to see a more direct path to the franchise in the philosophy of Emmeline Pankhurst. The difference between conservative American suffragists and the new breed of British "militants," Pankhurst told Belmont, was: "You talk. We act."

Belmont wanted to act and saw Mrs. Pankhurst's ideas manifest themselves in America in the actions of Alice Paul and Lucy Burns. So when Paul and Burns split off from NAWSA to form the Congressional Union for Woman Suffrage, and later the National Woman's Party, Belmont shifted her largesse to the new group, where her money could have more impact and she could have more clout. Belmont became the Woman's Party's primary financial backer. Alice Paul understood that while this generosity provided security, it also came with strings attached: Mrs. Belmont liked to have a strong say in the organizations she supported, and she was used to having her way. Paul was willing to accept the bargain and manage the difficult balance, and even though all policy decisions required Belmont's stamp of approval, Paul was able to keep the headstrong and prickly Belmont engaged while restraining her from taking over. It wasn't easy. In any case, even Mrs. Belmont's donations couldn't float the entire ship, so Paul was forced to plead for money constantly.

In contrast, Mrs. Catt had no such money worries. To Sue White's mind, and to the other Woman's Party staff, it seemed so unfair. Mrs. Catt had money to spare and no need to kowtow to any imperious benefactress. Catt was so lucky: her fairy godmother was conveniently dead.

How all this came to be certainly had the trappings of a fairy tale—or a dime novel.

In the fall of 1914, Catt was dining with Mollie and another friend in their Manhattan apartment when she was summoned to the telephone. Catt returned to the dining table flushed and stunned: "I am an heiress," she announced. The phone call was from an attorney; Catt had been named the major beneficiary in the will of one of the richest women in the nation, a woman she'd barely even met.

The woman was Miriam Follin Peacock Squier Leslie Wilde, Baroness de Bazus, the most admired businesswoman of her day and a gossip column celebrity who wore scandal like a personal fashion statement. Miriam Leslie crafted her own version of the American success saga, with a feminist twist: an ambitious girl from New Orleans, born with neither wealth nor social standing, who by dint of talent, grit, and abundant charm managed to climb the economic, professional, and societal ladders of New York City to become a media mogul of the late nineteenth century. She made her ascent with ruthless calculation and with panache.

She began her career onstage in a dance act with the notorious Lola Montez, managed to enter the circle of America's intellectual elite with her marriage to a distinguished anthropologist and diplomat, then subsequently took up a blue pencil as editor of popular women's magazines. She became an arbiter of taste and fashion, manners and mores, for American women, yet her private life was splendidly messy: she married four times, her lovers were numerous, her affairs—rumored and real—widely reported.

After dumping her second husband for her boss, the publisher Frank Leslie, whose eponymous *Frank Leslie's Illustrated Newspaper* brought a new kind of "sensational" journalism to America, Miriam seized the helm of the Leslie media empire when Frank died suddenly in 1880. She quickly rescued the faltering enterprise, nimbly reshaping the company, and soon she was among the nation's highest-paid executives, with a yearly salary of more than $100,000. She oversaw four hundred employees, and more than half a million subscribers read her publications each month. She evolved into that rare creature: a woman in charge of a large corporation and in full control of her own financial and personal affairs. The modern American woman indeed: the kind the Antis had nightmares about.

Miriam Leslie never joined the suffrage vanguard, but she did quietly support the movement with modest donations, good publicity in her periodicals, and occasionally the use of her office building for suffrage receptions. Carrie Catt had met her just a few times at these events, and they engaged in some conversation, but nothing more. So no one was more shocked than Catt when the phone call came from Mrs. Leslie's attorney in the fall of 1914, notifying her that the baroness (she'd made up the title and bestowed it on herself) had directed her estate to be given personally to Catt, with the instruction that it be used to "further the cause of woman suffrage."

The estate was valued at $2 million, an immense sum in 1914, equivalent to more than $50 million today. But it would take almost three years of furious legal wrestling for Catt to secure the bequest, as every distant relative and friend laid claim to the estate and tried to make the case that Mrs. Leslie was insane—what else could explain giving away her fortune to the suffrage movement? While Catt was taking control of the National and launching her "Winning Plan," she was forced to spend hundreds of hours in probate court hearings and attorney conferences, as well as countless sleepless nights, in her effort to win the Leslie estate. Finally, in early 1917, the court ruled to uphold the will, though almost half of the estate had been spent on legal fees and settlements.

Some of the bequest was in the form of jewels—Mrs. Leslie had a weakness for glittering gems—and a trunk full of them was brought to Catt's office at NAWSA headquarters on Madison Avenue. The trunk lid was opened, revealing a tangle of diamond necklaces and ruby earrings, emerald brooches and sapphire pins. Catt's staff gathered around the treasure chest and she motioned to them to come touch the jewels, touch the legacy of the woman who was buying the future for them. For a magical half hour the suffrage soldiers played dress-up, sashaying between the office desks in bejeweled splendor. One of the staffers picked up a diamond-studded tiara from the pile and placed it on the silver curls of Carrie Catt's head, crowning the Chief. After a while Catt clapped her hands and signaled for the jewels to be returned to the case; it was closed and latched and immediately sent off to be sold.

Catt used the Leslie money to finance the 1917 New York suffrage referendum campaign and her "Winning Plan," building a stronger central command base in New York and opening Suffrage House in Washington to lobby for the federal amendment. She established the Leslie Woman Suffrage Commission, which supported the Leslie Bureau of Suffrage Education, a sophisticated publicity and publication department, with a press bureau pumping out news articles distributed nationwide, the *Woman Citizen* magazine, thousands of pamphlets and educational materials, and the *History of Woman Suffrage* volumes. The Leslie Woman Suffrage Commission was also underwriting the costs of NAWSA's ratification campaign and the formation of the new League of Women Voters.

But even now, in summer 1920, Carrie Catt's fight for the Leslie money wasn't over. Another distant relative had recently filed suit to overturn Catt's claim on the estate, contending that Catt had somehow bewitched Mrs. Leslie into bequeathing her fortune to suffrage. Catt had to again wearily deny this, but the suit was going forward. The Leslie money hadn't exactly come without cost, not without a mighty amount of travail and headache and worry, but it had come, and Catt was grateful. Catt paid tribute to Mrs. Leslie every week, in every issue of *The Woman Citizen,* where above the masthead was placed a bold-bordered box containing a dedication to Miriam Leslie and "her faith in the irresistible progress of women."

•••

Mrs. Catt and Marjorie returned to Nashville on Thursday afternoon, August 5, the day of the Tennessee primary. Men around the state were going to the polls; all of the candidates expressed full confidence that they would win their contests. The results of the primary would determine who'd held on to power, who'd won it, and who had lost it. Governor Roberts's future, and his attitude toward ratification, would hopefully be clarified. He would, or would not, call the special session. The men who won the vacant seats in the legislature could tip the ratification polling numbers. But no one really knew.

Catt looked fatigued and had pale, dark rings under her eyes. She moved back into her room on the third floor of the Hotel Hermitage; in her absence, the hotel had filled with more Antis. Mrs. Ruffin Pleasant had arrived, wife of the former governor of Louisiana and, as Josephine Pearson described her, "the daughter of Maj. Gen. Ector, who had three horses shot under him at the battle of Lookout Mountain." Pleasant and her husband had been instrumental in defeating ratification in the Louisiana legislature, and they'd come to Nashville to apply their skills in Tennessee. Many more Antis from around the country were expected soon.

There was little to do but wait.

Upon her return, the weary Catt, who could have no fonder wish than for a quiet nap under the ceiling fan, found in her hotel mailbox a galling note from Josephine Pearson. It was the paper equivalent of a slap of white gloves on her cheek: a challenge to a duel.

Having warmed up with her scalding letter to James Cox, Pearson enjoyed turning her rhetorical flamethrower toward Catt, challenging her to a verbal duel—a public debate—against the Antis' knight-errant, Charlotte Rowe. Taking the role of a proper "second" in the code duello, Pearson laid out the offenses Catt had committed: "We have no objections whatever to your crying to Gov Cox for help, but when you have made a sweeping general charge meant to discredit Tennessee men and women, and their distinguished invited guests, we demand a bill of particulars."

The tone of the note was sarcastic and taunting: "We would not for the world convey the impression that we have any objection whatever to your presence here, for southern courtesy, as well as confidence that your presence here is helping us, would prevent our making such objections." But Pearson demanded that Catt debate Rowe "to allow the people of Tennessee to decide for themselves who is more 'inspiring,'" and no excuses or evasions would be acceptable. Catt would not lower herself even to reply. Catt did take a moment to write a quick note to Clara Hyde in New York: "I've had two rocky days and can only say please pity and pray for the cause, and for me."

After the polls closed, once the ballot boxes were opened and the votes counted, *Banner* reporters telephoned the latest tallies to the newsroom. A squad of editors there relayed these "hot off the wire" numbers to a team of typists, who sent them on to a projectionist, and the progress of the races was projected onto a screen hung across the street from the newsroom. A crowd of hundreds gathered on Commerce and Third Streets to witness the marvel of breaking news flashed before their eyes in the darkness, and they stood mesmerized, watching the numbers on the screen, until close to midnight.

By Friday morning, it was clear that Albert Roberts had prevailed over William Crabtree to win the Democratic gubernatorial primary by a comfortable margin of more than twenty thousand votes, and Alf Taylor had overwhelmed Jesse Littleton for the Republican nomination. Abby Milton and Catherine Kenny were disappointed by Roberts's victory, and Sue White thought that Roberts's win afforded a "slight advantage" in securing ratification, as now "his forces cannot claim lack of influence as an excuse for inaction." But all the Suffs were relieved to hear that most of the men elected to fill vacancies in the legislature were pledged to ratify.

Late on Saturday afternoon, August 7, Governor Roberts confirmed, or confounded, the rumors: he formally called the General Assembly to meet in extraordinary session beginning at noon on Monday, August 9. The decisive confrontation—anticipated, relished, dreaded—was finally set. It would begin in less than forty-eight hours.

Chapter 16

• • •

War of the Roses

ALL THROUGH THE WEEKEND, all over Tennessee, the men of the legislature were packing their bags, closing their shops and offices, canceling vacations, kissing their wives and children good-bye, and boarding trains. They might be gone for a few days or for three weeks (the full term of the session); no one could tell. The delegates who lived in the more remote sections of the state, where phone wires hadn't yet been strung or electricity service didn't yet exist, wouldn't receive Governor Roberts's call to convene until Sunday or Monday and would have to scramble to make their way to the capital.

They stormed into Nashville aboard steaming trains, riding the iron horses that had made the city great. Mercury was a busy god during this weekend, greeting the hundreds of men and women pouring into Union Station to attend the special session. He watched over everyone pulling into the station—the legislators and lobbyists, politicians and partisans, correspondents and conspirators—all the participants in what the newspapers were already calling "the Tennessee War of the Roses." And Union Station was a crazy place.

The special session was most especially a boon to florists: arriving passengers were met by welcoming parties of women who pounced upon them and attempted to pin a rose to their lapel, an Anti red rose or a Suff yellow rose. Yellow or gold had long been the American suffrage campaign's symbolic hue, signifying the flame of freedom's fires; the Woman's Party adopted a version of the British suffragists' tricolor of green, white, and violet/purple (a chromatic acronym for "give women the vote"); and the Antis had more recently adopted a patriotic red-blooded motif. A Tennessee delegate had to be careful about which color rose he accepted as his boutonniere, but whichever he chose, he would know no peace.

Josephine Pearson and Nina Pinckard were at the Hotel Hermitage, striking a pose for the camera. As the photographer set his bellowed Graflex camera on a tripod and fiddled with his flash, the women practiced their positions, standing at the doors of Anti-Ratification headquarters on the mezzanine level of the hotel. Red, white, and blue bunting, as well as miniature American flags, adorned the entrance, and Pinckard clutched a polished wooden pole bearing a large Confederate battle flag.

Pinckard was dressed all in white, from her hat to her shoes, a single red American Beauty rose pinned low on her breast; Pearson wore a dark dress and flat-brimmed hat, three red roses on her bosom; between the standing women was seated a very old, frail, white-mustachioed man.

When the photographer's flash exploded, it caught Pearson turned toward Pinckard, the corners of Pearson's mouth upturned in a satisfied half smile, her roses illuminated by the burst of light. Pinckard took a more assertive, defiant stance: her right arm outstretched upward, holding the corner of the Stars and Bars, spreading it out to its full glory behind her. Sitting beside her, sharing a grip on the flag's long pole, was the wizened man, wearing a bow tie and waistcoat, a huge rose pinned to his suit jacket. He was William Absalom Crutcher, a proud Nashville veteran of the War Between the States, a living symbol of all those who "fought and bled for Tennessee's States Rights" whose sacrifice, the members of the Southern Women's Rejection League wished to remind everyone, must not be squandered.

The Confederate veteran was just a boy when he joined the celebrated Tennessee cavalry unit led by General Nathan Bedford Forrest; he served as a scout, and all his life he was honored to belong to the Forrest group of Confederate veterans. The banner of the Forrest veterans was displayed prominently in the photo, hanging down from the Stars and Bars pole, and this was very much on purpose. The banner was a signal, a silent whistle to any Tennessean: General Forrest was popularly known not only as "the Wizard of the Saddle" for his lightning attacks on Union forces, but also as the brutal commanding officer at the Fort Pillow Massacre, where hundreds of surrendering black Union troops were slaughtered by Forrest's men. Forrest was also famous as a founder of the Ku Klux Klan, one of its first Grand Wizards. The photo made all the historical connections, raised the emotional stakes, expressed just what Pearson and Pinckard wanted it to convey. Pearson wrote a caption for the photo, displaying both her erudition and her heritage, saluting Jefferson Davis's use of poet William Cullen Bryant's battlefield hymn as a Confederate motto: "Truth crushed to the Earth will rise again."

A few floors above, Carrie Catt knew that Harriet Upton had arrived when she heard a booming laugh echo down the Hermitage hallway. That was Upton's distinctive laugh, and Catt was very glad to hear it. Upton, president of the Ohio state suffrage organization and recently appointed vice chair of the Executive Committee of the Republican National Committee, had been dispatched by Will Hays to demonstrate the party leadership's concern about Tennessee and also to placate Mrs. Catt. Catt had also wired a personal plea to Upton, at home in Warren, Ohio, to hasten to Nashville: Upton was needed to "straighten out" the Republicans.

Catt and Upton had been suffrage colleagues for thirty years. Upton liked to joke that she discovered Catt, then a young, unknown Iowa delegate to the National American Woman Suffrage Association's 1890 convention. Catt had delivered an impressive speech on Iowa's progress, and when the news reporters asked Upton, acting as publicity director for the convention, to identify the striking, dark-haired lady who'd just bowled over the audience, Upton admitted she had no idea. Needing some vital statistics, Upton passed a note to Catt: "Who are you? Where were you born? Where educated? What have you done? Are you married?"

Catt penciled quick answers to each query: "Born in Wisconsin, educated in Iowa, did newspaper work in California. Am married; he is in the back of the hall. Am not a big gun, never will be. Carrie Chapman Catt." And that, Upton liked to say, was one of the only instances she knew Carrie Catt to be absolutely wrong.

Upton, like Catt, had been one of Aunt Susan's girls, and Anthony had valued Upton's adroit political sense as well as her jovial nature. Besides her organizational and networking abilities, Upton had a talent for winning friends for the Cause with her good humor and could defuse tense situations with a witty aside. Upton served on NAWSA's board, was its treasurer for years, and for a time its headquarters was actually located in Upton's house in Warren.

Upton was comfortable with the rough-and-tumble of politics; her father had been an Ohio congressman, and she'd accompanied him on the campaign trail as well as to Washington. She also knew the ins and outs of Ohio political affairs: besides her Republican Party activities, she was in the thick of four failed attempts to convince the Ohio legislature to submit woman suffrage to a popular vote, had led two unsuccessful referendum campaigns

(1912 and 1914), succeeded in obtaining presidential suffrage from the legislature in 1917 (only to have it repealed), and piloted the effort for Ohio's ratification, which was still being challenged by the Antis. She'd faced off against the powerful liquor interests in her state time and again.

She knew both Warren Harding and Jimmy Cox quite well. In her role as head of Ohio Republican women, she'd attended the Harding Notification Day, seated on the stage behind the candidate while Alice Paul, Louisine Havemeyer, Anita Pollitzer, and Sue White watched from the far reaches of the pavilion. She knew Harding wasn't the strongest of suffrage champions, but she believed he was sincere, and she was in Nashville to convince Republican legislators that Harding, and the party, needed them to ratify.

Catt was delighted to see her comrade. Upton was a large woman and equally bighearted, pragmatic but tender, with a depth of experience few could match. Catt could be candid with Upton, rely on her judgment, and relish her wickedly funny ripostes; she could use some humor just now. But Upton was also an "outsider," another Yankee, and Catt was beginning to realize the double-edged nature of all her stinging "outsider" accusations: the Antis were having a fine time throwing them back in her face.

As a countermeasure, Catt now gave the signal to NAWSA headquarters to release to the press the small southern good-luck charm she'd been holding: a letter addressed to the men of the legislature of Tennessee from Lady Astor, the first woman to take a seat in the British Parliament. Nancy Astor was born a Virginia girl, one of the beautiful Langhorne sisters of that proper southern family; no outsider she. Catt had requested the note, and Lady Astor had gladly obliged:

"I want to send a message to the men of the South, because I come from the South, and feel that I know and understand it, as one only can understand the place of one's birth and childhood," Astor wrote.

> I know the strong sense of justice and honor that lives in the hearts of the people. I know their chivalry, too, and it is just because I appreciate that chivalry that I, as a woman, am anxious that it should be representative of the present and not only of the past—that it should be a progressive chivalry, equal to the needs and aspirations of the women of today, not content to give merely what was demanded of it in the old days.

Thirty-five states have given their hand and seal [in ratifying the federal amendment] but one is lacking. Will not the South give that one? Remember we are making a new world and women—mothers— long to have a share in the sort of world in which their children must live. We have moral courage and spiritual vision. Give us the chance to help you. . . .

Whether Lady Astor's plea had any real effect upon the legislators of Tennessee is questionable, but it helped drive home Catt's point: the whole world was watching.

Over the course of the weekend, as the opposing armies massed and the legislators assembled, the lobby of the Hotel Hermitage became the central gathering spot, the place to meet, talk and argue, cajole or confront friends and foes. It was neutral, but hardly tranquil, ground. The beaux arts grandeur of the space—its soaring marble columns and ornate vaulted ceiling, the swags, garlands, and rosettes carved into the wall borders, the Persian carpets below and cut-glass chandeliers above—gave a sense of both gravitas and gaiety to the animated conversations transpiring in the lobby. For more sensitive planning or clandestine plotting, the rattan chairs in the airy loggia or the dark banquettes of the lower-level (men only) Grill Room were favored.

By Saturday afternoon, the lobby was thrumming with conversation. Sun rays slanted through the painted glass skylight, bathing the room in a rosy glow, illuminating the puffs of tobacco smoke wafting above the feathered and flowered hats of ladies and the bare heads of linen-suited gentlemen. As viewed from above, from the balustrade of the lobby's mezzanine level, the number of Anti red roses seemed to multiply with each passing hour, swelling like a scarlet bloom of algae over the Tennessee marble floor tiles, overwhelming the smaller islands of yellow.

The Antis were descending upon Nashville in force. Mary Kilbreth, president of the National Association Opposed to Woman Suffrage, had come in from New York on the Saturday morning train, joining a brigade of Anti leaders landing throughout the day: Dolly Lamar from Macon, a leader of the Georgia Association Opposed to Woman Suffrage; Winifred Wyse of the Maryland antisuffrage organization; Frances Williams from Virginia; and Harriet Frothingham from Boston, president of the Massachu-

setts Antis, along with several of her associates. Beatrice Shillito, a leader of
the Ohio Antis, was comfortably settled into her room at the Hermitage and
had already delivered a rousing speech to an appreciative audience at Nashville's George Peabody College for Teachers. Dozens of Anti representatives
from other states were on the way. Expected on Sunday morning were Laura
Clay of Kentucky and Kate Gordon from New Orleans; their arrival promised to be especially delicious for the Antis.

Male antisuffragists, displaying all the chivalry expected of them, took
up their positions on the ramparts. Augmenting the team from the American Constitutional League who'd already arrived from New York and Baltimore were Ruffin Pleasant, former governor of Louisiana, and James
Pinckard of Alabama, joining their wives; Judge John Tyson of Montgomery
and Martin Lee Calhoun of Selma also made the trip. Two Maryland lawmakers traveled to Nashville on a mission to persuade their fellow lawmakers
to emulate Maryland in rejecting the amendment.

Besides these visitors, Tennessee's own Antis emerged from every corner
of the three Grand Divisions to make their way to Nashville. They were
heeding the call "To Arms, to Arms" that Josephine Pearson and her colleagues had issued earlier in the week, a summons presented in stirring verse:

> They are knocking, knocking, knocking,
> Knocking at your gate;
> Will you permit them entrance,
> Women of this state?
> Come, rally to our standard,
> Come show your pride of race;
> Beneath our unfurled banner,
> Come take your rightful place.

Everyone understood who "They" were. The call to arms was printed in
the state's major newspapers, mailed to sympathizers, and distributed
through clubs and churches. It reminded the citizens of Tennessee of the
larger issues at stake in this ratification fight: the threat that the federal
amendment posed to states' rights, the dangerous precedent of Negro
woman suffrage, and the frightening potential of racial equality. It asked
Tennesseans everywhere to don red roses to show their support and to gather

in Nashville beneath the Anti banner, the Stars and Bars that Nina Pinckard and Josephine Pearson had unfurled at the doors of their headquarters.

Those polished wood doors of Anti headquarters swung open at exactly five o'clock that Saturday afternoon for the welcoming reception. Josephine Pearson was a most gracious hostess, greeting her guests at the door while making sure the punch bowls were filled, the tea pitchers chilled, and the cookie trays replenished. Volunteer women from all the finest families in Nashville served as pourers and servers; the tables were beautifully appointed, and the room was decorated in the proper red floral hue. Nearly two hundred guests circulated around, chatting and quaffing, admiring the array of posters and broadsides, the assortment of informative brochures, and the museum exhibits.

There were, as promised, examples of the "force bills" that Congress could use to enforce the voting provisions of the Nineteenth Amendment, as well as, the Antis warned, the Fourteenth and Fifteenth Amendments. Congress had never yet exercised its power to protect black male voters from their blatant disenfranchisement in the southern states, but ratification might trigger a reassessment of that hands-off policy, the Anti materials warned, and "re-open the horrors of Reconstruction" when black men voted, and several even served in the Tennessee legislature. But the highlight of the exhibition was a dusty book, an 1895 first edition of Elizabeth Cady Stanton's *Woman's Bible*. It was a thick and homely tome whose bland exterior belied its power to provoke.

The book was Stanton's attempt to prove that the Bible, as interpreted by men and practiced by mainstream religions, had deliberately kept women in a subservient position, hindering their progress for millennia. Stanton had solicited contributions from women of different religious outlooks for this compendium of commentaries on Scripture with a feminist slant. She'd also invited suffrage leaders to contribute—including Carrie Catt—but most declined to participate in what they considered Mrs. Stanton's folly. In the end, Stanton wrote the majority of the commentaries herself, in her signature biting and entertaining style. So Carrie Catt was flabbergasted to find her name listed as a member of the book's "Revision Committee" when it was published; she'd never written a word for it.

The book had become a huge best seller in 1895 and a severe headache for the Suffs. It was, not surprisingly, denounced from the pulpit and in the press as the work of Satan. Stanton's position as honorary president of

NAWSA dragged the organization, against its will, into the squabble. The book's more blasphemous statements—that the Bible was not the Divine Word of God, but the creation of men, and that prayers ought to be addressed to "an ideal Heavenly Mother"—offended devout suffragists as well and spooked potential members, hurting the National Association's membership drives.

The younger women in the movement, including Catt, decided something must be done to limit the damage: at the next annual convention, they introduced a resolution denouncing *The Woman's Bible*, disassociating NAWSA from Stanton's book, and censuring its author. In addition, Catt insisted that her name be removed from subsequent editions. But the Antis had a first edition, and there it was, printed on the frontispiece of the volume in the ceremonial display. They labeled it "Mrs. Catt's Bible."

At the proper moment, Miss Pearson stepped onto a small raised platform to make the formal remarks of welcome. Her years as a teacher stood her in good stead now, as she effortlessly commanded her audience's attention. She saluted the guests of honor, all the visiting Anti leaders who'd come to defend Tennessee and the Southland. She led an ovation for the legislators wearing the red rose. She introduced the speakers, offering testimonials and pep talks. It was one of the most exciting moments of her life.

Nina Pinckard, Charlotte Rowe, and Mary Kilbreth spoke for the women Antis, exhorting antisuffragists of all stripes to join hands in defeating the amendment. Senator Walter Cameron of Marion County, near Chattanooga, spoke for those legislators who felt that it would violate their oath of office to vote on ratification in the special session. He'd voted for limited suffrage in 1919, he explained, but he would not vote to ratify the amendment. This was just the sort of switch the Suffs feared. There was spirited applause.

Another senator stood apart from the crowd, surveying the scene, listening to the speeches with only desultory interest. Lon McFarland was a lawyer who represented Wilson County in Middle Tennessee. Tall and dapper, favoring white linen suits, Panama hats, and string ties, he had a reputation for a sharp tongue and hot temper. He wasn't at all pleased about being dragged back to the statehouse in the middle of summer, and he didn't like being badgered about where he stood on ratification. He'd voted for limited suffrage in 1919, even supported it on the senate floor with a little speech saying that a man "would trust a woman with his name and his honor and with the rearing of his children, and there was no good reason why he should not trust her with the ballot." He was of two minds about this federal amendment. He could be persuaded by either side, but in any case, he wasn't going to broadcast his intentions, and on his lapel he wore his own small bicolored rosebud, tinged with both red and yellow petals. He enjoyed the look of confusion on people's faces when they saw it.

McFarland was not impressed with what he heard. As he strolled out of the party, the senator from the bluegrass horse country of central Tennessee was overheard to say: "That bunch of fillies was the longest on pedigree and the shortest on looks that I ever saw."

The Suffs stayed for the most part in their rooms, occasionally sending spies into the lobby who noticed one curious thing: as the evening wore on there was a steady exodus of men, wearing both red and yellow roses, from the Hermitage lobby, through the brass doors of the elevators, and up to the eighth floor. And they didn't come down. The Suffs were mystified.

Early on Sunday morning, August 8, aides to Governor Roberts bounded up the steps of the Capitol building for a scheduled strategy session with house Speaker Seth Walker. Roberts had appointed his young and progressive superintendent of public instruction, Albert Williams, to coordinate the administration's ratification efforts in the legislature. Williams, whose father had once been mayor of Nashville, supported woman suffrage for both idealistic and, as he called it, selfish reasons: in his experience, women cared more deeply about the education of their children, and if women could vote, they would likely make education a priority and force the state legislature to appropriate more money for schools. That was good for the children, good for the state, and also good for Williams's education department.

Williams eagerly accepted this tricky assignment from his boss, who, since winning the primary three days ago, seemed more enthusiastic about getting the federal amendment approved. It wasn't exactly a spiritual awakening, more of a political reckoning: Roberts realized that while he might have won the primary, his rival had won a goodly proportion of votes, the state Democrats were still fractured, and Republican Alf Taylor had made a strong showing. If he had any hope of winning the general election, he would need the support of the national Democratic Party and candidate Cox, and that meant proving to them that he was willing to put his own skin in the game to secure ratification, for the good of the party. Realistically, he also wanted the votes of Tennessee women, should the amendment go through, and he would gladly accept their electoral gratitude for championing their enfranchisement.

His closest advisers were still vehemently against ratification, arguing that his support for it was tantamount to political suicide. He would incur the wrath of not only the rabid states' rights and Bible-thumping folks, they screamed at him, but also powerful corporate interests, both within and out of the state, which viewed woman suffrage as a wrench thrown into the economic engines propelling the New South.

Roberts listened to his advisers' objections. Admittedly, they had some solid points, but he overruled them. Roberts knew what he had to do; he had to ram this ratification thing through the legislature. His protégé Seth Walker would carry the ball in the house, Andrew Todd would guide it through the senate, and Albert Williams would make sure it made it over the finish line. He had his team.

With the special session slated to open the next morning, Albert Williams had requested a meeting with Seth Walker to analyze the latest poll of the house: see where the various delegates stood, who might cause trouble, who needed convincing. In the last session, Walker, the governor's close ally, had adroitly maneuvered the administration's legislation, even the most contentious bills, smoothly through the chamber. He was a whiz at such things. And Walker was on board for ratification: he'd joined the Men's Ratification Committee, pledged to vote aye, and accepted the invitation to introduce the ratification resolution in the house, lending the prestige of the Speakership to the effort. Now the game plan needed to be perfected before the opening tomorrow, even if it was Sunday morning and everybody should be in church.

Williams and his deputies sat in the executive offices in the east wing of the Capitol building, going over the delegate lists, shooting the breeze, waiting for Walker to show. Walker was late. They waited for an hour and more. Finally, Walker marched in, flushed, agitated. He'd had a "change of conviction," he announced to a startled Williams. He'd decided to oppose ratification. And the governor was courting political disaster if he continued to support it.

With that, Seth Walker turned on his heel and walked out the door.

• • •

On Sunday afternoon, a caravan of forty shiny touring automobiles drove from the Hotel Hermitage out to Washington Hall, Mr. and Mrs. George Washington's country estate outside Nashville. The society pages of the newspapers called it a highlight of the summer social season. If women of refinement must be plunged, against their will, into the muck of politics, Queenie Washington and her hospitality committee believed, they should at least endeavor to retain the feminine social graces; an elegant garden party for the Antis was the proper thing to do.

The Washingtons' grand house was decorated with fragrant flowers from their garden, and the buffet table was graced by a bouquet of pink roses in a silver bowl. Among the guests sipping tea on the porch or strolling on the manicured lawns were many prominent Nashville ladies and gentlemen: sympathetic lawyers and businessmen, willing legislators, and all the distinguished Anti guests from out of state. Freshly arrived from Lexington was Laura Clay, whose charm and witticisms made her a popular conversation companion, and Kate Gordon, just off the train from New Orleans, both sporting red roses. They were the women Carrie Catt most dreaded encountering.

They were once her sisters in arms. Clay still treasured a photograph of herself standing together with Aunt Susan and the other "nieces" outside their mentor's Rochester home in 1900. The young women—including Clay, Carrie Catt, Harriet Upton, and Anna Shaw—NAWSA's new executive board, were poised to take over from Anthony, to lead the movement into its next phase. At the moment that photo was taken, Clay had already given almost twenty years of her life to the Cause and would devote nearly another two decades beyond. Her presence at the Anti garden party was a painful coda to a distinguished suffrage career.

Clay was the great gardener of southern suffrage, planting and nurturing suffrage societies in many states; she led the Kentucky suffragists for nearly a quarter of a century and became the leading southern voice within the executive council of the NAWSA. Gordon was a New Orleans public health activist who believed women's voice in government was the key to societal betterment. Both women were convinced that the South would accept woman suffrage only if it could be aligned with the region's larger political goals: regaining state sovereignty and retaining white social and political hegemony. The votes of white women could secure these goals.

Clay and Gordon urged NAWSA to adopt a "southern strategy" in promoting state-based woman suffrage, where local custom would determine how the franchise was achieved and implemented; if they chose to be racist, that was their decision. Catt, in her first term as president, acquiesced to this program in hopes of keeping the peace and softening the South for suffrage work. But in subsequent years, when Clay and Gordon (and several other southern suffragists) insisted that explicit white-women-only clauses be added to any suffrage proposals, the National Association, regaining a modicum of its moral fiber, rejected their policy demands. In response, Gordon and Clay created the Southern States Woman Suffrage Conference in 1913, promoting woman suffrage "as a solution to the race problem" with the franchise bestowed only by the states and only upon white women.

A secret sponsor of their new group was Alabama-born Alva Belmont, who wrote a big check and an encouraging note: she understood the "peculiar conditions" of her homeland and believed Clay and Gordon's approach might work in wringing woman suffrage from Dixie statehouses. Ironically, at the very same time, Belmont was also bankrolling Alice Paul's upstart Congressional Union; she was financing a state-suffrage-only approach with one hand and a federal-amendment-only goal with the other. Whatever might work. But the Southern Conference didn't last long.

When hope, and work, for the federal amendment was revived in 1916, Clay and Gordon were dismayed. They wanted the ballot, but they wanted it their way. On the day the U.S. Senate finally passed the amendment in June 1919, Clay resigned from both the National Association and the Kentucky suffrage organizations, and she and Gordon turned their energies toward thwarting ratification. Six weeks before, in June, they'd joined forces to fight ratification in Louisiana, where their awkward alliance with die-hard Antis, the ones who hated the idea of women voting at all, proved successful, even if distasteful. That same alliance was now assembled in Tennessee, and they were all sipping lemonade together on Mrs. Washington's lawn.

Queenie Washington stood on the top step of her porch to thank her guests for coming. This was an exciting time, she told them, and, at last, the Antis were poised for victory. And, she said, smiling, she had more happy news: the Southern Women's Rejection League had just received a cable from Governor Cox granting them a meeting! Following the garden party, she and Mary Kilbreth, as well as Nina Pinckard and a small delegation, would be boarding the night train to Dayton and meeting with Cox the following day. They would convince him to throw his weight toward defeating ratification!

Before the party ended, Mrs. Washington assembled a group of Rejection League women and their guests for a family portrait, posed on the porch steps of Washington Hall. Josephine Pearson was given a place of honor in the front row, alongside Nina Pinckard and Mary Kilbreth, near Laura Clay and Kate Gordon. Men in summer suits stood among the throng of women, and some of the more daring younger ladies sat perched, cross-legged, on the porch's stone parapet.

They all looked very happy. The most exciting news—that of Seth Walker's defection to their side—was not yet public and couldn't be celebrated at the garden party. But there were surely a few guests who knew all about it and had good reason to smile for the camera.

In the moments following Seth Walker's stunning reversal and abrupt departure from the Capitol, Albert Williams and his staff seemed shell-shocked. They slowly gathered their wits and phoned the governor at home. Roberts and Williams spent the rest of the day figuring out what to do, how to respond, how to control the damage. They tried to reach Walker, to reason with him, but his mind was set. Whatever—or whoever—had caused Walker to so suddenly change his "conviction" wasn't clear, and without a firm grasp of the rationale, the governor didn't have much leverage to threaten or force him back into line.

Roberts and Williams knew they had to keep a lid on all this, keep it from circulating around town, and certainly keep it from the press as long as possible. It was embarrassing, a demonstration that the governor was not in control of his allies, much less the legislature; it was a sign of his weakness. How could he explain this to Cox or to President Wilson? He needed time to think things through, to come up with an alternate plan. But this had to be the worst time and the worst place—a city crawling with political operatives and journalists—to try to keep a secret.

By evening, the governor's efforts to win back Seth Walker had come to naught and his normally scowling face—he rarely smiled—took on a look of abject dismay. His anxiety soaked through the words of the telegram he sent that night to Charl Ormond Williams, the Memphis schools' superintendent who'd recently been named vice chair of the DNC's Executive

Committee. Charl Williams was in Dayton (she'd attended Cox's acceptance speech on Saturday) and was about to depart for Nashville to help in the ratification fight. Before she stepped onto the train, Roberts asked her to deliver an urgent message to Cox:

> Suffrage situation very critical. Amendment will fail unless every possible effort is made to adopt it. Powerful organizations actively fighting it. It seems that the whole fight has centered here, and I suggest that you apprise Gov. Cox of the critical situation and of the necessity for doing everything possible. Certain influences here are making the fight very difficult.

"Certain influences" had gotten to Seth Walker. The governor braced himself: How many other legislators would follow Walker into the Anti camp?

On Sunday night, with the opening of the special session just hours away, the Chief faced her nervous field commanders. Assembled in her Hermitage suite for an intense strategy and intelligence briefing were the directors of all the different ratification committees—the Democratic women, Republican women, the Men's Committee, and the League of Women Voters. Anne Dudley, Harriet Upton, and Marjorie Shuler were there, too. Sue White was not.

White viewed her position in Nashville as the ambassador of an autonomous organization, a sovereign power, distinct from the workings of NAWSA. She would cooperate and coordinate with the National Association Suffs as necessary, but she would fly the Woman's Party's own flag and take direction only from Miss Paul. Even if she'd been invited to Mrs. Catt's room for the briefing, she would have refused.

The Chief took charge, acting as the professor-cum-general. She assumed both roles naturally, from long practice, always the teacher. She'd long ago established training schools for suffrage organizers around the country, and that summer tens of thousands of women were reading her syndicated "Mrs. Catt's Citizenship School" lessons in local newspapers, providing instructions on the workings of government and the democratic process, preparing women for the vote. Now she had to prepare her warriors to win the vote.

Catt reviewed the overall strategy: to maintain pressure on the presidential candidates and national parties, lean on state party leaders, keep close tabs on the legislators, and push for a quick ratification vote, while the delegates still remembered their pledges and before they could be enticed to change. "We are ready for a vote," Catt had told reporters earlier in the evening. "Enough men have promised to vote for ratification to put it over and there is no necessity for delay." The Antis, she understood, would be throwing every possible obstacle and motion to delay into the amendment's path. "If the Tennessee solons stand by their pledges, ratification of the 19th Federal Amendment is certain," Catt told the press. "I believe the favorable poll will stand."

But the women gathered in Mrs. Catt's room on Sunday night were, with reason, worried about that qualifier: *if.* The Tennessee Suffs had spent the weekend assiduously socializing, greeting the delegates at the train station, chatting up the politicos in the Hermitage lobby. They were hearing things—rumors, gossip, inside information—that disturbed them: about men changing their minds, planning to renege on their pledges, pledging both ways, or fixing to not vote at all. The reporters circulating around town were hearing these murmurs, too, and were writing cryptic allusions to "mysterious influences" and "certain vague, nameless forces." These forces, the papers said, "are reputed to have the unlimited financial backing of certain interests, which are opposed on principle and through interest to woman suffrage."

Anne Dudley did her best to neutralize all the dark, spooky rumors swirling around the city on Sunday, emphasizing her faith in the integrity of the Tennessee legislature: "Knowing its personnel as I do, and the high standard of the great majority of its members," Dudley told reporters, "I feel no hesitancy in saying that in a question involving the national honor, as this question of political freedom for women undoubtedly does, they will vote aye."

Pshaw! countered the Antis. "We know that pledges extracted under coercion and over-persuasion have no direct value," Nina Pinckard told the *Banner.* "A man will sometimes pledge a woman, as he would marry her, just to get rid of her."

On the eve of the legislature's convening, Sue White was trying hard to project the image of a calm and courageous commander, someone unfazed by the heat of the fight, the model Woman's Party warrior. But she struggled to hide her terror. White was staying in the Hermitage now, to be closer to the center of action, and from her room she wrote her daily round-up report and wired it to Miss Paul: "Speakers Walker and Todd will introduce resolution. . . . Republican Caucus called tomorrow, ten o'clock. . . . Nobody will say how bulk of Republicans will vote. . . . Some reports antis using money, and other reports that pledged men will not all show up. . . . If Republican caucus not favorable only desperate chance winning as Governor's forces doing nothing." The Suffs did not yet know of Seth Walker's betrayal.

Downstairs, in the Hermitage lobby, a strange sort of beauty pageant was under way. Anti headquarters had been alerted that the prettiest young Suffs were being deployed to mingle with the legislators in the lobby, and they were, as one reporter put it, "clad in the daintiest creations of the modiste and evidently making an impression." Alarmed, the Antis summoned a bevy of their own comely supporters, "all dressed and dolled to the limits of present-day fashions," to counter the Suffs' onslaught of pulchritude. Legislators certainly did not mind being caught in this middle, cajoled by cute representatives of both sides, and the Hermitage lobby was a smoky paradise for the uncommitted lawmaker.

The meeting in Mrs. Catt's room continued, as she delved into the details of the battle plan. Each woman would be assigned to track certain legislators. The local women who had gone out into the field to pledge the delegates of their districts would continue to ride herd on them. Leaders of the various ratification committees would act as liaisons to the men who answered to their constituency. And only Tennessee women were to lobby the legislators, attend sessions in the galleries, or even set foot in the statehouse. The Suffs under Catt's command agreed that they would present a 100 percent Tennessee-pure face in the Capitol; only those who possessed the proper Volunteer State pedigree and spoke with the correct regional drawl would be placed in the front lines. Mrs. Catt and Mrs. Upton agreed to remain in the background, "consulting specialists," as they were called. They would not venture to the statehouse at all, lest their presence be distracting and play into the Antis' hands.

Sue White's plan was very different. As a native daughter, she would be right out there on the firing line, on the floor of the chambers, but she also needed Pollitzer and Gram and Flanagan to guard their assigned men, whether they were Tennesseans or not. And Miss Paul, when she arrived, would definitely want to lead the charge in the statehouse herself. If Paul's presence inflamed the situation, so be it, White thought, but Miss Paul must come.

"Wish greatly you were here," White pleaded with Paul, "and if situation not more favorable after Republican caucus would insist on your coming to take hold if possible."

The strategy session in Catt's room ran long and late. The apprehensive suffragists went to bed after midnight, but few could sleep; they were kept awake by singing. All through the night the warbling voices of drunken legislators, some wearing red roses, some yellow, floated through the Hermitage hallways. The men had been enjoying themselves on the eighth floor of the hotel, where Anti lobbyists were pouring free Tennessee whiskey and old bourbon—including the local favorite, Jack Daniel's "in the raw"—in what came to be dubbed the Jack Daniel's Suite.

Chapter 17

◆ ◆ ◆

In Justice to Womanhood

On Monday morning, Anita Pollitzer and Catherine Flanagan herded the East Tennessee Republican delegation into Nashville. They hopped off the Knoxville special express train ahead of their flock and silently counted straw boater-hatted heads as the men filed out of the railroad car. They made sure no one slipped away.

Besides the contingent of East Division legislators, the women had rounded up an impressive collection of Republican political elders, including Alf Taylor, the newly minted gubernatorial nominee; Jesse Littleton, his defeated opponent; Congressman J. William Taylor; and former Tennessee governor Ben Hooper, who'd long been a friend of the Tennessee Suffs. Pollitzer was flashing her most beguiling smile as reporters approached her and her group on the platform. Brushing off the dust and cinders of the locomotive smoke and the fatigue of the journey, she looked remarkably fresh and fashionable in her flower-patterned organdy dress and her black hat trimmed with cornflowers. The reporters marveled at her entourage of heavyweight Republicans and she couldn't suppress her delight.

"These gentlemen, who do not belong to the legislature, came with us to help put suffrage over," she said, gesturing toward Hooper, Taylor, and Littleton with a grin. "They were a little shy of us when we first appeared in the mountains to solicit their aid, but now they eat out of our hands. They are suffragists."

Betty Gram puffed into Union Station on Monday morning, too, on board the overnight train carrying the Memphis and Shelby County delegation. Hers was an equally impressive constellation of West Tennessee Democrats, which included the mayor of Memphis, Rowlett Paine; Thomas Riddick, elected to the Tennessee House of Representatives specifically to help lead ratification efforts; and Joe Hanover, who had easily regained his house seat. Charl Williams and a large League of Women Voters group were also on the train, and the Memphis region's broad enthusiasm for ratification, encouraged by Mr. Crump, was displayed by the assortment of men's civic club representatives aboard. The Rotary, Lions, Kiwanis, American Legion, and Memphis City Club had all passed resolutions supporting ratification and sent delegates to lobby in Nashville.

U.S. senator Kenneth McKellar had already arrived in the city and immediately conferred with Carrie Catt. Her observations: The state Democrats seemed weak-kneed, the governor's strength puny, and Cox ineffectual. And she was hearing more rumors about the governor's men trying to sabotage the amendment. McKellar had better break out his whip to get his party men in line, she advised. She had no illusions about how political muscle was flexed. "I am here to do what I can for ratification and believe we will win," McKellar assured reporters after his consult with Catt. "There is an overwhelming sentiment in Tennessee for suffrage."

All through the weekend, porters had been cleaning and polishing, mopping floors and dusting desks, sweeping out the cobwebs of months of adjournment. Early on Monday, women took over the chores of readying the Capitol, both Suffs and Antis decorating the corridors with their own colors and regalia. The Capitol corridors looked more like a frenzied bazaar than any august halls of government, filled with vendors hawking their political wares. The Suffs tacked yellow bunting and banners to the walls and railings. The Antis lugged boxes of artificial red roses up the grand marble staircase, intended for the lapels of willing legislators and other sympathizers.

Mrs. Edwin Forbes, a stately, white-haired Boston Brahmin from the Massachusetts Anti organization, spent the morning poised with a red rose and pin, ready to pounce on every man who entered the building. As she attempted each conquest, she would point to the banner hanging on the wall above her head, a fabric rendition of the Southern Women's Rejection League motto: "We serve that our states may live, and living, preserve the Union."

Such a spectacle of women in the Capitol had never been seen before, and while some legislators were annoyed by the commotion, and others appeared befuddled, quite a few seemed to like it just fine. NATION WATCHES SOLONS; SOLONS WATCHING LADIES, was the headline in the day's *Memphis News-Scimitar*, and the reporter noted that "the eyes of legislators are upon the ladies, because they are fearful in wrath, and because some of them really are fair to look upon." The suffrage women who had canvassed the delegates in their home districts were assigned to watch over them in Nashville, and the diligent women tagged after their representatives at every turn. "The legislators are having the time of their gay young lives," the *News-Scimitar* writer observed. "They like to be lobbied with and everything. There are types of feminine lobbyists with argument, looks, and style to suit the most fastidious solon from the rural districts of the commonwealth."

At ten o'clock, the Republicans gathered for their caucus in a Hotel Hermitage meeting room. Herschel Candler, as state senate caucus chairman, presided, and he sat impassively as seven state party leaders took turns putting the ratification issue squarely to the members, with varying degrees of ardor and candor. Ben Hooper, who boasted of being the first southern governor to request his state legislature give women the vote, back in 1915, led off the series of presentations, followed by a string of East Tennessee party luminaries.

There were solid, practical reasons for Republicans to back ratification, they all emphasized. The party's minority position in the legislature could be worked to advantage: if the seven state senate Republicans and twenty-seven party members in the house voted together as a bloc, they had the power to swing the vote in each chamber, wresting credit from the splintered Democrats and turning Tennessee into a Republican suffrage victory. Good for the fall elections. At this point, Harriet Upton, ambassador from the Republican National Committee, read aloud the telegram she had received from Harding the night before, his version of a pep talk:

"You may say for me to Republican members of the General Assembly of Tennessee, that it will be highly pleasing to have the Republicans of that state play their full and becoming part in consummating the constitutional grant of women suffrage." Upton managed to read Harding's overripe prose with a straight face. "It is no longer a question of policy; it is a matter of Republican contribution to a grant of suffrage to which our party is committed and for which our party is in the main responsible."

Whatever their personal feelings or constitutional qualms, Hooper and the others told the Republicans, uniting for ratification was simply a smart move in an election year. It would put Alf Taylor in good position to defeat Roberts in November, too. When the ratification pitches were completed, Herschel Candler glanced around the room. "You have heard those in favor, is there anyone opposed?" he asked. No one responded. Candler himself made no arguments, but his colleagues knew very well where he stood.

Harry Burn sat toward the back, just listened, and did not speak. He admired Herschel Candler as an excellent lawyer and a judicious man, and

Burn was reading law under Candler's tutelage. A young, ambitious East Tennessee fellow could not find a better model or mentor than Herschel Candler, and Burn found the older man (Candler was just forty) to be unfailingly generous. Burn was probably impressed with the way Candler was handling this awkward meeting, too, using dry chill instead of expressive heat to shape the result.

The party leaders had come into the meeting aiming to nail down a unified Republican bloc to ratify, or at least a majority to pledge, but noting Candler's stony silence and the distinct lack of enthusiasm in the room, they backed off. The latest poll of the legislature's thirty-four Republicans counted thirteen supporting ratification, ten standing against it, and eleven still noncommittal, and few minds seemed to have been changed by this morning's meeting. It was obvious that more work, more vigorous prodding, was needed. Rather than risk a negative result, the Republican leaders adjourned. They had failed.

Anita Pollitzer was crestfallen. This was just the scenario she and Sue White had feared; there were evidently forces strong enough to embolden the Antis in the Republican delegation. Without the Republicans, there was no hope for a coalition ratification majority. A telegram swiftly went out to Alice Paul in Washington: "Please come at once, we need you badly."

While the Republicans were caucusing in the Hermitage, the Tennessee suffragists were attempting a unity conclave in the executive wing of the statehouse with Governor Roberts and his deputy Albert Williams. The governor laid out the situation: all the different ratification committees the Democratic suffragists had created were confusing to the legislators and allowed the men to shade their ratification stances depending upon which group they were answering. There needed to be a single, unified, Democratic Suff woman voice. Enough of tribal factionalism, the governor implored. Carrie Catt could only nod in exasperated agreement.

The rifts and rivalries she thought had been suppressed were back. Before the primary election, while the Roberts and anti-Roberts groups were still at loggerheads, she'd forced the heads of each ratification committee to sign a public letter forswearing any political partisanship and affirming their dedication to the single goal of ratification. Little good that had done.

Now that the primary was decided, and the Roberts camp victorious, the governor's allies were keen to extract some revenge on the Luke Lea–affiliated Suffs who'd plotted to defeat him. They were unwilling to deal with Abby

Milton or Catherine Kenny on ratification matters any longer. A more neutral, acceptable woman must be found, the Roberts allies insisted, ideally someone who hadn't been tangled in the internecine suffrage feuds of the past or the fisticuffs of the primary. That someone, the meeting agreed, was Memphis schools superintendent Charl Williams. She was the newly anointed vice chair of the Democratic National Committee and an ally of Boss Crump. Williams was named director of a new Democratic women's steering committee. Catt was glad for the gesture of unity, and she was told that Williams was an able administrator and conciliator, but Williams's inexperience in high-level, high-stakes legislative maneuvering made Catt a bit nervous.

Governor Roberts was pleased by the spirit of cooperation, and he promised the women he'd do everything in his power to win ratification. He just didn't tell them that Seth Walker had deserted them, double-crossed him, and made the whole ratification business much more difficult. It was up to Walker, damn him, to tell them that himself. Walker was no longer under Governor Roberts's power.

Shortly past noon Andrew Todd rapped his gavel, calling the Tennessee Senate into extraordinary session. At the same time, on the south side of the Capitol, Seth Walker pounded his gavel, bringing the House of Representatives to order. The chaplains offered prayers, and the clerks called the roll. There were quite a few empty desks, names called with no response of "Present," but a bare quorum was counted in each chamber, so the business of the day could begin.

Thomas Riddick, Joe Hanover, and the other freshly elected members were called up to take their oaths of office, the same oath some considered to be in dire jeopardy. They raised their hands, swore to uphold the Constitution of the State of Tennessee, as well as the Constitution of the United States, and sat down. The visitor galleries above the chamber floors were packed, mostly with women, but also with a healthy sprinkling of men. The Suffs were more energetic in their decorating, draping yellow cloths and flowers around the balconies, and yellow-flowered breasts outnumbered red ones in the rows. Clusters of women filled the doorways, both on the floor level and in the balconies, and both women and men were on the floor, circulating among the desks of the legislators, defying all rules of lobbying decorum.

Legislative item number one was consideration of the Nineteenth Amendment, and the next few dealt with establishing a process for women to register to vote, pay a poll tax, and other legal requirements. In addition, there were more than 140 other issues to address, a laundry list of state and local considerations that the governor had included as a special session sweetener, enabling the legislators to return home with a little gift for their constituents. The Suffs had qualms about all these other bills on the docket distracting the lawmakers and gumming up the works, perhaps purposefully so, but it was out of their hands.

Now came the ritual pageantry, the formal transmittal of the federal amendment from the governor to the legislature. Todd and Walker each ordered the clerks of their chambers to read aloud the governor's official submission of the amendment and his accompanying message to the legislature. Both Suffs and Antis held their breath slightly as the clerks began their recitations, as neither side knew just what the governor intended to say to the lawmakers or how strongly he would choose to say it.

To the Suffs' pleasant surprise, the governor offered an exuberant argument for ratification, urging the legislature to approve the amendment promptly. "Tennessee occupies a pivotal position on this question," he reminded the delegates. "The eyes of all America are upon us. Millions of women are looking to the Tennessee legislature to give them a voice and share in shaping the destiny of the republic." The lawmakers had an obligation to their constituents, the governor said, but also to their state and national party platforms: "Both parties have clearly and unequivocally declared for the ratification of this amendment," he told them. "But there is another and higher ground on which ratification may be made to depend, upon the ground of justice to the womanhood of America."

This was stronger stuff than the Suffs had expected. Roberts tackled the constitutional questions head-on, presenting the opinion of the Tennessee attorney general that acting upon ratification was legal and no legislator would be abrogating his oath of office. He covered all the bases, and his message conveyed a true sense of mission, even passion, a rare emotion for Albert Roberts to display: "I submit this issue to you as perhaps the most far-reaching and momentous one on which any body of men has been called to pass since the establishment of our government."

Seth Walker listened from the Speaker's leather chair, elevated on a rostrum at the front of the house chamber. Behind him was a bunting of stars and stripes, and above his head a bronze sculpted eagle watched over the assembly. Walker listened to the governor's message without showing any emotion or agitation. Only his gray eyes moved, surveying the room: a low gaze across the floor, where his colleagues sat, a flick of his vision upward to take in the partisans in the galleries. Walker was dignified and in control, methodically conducting his speakership responsibilities without a word about his change of heart.

According to the rules of the legislature, after the joint resolution to consider the Nineteenth Amendment was introduced, it would "lay over" in each chamber for a day and then be referred to the appropriate committee for consideration and recommendation. But the resolution wasn't introduced into the house. The delay was blamed on a clerical error: the governor hadn't attached the actual resolution document to his message, and without that piece of paper there was nothing to introduce. As it happens, this was a very convenient mistake for Speaker Walker, allowing him to delay the proceedings for a day, giving him extra time to quietly consolidate his forces.

On the senate side, Speaker Todd had to stall so as not to fall out of sync with the house. The only mention of ratification came when Lon McFarland brought greetings from the Maryland legislature and asked that it be read into the record. This "memorial" had been given to McFarland by the distinguished chairman of the Maryland Senate's Judiciary Committee, Senator George Arnold Frick, who'd led the successful effort to defeat ratification of the Nineteenth Amendment in his state legislature and sat in the senate chamber this morning as McFarland's guest. The message, signed by several dozen members of the Maryland General Assembly, asked their brother legislators of the Volunteer State to follow their lead in rejecting: Do not impose the federal amendment upon your kindred southern states, the Marylanders begged. Both chambers of the General Assembly adjourned until the next morning, taking no action on ratification. The Suffs groaned quietly.

Watching the proceedings, veteran Capitol Hill beat reporters privately told their fellow newspapermen: "Ratification doesn't have a chance."

The statehouse paralysis on Monday only shifted the political action to other arenas. The door to Governor Roberts's office swung open and shut constantly, with people crossing the threshold, in and out, all afternoon and evening. It was during this string of entrances and exits that the Democratic ratification leaders from Memphis—McKellar and Riddick—were slammed with the news of Seth Walker's defection.

Governor Roberts was forced to explain things to McKellar, who was enraged but also adamant that Walker's turnabout not derail ratification and endanger his own standing among national Democrats. McKellar and Riddick flew into action: they had to find a new legislative path before morning. McKellar made the rounds of Democratic delegates, while Riddick, still in his very first day as a member of the General Assembly, gathered together the Shelby County delegation. Before supper, he'd signed on all the Shelby representatives in the house to introduce the joint resolution on Tuesday morning. They would, as a group, take the place of Seth Walker.

Roberts told his advisers, his allies, and his political friends that he'd be defeated in the fall if he didn't secure ratification for the women; they told him he'd be defeated if he did. Roberts barely had time to catch his breath, and all the message slips on his desk reading "Call Gov. Cox" had accumulated into quite a pile. But there would be nothing to report until things were straightened out, in better shape. Roberts was using his time and energy to mend the gaping hole left by Walker's defection and to stop the rip from enlarging. Cox didn't need to know.

Hoisting umbrellas, both Suff and Anti women moved through the rain from the Capitol building to the Hermitage and ventured into the other hotels and cafés where legislators could be found. While they were busy buttonholing and beguiling, Mrs. Catt remained in her suite at the Hermitage, enmeshed in her own meetings, as both suffragist and political leaders came to consult with her. She was disturbed by the day's developments—the delay in introducing the resolution, the stalemate in the Republican caucus—and alarmed by more reports of mysterious men circulating among the legislators in the Hermitage lobby. It seemed these men did their business wearing camouflage, pretending to various names and professions. She was told they were slimy salesmen, fast-talking the legislators on the need to stymie ratification. Who sent them, no one knew. They were the sinister influences made incarnate, Catt was certain.

She handwrote a letter to Republican National Committee chairman Will Hays, warning him that Republicans seemed to be mixed up in all this. She sent the letter to her office in New York to be typed and delivered directly to Hays; she didn't want to dictate or wire this message from Nashville, it was too delicate.

"Outside people have supported a campaign here against consideration of the amendment upon the ground that if the legislature takes no action, there can be no question of constitutionality or violation of oath," she told Hays. "As many of the legislature are men of little mental training they are confused in their thinking by the conflict of legal opinion and think no action is a safe and sane escape. Curiously enough the Republicans have allowed themselves to be conspicuously connected with this attempt." The failure in that morning's Republican caucus certainly seemed to bear this out.

One of those outsiders was a man going by the name of Thomas Keith, who was hanging around the Hermitage and the Capitol. He said he represented the Acme newspaper syndicate, with interests in New York, Connecticut, and Vermont. He hinted that he was sent to Tennessee by the national Republican Party; his story changed daily. He talked a lot about the need to defeat the amendment. The Suffs found him suspicious enough that Catt had already engaged a private detective in New York to investigate Keith and get to the bottom of his mission. "I have a man on the job and will report when and if I can chase the thing down," Catt promised Hays in the hard-boiled lingo of her favorite detective novels.

As the special session got under way, a deputation of Anti women from Nashville were chugging toward Ohio, on their way to confront James Cox at his Dayton estate, Trails End. Cox's house was very different from Warren Harding's classic of American design; Cox's home was a sprawling, twenty-room French Renaissance–style mansion, definitely on the showy side. When the delegation finally arrived, they were ushered into Cox's study. He'd had a hectic few days, as he prepared for his first campaign swing. Warren Harding might hide all summer on his front porch, but Jimmy Cox was going out to the people, fighting for the League of Nations. Cox was consumed by meetings with his campaign staff and with Democratic Party officials; he was writing his stump speeches and recording the best ones on phonograph discs for distribution. The campaign was officially launched, and people were rallying round: one hundred prominent Democratic women had already signed on to stump for the Cox-FDR ticket. (Of course, if ratification failed in Democratic Tennessee, those women might not be too enthusiastic about stumping, Cox fretted.)

Cox was also looking forward to seeing his name up in lights. Soon thousands of electric signs, constructed by the new Cox Electric League, a group of electrical workers around the country donating their expertise to the campaign, would blaze from windows and rooftops. The signs were the ultimate in high-tech electioneering, consisting of a circle of bulbs with an X-shape of lights within: half of the circle would be illuminated into the letter "C," then the full circle would light up to spell an "O," and then the "X" would flash out his name. This gizmo was going to make Cox a household name. Cox was also getting himself in shape for the rigors of the campaign trail by taking brisk morning rides on his stallion, the Governor, galloping after rabbits for two hours before breakfast. He was fit and ready. He was not, however, particularly eager to meet his evening guests, the ladies of the Association Opposed and the Rejection League.

The women made their case, and Cox listened, for more than an hour. They asked that he use all his influence to defeat ratification in Tennessee, and if he could not promise that, he should at least stay out of the fight, exert no pressure on the legislature. Remember, they told him, states' rights was a sacred doctrine in the Democratic Party. They emphasized the states' rights rather than the woman's proper-sphere arguments of the Anti arsenal, perhaps realizing that they themselves were paying a political lobbying call. Cox asked questions and engaged in a polite exchange, but he ended the meeting without revealing his decision. He bade the ladies good night. At six o'clock the next morning, reporters caught Cox as he mounted the Governor for his morning ride. He told them he was standing pat on his decision to work for Tennessee's ratification.

Very well, then, Governor, was the Anti women's disappointed reply. This was obviously not the Democratic Party of their fathers: first Woodrow Wilson and now James Cox seemed very willing to desert the party's principles for cheap political expediency. The Anti delegation boarded the next train to Nashville, feeling miffed but certainly not defeated.

On Monday evening, in preparation for the next day's session, the Suffs approached Walker to review the latest poll of house members. That's when he revealed himself. No, he told them, he would not be introducing or sponsoring the ratification resolution. What's more, he could not support—or vote for—ratification. He told them this in a very matter-of-fact fashion, as if he were explaining a sudden whim to change the color of his tie. Then he departed. Once again, he gave his dumbfounded listeners no chance to respond, much less argue.

The shock waves of Walker's defection radiated outward in widening circles, knocking the Suffs off balance. Sue White and Betty Gram took it especially hard, as Walker had pledged to them personally. They had believed him; they felt like fools. In Mrs. Catt's room that night, the Suffs' strategy meeting was an angry affair. They railed against Walker, but they blamed Roberts and Cox. Roberts must have known his ally was planning this trickery; perhaps, the Suffs insinuated, he'd even encouraged it. In any case, he did not seem to be lifting a finger to stop it. And Cox surely must have known of Walker's desertion, too. (He probably didn't; Roberts hadn't told him.)

Catt tried to calm the rattled Tennessee Suffs, focusing their attention on what needed to be done to recover. She'd experienced this type of political betrayal so many times before; she was disgusted, but she wasn't surprised. She'd tried to warn them, right at the outset, that this sort of underhanded thing could, and probably would, happen in Nashville.

"We have long since recovered from our previous faith in the action of men based upon a love of justice," she'd told the Tennessee Suffs. "That is an animal that doesn't exist."

It was a rough night and a raw morning for the suffragists. Anxiety invaded their sleep, as did the noisy carousing of inebriated legislators in the hallways of the Hermitage. Sue White worked deep into the night with McKellar, Riddick, and Charl Williams, crunching the latest polling numbers of legislators' pledges, which appeared to be slipping. Anne Dudley babysat the joint resolution, making sure it was drafted correctly, every *t* crossed and *i* dotted in proper legal form, lest it be challenged. She also made sure that enough fair copies were printed so there could be no clerical mishaps again. Anita Pollitzer stayed up late with the Republican leaders, helping them to compose an SOS message to Harding and Hays. Then she was back at work well before sunrise on Tuesday, dispatching anxious telegrams to Alice Paul in Washington and Abby Baker in Ohio.

"Republican situation really fearful," she wired. "Hooper, Taylor, others working with me every minute, but we cannot get the men without national aid. Do not tell anyone."

She surreptitiously forwarded the text of the Republicans' fresh plea to Harding, containing their bleak assessment: "There are 3 Republican senators and 11 representatives strongly against us," the Tennessee Republicans informed Harding and named the men they knew to be pitted against ratification, including Finney Carter and Herschel Candler in the senate and

Representatives C. F. Boyer, H. T. Burn, and E. O. Luther. (It certainly pained Pollitzer to see the names of the East Tennessee men she'd personally lobbied, and thought she'd pledged, appear on this roll.) "They are all good party men," the Republican leaders told Harding, and they begged him to intervene. A less guarded note was sent to Will Hays, demanding he send a strong RNC man down to Nashville: Mrs. Upton was useless; the legislators considered her just a suffragist, not a Republican. They needed a respected party man who could knock heads in Nashville. "Please keep this in absolute confidence," Pollitzer insisted in her wire. "We must get national pressure . . . or all definitely lost."

By breakfast, the bleary-eyed Suffs were hit with another concussive blow from Seth Walker. He announced he intended to lead the opposition to the amendment on the house floor. He would "go down the line" to defeat the amendment, using his power as Speaker to bring as many house members with him as he could. And, he let it be known, he planned to refer the ratification resolution to a hostile committee.

The fallout was captured in a news story: "Speculation was rife as to what influence his move would have on other members of the lower body." No one had to speculate for very long: within hours five members of the house, previously pledged to ratify, were reported to have followed their Speaker to the Anti side.

The Antis could now openly call Seth Walker their friend and champion and chortle a bit when they did. They also received glad tidings from their co-workers in North Carolina: that state would definitely not ratify. The legislature had just convened, the governor was giving mixed, but mostly negative, signals, and the prospects for ratification were satisfyingly slim. Senator George Frick of Maryland was gleeful, telling reporters in Nashville: "If we hold Tennessee, the Amendment will never be ratified. The sentiment is turning against it."

At ten o'clock, Seth Walker stood on the Speaker's rostrum of the house, his left hand lifting the gavel, then swinging it down sharply to bring the session to order. In the senate chamber, Andrew Todd went through the same motion. The senator from Murfreesboro had never been a friend of suffrage; he'd voted against limited suffrage the year before, but he'd promised local suffrage leaders and state Democratic Party officials that he'd support ratification this time, even introduce the resolution into the senate. They had been burned by those types of vows before so were appropriately wary, but Todd did stand up and introduce Senate Joint Resolution #1 that morning. In the house, Walker sat calmly in his elevated chair while the six men of the Shelby County delegation rose to sponsor House Joint Resolution #1 in that chamber. The Suffs in the galleries murmured softly with relief. Both resolutions, in accordance to the rules, were laid over until the following day. The gavels in both chambers rapped adjournment. The battle resumed outside.

Betty Gram glimpsed the traitorous Seth Walker across the Hermitage lobby and headed over to challenge him: Was it true that he was going to violate his pledge to her and oppose ratification? she asked him. Walker appeared startled. People in the lobby turned to listen. Walker recovered his wits: "I'd let the old Capitol crumble and fall from the hill before I'd vote for ratification," he said boastfully. "I'm going to do all I can to influence friends to vote No."

Summoning her dramatic talents, Gram continued the interrogation: "What has brought about the change against the suffrage amendment in the house—the governor or the Louisville and Nashville Railroad?" she demanded loudly. "What kind of a crook are you anyway—a Roberts crook or an L&N crook?" Onlookers gasped.

"How dare you charge me with such a thing!" Walker bellowed. "That is an insult!"

Betty Gram only smiled. "Why, I am just asking you for information," she replied in a tone of mock girlish innocence. Visibly shaken, Walker stormed off. It was a moment of sweet revenge. But it might be costly.

Reporters, scurrying around to cover the fast-breaking events, demanded Carrie Catt's reaction to Seth Walker's defection. The Chief stuck to her strategy script. You must not let the public sense weakness or the enemy smell fear; that was a lesson she'd learned long ago. She declared that her poll was unshaken: "When I came to Tennessee three weeks ago I announced that a majority of both Senate and House were pledged to vote for ratification. No development has overturned that majority," she maintained. "I have absolute confidence in the integrity of the legislators of Tennessee and believe that they will stand by their pledges."

Catt was daring the legislators to prove their integrity. But in the corridors and stairwells of the statehouse, and in the parlors and alcoves of the Hermitage, the Suffs were learning that those pledges were not so much standing firm as keeling over. With little else to occupy their time, quite a few legislators adjourned to the Jack Daniel's Suite, the invitation-only speakeasy operating inside an eighth-floor room of the Hermitage, where hospitable hosts filled their glasses with forbidden liquors and filled their ears with persuasive arguments for why the Susan B. Anthony Amendment was bad for Tennessee.

Tennessee had been a "dry" state since 1909, at least on paper, and had enthusiastically ratified the national prohibition amendment in 1919. Many Suffs, and even some Antis, ardent prohibitionists themselves, asked why the law was not being enforced on the eighth floor of the Hermitage. "In Tennessee whiskey and legislation go hand in hand," they were told, "especially when controversial questions are urged. This is the Tennessee way," and Tennessee revered its traditions.

Nina Pinckard, the Southern Women's Rejection League president, was standing under the graceful high arches of the Capitol's second floor, engaged in intense discussion with a legislator, when a yellow-bedecked suffragist buzzed in from behind. "Don't speak to her," the Suff admonished the lawmaker, nodding dismissively toward Pinckard. "She's in the pay of the liquor interests."

Mrs. Pinckard, incensed by the slur, stared hard at the offending Suff, who'd already escaped down the corridor. Pinckard's rosebud lips tightened and flattened into a grimace. This was how the suffragists worked, she fumed, by innuendo and personal offense—by lies. Seth Walker might find his honorable revenge on the floor of the house, but Pinckard intended to seek a suffragist comeuppance in the newspapers and in court. She would pursue charges of criminal libel and public slander against the offending suffragist, and she warned—in a large, boldfaced notice in the *Tennessean*—that any Suff who made similar accusations would be "prosecuted to the full extent of the law."

"Such false and malicious charges are an example of what woman suffrage means in action . . . ," the Anti notice said, "cruel, unfair, dishonest, and unscrupulous attempts to blast the reputation of every courageous woman who dares to disagree with the politically ambitious fraction who demand 'votes for women' and 'offices for women.'"

The Antis vociferously denied that any of their members had received "one cent from any liquor or brewery interest." "This charge, ALWAYS CIRCULATED whenever the suffragists feel themselves BEATEN IN A FAIR

FIGHT, is founded only on the malice or ignorance of little minds which assume the public can be fooled by repeated falsehoods."

It was true that the Suffs repeatedly accused the "liquor interests"— brewers, distillers, bottlers, distributors, cork makers, hop and barley farmers, restaurateurs, and saloon keepers—of financing Anti activities in almost every state, as well as in Congress. But tracing the money, and the undercover political mischief, was extremely difficult, forcing Suffs to rely on mostly anecdotal evidence. They did uncover solid evidence that antisuffrage advertisements and resolutions were routinely circulated in saloons, often with a free drink as reward for signing an antisuffrage petition or voting "No" in a state referendum. Liquor industry workers were sent out as canvassers to warn nearby communities that their livelihood and well-being depended upon defeating woman suffrage. Liquor industry trade publications railed against suffrage. There were countless referendum election irregularities that Suffs felt could be laid at the feet of the liquor interests (and their suspicions were shared by many a governor, mayor, and representative), and liquor money undoubtedly changed hands in legislative halls; but there was little solid proof. It made sense that an entire industry, threatened with destruction by "dry" women voters, would work to protect itself. The problem was there were scant records; these were not transactions posted neatly in any ledger. So while the Suffs could competently connect the dots, they couldn't really follow the money. Their claims could be denied. Even with the Jack Daniel's Suite in full swing.

While Carrie Catt feigned calm confidence, a more honest hysteria gripped Sue White and her Woman's Party comrades. Telephone and telegraph wires strung between the triangle of Nashville, Washington, and Ohio pulsed with bulletins of alarm.

Pollitzer's before dawn telegram set Alice Paul on edge. The master micromanager was impatient with a lack of detailed information and frustrated by the limitations of commanding her forces at such a remove. But she couldn't afford to leave Washington, not until enough money was raised to cover her expenses and keep things going in her absence. Every rich woman she'd tried to put the touch on was away on vacation. She was reduced to asking her board members to pass the hat at their posh summer colonies in Maine and Rhode Island. She kept putting off her departure for Nashville.

What was going on down there? Paul demanded of Sue White in a testy midmorning telegram, sent while White was in the statehouse gallery. "We find it impossible to give help on Tennessee from this end as we have no information about Democratic attitude," Paul scolded. She demanded some basic info: Do we have a majority? Do you expect success? When will the measure come to a vote? Is there any evidence of Cox's promised efforts on behalf of ratification?

"Please do not spare money on telegrams," Paul chided White. Miss Sue was always carefully frugal, but that wasn't the only reason she'd not sent better reports. She had zero time to write any cogent analysis, but she also didn't know what to say. Tell Miss Paul that she'd lost control of the campaign? Explain that support for ratification was mysteriously evaporating—all on her watch? Not unlike Governor Roberts, White had been stalling for time, hoping to set things right before having to give a full accounting. Seth Walker had smashed her strategy, too.

The hottest gossip around Nashville on Tuesday was not the many rumors of defections and double crosses, or even the many elaborate conspiracy theories—though they were definitely swirling around—but Betty Gram's fiery confrontation with Seth Walker earlier in the day. The "Militant Oregonian" had insulted the Speaker, Walker's friends complained, questioned his integrity, and besmirched his honor. "Her language was offensive," one newspaper reported, "and the aftermath is a show of deep offense at the suffragists by Mr. Walker's friends, who are numerous in Nashville, both among the members and the residents."

Gram must apologize, Walker's friends insisted. Gram had no intention of apologizing.

"We are not going to be thrust aside easily," she said defiantly. "Some sinister underground influence is at work here. We are entitled to know just who is changing a majority to a minority. I rely on Alice Paul to uncover the real reason for the backset of our hopes here," Gram said. "If the liquor interests or the Louisville and Nashville railroad are responsible, she will find it out."

Gram's sisters in the Woman's Party were quietly thrilled by her nervy tackle of Walker, and even Carrie Catt would have to admit that the youthful provocateur was simply saying aloud what Catt herself was thinking. But the Tennessee Suffs were mortified by Gram's actions. This was just the kind of "unladylike" behavior that gave ammunition to the Antis, proving their predictions of the horrible "sex wars" that would attend suffrage and women's entry into politics. The southern suffragists had methodically fought against this stereotype for years, and they didn't have to wait long to feel the fallout: following his morning clash with Gram, Walker "began a vigorous opposition to ratification," the newspapers reported, "while his friends are irate over the militant policy here as a result of the speaker's defection."

Tom Riddick, always admirably blunt, applauded Gram's moxie and thought it might even do some good: "It will smoke out Seth Walker," he said, "and tell those confounded women to stop their cackle." It was assumed he meant the Antis.

By late Tuesday afternoon, when Alice Paul finally connected by telephone with her lieutenants in Nashville, they relayed the unfolding bad news: Seth Walker was working strenuously to peel away pledged votes. More legislators were suddenly altering their positions. "We are losing men right straight along."

Thomas Riddick barged into Governor Roberts's office and shut the door. Never a man to mince his words—he could slash a man to ribbons in the courtroom—Riddick told Roberts that suspicions about his sincerity and commitment were undermining the ratification campaign among legislators. People were saying that the governor was deliberately dragging his feet. The Suff women did not trust him, and Roberts's own men were fomenting trouble. Riddick delivered an ultimatum: If ratification failed in the legislature, if Democrats were shamed, Roberts's reelection was doomed. (This was, of course, the exact opposite of what Roberts was hearing from his advisers.)

Roberts protested, telling Riddick that he would be not only humiliated, but crushed, if ratification did not pass. He was in the ratification fight wholeheartedly, and in it to win. He vowed to bring pressure upon any straying friends and asked for the names of doubtful members, promising to go to work on them immediately.

While Riddick was browbeating the governor, almost a hundred Tennessee Suff women were conferring with about a dozen Democratic senators at the statehouse. (Quite a few invited senators decided not to show.) Responding to the furor over Betty Gram's public shaming of Seth Walker, Charl Williams assured the senators that the Suffs had no intention of trying to dictate their actions, and she soothed them by saying that the women willingly placed their cause in the hands of the men, relying upon their sense of justice and fair play.

If this smacked a bit too much of the type of female "soft suasion" historically favored by those opposed to woman suffrage, and if it echoed the Antis' willingness to put decision making in the hands of men, or if it brought to mind the classic image of the southern woman on her pedestal protected by her adoring menfolk, Charl Williams calculated that it was a necessary accommodation. It might not jibe with Mrs. Catt's admonition that a political man motivated by justice was an imaginary animal, but it was not, Miss Williams would insist, a capitulation. If it eased the minds of the senators and smoothed the path toward ratification, it was a worthwhile compromise.

By evening, Seth Walker had constructed a sturdy rationale for his revised ratification stance: "I have become convinced that it is my duty to my state and to my constituents to oppose this thing," he explained to a sympathetic reporter. "There is no question in my mind that a large majority of the people, both men and women in Tennessee, are against universal suffrage from principles, or are violently opposed to action through a federal amendment.

"The cities, no doubt, would vote for suffrage, but by no great majority, while the rural sections, which predominate in Tennessee, I know are strong against this ratification." Walker was relaxed and expansive with the reporter for the Anti standard, the *Chattanooga Times,* feeling well satisfied with the day's accomplishments.

"The method is wrong from every angle as I view it, especially from the standpoint of the South," Walker explained. "Tennessee has it in its power now to thrust upon every other state, whether agreeable to the people thereof or not, equal suffrage, and to enfranchise all elements of women. It is too much power to be wielded by a single state, especially since the present representatives have not been instructed in any way regarding it." Whether he consciously recognized it or not, Walker had just articulated, in vivid summary, every argument the Antis were advancing in Nashville.

Walker said he realized that his patron, the governor, was favorable to ratification and stood ready to push its passage through the legislature, but, Walker hinted, Roberts was only following orders from Democratic bigwigs. "I believe his stand is due to a sense of duty to the national party organization, which seems determined that Tennessee shall ratify," Walker claimed, making Roberts appear to be both a victim and a puppet. "My action is entirely independent, and there is no break between myself and the governor." This statement was also no favor to Roberts, making it seem as if a little matter such as betrayal of the suffragists and defeat of the amendment was no reason for discord between good buddies. It was just politics. "I think he will accord me full credit for acting as my own conscience dictates," Walker said of Roberts, "if I am placed in the position of refusing to vote as he may possibly ask me."

While Walker was giving fair warning to the governor—don't ask me to relent—and celebrating the purity of his own conscience, he did not attempt to explain the suddenness of his "change of conviction," nor did he bother to mention his legal work for railroad interests. He especially avoided any reference to whispers that a lucrative railroad position had been dangled before him as reward for his opposition to ratification.

Seth Walker was making Tennessee's junior U.S. senator Kenneth Mc-Kellar's job much harder, but McKellar kept at it all evening and into the night. He set up an office in his room at the Hermitage, loosened his tie, scrutinized the handwritten list he'd made containing the names of uncommitted or wavering senate Democrats, and summoned each man to his room, one by one. What he said to them, what he promised them, how he threatened them, we do not know. He probably brandished both carrots and sticks, offered both sugar and vinegar, but by late Tuesday night he could announce that fifteen Democratic senators had committed to voting for ratification. They made that promise to his face, gave him their solemn word; he would remember any man who reneged.

While McKellar was twisting arms in his Hermitage room, Judge Joseph Higgins, president of the Tennessee Constitutional League, was warning legislators that they dared not ratify the amendment. Should they be tempted to bow to suffragist pressure to ratify, Higgins explained, his organization "would be constrained to go into the courts and inhibit the Secretary of State from certifying the amendment." It was no idle threat—the league lawyers were already drafting the injunction papers—and it was a powerful one, promising both parties a disastrous fall of electoral chaos, putting the results of all contests, including presidential, into question.

Following the day's long string of fraught phone calls from Nashville, Alice Paul sent Abby Baker to see Cox again. Do something! she implored. Cox had sent another anodyne message to the Tennessee legislators through

Charl Williams, and his efforts appeared lackluster at best. In her visit, Baker discovered one reason why: "Cox appears worried," Baker reported confidentially to Paul. His aides were telling him that "women will double the Republican vote in Ohio and cause loss of state." The first wave of the Great Migration of southern black families into Ohio during the war had augmented the Republican voter rolls, and the votes of black women could only exacerbate the Democrats' problems in the state. Perhaps it was best not to push Tennessee, his aides were urging. Cox did, however, promise Baker that if Governor Roberts persisted in refusing to telephone him, he would call Roberts himself and demand a frank and detailed report.

Alice Paul had had enough. On Tuesday night she issued a blistering statement: "The majority for ratification of the suffrage amendment in the Tennessee Legislature has disappeared," she howled. Speaker Seth Walker's desertion was highlighted.

"The change in the Tennessee situation can be traced to one thing only—the failure of Governor Cox and Governor Roberts of Tennessee to put sufficient force behind their public pleas for ratification to insure a favorable action," she accused. "Defeat of the amendment in Tennessee would be a deliberate defeat."

Paul bitterly challenged Cox and Roberts, as she had Woodrow Wilson and so many other waffling politicians: Deeds, not words.

Chapter 18

* * *

Terrorizing Tennessee Manhood

I T WAS A STUNNING opening gambit. As soon as the chaplain finished his prayer on Wednesday morning, house majority leader William Bond rose from his seat. Bond was a friend of Seth Walker's, just a few years older than the Speaker, and they'd worked closely together to push through Governor Roberts's legislative agenda. They were both ambitious young lawyers forging political careers, and together they launched a meticulously orchestrated ploy.

Speaker Walker recognized Bond. He wished to introduce House Joint Resolution #4. Proceed, replied the Speaker. "Whereas," Bond read from the paper in his hand, as the floor and galleries suddenly went silent, heads tilted, ears strained. Bond's first set of six or seven "Whereas" pronouncements provided a history lesson, a pointed reminder of why the Tennessee Constitution contained that provision restricting the timing of the General Assembly's consideration of a federal constitutional amendment. There was good reason, Bond reminded his colleagues: the Fourteenth Amendment, giving all rights and protections of citizenship to the freed slaves, had been rammed down Tennessee's throat at the close of the Civil War, forcibly thrust through the legislature in 1866 by the radical Republican governor, the despised William "Parson" Brownlow. The legislature acted "against the opinion and sentiment of an overwhelming majority of the people of Tennessee," Bond recited, reading the resolution text in his practiced courtroom style. The legislators didn't ask the people—the white people—if they wanted the Fourteenth Amendment, he emphasized, it was forced upon them.

With that infuriating incident in mind, Tennesseans rewrote their state constitution in 1870, requiring legislators to face the public in an election before they considered any federal constitutional amendments. Bond acknowledged that the U.S. Supreme Court had ruled that the clause stood in conflict with the U.S. Constitution, and he didn't dispute that ruling but instead nimbly sidestepped the issue with a novel approach.

Resolved: The General Assembly must take no action on ratification until the voice of the people could be heard. The popular sentiment on ratification should be expressed by both men and women in mass meetings, held in every county seat of the state, at noon on Saturday, August 21—a postponement of nearly two weeks. A chairman in each county would then report the prevailing opinion of its citizens to the district's delegates in the legislature by August 24, and the legislators could then properly vote the will of their constituents. This would delay, and diminish, any chance for timely ratification.

The chamber erupted: shouts, cheers, and protests, on the floor and in the galleries, everyone on their feet. Reporters likened the reaction to a loud, breaking storm, thunderheads that had been building for weeks finally splitting open. The Antis applauded the resolution's brilliant stroke of promising a measure of populist democracy while delivering the desired delay—perhaps forever—of ratification. The Suffs were duly alarmed: the mass-meeting idea was a candy-coated and very palatable excuse for legislators to do nothing.

By house rules, the resolution should be held over to the next day for a second reading, but Speaker Walker made a quick, deft move, ruling to allow a suspension of the rules, placing the resolution immediately before the house. The hot debate began; faces flushed and voices rose.

"The members of this legislature must determine whether they are men or weaklings!" shouted Leonidas (L. D.) Miller of Chattanooga, a firm suffrage supporter who understood the seductive danger of the Bond resolution.

"Nothing could be fairer," to the people or legislators of Tennessee, "than this resolution," Billy Bond responded dismissively.

"This measure is not meant as an obstruction," Frank Hall, one of the resolution's co-sponsors concurred, "but to sound out popular sentiment."

Miller shook off their rationalizations. "Make no mistake," he insisted, "the authors of this resolution to defer are, in their hearts, bitterly opposed to suffrage ratification, and the purpose of it is not to secure the will of the people, but to delay action and defeat the ratification of suffrage in Tennessee!"

"Are you afraid to let the people express themselves?" Bond shot back. "Do you believe they will go against you, and that you will not be able to put over a measure they do not want?"

How much declaring do you need? Miller countered. The state conventions of both parties had declared for ratification, the national conventions, too. "And far and above the political party appeals," cried Miller, "comes the voice of the womanhood of America calling for justice long overdue." The Suffs in the gallery cheered. "Will you yield to the appeal of womanhood or the insidious influence at work to defeat the measure? To throw this question back upon the people will show cowardice," Miller boomed.

While the debate unfolded, Anne Dudley delicately circulated around the chamber. It was a safe assumption that just the lovely sight of her would remind certain legislators that they'd made a promise to support ratification, and for those who seemed to have already forgotten those vows, she could refresh their faltering memories with a sweet, sharp nudge. These were men she knew well, both politically and socially, and she could approach them in a certain easy way, a way they understood. She'd already pledged the delegates from Nashville and surrounding Davidson County, and they were all rock solid for ratification, they promised.

She'd gotten to know many of the legislators during the statehouse suffrage skirmishes of the past years, while others were friends or colleagues of her husband, Guilford, a prosperous Nashville insurance man who could amiably kid his pals about not being manly enough to support their wives in their desire for enfranchisement. Some of the men she saw in the chamber this morning had jeered her in the early years of the Nashville Equal Suffrage League, when she led that first public parade, with two thousand proper Nashville matrons dressed in white with yellow sashes making a spectacle of themselves on the streets of the city. These men had been taken aback when Anne, in a public debate, had smashed the Antis' trusty rationale—that women did not have the right to vote because they were not required to bear arms in wartime—with her poignant reply: "Yes, but women bear armies." And even the bitterest Anti solon had to admire Anne's sangfroid when that bomb was tossed through a window while she addressed a suffrage meeting in 1913. "Is that an anti-suffrage bomb?" she'd asked calmly, peering over the podium, pausing only a few beats. It didn't explode, so she continued on with her speech.

Yet today Anne Dudley seemed nervous. Mrs. Catt was professing confidence, but last night Andrew Todd had confided to the Suffs that he thought the senate might pull through on ratification, but the house was lost.

On the north side of the Capitol the senate was also in session, and the mood there was almost as edgy as in the lower house. Speaker Todd wanted to speed things along, allow no time for disruptions or space for delay, but he was struggling to stay on track.

The galleries of the jewel-box-like senate chamber were also packed, though the observers were quieter than their comrades in the house. Sixteen massive Tennessee marble columns, each hauled in one piece by slaves and convicts up Capitol Hill, surrounded the thirty-three desks of the senators like silent sentinels.

Joint Resolution #1, providing for the adoption of the Nineteenth Amendment, emerged from its overnight layover onto the day's docket. There was no attempt to introduce the kind of mass-meeting delay tactic that was being debated across the hall; Anti strategists were waiting to learn the outcome of that ploy before bringing it to the senate. But the Antis were prepared to strike in other ways.

Andrew Todd moved that the ratification resolution be referred for consideration to the Senate Committee on Constitutional Amendments, whose members were known to be friendly toward ratification. Herschel Candler immediately jumped up in protest. It should more properly be sent to the Judiciary Committee, he argued. (The Judiciary Committee members, it was understood, were less favorably inclined toward suffrage.) Candler did not like being railroaded like this.

He'd had enough of such tactics this morning. First he'd received an insulting telegram from Republican chairman Hays, telling him that for the good of the party, the good of the country, the good of the whole world, he should violate his oath of office to ratify. Such pompous claptrap was best ignored. Then he had to sit through another Republican caucus, where the same hollow arguments were pounded into the table. The state party leaders wanted everyone to file into a straight line, like stupid sheep, and swear to ratify, on the orders of Hays, Harding, and God. He wasn't having any of it. He was his own man. The ratification resolution should go to Judiciary! Candler insisted with fire in his voice.

In the house, Seth Walker stepped down from the Speaker's chair onto the floor to advocate for the Bond resolution. There was a stir in the galleries and fidgety anticipation among the delegates. Walker straightened his back and squared his shoulders, a tall, commanding presence in the well of the chamber.

"This resolution carries out the spirit of the law as enacted by our forefathers," Walker began. Remember, he told his colleagues, the Fourteenth Amendment was imposed upon the South by the vengeful Union states and forced upon Tennessee by a legislature "composed of Yankee carpetbaggers" who ignored the will of the people. He did not need to mention that accepting the Fourteenth Amendment was the price for Tennessee's readmission to the Union, nor did he choose to mention the legislators who tried to slip out of the statehouse to avoid voting on the amendment, prevented only by the gunshots of the Union soldiers on guard. Those bullet holes were still obvious on the marble staircase leading down from the house chamber.

The esteemed forefathers at the constitutional convention of 1870 corrected this procedure, prevented it from happening again, by writing that essential clause "in letters that stand immortal," Walker pontificated. Tennessee then rejected the Fifteenth Amendment, the one guaranteeing the voting rights of the freed slaves, and the General Assembly passed a joint resolution condemning federal "imposition" of black suffrage upon the states. "The constitution of this great state cannot be played with for political purposes," Walker insisted.

If the legislature was being forced, by a Supreme Court ruling, to act before an election, this resolution was a suitable and legal antidote, he explained. "We want to get an expression from the people, for that is the spirit of the constitution of 1870!" Walker declared to red-rosed applause.

Josephine Pearson watched the argument from her gallery seat; she'd never seen anything quite like this. Mr. Vertrees had not permitted her to set foot in the statehouse during the 1917 and 1919 debates, so this was her first opportunity to watch the legislature in action. Here were the brave Anti men of Tennessee taking their stand, upholding the honor of the South, and she was so proud of them. Especially that young, very handsome Seth Walker. She had suffered so long on account of her opposition to suffrage— lost so many friends, been snubbed too many times, turned down for jobs and appointments—and it was obvious to her why: because she was a proud Anti, willing to stand up for what she believed.

On the desk of each legislator was the latest set of Anti materials, which Pearson had helped to compose and distribute. She thought the new advocacy piece was especially fine: "CAN ANYBODY TERRORIZE TENNESSEE MANHOOD?" it screamed in big, bold type. "The Susan B. Anthony Amendment Will Never Be Ratified If Tennessee Representatives Do Their Duty NOW."

Tennessee had the opportunity to save America, the jeremiad announced. "The Federal Suffrage 'Drive' is Dead if Tennessee will answer the call of her own constitution, her own people, and that of her sister Southern states."

Face down the suffrage blackmailers and card indexers, the piece implored the Tennessee delegates. Ignore those who say woman suffrage is "bound to come" in an attempt to weaken your resistance; recognize that those distant party leaders and candidates—in Ohio and Washington—don't understand the South's "local conditions" and the threat of Negro domination. They don't see the looming danger of another era of southern reconstruction, brought on by federal control of elections. Only you, the legislators of Tennessee, stand in the way of calamity.

"The men who vote against Ratification will go down in American history as the SAVIORS OF OUR FORM OF GOVERNMENT and the true Defenders of Womanhood, Motherhood, the Family and the State," the document promised.

For Pearson and her allies, all this was neither hyperbole nor exaggeration; it expressed a deep truth and revealed a pernicious danger that was not being taken seriously enough. The nation had just fought to protect Europe, and itself, from the despotism of the Hun, but now the gravest threat to the American Republic was coming from within, from this federal amendment and its grave ramifications—racial, social, and political. It fell to the Antis, standing firm in Nashville, to safeguard the South's democracy.

Thomas Riddick, house floor leader for ratification, jumped into the debate. Many of the attorneys present had heard Riddick speak in a courtroom, but never before in the legislature; this was his debut performance. This resolution was ridiculous, Riddick railed, a legal sham and a logistic nightmare. Riddick's eyes blazed and his mustache bobbed up and down on his lip as he spoke. Not only was it simply a variation on the ratification referenda the Supreme Court had already struck down, and an outrageous shirking of a legislator's responsibilities, but these so-called mass conventions could never accurately gauge the public sentiment. How would popular opinion be measured—by who showed up first? by who yelled the loudest?—and who would interpret and report what was expressed? There was too much room for manipulation and possibly fraud.

The Suffs did a double take as they saw Governor Roberts appear in the back of the chamber. Sweating through his shirt and crumpled jacket, he was following the debate, consulting with Riddick and Miller, and writing strategy notes to certain delegates, dispatching the missives to their desks. He called some lawmakers over to his side for a few hushed words, an intense back-and-forth, then a pat on the back.

Roberts had finally spoken with Governor Cox on the telephone—told him things were under control—and had spent all last night and early morning working on iffy Democratic legislators. Now he was wrestling on the floor of the house; he was working.

Abby Milton saw the governor at the back of the room and saw her stepson, George Milton, Jr., scribbling away in the press gallery. Young George, barely twenty-five, was an eager, if callow, young reporter for his father's newspaper, finally assigned to a big story. He chronicled every event with gusto, as if he were a war correspondent or a sports reporter at an important race. He liked to relate who was jockeying for position, whether the red or yellow rose was drooping that day in the War of the Roses. And now he was taking notes on how Governor Roberts was rolling up his sleeves and doing his darnedest to stop this delay resolution. The Milton family had worked strenuously to defeat Roberts in the primary, putting the editorial pages of their *Chattanooga News* into the service of his opponent, but Roberts's very visible efforts on behalf of the amendment were causing them to view the governor in a new light.

Sue White and Anita Pollitzer, standing at the edge of the chamber, did not share this sunshine view of Governor Roberts; they still suspected that he was double-dealing. He's acting as if he's working for ratification, Pollitzer reported to Alice Paul, but his own men are working against us. Pollitzer also believed Roberts was giving inaccurate information to Governor Cox in an effort to keep the candidate from putting more pressure on state Democrats or coming to Tennessee himself. When Pollitzer mentioned the possibility of Cox coming to Nashville to help push for ratification, Roberts had visibly blanched.

Miss Paul took Pollitzer's suspicions seriously and issued new instructions to her organizers in Nashville: Backpedal on accusations against the liquor and railroad industries and instead emphasize the responsibility borne by Cox and Roberts if ratification should fail. The "sinister forces" charge was just too hard to prove concretely, even if true, and journalists were tiring of it; holding the Democrats accountable was more comfortable, and profitable, territory for the Woman's Party. Keep the pressure on. And talk to the wire service reporters in Nashville, Paul instructed her lieutenants, make sure they quote us rather than Mrs. Catt; it's important for fund-raising purposes that the Woman's Party receive credit and public attention for its work in Tennessee. Paul had already purchased a Pullman car ticket for Nashville.

As the house debate wore on, Joe Hanover of Shelby asked to be recognized by Speaker Walker. I wish to speak against this resolution, he announced. The Suffs paid particular attention to the words of this young attorney who so earnestly, and publicly, had come to their side. He'd made that heartrending speech during the limited suffrage debates last year, about the American Dream and the power of the vote, and his sincerity seemed to sway several on-the-fence delegates. Even though he'd resigned from the legislature to take a good job as a Shelby County district attorney, he'd decided he must return to the statehouse to help get ratification through, campaigned to regain his seat, and here he was. During the past few nights, he'd begun attending the Suffs' strategy sessions in Mrs. Catt's room, impressing them all, especially Mrs. Catt, with his political acumen and strategic vision. And his passion for their fight.

Hanover did not have Confederate pedigree or Tennessee forefathers. He was an immigrant whose parents had brought him as a boy to America to escape the pogroms against Jews in their native Poland. This was the land of opportunity, they told him, the land of equality and freedom, and he believed every word. He lived the American Dream: night law school, a fledgling legal practice, a seat in the legislature. But women—his own mother—didn't share in that equality, not as full citizens, and that seemed wrong, plainly un-American, to Hanover. Now he was in a position to do something about it.

"The people of Tennessee have already passed upon suffrage!" he declared. "The real voice of the people has already been heard in the expression of both party platforms." Hanover swiveled to look directly at Walker. "My colleagues, Mr. Bond and Mr. Walker, were both members of the Democratic state convention in June which wrote into its platform that 'we stand for woman suffrage in Tennessee,'" Hanover exclaimed, and suffragists all through the chamber burst into sustained applause.

Mrs. Catt was not in the chamber. In accordance with the new Suff strategy, she was to remain invisible, so she was sitting in her hotel room, quite miserable, staring at the Capitol cupola through an open window. Harriet Upton and Marjorie Shuler were with her, watching Catt closely for any sign that she was having trouble breathing, that the hot air and stress might be affecting her heart. As they sat in Catt's room, they could hear occasional cheers or shouts coming from the statehouse through the open window, but they had to wait for a breathless young messenger to run down from Capitol Hill and knock on Catt's door to deliver the latest report of what was actually happening in the house and senate chambers.

In the senate, Herschel Candler's motion to refer the ratification resolution to the Judiciary Committee hung in the air for just an instant before a pro-suffrage lawmaker made a countermove to table it. It was the custom of the senate, the senator protested, to allow the Speaker to refer resolutions to the committee he thought proper; that custom should be respected. The tabling measure was brought to a vote; it carried by a slim majority, and the Suffs were mightily relieved. Todd announced definitively that the ratification resolution would go to the Committee on Constitutional Amendments. This was a setback for Candler and his Anti colleagues, but they did not make any further fuss. It was just the first skirmish; there was time.

In the front row of the house chamber, Edward Oldham slowly rose to his feet to speak in favor of the mass meetings. He was a seventy-four-year-old farmer, and he was, he reminded his colleagues once again, a proud Confederate veteran. Oldham was only sixteen when he volunteered for the Tennessee cavalry, and he served for the full duration of the war; now, with his clipped silver beard and bare forehead, he bore a striking resemblance to his hero Robert E. Lee.

"The people of Lauderdale, whom I represent, do not want suffrage for women," Oldham pronounced confidently. Woman suffrage will cause divorce and dissatisfaction in many homes, he continued, and was a menace to family life. The people did not want it! "Is there any fair-minded man who is afraid to submit this question to the people he represents?" Oldham challenged his colleagues.

Man after man took his turn recommending or denouncing the mass-meeting resolution, but no one mentioned whether black citizens would be allowed to take part in these meetings; the answer was undoubtedly no. The delegates stood in the chamber just where Frankie Pierce had stood barely three months before, pledging the support of the Negro women of Nashville to the League of Women Voters, outlining her legislative goals, the programs her community needed. Catherine Kenny, who'd invited Pierce to the Capitol that day, had been so pleased with her presentation, and so impressed by the organizational ability Pierce had displayed in last fall's municipal elections in getting the black women to the polls, that she took real pride in this new alliance the women of Nashville had forged. It seemed to bring to life Mrs. Catt's concept of the league as an organization for all women voters: all colors, all creeds, all political parties. For Democratic Catholic women, for Republican black women, all together. But Frankie Pierce was not in the galleries this morning with all the other Tennessee Suffs. She couldn't be. Her presence could not help win ratification from the men of the legislature, it could only hurt. She wouldn't be allowed to sit with the white Suffs in the gallery anyway. Inviting her was simply out of the question.

The state party leaders were arrayed around the house chamber, in constant motion, pulling any strings they could reach. Kenneth McKellar was wielding the message that had arrived from DNC chairman George White that morning, urging Tennessee delegates to ratify. Republican leaders were impressing upon their delegates, especially the wavering ones, the importance of the special five-page telegram they'd just received from Will Hays of the RNC.

Hays had spent hours the previous night convincing a reluctant Warren Harding to agree to send direct notes to the list of resistant Tennessee Republicans that party leaders Ben Hooper and John Houk had requested. Hays had worked on Harding till midnight, badgering the candidate on the need for stronger, specific action on the ratification issue. All right, Harding finally agreed, you can send the messages—over your name, not mine. So Hays composed telegrams to the list of Republicans, including Herschel Candler and Emerson Luther in the senate, Austin Overton and Harry Burn in the house, and he pulled no punches.

"Democracy in the United States is really nothing but a sham unless election day gives all Americans the chance to express their political opinion effectively," Hays lectured the Republicans. The 1920 election will "influence our national life for at least the next 50 years," Hays argued, and women must be allowed to take part in that decision. "To hold American women bound by the result of an election, to train them in schools and colleges to think for themselves as well as a man, to accord them freedom of utterance as a constitutional right, and then to attempt to deny them the opportunity to stand up and be counted on election day is a governmental blunder of the first magnitude." Carrie Catt smiled when Harriet Upton showed her Hays's emotional plea. Will Hays sounded just like a good Suff. And for that reason, Herschel Candler had no intention of listening to his advice.

Across the hall in the senate, Lon McFarland, in his linen suit and bolo tie, rose to speak. He had his own resolution to introduce. Speaker Todd nodded for him to begin.

"The men of Tennessee, noted for their integrity and chivalry," he read aloud from the text of his resolution, "and being desirous of doing in this case for their women as they always have in the past, and having the greatest admiration and respect for the intelligence of our home women . . ." Those who knew McFarland's discerning eye for the ladies smiled, but no one quite knew where he was going with this odd oration.

"And Whereas, there are numerous lobbyists, both female and male, from all sections of the United States at the present time in the city of Nashville, some being for and some against the ratification of the amendment . . . ," McFarland pronounced in his smooth Tennessee drawl.

"Be it Resolved: That we most respectfully and earnestly request all of the ladies and gentlemen, and also all of the men and women from outside the state who are interested in lobbying for or against this measure, to please go away and let us alone, we feeling that we are fully capable and competent to fight our own fights without interference from any outside people whatsoever."

Back in the house, L. D. Miller stood again and moved to table Bond's delay resolution. Here was the first showdown, the first test of strength for both sides. If the Anti legislators could beat back this tabling motion, it would show they had the votes to delay, and possibly to kill, ratification. The galleries grew still. The roll call began. "Mr. Anderson," the clerk called out. "Aye," was the first response, in support of tabling the resolution, and the Suffs murmured approvingly. "Bell"—aye; "Bond" and "Boyer"—no. The Antis were pleased. "Boyd," "Bratton," and "Brooks"—aye. "Burn"—no. "Carter"—no.

Catherine Kenny kept a tally of the votes, mentally noting the men who had pledged to her canvassers to support ratification but who were now throwing their support to the delay resolution. One lawmaker from Dayton had sworn nine separate times—"I'm with you ladies till they call the roll up yonder," he'd promised—but now he was answering with the Antis. More optimistically, Kenny noted, four Anti delegates had now voted with the Suffs. Anita Pollitzer, who was keeping a similar tally for the Woman's Party, winced to hear the names of some of her East Tennessee Republicans, including Harry Burn, among those opposed to tabling the measure. Their pledges, their word, had been worth nothing.

The clerk moved down the roll: "Hanover"—aye. "Oldham," then "Overton"—no. "Riddick"—aye. "Turner"—no. And finally: "Speaker Walker"—no.

The Suffs did not have to wait for the clerk to announce his count; the delay resolution was dead. The Suffs burst into cheers, the Anti spectators were stoically silent. "The fight is won!" Governor Roberts gloated. "Victory for suffrage is certain." Speaker Walker banged his gavel and adjourned the house for lunch.

There was scant time for delegates to digest their hasty lunch before they were hit with the next Anti sally, a less nuanced, more lethal resolution introduced by representative W. F. Story, prohibiting the legislature from taking any action on ratification until 1921, but it was held over until the next day.

Joint Resolution #1, the ratification resolution itself, had already spent its overnight rest, and now Speaker Walker was obliged to send it to committee. He'd announced that he intended to send it to the House Judiciary Committee, chaired by his pal Billy Bond, but the outcome of the morning's vote demonstrated that Walker might face resistance to this move. He did. Walker reluctantly relented: the ratification resolution would be sent to the House Committee on Constitutional Affairs and Amendments, as it was in the senate, and Walker named Thomas Riddick to chair the committee.

Riddick was celebrated as an expert in constitutional law, and Walker's move appeared to be a generous gesture, but it was really a clever trap. Riddick, in only his third day in the legislature, now held significant additional power, and Walker understood that this might not go down so well with some of the veteran delegates, even if they were suffragists. Walker was carefully seeding trouble.

By late afternoon on Wednesday, the Hotel Hermitage was a hive of commotion. With both houses adjourned, assorted configurations of men and women, Suffs and Antis, Democrats and Republicans, held meetings, huddled in private, and hatched plans. Suffs congratulated themselves on their day's victories, while Antis dismissed the test votes as merely symbolic, no real measures of strength. They took courage in the communiqué they'd just received from their Anti brethren in the North Carolina legislature—signed by a majority of the lower body—promising a mutual pact to deny ratification. North Carolina lawmakers pledged not to inflict the Nineteenth Amendment upon Tennessee and begged Tennesseans to do the same.

The Tennessee Antis also floated a trial balloon: they let it be known that the men of the Constitutional League were not at all pleased with Governor Roberts's performance in the house chamber that morning, working so strenuously on the side of the Suffs, and might consider fielding an independent candidate to run in the fall election, siphoning off Democratic votes and weakening Roberts's chances. It was an appropriate punishment; they let the idea take off.

During the afternoon and evening, the League of Women Voters workers were again sent out to find and take the political pulse of their assigned delegates. The legislators were under tremendous pressure: from their party chiefs, their senior elected officials, their constituents. Adding to all this, they felt besieged by both Suff and Anti advocates, who were chasing them, pestering with questions, giving them no peace. It's little wonder that the league women often returned from their assignments frustrated, reporting that quite a few of the delegates could not be found or had skipped out on scheduled meetings. A favorite route of escape was the Jack Daniel's Suite.

A constant stream of legislators and politicians came to consult with Mrs. Catt in her room, and quite a few of them had whiskey on their breath, which unnerved her. At times the whole legislature seemed to be drunk. "Are none sober?" Catt asked incredulously. "Possibly," she was told.

Strike while the iron is hot, goes the old adage, so late on Wednesday evening Tom Riddick and Andrew Todd announced that both the house and the senate would vote on ratification on Friday. The votes appeared to be there, so why wait? But those keeping careful count with a more skeptical eye, including Sue White, recognized that things were not quite so rosy: while the Suffs had mustered enough votes to defeat the delay resolution, they had amassed the bare minimum—fifty votes—required for a constitutional majority in the house, the threshold that would be needed to ratify. There wasn't a single vote to spare.

"The opposition has yielded by barely a hair's breadth," White warned, throwing cold water on the Suffs' moment of joy, "and suffrage is not yet out of a hazardous position. The tabling of the referendum resolution was victory, but it is not the end of the fight. It will take further efforts and increased energy to accomplish ratification."

That night, Alice Paul sent Abby Baker to extract those increased efforts from Governor Cox. The presidential candidate was in a buoyant mood after the day's events in Nashville. "Boys, it looks like suffrage is going to go over in Tennessee after all," Cox told reporters at his evening briefing in Dayton. "I have just been talking with Governor Roberts over the long distance telephone. He is very confident. He believes a favorable vote will be taken by Friday."

While Cox was meeting with reporters in his office, Abby Baker was left to cool her tapered heels in a nearby anteroom. Impatiently awaiting her turn, she grabbed the ears of a few reporters herself and gave them a very different view of the situation. She openly questioned Cox's blithe confidence in Governor Roberts's optimistic reports and Roberts's ability to deliver ratification on his own. She came armed with a portfolio of documents, including the latest intelligence from Sue White and Anita Pollitzer on the ground in Nashville, attesting to the volatility of the situation and the dangers that lay ahead. Cox must switch around his campaign schedule, Baker insisted, go to Nashville immediately to take charge. He was relying too much upon an unreliable Roberts.

And Baker was carrying another bit of information, intended to neutralize the claims Cox was undoubtedly hearing from some southern Democrats, that woman suffrage would trigger an avalanche of Negro ballots—Republican ballots—spelling the demise of white hegemony and Democratic rule in the South. Baker carried her own statistics to reassure Cox: census data showed that there were more white women in the southern states (10.6 million) than black women and men combined (4.3 million). It was an old, and sad, suffragist argument, but as Baker knew from her years of lobbying in Congress and the states, it often worked. Woman suffrage would not imperil white supremacy in the South or harm the presidential ambitions of James Cox, she promised.

It was a late night and a bleary-eyed dawn for the Nashville combatants. Once Riddick and Todd announced plans for a Friday vote, there was little time for sleep. The Tennessee Suffs welcomed the promise of swift action, the Woman's Party workers were nervous about it, and the Antis were dismayed, but everyone knew they'd have to scramble to nail down the votes they needed within the next thirty-six hours. Most immediately, they were preparing for the expected morning showdown in the house over the Story resolution—if that passed, there would be no vote at all—and then for the joint house-senate hearing that evening.

The public hearing was shaping up to be a spectacular event, a kind of barefisted prizefight featuring an all-star card of Suff and Anti champions. The teams were still being assembled, the participants carefully vetted not only for their speaking prowess, but for their legal acumen, political clout, and popular appeal. It was reported that Governor Roberts might be on the Suff team, as well as Sue White representing the Woman's Party, and Anne Dudley punching for the Tennessee Suffs. The Antis were fielding notable judges, a U.S. congressman, and, of course, Charlotte Rowe. Pyrotechnics were anticipated.

Speaker Walker brought the house to order at ten o'clock on Thursday morning; the chaplain prayed, the clerk called the roll. The galleries were full again, ninety-four members were at their desks, Governor Roberts was working the floor. The proceedings moved swiftly and, for the Suffs, successfully. When delegate Story's resolution—prohibiting the current legislature from acting upon ratification—came up, the ratificationists moved quickly to table it, and the resolution went down in a voice vote.

Over in the senate, Lon McFarland withdrew his "please go away" resolution, aimed at all outside lobbyists, before it came up for consideration. He gave no explanation for the action, but his colleagues were both bemused and relieved. Both houses adjourned to prepare for the evening debate.

As the senate dispersed, Anne Dudley found Lon McFarland walking in the Capitol corridor and approached him with a smile. I'm not an outsider, she kidded him as she affectionately leaned toward him to straighten his string tie. I'm a Nashvillian born and bred, and if you want to honor Tennessee women, as you say you do, the best way is to vote for ratification, she continued as she nimbly pulled both ribbons of his tie even and firmed the knot. Tennessee men giving Tennessee women the vote; she thought that would appeal to McFarland's sensibilities. McFarland did not reply, nor did he back away. He simply reached into his jacket, pulled out his pocketknife, and in one motion sliced off the strings of his tie just below the knot. Dudley was left speechless, holding the limp strings in her hand, as McFarland walked briskly away. "Just keep it," he called over his shoulder.

The Anti ladies now went for the jugular. From their headquarters in the Hermitage they released a barrage of barbed propaganda publications, spiked with racist and sexist malice. Their matériel was only paper, but the words and images printed on those sheets had the lacerating proficiency of

a serrated knife. Some were original creations, while others were adapted
from recent Anti campaigns in other southern states, amounting to a roster
of greatest hits.

One was called *That Deadly Parallel,* using facing columns to compare
the provisions of the Fifteenth and Nineteenth Amendments, pinpointing
their similarities and warning of renewed federal oversight of Tennessee
elections and punitive enforcement measures, hearkening back to Reconstruction days. This theme was continued by an advertisement labeled "Shall
History Repeat Itself?," displaying a photograph of white women speaking
with uniformed black policemen and warning that "Negro policemen may
be appointed from Washington and sent to Tennessee to enforce the Federal
Amendment."

An equally dire tone was taken by *The Dark and Dangerous Side of
Woman Suffrage,* a pamphlet expounding the detrimental effects of political
equality upon marriage and the family. And this was amplified by perhaps
Pearson's favorite piece, titled "America When Feminized." This poster
featured a cartoon drawing of a hen, wearing a "Votes for Women" sash
across her breast, walking out the door, abandoning her nest and eggs. Her
mate, the rooster, calls after her: "Why, Ma, these eggs will get all cold!"
She replies dismissively: "Set on them yourself, old man. MY COUNTRY
CALLS ME!" The caption announces: "The More a Politician Allows
Himself to be Henpecked, The More Henpecking We Will Have in Poli-
tics. A Vote for Federal Suffrage is a Vote for Organized Female Nagging
Forever."

The Antis knew how to tap into the anger and confusion of southern
white American men at this nervous moment in 1920. Perhaps he'd returned
from the war to find his job taken over by a black or immigrant man—or,
worse, a woman—or maybe a machine was doing his job, making his skills
obsolete. Even if he kept his job, his pay didn't provide for his family as it
once did, as inflation eroded the dollar. Maybe his wife had donned coveralls
and taken a paying job in a munitions factory during the war, learned to
type and gone to work in a government office, or buttoned up a snappy
uniform to become a streetcar conductor. She wasn't keen on coming home.
Now she wanted to vote, even wanted to smoke, wanted everything a man
had; after the vote, who knew what else she'd demand. The comfortable
world he'd known was fast disappearing, and his sense of manhood was
under siege. The Antis seemed to understand him.

Laura Clay and Kate Gordon were working hard: handing out the provocative Anti literature in the Hermitage lobby and Capitol corridors, while
also buttonholing legislators sympathetic to their states' rights and southern
solidarity doctrines. The women's long experience as lobbyists served them
well now and made them particularly effective Anti advocates. Harriet Upton, who'd worked with both Clay and Gordon for years in NAWSA, felt a
wave of sadness to see them wear the red rose uniform. When Clay and
Gordon passed their erstwhile suffrage colleagues in the Hermitage hallways, they made no acknowledgment, pretending their former sisters in the
Cause simply weren't there.

While Nashville was preparing for the evening debate, the mood at
Woman's Party headquarters in Washington was tense and glum. "Tennessee rests as a heavy load on our minds," Alice Paul's secretary, Emma Wold,
wrote to a staff member on Thursday. "Anita Pollitzer telegraphs that the
vote will be taken tomorrow . . . and she has very little hope of a favorable
result. We have been hoping that Cox would go [to Tennessee] but Baker
wires this morning that Roberts still insists that ratification is safe and tells
Cox it is not necessary for him to come. It is needless for me to say how
stupid they all are, or how perfidious."

The public committee hearing and debate was the hottest ticket in town on
Thursday night. The house floor was jammed with legislators and officehold-
ers, judges and dignitaries, while the balcony was bursting with hundreds of
Suffs and Antis decked out in their team's floral colors. Hundreds more
people stuffed into the aisles and stood behind the railings and out the door.
Governor Roberts sat near the front; Luke Lea and Edward Stahlman were
separated by a careful distance. The boisterous atmosphere was more akin to
a baseball game played before rowdy fans than any staid legislative proceeding, and when Senator Lambert Estes Gwinn and delegate Thomas Riddick,
chairmen of their respective constitutional committees, called the hearing
to order at eight p.m., they warned that no spectator outbursts or demonstrations would be tolerated.

The lineups for both teams were being shuffled until the last minute. The
leaders of both sides had initially planned that only men speak, so as not to
ruffle the sensibilities of the more conservative lawmakers, but Charlotte
Rowe had demanded a speaking spot, and the Anti men reluctantly acquiesced. Then a woman should speak for the ratificationists, too, and Anne

Dudley was selected by the Tennessee Suffs, while Sue White insisted that the Woman's Party be represented, so White's name was penciled in on the agenda. In the end, it was a more neutral Charl Williams who appeared as the envoy for the Suffs, but just in the role of introducing the program.

"The women of this country have been fighting for suffrage for sixty years," Williams began in a strong voice laced with her smooth, oval West Tennessee vowels. The veteran schoolteacher continued with a brief history lesson of the suffrage struggle in her home state and concluded not with an argument, but with a plea pitched to fall softly on the ears of the southern gentlemen in her audience.

"We have asked the men of Tennessee to take the matter of ratification and solve it for us," she declared, using language that must have made Sue White wince. "We feel perfectly safe to place it in the hands of our own men. The eyes of the United States are upon Tennessee in this fight, and the women of the state and nation stretch out eager hands to our men in this fight." Williams's "damsel in distress" trope was irritating to some Suffs, and probably maddening to Anita Pollitzer and Betty Gram, but in this event of political theater it was the safest role for Tennessee Suffs to play.

Now began the debate, with each side allotted five speakers and ninety minutes to make its case. The tenacity of the nettlesome—or, as the Suffs would say, trumped-up—oath issue was obvious in the number of lawyers and judges tapped to argue the legal questions haunting ratification. For the Antis, this was the ideal forum for presenting a scenario of disgraced honor and impending chaos; for the Suffs, it was an opportunity to shoot down those canards once and for all.

The political realities were covered by Senator McKellar for the Suffs, hammering home the obligation of Democrats to follow their party platform and leaders—President Wilson and Governor Cox—to ratify. Tennessee congressman Finis Garrett, speaking for the Antis, did his best to strike electoral fear into the hearts of all present by conjuring a disputed election in the fall. If Tennessee illegally ratified the Susan B. Anthony Amendment and the nation's women were allowed to vote, it would throw the election into another Tilden-Hayes affair, he warned, referring to the 1876 debacle during which the results of the presidential election remained undecided for months. "You will place the election of our president, our congressmen, our governor, our legislature and every other election in jeopardy if you pass this Amendment," Garrett prophesied, and the Antis cheered. But Garrett's apocalyptic scenario paled in comparison with the one evoked by Charlotte Rowe.

"Under the pretense of political expediency and the fond dream of woman's emancipation from the laws of nature, suffrage leaders are working to destroy the states and enslave the American people," Rowe declared in her customary take-no-prisoners style. "The Federal suffrage amendment is a deliberate conspiracy to crush the will of the American public." The Antis in the audience bolted to their feet and clapped. "If the present legislature ratifies it will be due to the bolshevik and socialist influences at work on them," she insisted, and launched into a bitter tirade against Mrs. Catt and the Tennessee suffrage women. Though they were tempted to boo, the Suffs in the galleries just stuck their tongues out or made ugly faces at Rowe, silently expressing their displeasure. The legislators would be wise "to keep the counsels of honor and not the counsel of these women of Tennessee," Rowe advised rather flippantly.

"We are living in perilous times," Rowe warned. "The destroyers are at work. The wreckers are at our homes. The Bolshevists are at your door and seeking the centralization of power. Tennessee has the opportunity to immortalize itself as the savior of the republic," Rowe declared, "and redeem the principle of true representation and our union of states, without which American democracy must perish from the earth."

The Antis' delight in Rowe's fire-and-brimstone oration was curbed just a moment later when General Charles Cates of Knoxville, who'd served as Tennessee's attorney general for more than a decade, stood to speak on behalf of ratification. Cates immediately took the lady from New York to task for her slur on Tennessee women.

"When the men of Tennessee want to take lessons in honor they will take them from the women of Tennessee," Cates chastised to thunderous applause from the Suffs. "Let me say further to these distinguished ladies from outside the state who come here to preach against the women of Tennessee receiving the ballot—you can come here and preach to us for a thousand years before you could make us believe the women of Tennessee had lost their grip on womanhood!

"There is no socialism or bolshevism among Tennessee women," Cates thundered, and the Suffs roared. "The men of Tennessee trust their honor to their women," Cates rebuked Rowe as the galleries shook with more Suff applause, "and they should not hesitate to trust them with the ballot."

There were two shocking moments for the Suffs during the evening's jousting match. The unpleasant surprises weren't delivered by the abrasive insinuations of Miss Rowe or by the legal jujitsu of the Anti lawyers, but by a leaf of folded paper and the rap of a cane.

When Judge G. N. Tillman of Nashville rose to speak for the Antis, he slipped a sheet of paper from his jacket pocket, unfolded it, and began reading it aloud. It was a letter from Warren Harding, replying to a request from Tillman for clarification of Harding's position on ratification. The presidential candidate provided a startling reply: "I quite agree with you that members of the general assembly cannot ignore the state constitution," Harding wrote to Tillman. Eyebrows were lifted all around the chamber.

"I should be very unfair to you," Harding continued, "and should very much misrepresent my own convictions, if I urged you to vote for ratification when you hold to a very conscientious belief that there is a constitutional inhibition which prevents your doing so until after an election has been held." At this a few Anti legislators grinned, a few reporters looked quizzical, and all suffragists appeared extremely alarmed. Harding was giving credence, and approval, to the Antis' legally dubious and discredited constitutional objections.

"I do not want you to have any doubt about my belief in the desirability of completing the ratification, but I am just as earnest about expressing myself in favor of fidelity to conscience in the performance of a public service. Under these circumstances, please say to Republican members that I cannot ask them to vote for ratification."

Gasps of delight (the Antis) and disbelief (the Suffs) filled the chamber. The standard-bearer of the Republican Party had just given Tennessee GOP lawmakers permission to oppose ratification. More than permission, he seemed to be condoning rejection. The Tennessee Republican leaders, Hooper and Houk, felt a sudden chill and could only shake their heads in dismay. The morning papers would later describe Harding's letter as a "body blow" to the suffragists.

The Suffs in the chamber had barely regained their composure from this jolt when they were knocked off balance by another tremor, announced by the tap of Edward Stahlman's cane hitting the floor as he rose to speak. For the Antis.

Stahlman looked the part of a successful man, with his still powerful frame dressed in a finely tailored suit, his silver hair well cut and carefully combed, his expensive cuff links catching the light. His large head and firm features, together with the intensity of his blue eyes, projected the image of a man in control. He demanded attention, and every eye in the chamber was upon him.

"If you listen to these lawyers you will still be in doubt when they get through," Stahlman began with a smile, saying he decided to speak because the people wanted a little common sense. "It is easy for them to construe the oath which you took as members of the legislature. They didn't take that oath, you took it."

Color drained from the faces of suffrage women in the galleries. The man who was a charter member of the Men's Ratification Committee, who had repeatedly assured Mrs. Catt and all the Tennessee Suffs of his support for ratification, was suddenly changing his tune. "I am in favor of giving the women the ballot," Stahlman maintained in what had become a familiar Anti refrain, "but I am not in favor of giving them this power through any doubtful action by the Tennessee legislature." Suffs in the galleries held back tears. They were being betrayed again.

"We fought for democracy in Europe, but now we are apparently attempting to take it away from ourselves at home," Stahlman fumed in a rant against the federal amendment's centralization of power. "The most sensible expression I heard this evening was from Senator Harding," Stahlman said, lauding Harding's "good faith, good taste, and justice" while giving the Democrats in the room a shiver. "I hope Governor Cox will do the same thing Senator Harding did. The truth is neither one had any business meddling in our affairs."

Stahlman's comments went on for only ten minutes, but it seemed an eternity to the Suffs in the chamber. Stahlman was, without doubt, a powerful man in Nashville, and the editorial pages of his *Banner* were influential. Now both were arrayed against them.

It was nearing midnight when, the debate concluded, members of the senate and house constitutional committees withdrew into executive session to deliberate upon ratification. The potential damage of Harding's letter, and the infuriating betrayal of Stahlman, riled the pro-ratification members of the senate committee and spurred Senator Gwinn to move quickly. After some sparring, Gwinn emerged from the meeting to announce that the committee would return a favorable report, recommending ratification of the federal amendment, in the morning. Senate Speaker Todd said the

senate would vote on ratification within an hour of receiving the committee's recommendation.

Things did not go as smoothly in the house committee session, to the
Suffs' distress. Seth Walker, as Speaker, was an ex officio member of every
house committee, and while he rarely availed himself of this privilege, he
took good advantage of it now to attend the committee's deliberations. His
presence rattled Tom Riddick, the rookie committee chairman, and Walker
was able to easily outmaneuver him. Walker leveraged his personal friend-
ships and Speaker's muscle to force the committee to postpone consideration
of the ratification resolution, delaying any vote until the following week at
the earliest. The committee had the right to hold the resolution for up to
seven days, and there was some possibility it would. The ratificationists on
the committee were furious with Walker's interference and with Riddick's
inability to counter it. When they emerged from the conference, frustrated
and tired, they rushed into a series of additional strategy sessions that ran far
into the night.

Throughout the debate, and even while the committee deliberations were
grinding on into the new day, Governor Roberts retained his posture of
confidence. Senate ratification of the Nineteenth Amendment was assured,
he said, "unless something miraculous occurs." It was a strange way to put it.

Chapter 19

◆ ◆ ◆

Petticoat Government

THE POSSIBILITY OF supernatural intervention was also on the minds of the Antis. It was, after all, Friday the thirteenth. The day will be a "hoodoo" for ratification, several Antis promised reporters, elevating superstition to political analysis. The Suffs managed a condescending smile and assured their opposition that "old-time beliefs, both as to woman suffrage and Friday the 13th, are going to meet their Waterloo."

It was hard to tell what the fallout might be from Harding's bungling. Harriet Upton was speechless with rage. Republican chairman Will Hays was being pummeled by complaints: How could Harding do this? He was inviting Tennessee legislators to kill the amendment; he was undermining the Republican record on woman suffrage. Hays was furious with Harding.

Democratic vice presidential candidate Franklin Roosevelt, on the stump in the Midwest, took gleeful potshots at Harding's comic gyrations of opinion on Tennessee ratification and his flip-flopping on support for woman suffrage over the years. The GOP candidate's position on woman suffrage, FDR said with a broad grin, "was as clear as mud."

Neither Carrie Catt nor Alice Paul made any public comments on Harding's letter to Judge Tillman, though they fumed in private. They thought it best not to bring more attention to the unfortunate reasoning of the man from Marion, just let it die. But based upon the many newspapers, in Tennessee and across the country, that reprinted Harding's letter in their pages, it was not going to die.

The suffragists needed seventeen senators to vote their way today and another fifty votes in the house, whenever the ratification resolution managed to escape the clutches of Seth Walker within the Constitutional Amendments committee and make it to the floor. No one could predict when that might be. There was talk that Walker and his friends were trying to arrange for the resolution to be buried in the committee, never to emerge.

Tom Riddick's failure to protect the resolution in that committee the previous night was the last straw for the pro-ratification house Democrats.

Riddick might be a brilliant lawyer, but he was just too green a legislator, and his leadership, or lack thereof, was endangering the amendment, they contended. He didn't know how to work the system, no member owed him any favors or loyalty, and he had been elected only to serve in the special session. Riddick's somewhat arrogant, abrasive style rubbed many of the old-timers the wrong way, and the rural fellows found "Million Dollar" Riddick, the lawyer with a very lucrative practice, too rich for their blood. Early Friday morning, the house Democrats staged a mutiny, insisting on a new floor leader.

They found a suitable replacement: Joe Hanover. He was experienced, well liked, politically savvy, and devoted to suffrage. Carrie Catt heartily approved, as she had confidence that Hanover was well equipped to execute the Suffs' ratification strategy. By breakfast time on Friday, Hanover was the new house ratification floor leader. Have pity on good ol' Joe, his friends moaned, everyone knows the stiffest battle is going to be in the house. But the senate had to be won first.

Exhausted and demoralized, the Woman's Party staff in Tennessee had been looking forward to having their own commander provide leadership rather than Mrs. Catt, but Alice Paul was still in D.C., a victim of bad cash flow. But as much as Sue White yearned for Miss Paul to march into Nashville and relieve her of the awful responsibility of directing the party's role in this definitive fight, she also knew, deep down, that it might be best that Miss Paul stay away.

A harsh sentiment had arisen among many of the legislators against all outsiders, the Woman's Party in particular. The Betty Gram incident didn't help; both the Antis and the Tennessee Suffs were still angry about Gram's "scene" with Seth Walker. Miss Paul wouldn't care a fig about all that, she'd stared down tougher opponents and had no desire to do the polite thing rather than the right thing, but her presence in the city would be a distraction. More than a distraction: a gift to the Antis. They were already having a field day with Mrs. Catt; imagine what diabolical fun they could have with Miss Paul.

Sue White willed herself to be calm and brave and focused. She wasn't a little orphan anymore, feeling abandoned, having to make her own way. She was a confident, competent woman, and she knew what to do. Accent the positive: this proved Miss Paul's deep trust in her leadership abilities. She'd have to live up to that trust. She pinned a nosegay of purple, white, and gold asters to her open collar (those were the new special Woman's Party floral badges) and straightened her prison pin. Miss Paul wasn't coming to Nashville, and Miss Sue must lead the troops.

Josephine Pearson also willed herself to remain calm and collected. It wasn't easy for her; she was easily provoked. Her temper, when triggered by what she considered a moral outrage, expressed itself in emotional outbursts that could be embarrassing. "If I can get Josephine Pearson mad, we will win," Kate Warner boasted to another suffragist in the hallway of the Hermitage. Warner had witnessed a few of these episodes over the years. Pearson heard the boast and refused to give Warner such satisfaction. Whenever events in Nashville disturbed her, Pearson would lock herself in her seventh-floor room "for a spell" until the bubbling anger subsided and she regained her composure. Then President General Pearson would return to duty.

On Friday morning a throng of Suffs and Antis, in full floral regalia, pushed through the doors of the senate gallery, scrambling and shouldering one another to grab a good seat. In an impressive display of political symbolism, the pro-ratification senators had invited prominent Tennessee suffrage women to sit beside them at their desks, as guests, but also as future partners in the governing process. They were in for quite a show.

Andrew Todd gaveled the senate to order, and Estes Gwinn delivered the majority report of the Constitutional Amendments Committee. The report, hammered out in the early morning hours, was remarkably strong and unequivocal, even embellished by some rhetorical flourishes.

The committee "is of the opinion that the present Legislature has both a legal and moral right to ratify the proposed resolution," the report said, detailing the legal rationales for this judgment. "Its adoption is as certain as the recurrence of the seasons. . . ."

"National woman's suffrage by Federal amendment is at hand," the senators wrote, "it may be delayed, but it cannot be defeated; and we covet for Tennessee the signal honor of being the 36th and last state necessary to consummate this great reform." Cheers from Suffs in the balcony rang out as Senator Gwinn finished the report: "Fully persuaded of its justice and confident of its passage, we earnestly recommend the adoption of the resolution." More clapping. But there was a minority report, too, written by the two members of the committee who disagreed, insisting that the senate must refuse to act upon ratification. After sparring, and the first test vote, the minority report was tabled by a comfortable margin, and the majority report was accepted by a voice vote. More Suff hoorahs.

Ernest Haston, the Suffs' floor leader in the senate, rose to place the ratification resolution itself before the senate for passage, but Lon McFarland jumped to his feet. "Point of order," he yelled, and handed a written protest to the clerk, contending that the senate had no power or authority to act on the ratification resolution. Speaker Todd overruled the point of order and McFarland appealed the Speaker's decision, but Todd's rule was sustained by an overwhelming majority. These were the warm-up acts to the day's drama, and there was a rustle of movement, both on the floor and above, as the chamber braced for the main attraction. Senator Herschel Candler took the floor.

Candler was a man of the law, a husband and father, a former colonel in the army, but he felt like a lonely warrior, abandoned by his own senate colleagues and his party. They were all trying to defeat him in his crusade to prevent this abomination of woman suffrage from infecting the entire nation. He glanced around the chamber to see many of his colleagues sitting with women lobbyists at their elbows, sharing their desks, whispering in their ears: coarse, political women who should be at home, but instead they were invading the senate sanctum. A few of his fellow senators had political bosses sitting beside them, keeping them on a leash, making sure they voted the way they were told. It sickened him. He considered himself a man of patience and probity, but dammit, he was not going down without a fight.

"I know of the pressure that has been exerted here," Candler told his colleagues, "and I am humiliated to confess that southern Republicans are Republicans for revenue only." A segment of the men in the chamber grumbled. "I know of men who a week ago were against this thing are for it today, and I know why: Many of them now have their names on the state payroll," Candler continued, eliciting angry glares from the floor.

"I am here representing the mothers who are at home rocking the cradle, and not representing the low-neck and high-skirt variety," Candler said, pointing his finger at a group of suffragists, "who know not what it is to go down in the shade of the valley and bring forth children. Motherhood has no appeal to them." Women began to hiss at Candler, and an incensed Suff in the gallery shouted down: "I have six children!"

He didn't give up. The federal amendment was the dawn of "petticoat politics," Candler maintained, an era of radical feminine domination. "If there is anything I despise, it is a man who is under petticoat government!" he blasted. Men joined in the hissing.

"You are being dictated to by an old woman down here at the Hermitage Hotel whose name is Catt. I think her husband's name is Tom," Candler joked lamely. "Mrs. Catt is nothing more than an anarchist." The hissing grew louder, almost drowning out Candler's screed. "Have you read the speech of hers before an audience in New York, when she said that she would be glad to see the day when negro men could marry white women and it is none of society's concern? This is the kind of woman that is trying to dictate to us." Even some of his fellow senators were hissing Candler now. "They would drag the womanhood of Tennessee down to the level of the negro woman!" Protests rained down on him from every corner of the chamber. He was undeterred. He steadied himself to make his final terrifying point.

"Within a very few years after this amendment has passed, you will find that Congress has legislated so as to compel we people of the south to give to the negro men and women their full rights at the ballot box," he warned in a shrill voice. "Then you will find many of your counties, now dominated by the Democrats and white people, sending up negro representatives to this house.

"I have telegraphed to Senator Harding my unwillingness to violate the constitution of my state. I warn the majority in this chamber now that the next thing we know negroes will be here legislating in Tennessee as they did fifty years ago."

The chamber broke into a hissing, shouting, and jeering frenzy. Flushed and spent, he sat down. His colleagues were embarrassed by Candler's outburst, the Tennessee Suffs were outraged, and even the Antis found his statements offensive—and worse—possibly damaging to their efforts. Candler had managed to insult everyone.

Andrew Todd left the Speaker's chair to respond. He tried to calm the room, speaking in a stern but soothing, fatherly tone: "That is the most unfortunate speech that has ever been made upon the floor of the Senate," he lamented. "These slurs do not meet approval of the good women of Tennessee," he chastised Candler.

"I am convinced that there yet remains enough virtue among the womanhood of Tennessee and enough courage among the manhood of the state to see that no condition such as the Senator from McMinn has pictured would ever occur," Todd said in rebuttal. "We won't have negro rule.

Republicans and Democrats alike would take their muskets and go to the polls to prevent it." Todd was, unfortunately, correct about that.

"There are no sinister influences here," Todd said, trying to inject some humor into the tense proceedings. "Talk about petticoat government. If there is a man in this house or in the gallery who has not been under petticoat government ever since he was born, I want him to stand up. I am ready to go into petticoat government." The Suffs clapped their hands sore for Todd. "I have always been under that kind, and I thank God for it!" Todd received an ovation as he returned to the Speaker's chair.

Governor Roberts now entered the chamber, and all eyes followed him as he made his way to the Speaker's desk, sitting down next to Senator Todd. His silent presence gave the signal that he was keeping score. The Suffs applauded his appearance; the Antis viewed him with suspicion, and they noticed Roberts's surrogate, Albert Williams, circulating among the senators aligned with the administration, reminding them of what they'd promised. Congressman Will Taylor kept an eye on his fellow Republicans while he sat at the desk of one senator known to be opposed to ratification, never leaving his side until the roll was called.

The men of the senate felt compelled to explain themselves, to justify their positions, and for almost three hours a steady parade of wordy senators took the floor. Most rehashed the legal arguments or made the case for party obligation to ratify, but almost every speaker condemned—or, more painfully, ridiculed—Herschel Candler's vituperative remarks.

Republican National Committee member John Houk, who'd had a bad night after Harding's letter was revealed at the debate, stood to make a ringing speech. "There is no politics in this proposition, and there is no 'nigger' in this proposition," Houk declared. "It is a proposition of right and justice." Houk paused to accommodate the sustained applause from the gallery. "The time to split hairs is gone," he proclaimed. "In all my life I have never heard a sound argument against giving woman the right to vote: a woman is a human being and so is entitled to a vote in the making of laws affecting her and her children." Speaker Todd rapped his gavel to quiet the loud cheering.

Anita Pollitzer's favorite, Erastus Patton of Knoxville, also took after Candler: "I have never been a pie-hunting Republican," Patton protested, taking umbrage at Candler's insinuation that his fellow party members could be influenced by patronage. And he took exception to Candler's allegations that woman suffrage would be ruinous to state government: "If I thought for one minute it would work to the detriment of my little girl at home, I would vote against it," Patton vowed, "but you can't tell me that these magnificent women are going to turn the government into anarchy." Patton paused and then continued with a mischievous smile: "We have been accused of having petticoat government, but the Senator is mistaken there, he's behind the times, because they don't wear 'em anymore!" And the chamber broke into laughter. A few women blushed. Patton closed with a stirring appeal to the lawmakers to grant women their political freedom and a share in their government, ending with a rallying cry that brought all yellow-flowered spectators to their feet: "Let's make Tennessee the Perfect 36th!"

More senators stood to make heartfelt entreaties for ratification, including Senator C. C. Collins, who insisted on leaving his sickbed to attend the session and had to be helped to his seat, but who now rose shakily to his feet and, clinging to his desk, spoke up for ratification.

"I am voting for ratification because suffrage is right and just, not just because it aids either party," declared Albert Hill, upon whom the Suffs knew they could rely. "I believe that with equal suffrage we will have a better country and better government."

But one senator was less motivated by idealism than revenge. William Monroe was an avowed Anti; he'd opposed limited suffrage for Tennessee women the previous year and was listed as opposed to ratification, but he'd been bombarded with telegrams from Anti women in the North, specifically Connecticut, begging him not to impose woman suffrage upon their state by Tennessee's ratification. He didn't like Yankees telling him what to do. "Let's put back to Connecticut what she put on us," Monroe taunted gleefully, referring to the way that state, as well as other northern states, had readily ratified the Fourteenth and Fifteenth Amendments giving freed slaves civil rights and black men the vote.

"Connecticut was one of the first to take a position upon the question of Negro voting," Monroe explained. "Now that Connecticut took great pride in giving the south these amendments, it stands her in poor grace to say that we cannot hand back the question of woman suffrage. But I, for one, take great pleasure in so doing!" It was still and always about the Civil War, but if sour revenge brought another senator into the "aye" column for ratification, the Suffs were willing to clap for Monroe and his spiteful justification.

Carrie Catt and Harriet Upton waited impatiently in the Hermitage for word from the senate chamber. Catt kept busy with correspondence. She'd received a report from the private eye in New York digging for information about that mystery man in the Hermitage lobby, the one who claimed to represent a newspaper syndicate, or the Republican Party, or some other fiction. He was a fake, the investigator reported: his card bore a phony name, his company did not exist, his sponsors were shady. Stay away from him, the gumshoe advised Catt, make sure no one gives him any information. Catt wasn't surprised—she'd suspected the fellow was working for one of the corporate opponents of suffrage, one of the sinister influences—but this report just confirmed it. He wasn't the only such actor in the Hermitage lobby, she was certain.

It seemed long ago—but it was just last February—when Catt and Upton were so sure that they were on the verge of victory. So sure that at the NAWSA's final convention, after Catt made her valedictory speech launching the League of Women Voters, Upton had presented her with a beautiful victory brooch, a blue sapphire, the Chief's favorite color, surrounded by little diamonds. It was a gift of gratitude from suffragists across the country, and even schoolchildren had contributed their nickels and dimes to honor Mrs. Catt. The brooch would complement her ratification dress so well, and on that evening everyone had expected ratification to be completed within days. Catt was immensely touched by the gift, but she refused to wear the brooch until ratification was actually won. Here they were, six months later, marooned in a stifling room in strife-torn Nashville, still waiting for ratification. Upton longed for nothing so much as to see that brooch on Mrs. Catt's bosom.

There was also anxious waiting within the Woman's Party's town house in Washington as Alice Paul and her staff awaited bulletins from their colleagues in Nashville. "We are waiting, as women have had to wait thru all these ages, as patiently as possible for the results of the vote," Paul's secretary wrote that morning. "Our helplessness when we reach the final consummation of a piece of work, where we have to depend upon the judgment of men for the final word, is maddening even though it is an age-long helplessness."

It was well past lunchtime when the ratification resolution finally came to a vote in the senate. The roll call moved swiftly: "Bradley"—aye. "Burkhaiter"—aye. "Caldwell"—aye. "Candler"—no. One senator walked out of the chamber to avoid voting. Lon McFarland and two other senators abstained. An electric tension vibrated through the chamber as the "aye" votes climbed toward seventeen, the majority threshold needed to ratify in the thirty-three-member senate. "Houk"—aye was number fourteen on Sue White's tally sheet. "Long"—aye was number fifteen on Catherine Kenny's recording list. The Antis tried to raise a small ruckus of disapproval as the ayes mounted, and several men they'd been counting on buckled "under the lash of the bosses," as they put it, and deserted them. "McMahan"—aye was number sixteen, and the clamor in the galleries grew louder, with everyone wearing yellow up on their feet. "Matthews"—aye, and as the seventeenth vote in favor was cast, the gallery exploded in cheers and cries, waving of yellow banners, and deafening applause. The tumultuous demonstration continued, forcing a temporary suspension of the roll call.

Speaker Todd banged his gavel repeatedly, but the Suffs were still making so much noise that few people could hear the clerk continuing the roll or hear the senators' replies. The Suffs didn't care, they knew they'd won the senate. When the clerk finally shouted, in a hoarse bark, the final tally of twenty-five voting aye, four nay, one absent, and three not voting, the Suffs boomed again, and Todd had to call upon the sergeant at arms to subdue the rumpus. Catt and Upton could hear the cheers wafting up toward the hotel window.

The vote was a surprise, with stronger support for ratification than either side had expected. Several senators, card-indexed as Anti, had suddenly switched sides to bolster the margin. As the senators exited the chamber, they encountered a line of smiling suffragists who saucily lifted their skirts just enough to reveal a bit of ruffle beneath, proving that they still wore petticoats.

Streams of women and men, in distinct rivulets of yellow or red, cascaded down Capitol Hill from the statehouse toward the Hermitage. The Tennessee Suffs ran to Mrs. Catt's room to give her a full report. The vote was splendid, she agreed. The political leaders of both parties had done a fine job of keeping their men flying straight, and Republican senators hadn't taken Harding's free pass to abandon their pledges. But Catt was disturbed by Senator Candler's comments about her on the floor. She didn't care about him calling her an anarchist or a dictator, but she blanched when the Suffs related Candler's accusation that she favored intermarriage between the races. This could cause real trouble.

In a southern state such as Tennessee, racial taboos held tremendous power. In 1920, interracial marriage was illegal in thirty of the forty-eight states, including Tennessee, and antimiscegenation laws would remain enshrined in state constitutions for almost another half century, until declared unconstitutional by the U.S. Supreme Court. Even in those New England and upper midwestern states where interracial marriage was not against the law, it was widely scorned. Catt was right that mixed-race marriage was a toxic topic and woman suffrage could not afford to be in any way associated with it. She'd never said anything about marriage between the races; the allegation was a calculated lie, manufactured by the Antis and mouthed by their man Candler, but it could still be dangerous. She could not allow it to stand.

Within hours she'd written a firm, terse response and released it to the press: "It is an absolute fabrication that I have at any time advocated intermarriage between the white and negro races," she insisted. "Furthermore, I believe it to be an absolute crime against nature." Her statement was published in newspapers across the country.

Once again, Catt distanced herself from the ideal of true equality in pursuit of the franchise. She'd taken a similar position earlier in the year, during the South Carolina ratification campaign, when she'd refuted rumors circulating in the state capital that she'd "been entertained in negro homes and entertained negroes in my home."

"This is a most malicious appeal to sectional prejudice," Catt complained to a South Carolina senator. "I emphatically deny these stories." Whether her aunt Susan—who proudly welcomed many black guests to stay in her home and cherished her special place in Frederick Douglass's household—would have approved of her protégée's small-minded defense of the amendment that bore her name can only be surmised.

When pressed for the source of his allegations about Catt's views on interracial marriage, Candler had to admit he'd stretched things a bit, connected dots in a most haphazard way. He said he'd based his claim on a published interview with Catt in which she was quoted as saying, "Suffrage knows no bias of race, color or sex." Catt did believe that, at least in the abstract.

Though both houses of the legislature were adjourned until Monday, and the house vote wasn't yet scheduled, the pace of activity in the Hotel Hermitage did not abate on Friday afternoon. The Antis were not downcast by the senate's action; the senate vote was no indicator of suffrage's strength, Charlotte Rowe told the press. "This happened in other southern states," she said. "It will be remembered that in both Mississippi and Delaware the senate ratified, but defeated the amendment in the house by 2 to 1. These two states were working under the same 'party pressure' as Tennessee is now." The Antis were setting their sights on the house, a more fertile field for their activities. They brandished copies of the Friday afternoon *Banner,* which, as expected after Major Stahlman's public denunciations the night before, had turned its editorial pages against ratification.

While the Antis held strategy meetings on the mezzanine level of the Hermitage, the Suffs held their own in the assembly rooms below, just off the lobby, and then broke into smaller conclaves throughout the hotel and statehouse. Joe Hanover took charge, projecting confidence and determination. Hanover ordered another canvass of the house members, to solidify the pledges and identify any weak reeds among the members. Hanover was hearing things about legislators having second, and third, thoughts. The Tennessee Suffs were assigned to find their delegates once more.

Finding those delegates was made decidedly more difficult, as many had packed their bags and headed home for the weekend. The legislators were tired and grumpy, and staying in Nashville cost more than their per diem salary could cover. For those who lived close enough to make a weekend sprint home feasible, it was a chance to unwind, see their family, and consult with constituents. This made the Suffs very nervous, to think of the house members moving beyond their grasp and into the grip of unknown persuaders. Suffragists in the home districts were put on alert to keep an eye on their solons, while those in Nashville were ordered to stick close to the delegates who remained in the city.

The suffrage women were each assigned two delegates and took their responsibilities seriously, inviting their designated men to lunch and to dinner, for a ride in the country, a game of cards, or a moving picture show, anything to keep them out of the clutches of Anti workers, corporate lobbyists, or a bender in the Jack Daniel's Suite. The legislators certainly enjoyed the attention of some very attractive and socially prominent women, including Annie Laurie Stahlman, an energetic suffragist who was seen hosting a delegate at the tony Belle Meade Country Club, against the vehement protests of her father-in-law. The Suffs' work was to "cajole and coddle, entertain and amuse" the delegates, as Harriet Upton described it, all the while making strong, logical arguments for ratification. Some newspapers took a more hyperbolic view of the suffragists' attentions: "Automobile rides, hugs, kisses, even the absurdity of polishing the members' noses and rouging their cheeks in the assembly hall were frequently witnessed," one observer claimed.

Warren Harding did not send any note of congratulations to the senators of Tennessee. He was baffled by the negative reaction to the letter he'd written to Judge Tillman about fidelity to conscience and honorable reluctance to violate one's oath of office. It proved he was a man of principle, he believed. He'd gladly given Tillman permission to read the letter aloud in the state-house in Nashville last night, but now Will Hays was furious with him. Harding couldn't fathom why. While the senators of Tennessee were voting on Friday afternoon, Harding was speaking from his front porch, advocating a new "baptism in righteousness and a new consecration in morality" for the nation, a return to honesty and unimpeachable virtue in civic life. His wife, Florence, smiled approvingly from the shadows of the porch.

At the White House, Woodrow Wilson was feeling chipper, much improved, so much so that his physician, Dr. Grayson, had left his side to take a long-delayed vacation. Wilson spent his days sitting in his wheeled chair, reading in the sun of the south portico, keeping up with the dreadful news of renewed fighting in Europe—Warsaw was under fierce attack by the Red Army—and taking long automobile rides through the Virginia countryside with Edith. He tended to public affairs for as many hours as his strength allowed, working with his secretary, Joseph Tumulty. Upon his return from his daily car excursion on Friday afternoon, Tumulty briefed him on the situation in Tennessee. Ratification in that state was halfway there, Tumulty told the president, national woman suffrage almost clinched, his League of Nations legacy possibly made secure, but there was an obstacle: the Democratic Speaker of the Tennessee house, Seth Walker, was standing in the way.

Tumulty, the Suffs' best friend in the White House, kept in close contact with Mrs. Catt and with Helen Hamilton Gardener, NAWSA's liaison to the president. Mrs. Gardener, recently appointed by Wilson to the Civil Service Commission, was very generous to Tumulty, sending his family boxes of flowers, fresh apricots, and other delicacies (she sent such gifts to Mr. and Mrs. Wilson, too), and building on this friendly relationship, Gardner could comfortably approach Tumulty with occasional requests. On Friday evening, the president sent a telegram to Seth Walker:

May I not in the interest of national harmony and vigor, and of the establishment of the leadership of Americans in all liberal policies, express the earnest hope that the house over which you preside will concur in the suffrage amendment.

As soon as the wire was sent, Tumulty sent a second telegram to Carrie Catt at the Hermitage, informing her of the president's message to Walker, knowing she'd be pleased. When Alice Paul learned of Wilson's gesture of help, she was also immensely pleased. Paul did not enjoy a close relationship with the White House, for understandable reasons, but she thanked the president, publicly and warmly: "The message sent by President Wilson to Speaker Walker was without solicitation on our part, and we are deeply grateful for the aid he has given the suffrage cause since the fight for ratification by Tennessee began." In her glee over the combined successes of the day—the senate ratification and the president's assistance—Paul got a bit carried away: "We have won the long fight for suffrage," she announced on Friday night. But Miss Paul was mistaken.

The weekend of waiting developed into a strange interlude, marked by intensifying anxiety and hostility, move and countermaneuver. On Saturday morning, Seth Walker answered President Wilson's personal plea, and the defiant tone of Walker's telegram was remarkable, even shocking:

"I have the profound honor to acknowledge your wire of Aug 13," Walker wrote to Wilson. "I do not attempt to express the views of other members of the lower house of Tennessee, but speak for myself alone, which on the Anthony amendment are contrary to yours. You were too great to ask it, and I do not believe that men of Tennessee will surrender honest convictions for political expediency or harmony."

The arrogance of Walker's reply, and its air of condescension, angered many Tennessee Democrats but made Walker an even greater hero to the Antis. He was their leader in Tennessee now, and he was showered with congratulatory messages from around the country. "I thank God that the spirit of Andrew Jackson still exists in the old Volunteer State," wrote an admirer in Texas. "May your message awaken the old mountain patriots to a realization of the imperialism that threatens the rights of the states and individual liberty of the citizens." Walker also received a pat on the back from the Ochs family, publishers of the *Chattanooga Times:* "We are with you in spirit and heartily congratulate you on the masterly manner in which you have expressed your convictions . . . your courage to maintain virtue will shine resplendent in the hearts of worthy Tennesseans."

At the same time, Carrie Catt found herself forced into an uncomfortable defensive crouch, as she spent the weekend deflecting the Antis' vitriolic personal attacks. First she'd had to publicly refute Senator Candler's racially loaded allegations, and on Saturday she felt obliged to push back against the newest Anti claims concerning her connection to *The Woman's Bible*. They'd taken out a big half-page ad in the *Banner*, denouncing Mrs. Stanton's tome as a "suffrage tract" that questioned the divinity of Christ, denigrated Christianity, and ridiculed the Christian Church. The ad even lambasted the suffragists for desecrating the Sabbath by holding convention meetings on Sundays. "This is the teaching of national suffrage leaders," the ad screamed, with Carrie Catt's name in bold type. "Are you willing for women who hold these views to become political powers in our country?"

Catt was tired of this *Bible* nonsense and responded, "I spoke and voted for a resolution repudiating the bible." But it was all a red herring, she averred, a distraction from the real issue facing Tennessee—justice for women.

Catt's reply was duly published in the papers, but it didn't restrain the Antis from using *The Woman's Bible* as a grenade. They invited sympathetic clergymen to view the *Bible* exhibit at their Hermitage headquarters and convinced more than two dozen men of the cloth to sign a petition to the legislature condemning Mrs. Stanton's heretical book and denouncing woman suffrage in general. Quite a few sermons on Sunday were devoted to demonizing the long forgotten *Bible,* its long dead author, and the beleaguered, but still living, president of NAWSA, perspiring in her room at the Hermitage.

Catt had reason to feel like a punching bag. Besides the Antis' crude aspersions, she was being flooded with anonymous letters, dutifully delivered to her room by the bellboy, letters that were "vulgar, ignorant, insane," as she characterized them, attacking her personally and denigrating all suffragists in the most sordid manner. Catt was also convinced that her phone was being tapped at the hotel. Upton, the veteran of many a dirty Ohio campaign, told Catt that almost every day, when she opened the door to her room, she found a man just outside, leaning with his ear to the door, trying to listen to her conversations. Pardon me, she'd bark with great annoyance, and he would scamper away. Other Suffs also reported men loitering in the hallways near their rooms, trying to overhear their discussions and meetings. They took to closing the transoms above their doors, making it harder to eavesdrop but also making their rooms unbearably hot and stuffy. Soon Upton would find that her telegrams were being intercepted on their way from her room to the hotel's Western Union desk and handed to Anti headquarters.

The Antis also felt aggrieved. Charlotte Rowe announced that she was lodging a civil suit, seeking damages against Catherine Kenny for public defamation. Rowe claimed that when she recently came upon Kenny talking to another suffragist in the Hermitage lobby, Kenny warned her companion: "Let us move away from that notorious woman." Rowe, outraged, followed Kenny across the lobby, making quite a scene. Now the incident was the city's favorite piece of gossip—did Kenny use the phrase "notorious woman" or "notorious creature"?—while Kenny protested that she didn't say Rowe was "notorious" in the sense of character, just reputation. Rowe was not mollified; see you in court, she told Kenny.

The Antis also complained that Suffs were conspiring to suppress the distribution of antisuffrage-inclined newspapers, such as the *Chattanooga Times*, in Nashville. The paper was suddenly hard to find at the newsstand in the Hermitage lobby or at most other vendors in town, and the Antis alleged that Suffs were buying bundles of the paper off the delivery truck and destroying each day's issue before it could reach the hands of readers. The *Times* launched an investigation.

The Antis were well aware that their backs were pressed against the wall, but they adopted a defiant swagger during these intervening days, boosting their image among impressionable legislators. The looming confrontation in the house was possibly the Antis' last stand, their Alamo, though they were confident of a more favorable outcome than experienced by that former Tennessee legislator Davy Crockett. Along with their more aggressive stance, the Antis' language and actions grew more belligerent. Friction with the Suffs became physical. Upton was jostled in the Hermitage elevator by a group of Tennessee Anti women (whether Miss Pearson was among them isn't known) who made clear that she wasn't welcome in Nashville. Joe Hanover also found himself roughly shouldered in the hotel and was subjected to vile slurs as he walked through the lobby: "Kike!" the Jewish legislator was called. "Bolshevist!" It was getting nasty.

On one afternoon during the weekend, Catt lay down on her bed to take a nap. The heat, tension, and constant stream of visitors sapped her strength by midday, and she found forty winks to be a tonic, keeping her going for the late night meetings. As she stretched out on the mattress, she slipped her hand under the pillow, and her fingers hit something hard. Bolting upright, she grabbed the thing under the pillow and pulled it into the light. It was a whiskey bottle.

The Antis. The Antis planted the booze, she was certain, to discredit her. It was another of their devilish plots to malign her and embarrass the Cause. She didn't scream, but she did panic. She must hide it before she was caught in possession of the forbidden booze by an Anti search party, obviously the next stage of their plot. She considered hiding it in a suitcase, but that seemed too obvious; she thought of flushing it down the toilet, but the liquor smell might linger. She heard someone enter her sitting room and braced for the raid.

It was only Harriet Upton walking in. Oh, that bottle, Harriet tried to soothe the Chief, there was nothing to it. A friendly woman reporter had asked if she could stow it in the suite for safekeeping, Upton had agreed, and there was nothing to be alarmed about. But Catt was still alarmed. The Suffs couldn't afford a tawdry, trumped-up scandal like this. Catt insisted that she be driven far out into the countryside, where she was finally relieved to see the whiskey bottle safely disposed, buried in the crevice of a stone wall covered with poison ivy. Paranoia had set in, but with good reason.

In the wake of the senate ratification, the Antis redoubled their efforts to swing house delegates against ratification. Whether a delegate was still non-committal, confused, or simply ripe to have his mind changed, the Antis made a fresh push to get to him. If he remained in Nashville over the weekend, they found him; if he was at home, he was visited. There were many means of persuasion.

A thriving industry of bribery and influence peddling developed, and there were rumors of sacks of money being shipped into Nashville over the weekend in advance of the house deliberations. Both the Antis and the Suffs claimed their opponents were trafficking in illicit inducements, and there were so many reports of bribes being offered and taken that a Nashville judge would soon convene a grand jury to investigate. Some legislators and politicians were said to be acting as middlemen, bringing the names of sus-ceptible lawmakers to Anti campaigners, then arranging the payments, with a finder's fee cut for themselves.

Harriet Upton learned that one Republican legislator was being offered $100 by a rogue Republican lobbyist working against ratification, on condition that the lawmaker simply go home before the house voted. The legislator decided to stay. But the delegate who'd tried to strike a bargain with Upton—I'll vote for ratification if you can arrange for a new post office in my hometown—walked over to the Antis when she refused.

Joe Hanover was swamped by reports of money being slipped under the table to influence house members' votes or to keep them from voting at all. Hanover didn't possess the usual political tools to counter these blandishments—patronage, pork, and legislative favors, such as greasing the wheels for bills sponsored by a delegate—because he was only a rank-and-file legislator with a battlefield promotion to floor leader. The Suffs also didn't have the corporate support—or cash—that the Antis seemed to possess. Hanover's most useful tool was his popularity and respect in the house. Some of the less educated legislators from the rural districts had come to rely upon Hanover to draft the bills they wanted to submit for passage, and he used his legal skills to help them. That generosity now paid off. One of those veteran members, a fiddle-playing farmer who was counted safe to vote for ratification, came to Hanover's room over the weekend to report that he'd changed his mind. "Sorry, Joe, but I'm going to have to leave you suffrage boys," the fiddler said, a bit bleary-eyed from a long night in the Jack Daniel's Suite. "The Antis just paid me two hundred dollars."

The way Hanover told the story, he put his arm around his colleague and said: "You sold out too cheap. I hear they're paying the others five hundred."

The legislator was miffed. "Well, them crooked sons of bitches!" he cried. "I'm gonna vote for you, Joe." And he returned to the suffragists' camp.

There were other modes of persuasion available to the Antis besides cold cash: jobs and positions could be offered, business and personal loans proffered, lucrative deals dangled. And if these didn't work, there were other techniques besides logical argument to convince a man that it was in his interest to vote against ratification. Edward Stahlman, once a professional lobbyist for the railroads and still their outspoken ally, could be seen all over the Hermitage, hard at work on legislators who'd pledged to ratify but now might be convinced to waffle and tilt. His efforts were meeting with success, and reporters were beginning to notice that in the past few days, Stahlman "has done more to change the minds of men who were for suffrage when they came here a week ago than any other individual." Luke Lea's *Tennessean* began to refer to Stahlman as "the Prince of Lobbyists" with grudging admiration.

"Enough votes are pledged to adopt the resolution in the house," a veteran statehouse reporter noted over the weekend, "but the members do not look you in the eye when they say they will vote for it." Sentiment for ratification had cooled, and "a sort of reversal of enthusiasm has been spreading over the members like wet blankets," the reporter observed. "The house would like to postpone action another week or another month or another hundred years. . . ."

John Houk noticed eyes averting, too. He was losing pledged men. His senate colleagues had held firm, but lower chamber delegates were deserting the ratification ranks all through the weekend. Those smooth-talking corporation men in the Hermitage lobby were the reason, he believed.

"There are signs of the old railroad lobby against ratification on the surface," Houk warned RNC chairman Will Hays in a searing telegram. After years in the statehouse, Houk could spot them—the railroad men and the factory men, the steel men and the liquor men—from across the Hermitage dining room, with one eye shut. He could almost smell them.

In an extraordinary step, Houk went beyond his confidential note to Hays to sound a very public alarm on Sunday evening: "I believe one of the most powerful lobbies in the history of the Tennessee legislature is now at work to defeat ratification," Houk announced to reporters, "and if ratification is defeated the special interests of the state will be responsible." He called for a legislative inquiry into the reports of corporate influence and bribery.

Sue White knew what John Houk was talking about: her latest polling numbers kept slipping through the weekend, as men who had once pledged for ratification hesitated yet again. It was the Louisville and Nashville influence, she, like Houk, was convinced. The L&N had kept a stranglehold on the Tennessee legislature for generations, and now Edward Stahlman and Seth Walker could forcefully represent the company's position against ratification in persuasive confabs with (often) intoxicated delegates. There was a powerful synergy in the workings of the Anti lobbyists.

In retaliation, White threatened to reveal the names, and publish the written pledges, of any delegate trying to wriggle out of his promise to vote for ratification. No man would be allowed to execute a double cross quietly. Show them for the hypocrites they were, Miss Sue insisted.

"Blackmailers!" screamed the Antis.

The developments over the weekend seemed to confirm the shape of what might be called the suffragists' grand unified conspiracy theory, a political hypothesis that was far-reaching but not so far-fetched. It tied together the L&N, Seth Walker and Edward Stahlman, and the mysterious "syndicate" man in the Hermitage lobby, with the money passing hands in the rooms above; it linked the refusal of the governors of Connecticut and Vermont to call special sessions with Warren Harding's infuriating ambivalence.

On Sunday night, Alice Paul articulated this theory to the press: The L&N, owned by the Connecticut-based Atlantic Coast Line holding company, was financing and directing a furious antiratification lobby in Tennessee in order to protect the reelection of Connecticut senator Frank Brandegee, who faithfully advanced the interests of the company in the U.S. Congress. With the railroads just emerging from wartime federal control, facing labor demands and capital improvement expenses, they needed to keep their friends in Congress, especially ones such as Brandegee, who held a seat on the Interstate Commerce Committee.

Brandegee was also a vociferous antisuffragist who'd helped block congressional passage of the Nineteenth Amendment for years, working in harmony with Senators James Wadsworth of New York and George Moses of New Hampshire, all of whom were up for reelection in the fall. These incumbents had good reason to fear that if the women of their states were allowed to vote, they might exact revenge on them at the ballot box. Mollie Hay was at that very moment leading a revolt within the New York State Republican Party against Wadsworth's renomination. These three senators were Republicans, and they'd been instrumental in choosing Warren Harding as the party nominee inside that famously smoke-filled room in Chicago earlier in the summer. Now they were asking Harding to protect their careers by putting the brakes on the Nineteenth Amendment and keeping women from the polls. The Connecticut and Vermont governors were also under the Atlantic Coast Line's corporate influence, the theory posited, and the company had probably sent that mystery man—who claimed to represent a syndicate of New York, Connecticut, and Vermont interests—to the Hermitage.

"Some of the poor dupes in Nashville do not realize that they are victims of a plot," Paul told the press, blithely insulting the Tennessee legislators, "to return this bitter anti-suffragist [Brandegee] to the senate this fall." Amplifying Betty Gram's accusations against Seth Walker, Paul let the fur fly:

"Mr. Walker, speaker of the house, is a young attorney who has, on many occasions, given the most fervent assurances that he would support suffrage. Recently he was made an attorney for the L&N Railway and the result is the otherwise inexplicable change of attitude evidenced in his message to President Wilson yesterday refusing to support the suffrage amendment." It all fit together, alarmingly well.

That night, Paul sent Abby Baker on another emergency mission to see Warren Harding. She was to impress upon him the damage Senator Brandegee and his railroad minions were causing in Tennessee and to urge the candidate to do something about it. Baker took a taxi to Harding's house in Marion and was ushered into his study by Florence. Harding was evasive, as usual, but beyond that, Baker found him to be stunningly obtuse. "Frank Brandegee has no influence in the Senate or anywhere else," Harding told Baker, dismissing her concerns about him. "He only has $100,000." It seemed a bizarre assessment of a prominent lawmaker, but she let it go.

When she told Harding that his letter to Judge Tillman was being used by the L&N lobbyists in Nashville to convince legislators not to ratify, he responded: "I could not stultify myself by asking a man to vote for ratification if he had conscientious scruples about constitutionality." Baker explained that those constitutional questions had already been ruled moot by noted legal experts, but Harding only looked at her blankly and repeated robotically: "I cannot stultify myself . . ." No matter the argument she put forward, regardless of the evidence she presented, Harding parroted this same answer, "I cannot stultify myself . . . ," punctuated by a wiping of his brow.

"Harding looks perfectly stupid," Baker relayed to Alice Paul. "So much so that the newspapermen call him nothing but 'Old Stupid.' They say he is drinking again and his appearance confirms the report." Even in this state, Harding did manage to make a pass at Mrs. Baker. But he said he'd have to ask his campaign manager, Harry Daugherty, whether he should play any further role in Tennessee. Daugherty would tell him: No.

By Sunday night, August 15, things seemed murkier than they'd been before, the outcome in the house even more uncertain. The Suffs had come into the special session with sixty-two signed pledges for ratification from house members; the Woman's Party now reported between forty and forty-three firm commitments, with another dozen pro-ratification votes possible. The Antis claimed some of those "firm" legislators had pledged to them as well. Both sides projected confidence, both sides predicted victory, but both began to hedge a bit.

Joe Hanover went from an unequivocal declaration on Saturday—"There is absolutely no chance of defeat"—to a more measured statement on Sunday: "There is no doubt in my mind" that Tennessee would ratify. Sue White admitted that the issue was "undecided" but took a literal approach to predicting victory. "We have the votes pledged," she said, "and many of these pledges are in writing, and in my possession." Those were old pledges, she knew, minds had been changed in the meantime, but she'd use those original promises to shame any deserter. Seth Walker insisted he was "reasonably sure" the house would reject ratification. Reporters understood that neither side had any idea how things might play out, polls had become meaningless, everything was in flux.

On Sunday evening, a weary Carrie Catt sat at the writing desk in her room and penned a letter to her friend Mary Peck in New York, offering her candid view of the situation in Nashville:

We now have 35 1/2 states. We are up to our last half of a state. With all the political pressure, it ought to be easy, but the opposition of every sort is here fighting with no scruple, desperately. Women, including L. Clay and K. Gordon, are here appealing to Negro phobia and every other cave man's prejudice.

Men, lots of them, are here. What do they represent? God only knows. We believe they are buying votes. We have a poll of the House showing victory but they are trying to keep them at home, to break a quorum and God only knows the outcome. We are terribly worried and so is the other side.

I've been here a month. It is hot, muggy, nasty, and this last battle is desperate. We are low in our minds—even if we win we who have been here will never remember it with anything but a shudder. Verily the way of the reformer is hard.

Chapter 20

♦ ♦ ♦

Armageddon

O N MONDAY MORNING, the mood in Nashville was volatile, even violent. This was the suffrage Armageddon, as both sides considered the impending clash as a defining battle between good and evil, a struggle for the soul of Tennessee and the heart of the nation. When the legislators returned to the city, they were welcomed by a new Anti broadside that made the stakes perfectly clear:

BEWARE!

MEN of the SOUTH: Heed not the song of the suffrage siren. Seal your ears against her vocal wiles. For, no matter how sweetly she may proclaim the advantages of female franchise—

REMEMBER, that Woman Suffrage means a reopening of the entire Negro Suffrage question; loss of State rights; and another period of reconstruction horrors, which will introduce a set of female carpet-baggers as bad as their male prototypes of the sixties.

DO NOT JEOPARDIZE the present prosperity of your sovereign States, which was so dearly bought by the blood of your fathers and the tears of your mothers, by again raising an issue which has already been adjusted at so great a cost.

NOTHING can be gained by woman suffrage and much may be lost.

With the reconvening of the legislature, the Hotel Hermitage lobby became a petal-strewn battlefield, with men and women shooting suspicious glances at one another, flinging insults and insinuations, hurling accusations of deceit and skulduggery. The opulent lobby, chandeliered dining rooms, and potted-palmed loggia were scenes of shouting matches and shoving, often escalating into fistfights.

Overnight, Governor Roberts had been visited by a powerful group of newspaper publishers and warned that unless he reversed course and "pulled

off his men" working for ratification, his political career was over. Stahlman's *Banner,* the Ochses' *Times,* and other Democratic papers that had
supported Roberts in the primary would turn their editorial pages against
him in the general election, go Republican. Roberts swallowed hard.

Joe Hanover began receiving telephone calls in the middle of the night,
from women and from men. The women spoke in sugary tones, professing
to be devoted Suffs who wanted to give Hanover some vital information.
Meet me in room something or other, they'd purr. He had to laugh, it was
so obvious. He knew that if he walked into that room, the Anti-hired photographers would flash their camera bulbs, purporting to catch him in a
compromising situation. No thanks, he answered. But the men's voices on
the phone were gruff and sinister as they delivered naked threats: If he knew
what was good for his health, he'd do an about-face on ratification. Governor
Roberts ordered Hanover placed under police protection. Captain Paul Bush
of the Tennessee State Police was assigned as Hanover's bodyguard, and the
strapping trooper took up residence in an adjoining room on the third floor
of the Hermitage, monitoring Hanover's mail, telephone calls, and visitors.

The delegates, especially those who'd signed pledges to ratify, were also
reminded of just how much they, and their families, might lose if they continued to support ratification. Those who hadn't succumbed to bribes began
to be pelted with threats: job loss, political ruin, career destruction; their
house mortgage just might be foreclosed, their loan called due, their business
met with unexpected disaster. Carrie Catt was appalled by reports of blatant
extortion, horrified by the idea that shadowy men working for the Antis'
corporate friends were "applying the third degree" to lawmakers in hotel
rooms around the city.

If house members weren't persuaded by these techniques, perhaps they
could be dissuaded—or prevented—from voting at all. Some began receiving phony telegrams claiming their wife was ill, their child injured, their
house on fire, to compel them to hastily leave Nashville. Other lawmakers,
known to have a weakness for liquor, were entertained for hours in the Jack
Daniel's Suite, plied with whiskey until they were in a stupor, and the resulting hangover was expected to be powerful enough to keep them from the
next roll call. When the Suffs learned that one such legislator, listed as favorable to ratification, was careening down the Hermitage hallways, they made
sure he was escorted by friends to his room, put under a cold shower and
sobered up under a fan, then put to bed. He made roll call.

Both the house and senate convened at two o'clock. The senate, relieved of
the burden of ratification and unencumbered by hordes of spectators, took
up more routine measures. But the house floor and galleries were again
crowded with red- and yellow-rosed partisans, and similarly bedecked men
and women were in animation on the floor, darting from one delegate to the
next. Disproving fears about a quorum, attendance was unusually high, with
ninety-five of the ninety-nine delegates in their chairs. There was a height-
ened buzz of anticipation, as there was some possibility that the vote might
be called right then and there.

But the Constitutional Amendments Committee hadn't yet met to decide upon its recommendation, and while the Suffs might attempt to drag
the resolution out of committee onto the house floor for a vote, that would
be risky, as such a move required two-thirds of the members to agree, not
just a majority. Ratification leaders would execute this maneuver only if they
felt very confident of their strength. They were not confident; the Antis
noticed. The house adjourned until Tuesday morning, pending the decision
of the committee. The intervening hours were frantic.

As the delegates emerged into the Capitol corridors following adjournment, they were backed into corners by teams of women, adorned with red
or yellow, making another round of soprano supplications and alto advoca-
cies. As the lawmakers walked on the sidewalks leading from the statehouse
to the Hermitage or any of the adjoining streets, they were accosted by zealous proselytizers trying to convert them. Knots of arguing advocates formed
on the streets and in the Hermitage lobby, attracting curious onlookers and
wisecrackers the way a brawl or a cockfight might. "Campaigners were working in relays," wrote reporters on the scene, "and when one enthusiastic advocate or antagonist of votes for women became exhausted there was another
one near to take up the task."

More bad news was delivered to the Suffs during the day: nearly the
entire Nashville-Davidson County delegation, five of the seven men who
had been pledged solidly for ratification, had suddenly defected to the Antis.
This was the stuff of nightmares. The Davidson delegation was a keystone
Democratic bloc and was the responsibility of Luke Lea and his political
apparatus to manage. Lea had obviously lost control of his men—or let them
go. Or the railroads—with offices, facilities, and tracks in Nashville—had

captured them. Anne Dudley, who'd pledged these Davidson men of her home district, was distraught; Carrie Catt was dismayed, but not deeply shocked, to find that, once again, the freedom of American women might fall victim to the egos and ambitions of powerful men. As might be expected, the Antis were jubilant.

Opponents of the federal amendment were emboldened to take daring new steps. The same band of Democratic newspaper publishers who'd visited Governor Roberts was now making the rounds of state Republican leaders, offering a sweet deal: Make sure enough Republican delegates in the house swing against ratification, preventing a majority coalition, and the Democratic newspapers would come out for the Republican ticket, from Harding on down. To stimulate more defections, Charlotte Rowe publicly offered to defend any delegate who might wish to withdraw the ratification pledge he'd given to the Suffs. If Sue White was threatening to expose delegates who reneged on their pledges, Rowe promised to protect them from such disgusting blackmail. She could provide beleaguered legislators with incriminating information about the Suffs; it was the Antis' own type of card-indexing system—they could play that game.

The Antis also beefed up their Constitutional League legal team with the arrival of Judge Oscar Leser, a noted legal scholar who'd piloted efforts to defeat ratification in Maryland. And they augmented their lobbying brigade with former Chattanooga mayor (and recent gubernatorial contender) Jesse Littleton—who'd so unctuously assured Anita Pollitzer he was a firm suffragist—now openly working for the Antis.

In Marion, Warren Harding did the Antis another favor. When pressed by reporters for his latest opinions on ratification, Harding speculated that should Tennessee ratify, the constitutional questions swirling around the legislature's action, and the legal challenges that would surely follow, might throw the fall elections into chaos. Harding was reciting, almost verbatim, the Antis' script; he was skilled at repetition, if not reasoning. His fears about Tennessee's ratification would appear on the front pages of newspapers the next morning.

Governor Roberts was just trying to keep his head above water. On his desk was a barbed message from DNC chairman George White: "I insistently hope the Volunteer State, under your magnificent leadership, will keep step with the times," just as he received another "I'm depending upon you" telegram from Governor Cox. James Cox was receiving panic-tinged reports from Tennessee all day. Sue White and Anita Pollitzer wired to him the details of their findings about the probable Walker-L&N-Brandegee–Atlantic Coast Line connections, and he took them seriously. He mentioned the alleged conspiracy in his daily press briefing, and he authorized a special message, sent specifically to Democratic members of the Tennessee house known to have business ties to the L&N, asking them to stand fast for ratification.

"Asinine," a spokesman for the railroad called all the rumors about the Louisville and Nashville interfering in Tennessee's ratification fight. The accusations were "too absolutely absurd to need a denial," he contended. "What would the L&N be bothering about suffrage for?" he asked. "We have troubles enough of our own."

At eight p.m., the House Committee on Constitutional Amendments, a body of eighteen delegates drawn from both political parties, with Speaker Walker attending in an ex officio capacity, convened in the hotel room of its chairman, Tom Riddick, to decide whether to recommend ratification. Hundreds of people gathered in the Hermitage lobby, in the hallways and public rooms, awaiting word of the committee's decision. At a few minutes before the hour, Joe Hanover, who served on the committee, glanced at his pocket watch. Two committeemen, both pledged for ratification, were absent. Alert suffragists rounded up the two, who were obviously trying to duck the meeting, and hustled them over to Riddick's room.

The meeting was brief, little more than fifteen minutes: no debate, not even any real discussion. The first ballot was tied. Joe Hanover was disturbed to see that one of Governor Roberts's close allies, Banks Turner, voted with the Antis. Then, without explanation, another of the delegates who'd voted with the Antis asked to change his vote: put him in the aye column, favoring ratification. It is possible that Seth Walker signaled him to do this. The committee vote had demonstrated the strength of the Antis, and under these circumstances, the quicker Walker could herd his men to a full house vote, the better. The committee, by a vote of 10 to 8, recommended ratifying the federal amendment.

Joe Hanover left the room quickly. The Suffs had won, but the vote was too close. It didn't bode well for the full house vote. When Seth Walker strode out of the committee meeting, he told reporters: "We've got 'em whipped to a frazzle. We have ratification beaten, that is all there is to it."

Nashvillians awoke on Tuesday to a boldfaced and boxed advertisement in the morning *Tennessean:*

AN APPEAL TO THE CITIZENS OF NASHVILLE

Will you, by your presence in the Capitol this morning, help to DE-FEAT the Susan B. Anthony Amendment? This is the most important issue that has confronted the South since the Civil War.

We appeal to you in the name of Tennessee, in the name of the South to help us maintain a righteous cause.

Wear a red or pink rose. Show your loyalty to the people of your own land.

In the name of millions of Southern women we appeal to the unquestioned chivalry of the South.

Josephine Pearson was very proud of this bugle call from her Tennessee women of the Rejection League—fighting on the front lines—to their kinsmen on the home front. This was the day of the vote, and just as valiant Confederate soldiers had attempted to storm the statehouse in 1864, to oust the blue-belly Federalist soldiers and release the city from Union occupation in the Battle of Nashville, so she and her fellow Antis were willing to face the barrage on Capitol Hill today, for the glory and future of Tennessee. And Pearson was confident that the people of Nashville would turn out today to defend their state and protect their heritage. She pinned on her three red roses, her president general insignia, and headed to the statehouse.

The statehouse was looking a bit too yellow for Miss Pearson's taste. Squads of Suff decorators had been busy since just after dawn, tacking up bunting and banners, hanging flags. Saffron-colored cloth was draped from the columns of the building's portico, while the golden satin banners of the Tennessee suffrage organizations—as well as the Woman's Party's purple, white, and gold standards—were suspended between the Corinthian columns of the house chamber. Some daredevil suffragist had lashed a big yellow sunflower to the spread-winged eagle above the Speaker's chair.

Waves of people, thousands of people, surged up Capitol Hill in the hours before the session was to begin. The impassioned, the incensed, and even the indifferent came trudging up the Hill. Women who'd been in the suffrage fight for years, as well as those who'd ignored it all that time, came to watch a moment of history unfold before their eyes. Mothers brought their daughters. A car filled with women factory workers arrived, all wearing red flowers; they'd been given the day off by their boss to swell the ranks of the Antis.

The galleries were packed long before the first gavel, as Suff and Anti sympathizers fought over the seats and benches, elbowing one another for a standing room spot. On the floor of the chamber, the area behind the brass bar was already stuffed with standing spectators, and those who couldn't squirm their way in were pushed back into the hallway, where they stood four deep. The chamber floor looked like Union Station's waiting room, with nearly 100 members seated and more than 250 lobbyists milling around them.

Seth Walker, his eyes swollen from lack of sleep, stood on the Speaker's stand and rapped his gavel at half-past ten. The moment the roll call was complete, ninety-five legislators present, the Antis made their first move: they demanded that the floor be cleared of all lobbyists and spectators. A howl of protest went up from the ratificationists. House Rule #17 stipulated that no one but legislators were allowed on the floor except as guests of the Speaker; the rule was rarely enforced, but it should be now, the Anti delegate insisted. Speaker Walker agreed. Joe Hanover jumped up to protest: "There is no reason to ask America to leave the chamber," he yelled, the people are entitled to petition their representatives in person; we have nothing to hide. Hanover moved to suspend Rule #17. Walker smiled; he'd maneuvered the first test vote.

Suspending a house rule required a two-thirds majority. There was no way the Suffs could muster that many votes. The roll was called, with fifty-one voting aye to allow spectators to remain on the floor, forty-five voting no. Not enough. Speaker Walker ordered the sergeant at arms to remove all spectators from the chamber floor. It took some minutes for all the Suff and Anti workers to be escorted off the floor—the women did not go willingly. Only then did the real dueling begin.

Tom Riddick, as chairman of the Constitutional Amendments Committee, submitted the majority report recommending ratification and kicked off the debate. He put his courtroom dramatic skills to good use and opened with a bang: "Isn't it time for the South to quit being the tail-end of creation, the backyard of civilization, remaining backward on the march of progress?" he cried, calling opposition to woman suffrage "a relic of barbarism."

Riddick's arguments ranged from quoting the Golden Rule and Declaration of Independence—"If women are human beings, why shouldn't the first sentence of the Declaration of Independence apply alike to them?"—to dismissing the "Negro question" along with the various legal complications supposedly impinging upon ratification. And he made a threat: "I have here the pledges of 62 members of this House to ratify the 19th Amendment, right here in black and white," he announced, "which the people of Tennessee will have the opportunity to read." A few legislators looked queasy. "You speak of your conscience?" Riddick demanded. "What about your conscientious objections to violating your pledge?" More cheers from the yellow-breasted men and women. "If those men fail to keep faith, and this resolution is defeated," Riddick said slowly and solemnly for emphasis, "I shall go from this chamber a dishonored man. Ashamed of being a Tennessean, and doubly ashamed of being a Tennessee Democrat!" Flushed and quivering, Riddick sat down.

For the next three and a half hours, the friends and foes of ratification made their case in the well of the house. Almost every argument ever voiced over the past seven decades, both for and against woman suffrage, was revived, with the addition of concerns such as states' rights, southern chivalry, home rule, and the Negro question. And, of course, the loudest themes heard in Nashville during the past weeks—constitutional qualms, oaths of office, *The Woman's Bible,* and "certain influences" trying to sway the legislature— all popped up during the overheated debate. Frustrated spectators relegated to the statehouse corridors had to rely upon those standing closer to the chamber door to relay what was being said inside. All they could hear was the ballyhoo.

Each time a speaker made a clever remark or a cogent point, fans adorned in either floral yellow or red applauded and cheered, whistled and stomped. Decorum was completely abandoned by both sides. It was the political version of talent night at the local vaudeville house, and the speakers definitely played to the audience, each trying to outdo the other and win the crowd's approval.

Creed Boyer took the homespun approach: "Women are the best thing God ever made," announced the seventy-four-year-old Republican from the mountains of East Tennessee, "and I honor women above all humankind.

But I would not pollute them by allowing them to wade through the filthy waters of politics." The Anti women lobbyists clapped.

He was blessed with a wife, nine daughters, eight sons, and eight daughters-in-law, Boyer told his listeners, and all of his womenfolk agreed that he and his sons could adequately represent them at the polls. "And I guess what's good enough for them will have to be good enough for the rest." Catherine Kenny remembered Boyer. He'd pledged to ratify "until the cows come home." Now he was proud to be voting against ratification, for the sake of his eighteen female family members. The Suffs' hisses were drowned out by the Antis' applause.

Carrie Catt again kept vigil at the open window of her room, straining to hear the periodic bursts of cheering that spilled down from Capitol Hill. The imposing visage of the statehouse filled Catt's window frame, just as it dominated the skyline of the city. In that building, at that moment, her Cause and the future of American women was being debated and decided—by men. She could only watch.

Catt was, however, amused to learn that the Tennessee Suffs had gotten hold of a replica of the Liberty Bell, that famously cracked symbol of American independence, and installed it in the house chamber this morning, ready to be rung the moment the vote to ratify was won. When it was won; if it was won.

For years, in so many of her speeches, Catt had spoken of the moment heralding women's political freedom. The bell of liberty would surely, inevitably, ring, she'd say, because there was nothing so powerful, so irresistible, as an idea whose time had come. She'd told that to her Suffs in 1916; she'd told that to Congress in 1917; she'd told it to President Wilson in 1918. But sometimes, like this morning, she had to wonder. Some men in that statehouse across the way were undoubtedly making the same arguments against woman suffrage that Susan Anthony had heard. And some women were still frightened, or deluded, enough to be applauding them. The vote was likely to be excruciatingly close. Even at this late date, there was no firm consensus, no overwhelming mandate, for giving women the vote or permitting their full citizenship. She tried not to wonder whether America was ready to hear the Liberty Bell.

They went on and on, hour after hour. George Canale, a fruit merchant from Memphis, took the floor: "As a Southern man, I could not refuse to allow women to shed their refulgent rays across the path of politics in the South," Canale gushed. "Woman is God's chosen creature, and won't she, if taken into our political life, scatter her purity and fragrance into the muddled waters of our political life, and make it as clear as a crystal?"

Percy Sharpe, one of the Davidson County defectors, stood to speak of his sleepless nights, worrying about the violence that might be unleashed in the South if universal suffrage was imposed and black women and men were allowed to vote. He could not subject his elderly mother to such indignities. "I reached the decision that I would never put this thing upon my people," he proclaimed, or "force woman suffrage upon the states which don't want it."

The parade of speakers continued:

"Taxation without representation should no longer apply to the women of the United States," cried a speaker for the Suffs.

"This issue has nothing to do with woman's suffrage," insisted an Anti advocate, "it is a matter of the constitution and violation of our oaths."

"I would be ashamed to admit that my wife, my mother, or my sisters were not as capable of exercising the ballot as I am."

"The so-called elevation of woman in politics means instead her degradation."

"The working women of this country should have the same right accorded to Negro chauffeurs or a Negro porter."

"Tennessee must place the capstone on the temple of justice by becoming the 36th state."

The luncheon hour came and went and stomachs began to growl; the delegates got a bit fidgety. The Suffs noticed and kicked into action. They'd already bought sandwiches and iced tea to feed the hungry legislators, keep them from adjourning, and hold them for a vote. But the house sergeant at arms, under strict orders from the Speaker to allow no unauthorized person onto the floor, refused to permit the Suffs to distribute the food or even allow the pages to do it. The sandwiches sat uneaten, and the hungry legislators grew grouchier.

At some point between a speaker offering a tribute to the glories of womanhood and an orator launching another tirade against Mrs. Catt and *The Woman's Bible,* a page approached the desk of delegate Charles Wesley Brooks, Democrat from Carroll County, and slipped him a telegram. Brooks read it quickly and the color drained from his face. He sprang out of his chair and made his way to Joe Hanover. Brooks was in the ratification camp.

The note brought Brooks the awful news that his wife was seriously ill, and her doctors were imploring him to return home. I have to go, Brooks whispered into Hanover's ear, explaining the situation. Hanover had to wonder whether the dire warning was real, as there'd been so many fake telegrams of emergencies in the past few days. It was real, but Brooks was needed for this next vote; Hanover begged him to stay. Brooks slipped a folded train schedule from his inside jacket pocket and scanned down the tables. It was a long trip back to his home in West Tennessee. He needed to catch the next fast train.

Sue White, Betty Gram, and Anita Pollitzer stood just behind the brass bar at the rear of the chamber, paying close attention to the speeches but also watching the delegates themselves: who was listening, who was doodling, who was walking around, who was whispering to whom. They recorded each procedural vote, and they kept closest tabs on their men, the men they'd pledged or attempted to sway, the ones they could trust, and especially the ones they could not. They noted with irritation, but also a touch of sadness, that Harry Burn of Niota was wearing a red rosebud in his lapel this morning.

Burn was infuriating; he seemed willing to tell each side what they wanted to hear. Most recently he'd declared himself "undecided"—but he was voting with the Antis. Pollitzer noticed that Burn appeared agitated, his baby face lined with worry, his eyes betraying strain. She and Gram felt rather sorry for him; he was their age, he could have been their brother or boyfriend. He was awfully cute. He wasn't a smooth politician, he had an endearing awkwardness about him, an almost comical earnestness.

"I cannot pledge myself," he'd whispered to Pollitzer and Gram when they'd last confronted him. "But I will do nothing to hurt you." What did that mean? All they knew was that they couldn't trust Harry Burn.

After more than two hours of bitter back-and-forth, with tempers sparking and stomachs growling, Seth Walker relinquished the Speaker's chair and walked down to claim the floor. Before he could open his mouth, the Antis in the chamber began a long, loud ovation for him, which he accepted graciously, with a nod. He looked paler than usual, his eyelids heavy, his voice tighter, his manner agitated. Reporters noted that his nerves seemed "more or less unstrung." Nevertheless, the chamber hushed as he launched into what Tennesseans call a "real bearcat" of a speech.

"I thank God I can stand here unfettered and unhampered by political influences or by political aspirations," Walker opened. He won a loud cheer from the Antis while Suffs grimaced. "I resent the statements made by Mr. Riddick that the South is the tail end of creation," he fumed, his voice rising. "I am a southerner from the bottom of my foot to the crown of my head! . . . We want this to remain a white man's country!" There was deafening applause from the red-rosed.

"I resent charges that I've been influenced by a certain railroad, or that railroad has tried to change the opinion of some members of this body," Walker shouted. He held up a copy of the General Assembly's oath of office. "We are asked by some to disregard this oath. I don't believe the men of Tennessee will do it. The man who asks you to sacrifice your conviction is not worthy to be called a Tennessean."

Walker read the oath aloud, emphasizing the section where members swear they will "not vote for anything injurious to my people." The Nineteenth Amendment was most certainly injurious to the people of Tennessee, and to the rest of the South, Walker boomed. "Just as soon as this 19th Amendment—this Susan B. Anthony Amendment—is put upon a state like Georgia," a state with a large black population, "Hell's going to break loose in Georgia!"

Are we going to force suffrage upon another southern state that has rejected it? Walker challenged his colleagues. He read a letter he'd received from "certain colored ladies of California" urging the Tennessee legislature to ratify. "The Negro women of California always voted 99 per cent," the letter writer said, pointing proudly to the active participation of black Californians, who'd been able to vote since 1911. "While our white sisters vote only about 20 percent."

"I say this is infamous!" Walker shouted.

Walker held a sheaf of documents in his hand and methodically read aloud one, then the next, to make his various points. He gave a dramatic reading of Harding's letter to Judge Tillman, praising Harding's good judgment and character, while provoking a shiver in his fellow Democrats. "I don't know whether Harding or Cox will be elected as President," Walker said slyly, "but if Harding should be elected, you will have an honest man."

He then read President Wilson's recent telegram to him, urging ratification, and at this point the galleries exploded again, but now it was the Suffs causing a ruckus. At Walker's mention of Wilson's name, Anne Dudley climbed atop a bench at the very back of the room, behind the railing where spectators were still permitted to stand, and began shouting, "Wilson! Wilson! Wilson!" followed by a shrill cheer. "Little would one have dreamed that this little mite of a woman could possess such vocal powers," wrote the *Chattanooga Times.*

Wilson, the southern president, was still a demigod to Tennessee Democrats, though he was being branded a traitor by Antis of the party. Dudley's call was taken up into the galleries, where Suff women echoed Dudley's "Wilson" cry, with whoops, trills, yells, whistles, clapping, and foot stomping. It was quite a scene, and it went on for several minutes, drowning out Walker's speech.

He paused, waited, and then, sensing a lull in the rumpus, regained control. He read aloud his defiant reply to President Wilson, which elicited an outburst from the Antis almost as rowdy as the Suffs' had been. Walker then glanced up toward the galleries to address his yellow-sashed tormentors:

"Last year, standing about where I am now, I made the fight in this house for the suffrage bill, which you seemed to desire so ardently then. After the fight had been won I was proclaimed a hero. Today you same women are denouncing me as a Judas, as a Benedict Arnold, as a traitor. I have been insulted right here in this city. It has been said that the Louisville and Nashville Railroad had something to do with dictating my attitude." Betty Gram may have felt eyes all around the chamber burning into her, but she retained an impassive mien. Walker brushed away those claims, but as the Suffs noticed, he never actually denied that he'd been influenced by the L&N.

Walker resented yet another thing Tom Riddick had said earlier in the debate. He was angered by Riddick holding aloft the pledges of legislators who had once promised to ratify and threatening to expose those who'd changed their minds. Walker had his own pile of pledges:

"I have right now in my pocket the written pledges of more than a majority of members of this house that they will vote to defeat this amendment," and a gasp could be heard in the galleries. "But before I would show that paper to a living soul, and thus keep any one of these men from voting according to his own conscience, or even threaten to publish the list in an effort to coerce them into voting as they may feel they should not, I would suffer this right arm to be cut off," he cried, extending his arm for effect. He excited the crimson-corsaged to another wild ovation.

"Men of Tennessee, be men today!" Walker exhorted, bringing his admirers to their feet. "I don't want Democrats or Republicans. I call upon you as men!

"In good faith and good morals, we cannot ratify!"

Walker's concluding words coaxed another round of jubilant acclamation, and the substitute Speaker rapped the gavel repeatedly, to no avail. Walker had spoken for almost an hour, his passion and fury mesmerizing the chamber. His stem-winder seemed to galvanize the Antis.

With the vote expected to be so close, even the slightest swing in sentiment could spell the difference between success and failure of the amendment. When the delegates emerged from Walker's oratorical spell, they remembered they were hungry. Charlie Brooks slipped his watch from his vest pocket: he couldn't stay very long.

It was Joe Hanover's turn, and he was under pressure to score. "Ours is the great Volunteer State," he began, "and women from the East, West, North and South are looking to us to give them political freedom." The Suffs in the gallery gazed down upon Hanover's head and beamed. "The entire world today has cast its eyes on Tennessee. This is a moral question, and that's why I am here, voting for this amendment." Applause.

Hanover wanted to make a soaring oration for suffrage, but he couldn't allow Seth Walker's assertions and allegations to go unchallenged. He tackled them one by one: he countered Walker's slights about black women voting in California with a testimonial from the governor of that state, attesting that "politics is cleaner and government is better" since California women were given the ballot. Cheers. He refuted the picture Walker had painted of woman suffrage bringing about Negro domination in the South by quoting the suffragists' favorite population statistics, showing that white women voters outnumbered eligible black citizens in the southern states. Then he tackled Walker head-on.

"There has been so much said about the constitution of Tennessee and oath of office," he said in an even tone, but then allowed his voice to rise, "but certain interests have sent their lobbyists to ask members of this legislature to violate their pledges!" Suffs in the galleries rained down boos. "And their agents are down at the Hermitage Hotel right now!"

While Hanover was speaking, a knot of Anti legislators gathered behind the screen of the Speaker's desk, out of view. They whispered to one another, gesticulated, nodded in agreement, and returned to their desks. Charlie

Brooks looked at his watch again. It was going on so long, he really couldn't wait around for the vote. His train would be leaving soon and he had to get home to his Ida.

"Tennessee never does things by halves for women," Hanover continued, but he could see his colleagues were getting restless, and he rushed to finish. "What we do for them as Southern men we should have the privilege of doing for other women, that ours may be truly a democracy."

As soon as Hanover concluded, while the cheers for him were still reverberating, before he could even return to his chair, a rush of voices and raised hands clamored to be recognized. The voices and hands belonged to the same delegates who'd gathered behind the Speaker's desk moments before. Finally it was Seth Walker, still on the floor, who was recognized. "I move this House adjourn until tomorrow morning," Walker announced, saying that the delegates needed more time to consider so momentous a decision. Chaos broke over the chamber.

"No, no!" shouted Hanover and Riddick and other ratification leaders. "No, no!" was the echo from Suffs in the gallery. Further delay played into the Antis' hands, the Suffs feared, gave them more time to pick off swaying delegates. More time for bribes, more time for intimidation, more time for simple confusion and doubt. The postponement over the weekend had been disastrous for the Suffs' count. The test vote on clearing the floor had given the Suffs a hairbreadth majority of fifty-one. They needed to vote—today. But Walker's motion to adjourn took precedence. The roll call on the motion to adjourn began.

The delay was too much for Charlie Brooks; he had to get home. He was sorry to bother Joe Hanover again about his personal problem, but Brooks's problem was the Suffs' problem, as they couldn't afford to lose a single vote now. Just stay to vote against adjournment, Hanover pleaded, then darted to the back of the chamber and found Luke Lea, explaining Brooks's situation. Lea went up to the gallery, where Newell Sanders was sitting (after being chased from the floor), and they rushed out of the statehouse together.

Brooks did stay and voted against adjournment, but it was to no avail. With a solid Anti phalanx augmented by the merely hungry and testily tired, the motion to adjourn was approved by a vote of 52 to 44. The gavel rapped: the house was adjourned until ten thirty Wednesday morning. The Suffs in the gallery were silent and stunned. Josephine Pearson and her comrades were all smiles as they bustled down from the galleries. The hundreds of spectators still standing in the hallways looked confused.

Luke Lea and Newell Sanders ran back to the statehouse with a plan: Sanders laid out $495 for a chartered train to take Brooks that afternoon directly to the nearest depot to his house, then wait. If Brooks's wife was well enough, the train would return him overnight to Nashville, and he'd be able to vote with the Suffs tomorrow. Lea and Sanders drove Brooks to Union Station.

If any delegate who'd agreed to adjournment thought he was buying himself a respite, he was sadly mistaken. Even as they escaped down the Capitol steps, the delegates were overtaken and surrounded by red and yellow advocates; they were accosted on the sidewalks and barricaded on the curbs; they had uninvited companions at their luncheon table; they were pulled aside into Hermitage alcoves. The screws were tightened.

At the Hermitage, Catt and Upton were livid, and they lashed out at the man they felt responsible for precipitating this turn of events—Warren Harding.

"Opposition only claiming unconstitutionality and you fall into their trap," Upton berated Harding in a blistering telegram. "This morning Democratic speaker of house read your letter and declared you upheld position of constitutional objectors. Not only Republican but Democratic votes at stake."

Upton went on to the candidate's latest outrage: "Your published interview on possibility of election contest will absolutely kill ratification unless counteracted. No such question exists. Imperative that you should send message that having been convinced constitutional objection is not well founded you still urge Republicans to vote for ratification. That message must come before ten o'clock Wednesday morning. Notify me."

Carrie Catt didn't bother writing to Harding, addressing her complaint directly to RNC chairman Will Hays: "Harding's letter to Tillman and morning paper interview has lost us votes and unless counteracted will bring defeat. The world will lay entire responsibility for defeat upon Harding. Immediate action is necessary. See Upton telegram to Harding. CCC."

Hays, traveling between Marion and New York, didn't see Catt's wire until late Tuesday night. He telegraphed her near midnight: "Wire me any suggestions as to just what I should do."

Upton received no reply from Harding.

•••

The move to adjourn was a stealth act perfectly executed. Seth Walker was a masterful parliamentarian, manipulating rules and procedures like a scalpel in the hands of a skilled surgeon. He'd outmaneuvered the Suffs again. On the other hand, it might be taken as a sign that the Antis were frightened of a vote, that they were delaying in an effort to postpone defeat. That was a comforting notion to the Suffs, but they knew it was overly optimistic: the Antis were most likely postponing in an effort to fortify their numbers. Walker claimed a majority already, and the adjournment vote showed fifty-two siding with the Anti-led move, forty-four resisting. Several men who were on the Suffs' lists as favorable had voted to adjourn; had they jumped the fence to the Antis? Or was it hunger and fatigue, and perhaps fear, propelling some of those "aye" votes for delay? The problem was, no one knew.

Both sides scrambled through the afternoon to fortify, and possibly augment, their lines. Charl Williams, with the encouragement of Mrs. Catt, called all suffragists to the Hermitage assembly rooms for a pep talk and assignment sign-up. Another poll must be taken by nightfall—find your delegates. Take them to dinner if you can, take them for a walk or drive if you're able, take them to the moving pictures if you must, just keep them in your sight. Volunteers were needed for policing duties: the Hermitage hallways must be patrolled throughout the night to make sure delegates could not attempt to slip—or be spirited—away. Suffrage soldiers must guard the platforms and passenger rooms of Union Station, so no cowardly, or coerced, delegate could leave town before the vote. Be prepared for a night without sleep.

Joe Hanover hadn't slept for several nights, and he hadn't eaten much, either. He never did get lunch after the adjournment, and he wasn't going to get any dinner tonight. He'd lost several pounds from his thin frame since the special session began. He reached into his jacket pocket for one of the graham crackers he kept there, his battlefield rations, and came up with crumb-coated fingers. With his clean hand he went through his delegate poll again, checking off the men who were solid and those who were not. Then he made his rounds.

By early evening the Hermitage lobby was more crowded and noisy than ever, the whole scene blanketed by a layer of cigar smoke. Suddenly a reporter for the Associated Press ran into the lobby, waving a long, narrow strip of paper torn from a newswire teletype machine. He stood in the center of the lobby and began reading the bulletin aloud in a booming voice: "In a surprise maneuver, the North Carolina Senate has voted to postpone consideration of the ratification of the 19th Amendment until the 1921 legislature. The vote was 25 to 23 to postpone."

Anti sympathizers in the lobby lustily cheered the news, and red-corsaged women laughed with glee as word spread throughout the hotel. Seth Walker was especially pleased. Those women wearing yellow were visibly shaken and tried to hold back tears, and some men looked grim and shook their heads.

The vote in Raleigh was ominous to the Suffs in more ways than one. Not only did it mean that ratification was dead in North Carolina—the senate had been possible, in the house there was no chance—but it was the manner in which the Carolina Antis had finessed the senate vote that gave all suffragists in Nashville a fright. After hours of vicious debate the senators had been ready to vote, and the Suffs seemed to possess a slim margin to pass ratification. But before a motion to ratify could be proposed, the Anti floor leader jumped in to make a motion to postpone. Nervous senators welcomed this easier route, a way to opt out of a contentious issue. It was much safer to simply avoid voting; they could claim they'd not really voted against woman suffrage, just wanted to think about it a bit longer. This was a ploy that might be replicated in Nashville tomorrow.

Lights burned late in the Hermitage as meetings and plotting continued, pleas were made and pressure applied. A knock on a delegate's door might bring a visitor bearing gifts, or the promise of sex, or even the threat of kidnapping. Harriet Upton was awakened several times in the wee hours to learn that a Republican member was missing; a hunting party went out to find him. Men of the Ratification Committee began knocking on delegates' doors every few hours to check on them.

Suff and Anti leaders plotted their moves and developed contingency plans in conferences that stretched well into the night. The mood at the nightly strategy meeting in Mrs. Catt's room was particularly bleak, and the Suffs tearfully confessed their despair to one another. Even Catt gave up on any confident proclamations of majorities and victories. Every man who had been marked as "bribable" on her ledger had proven himself and moved to the Anti side. The latest poll showed that whatever majority the Suffs may have once possessed had evaporated. The count predicted ratification to fall short by two votes. The amendment, the Cause, and Carrie Catt's life's work, falling short.

As the meeting broke up and the Suffs returned to their rooms for a restless night, Carrie Catt caught Abby Milton's sleeve. Milton's heart ached to see the Chief appear so despondent, so close to seeming helpless. Milton was a religious woman, and she knew Catt was not, so she was startled when Catt leaned in to whisper: "Mrs. Milton, there is one more thing we can do—we can pray."

Chapter 21

• • •

The Hour Has Come

HOUSEWIVES LEFT the breakfast dishes in the sink. Clerks took the morning off, and shop attendants might even have called in sick. Farm wives gave the cows an early milking and hopped into the truck for the bumpy ride to the city. Whole families arrived on the street-cars, carrying picnic baskets.

On Wednesday morning, the citizens of Nashville and residents of Davidson County came to Capitol Hill again in hopes of glimpsing a historic moment. They arrived early, while the limestone statehouse still glowed pink in the sidelong rays of the morning sun, when the air was still blessedly cool. They surged up the hill, climbed the steps, attempted to enter the galleries or even just the corridors, but those were already jammed, so they perched themselves on the outdoor porticoes and the parapets, spilled down the steps, and spread out on the sloping lawns. From Carrie Catt's window, the scene looked like a giant carnival.

The mood was decidedly less jolly within the Hermitage, at least on the floors where the Suffs resided. Whether or not Mrs. Catt and her comrades prayed for divine intervention during the night, they surely did not sleep and arose facing a day when they would be more dependent upon the whims of men than the grace of God. They did not have the votes to win ratification, and they knew it.

The Suffs donned their white dresses and their yellow sashes, their marching clothes. Sue White, Catherine Flanagan, and Betty Gram attached their prison pins. Anita Pollitzer stuck a fresh yellow flower onto the brim of her hat. They went to find their men, get their pledged delegates to the Capitol. Scores of other suffrage workers were doing the same, going about the task with grim resolve and a quiver of foreboding.

It had been a hellish night for many of the legislators. They'd been trapped in late night conferences, woken in the night, and badgered in the morning. They were sick of being hounded by women and pounded by their party leaders. They were exhausted and irritable, and quite a few were frightened.

Governor Roberts was in his office on the first floor of the Capitol hours before the gavel was to rap. He looked frazzled, his eyes sunken, his forelock already stuck to his forehead by perspiration. He was conferring with his lieutenants and with ratification leaders, going down lists of names. He summoned certain delegates to his office for a "talking-to." He'd already fielded a couple of nervous phone calls from James Cox, pressing for reassurance, which made Roberts only more agitated. And now Cox was calling again.

"Governor, the mothers of America want the League of Nations," Cox told Roberts, and Roberts nodded as he held the telephone earpiece a few inches from his head. The meaning was clear: women voters would demand America enter the league and so would vote Democratic, vote for Cox and for Roberts. The party needed women voters. Get it done, Cox was telling Roberts.

One of Roberts's men in the legislature, a dependable ally, was sitting on the other side of the governor's desk, waiting to receive his talking-to. Banks Turner, a thirty-year-old farmer from West Tennessee, was giving Roberts trouble, siding with the Antis on every vote. There seemed to be no persuading him, he was stubborn as a mule, and he wasn't thinking long-term, Roberts fretted. Turner waited, not very patiently, while Roberts spoke into the telephone mouthpiece.

"Governor," Roberts told Cox, "I have right here in my office the man who could furnish the necessary vote for ratification."

The press box at the front of the house chamber was jammed, the reporters ready. This was turning into a plum assignment; their editors were giving them lots of column inches, putting their stories on the front page. For decades, the suffrage fight—if reported at all—had been relegated to the "women's page" of most newspapers, alongside household tips, recipes, and club activities. It might peek into the news section if a referendum campaign was being waged in the home state. Now the culmination of the battle in Tennessee for the thirty-sixth state was being treated as breaking news of significant consequence to the nation—which indeed it was.

The Tennessee newspapers were, naturally, consumed by the ratification events, and the regional southern papers paid close, if nervous, attention to the fate of the federal amendment. The major national newspapers, along with the Associated Press, dispatched some of their star political reporters and columnists to Nashville to cover the finale of the ratification drama; *The New York Times* sent a female journalist to provide lively commentary, supplementing the paper's straight news accounts. Editorial cartoonists were mining the ratification story for its more comical gems: drawing flirtatious women wooing Tennessee colonels, Republican elephants and Democratic donkeys courting fickle females, a frustrated suffragist trying to fasten the thirty-sixth button on her blouse, and a Tennessee legislator using a Ouija board to predict the outcome of the fight. But there was no doubt: this was a big story.

Joe Hanover made the rounds, shaking hands, patting backs, whispering in ears. Charlie Brooks wasn't going to make it, Hanover told his ratification troops; his wife wasn't out of the woods yet, so he couldn't return on that special train. The Suffs were down another vote.

Anita Pollitzer and Betty Gram watched the delegates walk hesitantly down the corridor and into the chamber. It seemed there were more red roses on male lapels than yesterday, but perhaps that was an optical illusion. They spied Harry Burn walking in, again sporting a red rose. "We really trusted you, Mr. Burn," they hissed at him, "when you said that you would never hurt us."

He turned toward them. "I mean that," he mumbled. As Burn made his way to the left side of the chamber, to his place in the middle of the third row, a page brought an envelope to his desk.

It was a small irony that the Antis were forced to get their most urgent messages out to the public by buying large display ads in the suffragist morning *Tennessean,* lining the pockets of their nemesis Luke Lea. That morning they'd taken most of a page to repeat their appeal for Nashvillians to rally to the Capitol in red roses, and they bought another page to rattle any legislators still reluctant to tilt their way. "The Truth About the Negro Problem" grabbed eyeballs with bold type, capital letters, and apocalyptic warnings of RACE WAR:

> For the sake of Southern civilization, for the sake of womanhood and
> for the sake of the welfare of the negro race as well as the white race,
> the Susan B. Anthony Amendment should be defeated. Nowhere on
> earth have two races lived in the same territory with such harmony as
> has always existed between Southern whites and negroes. Except when

hurled into political combat with each other by politicians . . . the two races have always gotten along well in the Southern states. This amendment will not only hurl women into political competition and battle with men, but it will and must involve political warfare between the races—a thing that no thinking American, white or black, should advocate.

Making the threat more personal, the advertisement warned that white elected officials in the southern states would be placed in peril by the amendment, likely to be thrown out of office by the combination of women and black voters.

The better class of NEGROES THEMSELVES know they are better represented by able white men than they would be by designing politicians of their own race, just as the majority of the women themselves feel they are better represented by the fathers of their children than they would be by politically ambitious office seekers of their own sex.

"The Federal Amendment brings with it race antagonism as well as sex antagonism and the hazard is too great," the piece proclaimed. Besides its prominent space in the morning newspaper, every house delegate had a copy of the polemic on his desk. Josephine Pearson could see the flyers from her seat up in the balcony of the chamber.

Speaker Walker gaveled the house to order at ten thirty-five a.m., with ninety-six of the ninety-nine members at their desks, lobbyists for both sides surrounding them. The senate had adjourned its session across the hall to observe the house proceedings, bringing senators to mingle on the floor. Rule #17 was again enforced, and the sergeant at arms moved through, clearing the floor of everyone but legislators and reporters. This time women Suffs resisted more strenuously, and the sergeant had to call for his deputies to help evacuate the ornery women. Some walked back onto the floor and had to be removed again. Finally, the debate on the motion to concur with the senate in ratifying the amendment, interrupted by yesterday's abrupt adjournment, was resumed.

The Suffs applauded L. D. Miller's call to his colleagues to free themselves from the grip of special interest lobbies that had controlled the legislature for fifty years. But they felt their stomachs clench when yet another faithless Davidson County delegate who'd been counted on the Suff side announced that he was defecting to the Antis. "I have considered it in the secrecy of my closet at home, and I am frank to say to you that I come here this morning with doubt in my heart as to whether it is best for the women of the country." To the Suffs, his change of mind sounded very suspicious. The Antis gave him a long ovation.

Speeches droned on for most of an hour, and the chamber seemed to slip into a stupor. The day was growing warmer, and the heat seeped into the assembly hall. Delegates gazed into space. Women in the galleries fanned themselves with quick flicks of the wrist. Joe Hanover jumped from one man to another, whispering into their ears. Harry Burn, over in desk forty-four, read the letter that had been delivered by the page, refolded it, pushed it back into its envelope, and tucked it into his inner breast pocket.

Up in the Speaker's chair, Seth Walker sensed this restlessness and the glum spirits among the suffragists. He'd done the calculations; he knew he had the votes he needed. He signaled for his Anti colleague Austin Overton to take over the Speaker's chair while he stepped down onto the floor. Walker asked to be recognized. Suffs snapped their eyes toward him and held their breath.

"The hour has come," Walker shouted with a melodramatic flair. "The battle has been fought and it is won. The measure is defeated." Some Suffs in the gallery began to sob. "Mr. Speaker, I move that this measure goes where it rightfully belongs—to the table!"

The chamber exploded, with wailing in the galleries and tumult on the floor. Joe Hanover and other Suff delegates jumped into the aisles, clamoring to be recognized, while a chorus of Anti delegates yelled, "Second the motion!" from their desks. A suffragist in the gallery blew a siren horn in protest, adding to the turmoil.

It was a masterstroke, long feared. Tabling would effectively kill the ratification resolution, bump it off the docket, knock it out of consideration, but in a safe, passive way—an attractive escape path for any man still nervous about the consequences of his suffrage decision.

Bang, bang, bang went the gavel, barely audible over the din, and it was several more chaotic, cacophonous minutes before delegate Overton, overwhelmed in his role as Speaker pro tempore, could regain enough control to order a roll call on Walker's motion to table. Then the chamber quickly grew still.

Sue White stood at the rail at the rear of the floor, a tally sheet in one hand, a pencil in the other. She concentrated completely on the replies of the delegates, going methodically down the alphabetical list in sync with the clerk, making her marks next to each name. She tried not to think about what the final count might be and what it could mean. By all reckonings, with several new additions to their ranks, the Antis had the votes to defeat the amendment. They had forty-nine firm votes, the Suffs only forty-seven. She was an optimist, but she wasn't naive. This was most likely the death of ratification in Nashville and quite possibly a mortal blow to the Susan B. Anthony Amendment. Tennessee was her home state, and this vote, to her mind, was a test of Tennessee's commitment to justice and liberty. This was her campaign, she was in charge for the Woman's Party, and she had failed. She kept her eyes steady on the tally sheet.

The vote seesawed as the roll call progressed. The first set of names ("Anderson"—no; "Bell"—no), rejecting the tabling, gladdened the Suffs. But the next set (Bond, Boyd, Boyer, Bratton, Burn), all voting "aye," sent them spiraling into despair. Anita Pollitzer crossed off Harry Burn's name on her stubbornly hopeful "doubtful" list and moved him decisively to the Anti column. The Antis began to clap and cheer for every vote cast their way, and the Suffs tried to keep pace. Back and forth it went.

There were many scribes keeping tallies besides the official clerk of the house: Suffs, Antis, politicians, corporate lobbyists, and news reporters were all working their pencils on the narrow tally sheets. The room resembled a small baseball stadium filled with fanatic fans, all keeping their own box score. It wasn't easy to keep up, as the clerk's call of names and the responses were often drowned out by some sort of sonic interference.

"Story," "Swift," "Thronesbury"—aye, and the Antis were up on their feet as the roll entered the homestretch and they appeared ahead. The roll sped up: "Travis," "Tucker," "Turner"—no, and the score evened up again. Few of the tally takers, or even those just following, had time to pause or think about any anomalies, any strange surprises, among the responses. But Seth Walker and Joe Hanover did notice: Banks Turner had just voted not to table. The roll rushed on.

The Antis seemed to own the end of the alphabet: "Weldon," "Whitfield," "Wilson," "Wolfenbarger," "Womack"—all voted aye. Women wearing yellow were weeping openly as Speaker Walker shouted the final "aye" and the Antis burst into a wild ovation. Their tallies showed the vote as 49 to 47 for tabling. The amendment was dead in Tennessee! But the clerk had a different accounting: his tally was tied, 48 to 48. By the clerk's tabulation, the motion to table had not achieved a majority, so it was defeated. And now the entire chamber went berserk.

Delegates sprang out of their chairs and rushed to the base of the Speaker's stand, forming a seething scrum, shouting, arguing, waving tally sheets in the air. The galleries burst into confused but loud protest: there was something for everyone to complain about. Seth Walker was running up and down the center aisle, and he was fuming: this cannot be, the clerk is mistaken, he insisted. Delegates vied for attention from Overton, the besieged substitute Speaker, the Antis demanding another vote, the Suffs maintaining it wasn't necessary.

Overton found his gavel useless, so he called on the sergeant at arms to force all members to take their seats. Thomas Riddick would not sit down. He was still vigorously arguing that the clerk's tally was official, the tie vote should stand, and tabling had been defeated. The sergeant pressed him. "I have as much right to be in the aisles as Walker does!" Riddick yelled as Walker passed by him in the aisle. Then Riddick said something else in a low voice that only Walker and those nearby could hear. Seth Walker wheeled around and advanced toward Riddick in what onlookers described as a "menacing" manner. Riddick stepped forward to confront Walker and the men almost came to blows before delegates jumped between them and pulled them apart. Riddick's friends calmed him and persuaded him to sit down. Overton, taking his cue from Walker, instructed the clerk to call a second vote.

The roll began again. "Anderson," "Bell"—no. "Bond," "Boyd," "Boyer," "Bratton," "Burn"—aye. And so on down the list, with no change in stance. The clerk repeated each delegate's name and his vote, just to make certain. The roll was orderly, but the chamber was in turmoil, as the tally remained neck and neck. As the roll continued, Seth Walker walked up the central aisle to the desk in the fifth row occupied by Banks Turner. He pulled up a chair, sat down beside Turner, and draped his arm around Turner's shoulders. Turner was Walker's contemporary, both a colleague and a friend, and someone Walker had come to trust: Turner had voted right in all the test ballots and had given a good thumbs-down to the ratification resolution in the Constitutional Amendments Committee. Walker couldn't fathom what was going on with Turner now. Walker kept his arm wrapped around Turner's shoulders as he whispered urgently into the renegade delegate's ear. Denizens of the gallery strained their necks to watch Walker applying muscle to Turner, both literally and figuratively. Suffs watched the embrace with alarm: the powerful Speaker was cajoling, perhaps threatening, the one delegate who might save the ratification resolution from immediate doom. Governor Roberts watched intently from the back of the floor.

The roll call headed toward the tail end of the alphabet, the Ss and the Ts. "Tarrant"—no. "Thronesbury"—aye. "Travis"—aye. "Tucker"—no. "Turner . . ." There was a pause, a collective breath holding. Suddenly Banks Turner shook off Seth Walker's arm from his shoulders, bolted up from his chair, and declared: "Nay."

"The second ballot is tied, 48 to 48," the clerk reported amid the Suffs' shrieks of joy. From high in the Speaker's chair, Overton announced: "The motion is lost for want of a majority." Walker stormed away from Turner's desk, but he quickly realized the new opportunity presented to him by the tie vote: the tabling motion was lost, but the larger battle might still be won. A vote to concur with Senate Joint Resolution #1, ratifying the Nineteenth Amendment, was instantly called.

The sun was high in the sky as noontime approached, baking the heads of the people spread out on the steps, ledges, and lawns of the Capitol. There was a festive mood among those lounging on the grounds as they waited for the periodic reports of what was happening inside. Waiting to hear of the big moment, whenever that might come, whatever it might be. Carrie Catt watched the crowds from her window as she, too, waited. Thirty-five and a half states. In 1908, when she and the Suffs asked President Theodore Roosevelt what it would take to win presidential and congressional support for a federal woman's suffrage amendment, he told them: "Go, get another state"—get another state to approve woman suffrage and impress the Congress. Now they were down to the last half of a state. It was still excruciating, this waiting.

Joe Hanover was in antic motion on the floor. He was threading between desks, grabbing elbows, thrusting his chin toward ears, confronting and cajoling delegates in the minutes before the vote on ratification began. If he needed to speak to one of the men privately, he pulled him into one of the committee rooms or cloakrooms at the side of the chamber. Hanover was

Sue White (center), Betty Gram (far right), and the National Woman's Party picketed the Republican National Convention in Chicago in June 1920, protesting the party's lack of commitment to ratification of the Nineteenth Amendment.

The grand Hotel Hermitage became the headquarters and home for both Suffs and Antis during the six weeks of the ratification battle; the hotel lobby became known as the "third house" of the legislature.

From a boat bobbing in the Hudson River, Louisine Havemeyer (right) passes the Suffrage Torch to New Jersey colleagues during the 1915 woman suffrage referendum campaign in New York and New Jersey. Neither state approved the vote for women.

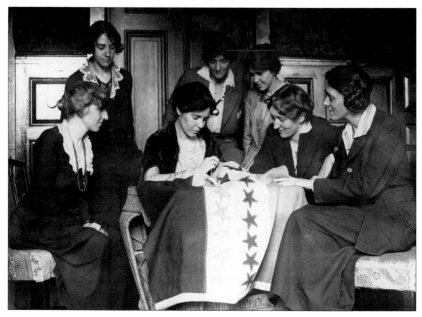

Alice Paul was a master designer of pageants, demonstrations, and photo ops to promote suffrage. As each state ratified, it earned a star on her ratification victory banner. The thirty-sixth star was elusive.

Alice Paul awarded these small silver medals of valor to Woman's Party veterans who endured imprisonment for their civil disobedience. Sue White, Catherine Flanagan, and Betty Gram wore their pins proudly in Nashville.

Seth Walker, Speaker of the Tennessee House of Representatives, promised suffragists he would pilot the Nineteenth Amendment ratification resolution to success in his chamber.

Delegate Joseph Hanover of Memphis was a staunch woman suffrage supporter; his sincerity and political acumen impressed Carrie Catt, and he became the ratificationists' floor leader in the House.

Edward "Boss" Crump, former mayor of Memphis, led the Democratic party machine in Shelby County and made sure Memphis area delegates were on board for ratification. He wanted women to vote.

Sue White used her knowledge of her home state to guide the Woman's Party campaign in Tennessee. Here she is meeting to plot strategy with (from left to right) U.S. senator Kenneth McKellar, state senator Ernest Haston, Governor Albert Roberts, and Memphis delegate Joe Hanover.

Josephine Pearson, at right, presides over a busy workshop of volunteers at Anti headquarters in the Hotel Hermitage.

Nina Pinckard, president of the Southern Women's Rejection League, poses with Josephine Pearson at Anti headquarters. Between the women sits an elderly Confederate veteran.

Nina Pinckard of Alabama, Charlotte Rowe of New York, and Anne Pleasant of Louisiana held red roses as they lobbied against ratification in Nashville.

Josephine Pearson reveled in her role as Anti leader, even though she believed women shouldn't be involved in politics.

Speaker Seth Walker presided over the House of Representatives' bitter debates over ratification.

America When Femininized

SUFFRAGIST—FEMINIST IDEAL FAMILY LIFE.

**The More a Politician Allows Himself to be Henpecked
The More Henpecking We Will Have in Politics.**

**A Vote for Federal Suffrage is a Vote for Organized Female
Nagging Forever.**

"American pep which was the result of a masculine dominated country will soon be a thing of the past. With the collapse of the male ascendancy in this country we can look forward to a nation of degeneration. The suppression of sex will ultimately have its harvest in decadence, a phenomenon already beginning. The effect of the social revolution on American character will be to make "sissies" of American men—a process already well under way."—Dr. William J. Hickson, Chicago University.

WOMAN SUFFRAGE denatures both men and women; it masculinizes women and femininizes men. The history of ancient civilization has proven that a weakening of the man power of nations has been but a pre-runner of decadence in civilization.

Will you stand for this? Prove that you will not by voting to **Reject** the Federal Woman Suffrage Amendment to the Constitution of the United States.

**SOUTHERN WOMAN'S LEAGUE FOR REJECTION OF THE
SUSAN B. ANTHONY AMENDMENT**

WE SERVE THAT OUR STATES MAY LIVE, AND LIVING, PRESERVE THE UNION

The Antis sought to irritate male egos with this poster depicting a "henpecked" rooster whose hen wears a suffrage sash. "A Vote for Federal Suffrage is a Vote for Organized Female Nagging Forever."

Mrs. Catt's Defamation of Her Country

From The Woman Patriot, June 29, 1920

MRS. C. C. CATT, President of the International Woman Suffrage Alliance and the National American Woman Suffrage Association, never fails to take advantage of any opportunity she can get *to denounce her own country*. In the midst of the great war, she went to Toronto, Canada, and so disgusted her hearers by her diatribes against the United States that the Toronto Daily News of May 12, 1917, says of her:

"She was distinctly unpatriotic. The position of women of Vacation was compared with that of the women of the United States to the disadvantage of the latter—an insult to the intelligence of her audience and a defamation of her country. Another patriotic utterance to put forth in a foreign country was 'You never can tell when you are going to have an honest election in the United States'—and this from a woman who, we hear, has been honored by appointment on the National Defense Committee! Surely even the most ordinary ideas of decency would be sufficient to suggest that her diatribe be confined to the borders of her own country."

"UNITED STATES HAS NO RIGHT"

Earlier in the war she went to St. Louis (February 10, 1916), and told the pacifists and pro-Germans there that

"The United States has no right to ask any of its large number of citizens of foreign birth to bear arms against the countries of their kin." (St. Louis Post-Dispatch, Feb. 10, 1916.)

Her perpetual "knocks" against the United States would fill a book, and that she is still doing her utmost to defame her native country is proved by her remarks at the Geneva suffrage convention on June 6, 1920, extracts of which are quoted directly from the official suffrage organ for June 12:

"No other country has repudiated its Constitution, principles and history in its denial of votes to its women, and that is why the extension of suffrage to the women of all Europe has so astounded and humiliated the women of the United States. . . . Aliens, illiterates, drunkards, paupers, criminals and feeble-minded may all vote in the United States. . . . It is not pleasant to record such damning facts concerning one's own nation. I do it in order that you who come from many new European republics may know that reaction may seize republics, too, and that resistance to the inevitable amount of human progress may be surprisingly stubborn. Not only in the United States of America a curious example of tardy action, but the two European republics, France and Switzerland, are conspicuous in the midst of an enfranchised Europe for their disregard of this question."

Mrs. Catt's denunciation of her own country is a matter of habit with her, but in aligning the United States, the Republic of France and the Republic of Switzerland together against woman suffrage, she merely proved again what Mrs. Rossiter Johnson so ably demonstrated thirty years ago—that monarchies, *empires* and *autocracies* are all more favorable to feminism than republics. (Woman and the Republic.)

Switzerland recently defeated woman suffrage by a three to one majority in three cantons—after a year and a half of Mrs. Norman de R. Whitehouse and Frau Rosika Schwimmer, and we print elsewhere an interesting communication showing that *the Women Patriots of Switzerland* are now organizing against woman suffrage, and asking American anti-suffragists to participate in a European anti-suffrage conference this fall.

DEMOCRACY VS. WOMAN SUFFRAGE

The whole truth of the matter is that where there is real democracy—where the people have a chance to express their *reverence for womanhood* by popular vote—woman suffrage is usually snowed under as is the United States and Switzerland. For, as it was when Thomas Jefferson wrote these words to Mrs. Bingham from Paris in 1787:

"It is in honorable circumstances for man that the first moment he is at his ease he alters the internal employments to his female partner and takes the external upon himself. And this circumstance, or its reverse, is a pretty good indication that a people are or are not civilized. Men, in a civilized country, never subject their women and children to labor above their force and sex."

Under tribal conditions—where woman is in absolute drudge—she has all the rights that the most modern feminists demand, the "squaw rights" of the Iroquois, the Hoppis, etc., to do all the rough work of the tribe and take part in its councils. In countries where a monarch can enfranchise women by edict to please some suffragette courtesan, there have been other parallels like the Female Senate of Rome given power by the emperor to make laws for women, and called a Senate of Etiquette. (See Dill, Roman Society, pp. 77, 81). In countries where parliaments of politicians, influenced by lobbies of nagging suffragettes, can confer the vote without reference to the will of the people the suffragists also succeed—but in *civilized* countries, where the will of the people may be expressed at the polls on this subject, women are honored, reverenced and so highly valued as the mothers of the race that they are protected from politics, strife, military service, jury duty and other hardships that women are *forced* to endure under tribal conditions and urged to revert to by modern feminists.

BOSTON REVIEW ON MRS. CATT

Mrs. Catt's unpatriotic utterances are well and ably criticized in the following editorial from the Boston Review of June 12:

"That eminent and conservative exponent of equal suffrage, Carrie Chapman Catt, is enlightening the conference of suffragists in Geneva, Switzerland. In spite of her name; she is dogmatic. Referring to the country which she claims to represent, she remarks:

"'No other country has repudiated its constitution, principles and history in its denial of votes to women.'

"That is only a fraction of the libelous misstatements made by Mrs. Carrie Chapman Catt, as reported by the Associated Press. This country has not repudiated its constitution, its principles nor its history by refusing to grant votes to women. The idea that women should have, equal rights with men at the polls was never seriously entertained by the founders of this country. What women have obtained has been largely through careful and intelligent work for years by suffragists of far more discretion and intelligence than Carrie Chapman Catt. The present generation of suffragist seekers consists mainly of a loud noise, and man, alas, is today influenced by loud noises rather than by logic.

"That is why the Catts have got so close to constitutional writings. That is why they are now mouthing in foreign lands concerning the obliquity of their own nation. Here in Boston men and women have been held for deportation and imprisonment for saying things less treasonable than the Catts are saying almost every day."

The Antis attacked Carrie Catt—personally and politically—at every opportunity, and used this broadside to accuse her of being unpatriotic, even treasonous.

This Anti broadside insists Tenneessee legislators "do their duty" to protect the state from the Nineteenth Amendment. The federal government should have no say in who has the right to vote.

Can Anybody Terrorize Tennessee Manhood?

The Susan B. Anthony Amendment Will Never Be Ratified If Tennessee Representatives Do Their Duty NOW

Because the People Do Not Want It

Federal Suffrage Not "Inevitable"

VICTORY is merely a question of MANHOOD and MORALE.

The Present Situation

Only Five States Yet to Act

Tennessee's Opportunity

The "Card Index" Pressure System

A Peril to the South

The Constitution vs. Platform

The Acid Test of Experience

This is the opening argument in a great campaign to save the States from destruction.

If YOU believe in the right of the people of each State to control their own elections, we ask your active support

SOUTHERN WOMEN'S LEAGUE FOR REJECTION OF THE SUSAN B. ANTHONY AMENDMENT

Headquarters, Mezzanine Floor, Hermitage Hotel

| Don't Fail to Visit the Exhibition | Come and See "The Woman's Bible" | Have You Seen the Three Force Bills? |

Mass Meeting
TONIGHT
Ryman Auditorium
8 O'CLOCK
TO SAVE THE SOUTH

FROM THE SUSAN B. ANTHONY AMENDMENT
AND FEDERAL SUFFRAGE FORCE BILLS

Senator Oscar W. Underwood, of Alabama, and Ex-Gov. Ruffin G. Pleasant,
of Louisiana, Have Been Invited to Speak

MAJ. E. B. STAHLMAN
MISS CHARLOTTE E. ROWE
HON. FRANK P. BOND
AND
PROF. GUS DYER
WILL SPEAK
MRS. THOMAS H. MALONE, JR.
WILL SING
JUDGE J. C. HIGGINS
WILL PRESIDE

EVERYBODY INVITED

Antis advertised this rally "To Save the South" from the threat of federal pressure on southern states to allow black women, and men, to vote.

On Friday, August 13, the Tennessee Senate voted to ratify the Nineteenth Amendment.

Harry T. Burn of Niota, the youngest member of the Tennessee General Assembly, wore a red rose when he entered the House chamber to vote on ratification on Tuesday morning, August 18.

Phoebe (Febb) Burn, Harry's widowed mother, wrote a letter to her son offering advice on how he should vote on the ratification issue.

Memphis suffragist Charl Williams watched Governor Roberts sign the official ratification certificate on August 24, after a week of Anti manuevers to reverse Tennessee's decision.

When news of Tennessee's ratification reached Alice Paul on August 18, she sewed the thirty-sixth star onto her ratification banner and unfurled it from the balcony of Woman's Party headquarters in Washington.

Alice Paul lifts a glass—filled with a Prohibition-compliant beverage—next to the completed ratification banner outside Woman's Party headquarters.

The Nineteenth Amendment officially entered the U.S. Constitution on August 26, and Carrie Catt returned home to New York City greeted by a joyous parade. She held a giant thank-you bouquet "from the enfranchised women of America."

A WOMAN LIVING HERE HAS REGISTERED TO VOTE THEREBY ASSUMING RESPONSIBILITY OF CITIZENSHIP

Recruitment drives urged newly enfranchised women to register to vote in the fall 1920 elections. This sign celebrates the woman of the house as a full and patriotic citizen.

Uncle Sam holds his wife's hands—who wears the cause of suffrage on her sleeve—and announces: "Equal Partners Now, Ma," as editorial cartoonists celebrate American women's full citizenship.

SUFFRAGE

GREETINGS

SATTERFIELD

"EQUAL PARTNERS NOW, MA"

Life

October 28, 1920

Price 15 Cents

Vol. 76. Copyright, 1920, Life Publishing Company No. 1982

"Congratulations"

A classically robed Liberty hands the ballot to a tired but hopeful American woman, offering her "Congratulations" in this Charles Dana Gibson illustration on the cover of *Life* magazine in October 1920.

"The Mystery of 1920" is the new woman voter, as a fashionable lady pauses at the door of a voting booth on the cover of *Leslie's Illustrated* magazine in September 1920.

On Election Day 2016, thousands of American women visited the graves of suffrage movement leaders, honoring their legacy by pasting "I Voted" stickers on their headstones. Susan Anthony's grave in Rochester, New York, was festooned with stickers, flags, and flowers.

A statue by Alan LeQuire celebrating Tennessee's role in securing the Nineteenth Amendment was dedicated in Nashville's Centennial Park in 2016. It depicts suffragists (from left to right) J. Frankie Pierce, Carrie Chapman Catt, Abby Crawford Milton, Anne Dallas Dudley, and Sue Shelton White.

pulling over delegates who still might be wobbly, and there weren't too many of them left; the lines were fixed. Banks Turner had saved the day on that last vote to table—that roll call had felt like a near-death experience to Hanover—but there was no knowing whether Turner was going to stick with the Suffs on this next, decisive vote. And even if he did, even if Turner defied Seth Walker again, it wouldn't do the trick: the vote would be tied and ratification would die. Hanover needed two more solid votes, and he had no hope of finding them.

The clerk shuffled the papers on his desk in preparation for beginning the roll call once again. The tension in the chamber was almost painful, given the stress and heat. Josephine Pearson felt a surge of excitement. Abby Milton and Catherine Kenny recognized they could do nothing more to steer the decision; it was out of their hands. It was just as Mrs. Catt had predicted, just as she'd told them: "No matter how well the women may work, or how effective their results may be, ratification in Tennessee will go through the work and action of men," she'd warned, "and the great motive that will finally put it through will be political and nothing else." Not justice, not fairness. Politics—Tennessee politics, presidential politics—might put ratification through, or it would kill it.

Chief Clerk John Green started from the top again, in a slow, careful cadence. "Anderson . . . Bell . . ."

Harry Burn heard his name called. He knew most of his constituents in McMinn County didn't want woman suffrage and were even more vehemently opposed to the federal amendment. His colleague and legal mentor, Herschel Candler, was dead set against ratification. Certain political leaders had warned him, in graphic terms, that for the sake of his own political career he'd best vote for rejection. He was painfully torn. Personally, he favored giving women the vote, he thought it was only fair and right, but Burn wanted his constituents to reelect him in the fall. He wanted a political career. He was supporting his widowed mother back in Niota as an agent for the local railroad, and his father had been stationmaster of the Niota depot for thirty years. The railroad was against the amendment, too. Rejection was the safest course. But now, with Banks Turner possibly flipping, suddenly siding with the Suffs, and maybe creating a tie, ratification could hinge on a single vote. His. It was the scenario he'd most feared. The sound of his name echoed in his ears.

In his jacket pocket, inches below the red rose on his lapel, sat the letter that had arrived earlier in the morning, addressed to him at the Capitol building, written in a fine, very familiar hand: "Dear Son: Hurrah and vote for suffrage and don't keep them in doubt. I noticed Chandler's [*sic*] speech, it was very bitter. I've been waiting to see how you stood but have not seen anything yet. Don't forget to be a good boy and help Mrs. Catt. . . . With lots of love, Mama."

"Aye," said Harry Burn.

Sue White's pencil froze on her tally sheet. The clerk moved on to call George Canale. Burn's reply was so unexpected, uttered so quickly and flatly, that few in the chamber reacted at all for several moments. Perhaps they'd heard it wrong. Perhaps the young legislator had gotten confused. But as the clerk moved deeper into the "C" names, a low murmur bubbled up in the galleries and swelled to fill the chamber, a throaty rumble of astonishment as it all sank in: Harry Burn had just voted "aye" for ratification.

Suffs rose to their feet and roared, overpowering the clerk's voice. The roll call had to be suspended, and it took several minutes to regain order. Seth Walker and the rest of the Anti delegation of the house drilled their eyes on Burn and slapped their knees in disgust with the fickle young lawmaker who'd said he was with them. Anita Pollitzer and Betty Gram, squeezed by the crowd, expressed their amazed joy vertically and vocally, bouncing up and down while shrieking.

"My vote will never hurt you," Burn had told them, but he'd given them no good reason to believe him. So this was what he'd meant.

Of course, Burn brought them to a tie, and only if Banks Turner remained with them could they inch ahead to win. They hushed themselves and sat through the rest of the roll call in agony.

Seth Walker did not. He walked over to stand next to Banks Turner. The hall hushed as the clerk rounded past the S names and headed into the Ts. Walker was again whispering to Turner. The clerk called, "Tarrant"—aye. "Thronesbury"—no. "Travis"—no. "Tucker"—aye. "Turner . . ."

Silence. Banks Turner did not reply. "Mr. Turner," the clerk called again. Again silence. A great shout of satisfaction went up from the Antis on the floor and in the galleries. Suffs bit their lips. Joe Hanover stood frozen at his desk. Harry Burn swiveled his head over his left shoulder to watch Turner. Seth Walker stood in the aisle next to Turner. "Mr. Turner," the clerk called once more. Turner remained silent, his face contorted by the strain of the moment. The clerk marked Turner as not voting and moved on: "Vinson"—no. Soft sobbing could be heard in the balconies.

The roll call spiraled toward its conclusion with the Ws, and the Antis leaned forward in happy anticipation as the final set of names was called, a solid phalanx of seven nays. Then the clerk called: "Speaker Walker." And Seth Walker shouted, "No." The tally was 48 to 48. The amendment was defeated. All the Antis, including Josephine Pearson, were on their feet again, ready to cheer, but before any sound could leave their throats, Banks Turner abruptly stood up from his chair.

Turner was a thin man, and even though he was still young, his reddish hair was thinning and receding, making his forehead, covered with beads of perspiration, prominent. His eyelids drooped and his lower lip jutted out as he took a breath, then spoke.

"Mr. Speaker," Turner said, "I wish to be recorded as voting Aye."

There was a long moment of silence, silence and shock. Then an explosion, a roar never before heard in the old statehouse. The chamber shook with screams and cries, with thumping and whooping. Anne Dudley's shriek pierced the chamber. Those who could dance in the jammed chamber did, and there was weeping among both men and women. The winners frantically waved hundreds of tiny yellow flags and threw yellow flowers down onto the heads of the legislators on the floor. Joe Hanover was mobbed by delegates, like the winning pitcher of a ball game. Hanover and his ratification men ripped the yellow roses from their lapels and tossed them up into the balconies, where they met the yellow petals raining down.

Overton, helpless in the Speaker's chair, didn't even try to gain control of the chamber. The clerk hadn't even announced the tally, but the Suffs didn't care, they could count. With Burn, and then Turner, it was 49 to 48. But through the uproar a loud voice rang out. It was Seth Walker, his arm outstretched, his face flushed. "Mr. Speaker," he called out, "I wish to change my vote from Nay to Aye." The Suffs were too busy celebrating to pay much attention. "And," Walker shouted over the din, "I wish to move for reconsideration." It was a Machiavellian move, buying his side time. By changing his vote to the winning side, he could claim the right to bring the ratification question back for another vote anytime within the next two days.

But none of that mattered at this moment. The winners were too relieved, too overjoyed. Walker's vote gave the suffragists a valuable gift: the fiftieth vote, an unassailable constitutional majority. An emotional chorus of "My Country, 'Tis of Thee" drifted through the statehouse.

Carrie Catt could hear the wild commotion from her window, and she knew. Yellow-draped messengers were running down the hill toward the Hermitage to give her the news she had been waiting a lifetime to hear. Harriet Upton's heart began to pound in her chest as she watched the Suffs cascade down the hill.

Alice Paul, waiting in Washington, received a rush wire from Nashville. She rose, went to her worktable, stitched the thirty-sixth star onto the long cloth banner she'd created to chart the course of ratification, and unfurled it from the window of National Woman's Party headquarters.

But the fight was not over.

Chapter 22

· · ·

Liberty Bell

THE SUFFS CELEBRATED while the Antis seethed. The happy pandemonium in the house chamber gave way to visceral anger as the Antis focused their rage upon Harry Burn.

They hurled insults and threats from the galleries. Governor Roberts ordered the sergeant at arms to protect Burn, who decided to take matters into his own hands and slipped into the clerk's room at the side of the chamber, climbed out a window, scooted along a narrow ledge, then climbed back in the next window, into the state legislative library. A startled librarian watched Burn jump into the library, descend its wrought-iron spiral staircase, make his way into the lobby, around the back of the sergeant at arms, and out of the Capitol. Although Burn could make this swashbuckling physical escape, the Antis would pursue him in other ways.

The Suffs' bubble of euphoria was quickly pricked by a disturbing realization: Seth Walker's move for reconsideration in the final chaotic moments of the session had put a giant question mark over the ratification. House rules gave Walker control of the reconsideration motion for the next three days, and he could call it up for a vote at any time. If a majority of the members present in the chamber agreed to reconsider the ratification, erasing the original vote, the amendment could still be rejected. In this game of legislative do-over, it was a matter of which side could muster the most men at any instant. In the skilled hands of a parliamentarian such as Speaker Walker, reconsideration could be a lethal weapon.

The Suffs needed to maintain their strength, and their forces, for several more days. They couldn't afford to lose a single one of the forty-nine men who had voted for ratification, and all of them must remain on call to rally to the statehouse in defense of ratification at the drop of a hat. If the Antis could pick off just one of those ratification delegates, everything the Suffs had accomplished could be reversed. The Antis were defiant, insisting that their victory had been only slightly postponed. "The fight is not over by any means," insisted Judge Higgins of the Tennessee Constitutional League. It was going to be a very long seventy-two hours.

Despite their frustration and continued anxiety, there must have been quite a joyous scene in room 309 of the Hermitage, when the singing, dancing Tennessee Suffs returned from the Capitol to celebrate with Carrie Catt. Catt wanted to share this moment with Mollie, but Mollie was a thousand miles away. She could, however, improvise a happy little ratification dance, a reprise of the jig she'd stepped to express her glee in celebration of congressional passage of the amendment. A jubilant Anne Dudley could finally feel that her faith in the men of the legislature was vindicated, as enough of them had proven gallant and brave when it counted. "It has been the greatest battle ever fought in the history of Tennessee, against such odds that it seemed that only a miracle could save us," she gushed, "but the honor of Tennessee has been upheld by the men of the Volunteer State." Abby Milton called it the happiest day of her life and truly believed it was divine providence that moved Seth Walker to unwittingly give the Suffs that fiftieth vote, affording them an unassailable constitutional majority. Now they must hold that majority intact.

A breathless Sue White dictated a report to Alice Paul; White's colleagues at headquarters replied: "Splendid Work. Hold the Fort."

While the Suffs in Nashville understood that their work was not yet done, the rest of the world assumed the house vote was the final step for women's enfranchisement, and thousands of congratulatory messages from around the world poured into Nashville, NAWSA's offices in New York City, and National Woman's Party headquarters in Washington. Some gave full credit for the victory to Carrie Catt ("Only you could have brought victory"), while others accorded that honor to Alice Paul ("I know who won it for us all! Almost single handed you've given this generation of women their political freedom").

"The civilization of the world is saved," exclaimed James Cox, in anticipation of women voters supporting the League of Nations.

"All along I have wished for the completion of ratification and have said so," Warren Harding said rather defensively, "and I am glad to have all the citizenship of the United States take part in the presidential elections."

Catt had had lots of time to think about what she might say when the time came, and true to form, she projected nothing but certainty that ratification was won and the "hour of victory" arrived. She issued a statement of fierce optimism and simple eloquence:

> Our mothers began it. So it came on to us as, in a way, a sacred trust.
> And a great part of our rejoicing today in the hour of victory is compounded of our feeling of loyalty to the past and our satisfaction that we have stood faithful to its trust.
>
> Now that it is all over, the feeling of "ceaselessness" is probably the sensation uppermost with us all, and perhaps that is just as well that it should be. For women cannot stop. The National cannot stop. With a new purpose, the purpose of making the vote register for an improved citizenship, the women of the National are already lined up under a new name, the League of Women Voters.

Sue White enjoyed a congratulatory telegram from her brother in San Francisco and from friends who wired, "Bully for Tennessee and Hurrah for You," while a North Carolina admirer cheered: "Remember Stonewall, Hold the Line for the Honor of the South. God Bless You." But she could take special delight in the compliment given to her and the Woman's Party by former Tennessee governor Ben Hooper, who wired to Alice Paul: "I want you militants to join the Republican party. I know live people when I see them and you are the kind we need."

Alice Paul had already given the press a prime photo opportunity: the well-rehearsed unfurling of her ratification banner from the balcony of headquarters, a Rapunzel-like scene complete with young Woman's Party staffers, dressed in white, applauding the long, starry banner. Then she posed beside the banner, raising a celebratory wineglass (filled with grape juice, no doubt) to toast the thirty-sixth state. By afternoon she also gave reporters a valedictory statement, but Paul's vision for the enfranchised woman was not merely as an educated voter, but as a committed activist for true equality:

> The victory of women today completes the political democracy of America and enfranchises half the people of a great nation. . . . With the power to vote achieved women still have before them the task of supplementing political equality with equality in other fields. In state and national legislation, as well as in other fields, women are not yet

on an equal basis with men. The vote will make it infinitely easier for them to end all discriminations and they will use the vote towards that end.

Paul could not possibly imagine just how long that task would take or that she would devote the rest of her life to achieving it.

They didn't have to wait long for the first assaults.

In a series of closed-door meetings throughout the afternoon and evening, the Anti leadership hammered out a multipronged plan to discredit the legitimacy of the house's ratification vote while pumping up pressure on those delegates who'd voted to ratify. They generated an avalanche of reproach directed at those who'd supported ratification, with the goal of delivering to each man at least a hundred protest telegrams. They also announced a mass meeting "To Save the South" at Nashville's Ryman Auditorium for the next evening and planned "indignation" rallies around the state in the districts of legislators who voted for the amendment. If they could frighten one man, they could win.

And they had special plans for Harry Burn. By evening a group of leading Antis, including Edward Stahlman and Charlotte Rowe, had invented an elaborate scenario to explain Burn's sudden reversal on ratification: he'd been bribed. By Joe Hanover.

They came up with "witnesses" willing to describe a sordid scene of corruption in the minutes before the final vote on ratification. It was a complete fiction, something out of a pulp novel: Harry Burn dragged by his lapels into a side room off the chamber, where Joe Hanover roughed him up and offered the guileless legislator "anything in the world he wanted," with the promise of making him "the biggest man in Tennessee" and a payment of $10,000. Dazed and frightened, Burn was then shoved back into the chamber, the convenient witnesses claimed, where he immediately changed his vote to "aye" and put ratification over the top. Late on Wednesday, a delegation of Antis confronted Burn with these affidavits and gave him a choice: Don't show up for the vote to reconsider ratification tomorrow, and we won't publish these accusations in the *Banner*. Stick with the Suffs and your reputation will be destroyed.

The first thing Harry Burn did after escaping from the statehouse and returning to his hotel room was to place a long-distance telephone call to his mother in Niota. Febb Burn was delighted to hear from her son and even more delighted when he told her he'd received her letter and taken her advice and his vote for ratification had put it through.

Phoebe (Febb) Ensminger Burn was a sharp-witted, college-educated woman who read several newspapers every day and kept abreast of current events. Febb thought it was ridiculous that women couldn't vote: her hired hands, who owned no land and paid no taxes (and in some cases couldn't even read or write), were permitted to vote, but she, an educated, tax-paying woman, could not. It was the same predicament Carrie Catt's mother had faced in Iowa a half century before. Febb Burn resented having no say in her country's affairs and believed giving women the ballot would purify politics. "I am for progress," she'd say, explaining her pro-suffrage attitude, which was not a popular stand in Niota.

She'd been keeping track of the special session in Nashville while Harry was away and was disappointed to find no mention of her adored son in the local papers' reports. She was hoping and praying that Harry would support ratification. She knew he was under a lot of pressure about it. So she'd written a seven-page letter to him, filled with family news, complaints about the rainy weather, a request for some piano sheet music, and that crucial maternal advice. Within hours of Harry's vote for ratification, reporters, photographers—and Anti agents—were on their way to the hilltop house in tiny Niota to find Febb Burn.

It wasn't hard to find Governor Roberts. He was in his office at the Capitol, receiving well-wishers, thanking the men who'd stuck with him. He'd proven to be among the most faithful, and courageous, suffrage men in the capital. Alice Paul wired her personal thanks for his "splendid fight" for ratification, which the governor must have especially enjoyed, given the disdain her workers displayed toward him. And Roberts could take pleasure in the congratulations of vice presidential nominee Franklin Roosevelt: "The action of Tennessee assures the greatest step that could possibly be taken for human rights and better American citizenship." But there were other telegrams of a more menacing nature, such as the one signed by more than a hundred men in Fayetteville: "Protect the rights of our states against federal encroachment and force laws. Dissatisfaction that exists here will seriously endanger your election in November."

The Suffs knew they must be constantly vigilant. Quite a few delegates were already grumbling that they wanted to go home, they were tired, they missed their families; asking them to stay for another three days was too much. The Antis, of course, were providing ample inducements for the delegates to leave: fake telegrams calling delegates home for family emergencies again proliferated, and threats of all kinds were deployed to break the ratification bloc. But the Suffs were not going to allow it. The Hermitage halls and lobbies were patrolled day and night even more vigorously, as were the other hotels and boardinghouses. Union Station waiting rooms and platforms were also guarded; taxi stands were surveyed hourly, ticket booths monitored. Rotations of suffrage men checked on ratification delegates through the night. Any man found walking with a suitcase was intercepted and escorted back to his room.

The Jack Daniel's Suite did a more robust business than ever. Harriet Upton was again awakened by frantic reports that Republican men were missing. Kidnappings were rumored, and some appeared to be real, as search parties were dispatched. Two suffragist legislators complained that they were woken repeatedly, every half hour, by phone calls; they knew the calls were a ruse to keep them awake and cause them to be groggy when it came to vote the next morning. The Antis were stooping low, but they were desperate. During the night, Joe Hanover was warned by Antis to "get out of the way" during the next day's confrontation over reconsideration. The Antis held embarrassing affidavits chronicling his bribery of Harry Burn, Hanover was told, and if he didn't stand down in his defense of ratification, the Antis would unleash the documents.

On Thursday morning, the Antis received a jolt when they opened the morning *Tennessean*: the affidavits they'd fabricated, alleging Harry Burn's corruption by Joe Hanover, were splashed over the front page and exposed as fraudulent. It was a scoop that neutralized any threat. It seemed the stenographer who'd been hired to take the dictation for the affidavits was a suffragist and, realizing the bogus nature of the testimony, handed copies of the texts over to the *Tennessean*. This morning they were in print—before they could appear in the afternoon *Banner*—along with strong denials and refutations from Joe Hanover and Harry Burn. The blackmail had been foiled.

Everyone returned to the house chamber for the morning session: the frazzled legislators and anxious onlookers. Cheers and applause rang from the galleries as the delegates filed in, with loud ovations for the heroes on both sides: Seth Walker, Joe Hanover, Banks Turner, and Harry Burn. All of the Anti delegates were in attendance, as well as all the men who'd voted for ratification. The question was whether any of the Suff men had been induced to change their minds overnight.

After the gavel and preliminaries, Harry Burn rose from his desk and asked for a point of personal privilege. The galleries buzzed. Burn handed a written statement to the clerk to be printed in the house journal: "I desire to resent in the name of honesty and justice the veiled intimidation and accusation regarding my vote on the Suffrage Amendment as indicated in certain statements," Burn opened, "and it is my sincere belief that those responsible for their existence know that there is not a scintilla of truth in them.

"I want to state that I changed my vote in favor of ratification first because I believe in full suffrage as a right; I believe we had a moral and legal right to ratify; and I knew that a mother's advice is always safest for a boy to follow, and my mother wanted me to vote for ratification."

Suffragists in the gallery could take extra pleasure in noticing that Harry Burn had chosen to accessorize his suit with a suffrage white tie. "I appreciated the fact that an opportunity such as seldom comes to a mortal man to free seventeen million women from political slavery was mine; and I desired that my party in both State and nation might say that it was a Republican from the East mountains of Tennessee, the purest Anglo-Saxon section in the world, who made national woman suffrage possible at this date, not for personal glory but for the glory of his party."

Burn's earnest, emotional statement only enhanced his stature among his colleagues and the public, effectively thwarting the Antis' attempts to smear him. The scheme was even belittled by the Anti hero of the senate, Herschel Candler: "There never was a finer, cleaner man than Harry Burn," Candler said, defending his protégé. "The present charges are too ridiculous for utterance."

Seth Walker never made a move for reconsideration on Thursday. It was obvious the Antis had not yet budged any one of the "Sterling 49," as the Suffs called their house stalwarts. Walker needed more time. The house adjourned until Friday morning.

Having failed with Harry, the Antis trained their sights on his mother. On Thursday afternoon, Febb Burn sent a telegram to Abby Milton, complaining about the uninvited appearance of Anti leader Anne Pleasant on her doorstep: "Woman was here to-day, claims to be wife of Governor of Louisiana, and tried by every means to get me to refute and say that the letter I sent to my son was false. The letter is authentic and was written by me. . . .

I stand squarely behind suffrage and request my son to stick to suffrage until the end. This woman was very insulting to me, and I had a hard time to get her out of my home."

That same afternoon, Febb Burn received a much more welcome communication from Carrie Catt: "You are blessed with a brave and honest son, whatever the enemies of justice and decency may do now to show their vengeance upon him. He is bound to have a great future. You will ever be proud of him."

The band in the Ryman Auditorium struck up "Dixie" when Seth Walker came onstage at the Antis' rally to "Save the South" on Thursday night. He was introduced as "a young Andrew Jackson" and given a thunderous standing ovation. An all-star lineup of speakers, including Charlotte Rowe and Edward Stahlman, fed the crowd some of the reddest meat yet served during the campaign.

Walker lauded the Anti delegates who'd rejected ratification, who'd "signed their names in the blood of the South to keep this a white man's country and a white man's government," and he boasted that he'd persuaded several more legislators to join his side; he claimed he had enough votes to rescind ratification. The crowd went wild. The Suffs got scared.

Before the session convened on Friday morning, Joe Hanover faced another ulcer-inducing problem. Charlie Brooks, though he'd hoped to make it back to Nashville, still hadn't returned, putting a chink in the Suffs' protective shield. And now Tom Dodson, a young East Tennessee lawyer who was an enthusiastic suffragist, needed to go home: his baby, who'd been sick for a few days, was reported to be dying. This wasn't a spoof, it was real, and a heartbroken Dodson was intent upon taking the next train home. Dodson was on his way to Union Station when Hanover and the ratification leaders realized he was gone; his vote was needed to thwart reconsideration.

In a hasty conference, Newell Sanders again offered to charter a special train to get Dodson home if he would stay for the pivotal votes, and a delegation of Suffs dashed to the station, arriving just as Dodson's train was blowing its departure whistle. In a scene straight out of a *Perils of Pauline* melodrama, two nimble suffrage men jumped onto the train, pleaded with Dodson to stay, and promised that the special express train would speed him home once the vote was complete. Dodson hesitated for a moment, then grabbed his bag. The three men jumped off the moving train and Dodson returned to the Capitol.

The delegates filed into the chamber, cheered by their sympathizers in the galleries, eyed suspiciously by their colleagues on the opposing side. The desk of one delegate, whose teaching position had been threatened by Antis if he didn't vote to reconsider, was surrounded by state schools commissioner Albert Williams and other members of the Roberts administration in a demonstration of protection and defiance. Joe Hanover looked haggard. Harry Burn and Banks Turner wore yellow roses.

Seth Walker was pale and agitated. Despite his claims of the night before, he really didn't have three solid defections in his pocket. He needed more time and tried to adjourn until Monday; he could surely pry a few more votes by then. But the suffrage line held firm, and the Monday adjournment was voted down 49 to 47. Walker looked crushed and made no motion to reconsider. Josephine Pearson and the Anti women in the galleries were disgusted. The Suffs swiftly moved to adjourn until Saturday morning, by which time Walker's control over the reconsideration motion would have expired. The Saturday motion passed. The Suffs had prevailed.

Suff women burst into applause and broke into song, leaving the chamber singing patriotic airs, tears flowing down their cheeks. They stopped at Governor Roberts's office on the first floor and serenaded him in thanks for his help. Out the doors and down the steps of the Capitol they sang "My Country, 'Tis of Thee" over and over, their voices ringing especially loud as they emphasized the phrase "sweet land of liberty."

"You are all heroes," exclaimed Carrie Catt in praise of the ratification delegates who'd held fast, "your names will forever be written on the hearts of American women." The Suffs began to believe that ratification was finally safe.

"The victory is complete," Alice Paul crowed. "It is a victory for humanity."

The Antis grew more frantic now. They'd run out of time and made little headway. They came up with a new plan. In the middle of the night, around two o'clock on Saturday morning, Josephine Pearson's phone rang in her Hermitage room, an urgent summons from Anti headquarters. She quickly dressed and made her way down a side stair, joining her fellow Antis in a secret mission. Shielded by darkness, twenty-five delegates opposed to

ratification had left their beds and, in small groups, made their way to a
train stop on the south side of the city. Pearson and her comrades bade an
emotional adieu to their brave soldiers; Seth Walker gave instructions to his
men. At three thirty a.m. the delegates boarded a special L&N train bound
for Alabama, over the state line, on an assignment to break the house quorum and delay a final vote on reconsideration until Walker could drum up
a few more votes. The "Red Rose Brigade" reached Decatur by daybreak.

When the forty-nine pro-suffrage delegates, including the returned
Charlie Brooks, entered the house chamber on Saturday morning, they were
met by only eight Anti legislators, plus Speaker Walker. The rest were gone.
In a delicious move, Tennessee suffrage women sat at the desks of the missing Anti delegates. Walker's control of reconsideration had expired, so Tom
Riddick gleefully took hold, moving that the house table the reconsideration
motion. Walker protested, but the Suff delegates took pleasure in tweaking
their Speaker as they merrily rolled on to the final procedural steps, reaffirm-
ing the house's ratification and sending it on to Governor Roberts's desk for
his certification.

It was done. Ratification was complete. The finale brought a round of
delirious cheering, and a suffragist on the floor rang the mini Liberty Bell.
But Carrie Catt couldn't yet go home.

What followed has been described as an opéra bouffe, a wild, theatrical
attempt by the Antis to stall and stymie enactment of the federal suffrage
amendment. But the Antis' machinations were desperate and dangerous
enough to cause the Suffs significant worry. The legal jousting began immediately, as the Constitutional League obtained an injunction restraining
Governor Roberts from certifying the legislature's ratification, which froze
matters for a maddening few days. Catt was forced to remain in Nashville
to supervise the Suffs' pushback while Alice Paul screamed from Washington that the Antis' legal maneuvers could postpone women's enfranchisement for months or years, certainly keeping women from the polls in
November. That's definitely what the Antis intended.

And the "indignation meetings" began, targeting the legislators who'd
supported ratification. The rallies debuted in Harry Burn's county of Mc-
Minn, where Anne Pleasant denounced Burn in the Athens courthouse and
seven hundred people reputedly signed a petition demanding that he change
his vote.

The Antis' goal was to foment such public reaction against ratification, and the delegates who'd supported it, that the men of the legislature would be forced, for their own political survival, to return and rescind approval of woman suffrage by a majority vote. The rallies also demonized Governor Roberts, calling for his resignation and, failing that, his defeat in November. As these protest rallies continued around the state, with Seth Walker, Charlotte Rowe, and Edward Stahlman featured speakers, they grew more virulent, tainted with the danger of mob action. The theme of "Save the South" and the overtly racist tone of the rallies resonated with sympathetic citizens who were affiliated with the newly rejuvenated Tennessee Ku Klux Klan. One observer at the scene of a particularly vicious indignation meeting targeting senate ratification leader Andrew Todd asserted that Charlotte Rowe and the other speakers had inflamed the crowd's anger to a boil, and if Todd had come anywhere near the meeting in the courthouse square, he likely "would have been lynched."

The Suffs deployed their own legal teams in the courts. When the Tennessee attorney general was finally able to convince a judge to dissolve the injunction against the governor, the Antis moved their legal assault to the federal level, attempting to enjoin the U.S. secretary of state from accepting Tennessee's ratification and proclaiming the Nineteenth Amendment as law. Still, on Tuesday morning, August 24, Charl Williams stood vigilantly watching over the shoulder of Governor Roberts as he signed the certification of Tennessee's ratification at his messy desk. The certification papers were immediately placed in an envelope and mailed special delivery to Secretary of State Bainbridge Colby in Washington. Carrie Catt could finally pack her bags.

On Wednesday, August 25, Catt, Harriet Upton, Marjorie Shuler, and Charl Williams, under the watchful eyes of the angels of commerce, left Nashville's Union Station aboard a train connecting through Chattanooga. During the layover, Abby Milton brought Mrs. Catt to her home for a goodbye kiss from the three little Milton daughters, whom the Chief had befriended during her brief convalescence weeks before. Catt taught the girls the steps of her ratification dance, her expression of victory and relief, which the girls enjoyed reenacting long after Mrs. Catt had waved good-bye.

Catt and her traveling companions hoped to arrive in Washington in time to attend the proclamation-signing ceremony in Secretary Colby's office. So did Alice Paul, who arranged for photographers and movie cameras to record the historic event. Neither group wanted to share the limelight with its rival; even in their hour of mutual triumph, the rift between NAWSA and the National Woman's Party could not be healed. Bainbridge Colby had no desire to be caught in the messy middle of a suffragist feud or give the Antis any more time to invent another obstruction. When the Tennessee documents were delivered to him in the early morning hours of August 26, he decided to simply sign the proclamation in the privacy of his home: no women, no cameras. The Nineteenth Amendment entered the Constitution of the United States with neither Carrie Catt nor Alice Paul present.

News of the proclamation of the Nineteenth Amendment reached Tennessee by midmorning, prompting jubilation among the Tennessee Suffs and sour denunciation by the Antis. "Tennessee has not ratified Nineteenth Amendment," Seth Walker wired to Bainbridge Colby. "This legislature has no power to act, and has not acted," he insisted. Within days, Walker would summon the Red Rose Brigade back to Nashville and, in the absence of the pro-suffrage delegates, ram through a repeal of the house's ratification. The senate acquiesced when Walker cleverly tied the legislators' per diem pay to the nullification measure, and a frightened Governor Roberts, trying to appease the Anti Democrats, signed it. The papers were sent to Secretary Colby, and Walker himself went to Washington to convince Colby, but it didn't matter: the Nineteenth Amendment was safely within the Constitution. Later in September, under intense pressure from Republicans who wanted a modicum of credit for giving women the vote, the governor of Connecticut relented, allowing the legislature to ratify, though it made no difference. Still, Constitutional League lawyers would pursue their legal efforts to strike down the validity of the amendment all the way to the Supreme Court. Not until 1922, in an opinion written by Justice Louis Brandeis, would the Supreme Court finally bring the Antis' legal crusade to an end.

On the night of the amendment's proclamation, a devastated Josephine Pearson retired to her room "tired and heart-sick to have fallen a victim of Perfidy," as she described it. Losing the ratification fight "embarrassed my self-respect, and also lost something of trust, never quite restored," she confessed. She felt an emptiness, "a void," such as she had never experienced in her life. "Lost Ideals! Not defeat, but disgrace for my native state and my country."

The next afternoon, Carrie Catt went to the White House to personally thank Woodrow Wilson. Catt was stunned by Wilson's appearance; she hadn't seen the president since his stroke and wasn't prepared for the sight of a shriveled man, his legs covered by a shawl, unable to rise to greet her. Edith Wilson stood by her husband's chair. Catt thanked Wilson for all the help he'd provided in the ratification fight, especially his efforts in Tennessee, but she sensed the bitter sadness in Wilson, even as he was congratulating her: she'd successfully finished her fight for woman suffrage, but he would never be able to finish his for the League of Nations. Tears were streaming down Carrie Catt's face as she departed the White House.

The National American Woman Suffrage Association held a jubilee celebration at Poli's Theatre in downtown Washington that night. Alice Paul was not invited. She was on her way to New York to meet with Alva Belmont and the National Woman's Party executive committee to make plans for the convention that would chart the future of the organization and decide whether it would form an independent women's political party. Sue White intended to be at that meeting. This phase of White's life, so exciting and exhausting, was over; what was next, she didn't know. As Miss Paul said, winning the vote was only the first step, now the fight for women's equal rights in all other facets of life must begin. White wanted to play a part in that next phase of the work.

Poli's Theatre was filled to overflowing with giddy suffragists eager to hear celebratory speeches and tales from Tennessee. Relieved of having to hide and hold her tongue, Mrs. Catt blasted the corporate interests that tried to thwart ratification and belittled the religious and racial attitudes at the core of the Antis' arguments against the amendment.

But while suffragists were celebrating the dawn of a new political era, an editorial writer for the *Baltimore Afro-American* newspaper offered his readers a chilling, and prescient, view of the situation:

Woman's Suffrage is now a fact. Candidate Harding and candidate Cox importuned the Tennessee legislature to join in the ratification of the 19th Amendment, but it was not until after the solons were assured that it would be as easy to disenfranchise Negro women as it has been to disenfranchise Negro men that they consented to lift the ban and permit the passage of the Suffrage measure. Under the "wide discretion" allowed the election officials in the state of Tennessee it has been a very easy matter to disqualify a male Negro applicant for certificate to vote. It will be just as easy to disqualify the female Negro applicant. And thus we take another step in the great work of making the world safe for democracy.

On Friday morning, August 27, Catt arrived home. When she reached New York's Pennsylvania Station, hundreds of Suffs were waiting, and a band struck up "Hail, the Conquering Hero Comes" as the train sighed to a stop. Mollie Hay was the first to greet Catt on the platform when she stepped from the railcar, looking a bit pale, overwhelmed by the emotion of the moment. Mollie escorted Catt upstairs to the station's palatial beaux arts waiting room, where New York governor Alfred Smith and a delegation of politicians were waiting to congratulate her. The Suffs of New York City presented Catt with an enormous bouquet of blue delphiniums (her favorite flower) and yellow chrysanthemums, tied with a suffrage-yellow satin ribbon inscribed: "To Mrs. Carrie Chapman Catt from the Enfranchised Women of the United States."

The triumphant procession began. Carrie, Harriet Upton, and Charl Williams rode in an open limousine decked out in suffrage colors while Mollie Hay and other national and state suffrage leaders marched in a guard of honor around the car. The parade was led by a troop of mounted police, a column of soldiers from the Seventy-First New York Infantry Regiment, and a military brass band. As the auto bearing the Tennessee victors swung into the parade line, a great cheer went up, and Mrs. Catt rose to her feet in the rear section of the car to acknowledge the ovation. She stood, tall and smiling, her hat slanted on her head, her left arm holding the gigantic arrangement of flowers, her right arm raised high, saluting the crowd. She seemed at once the victorious general and the beloved queen. This homecoming, she would later say, was the happiest moment of her life.

Hundreds of parading women wore their traditional marching clothes, white dresses with yellow sashes, and carried the banners of their local suffrage societies. Thousands of spectators on the sidewalks cheered and clapped, office workers leaned out the windows of the tall buildings lining the route to add their huzzahs, and the trumpets blared as Carrie Catt led the last suffrage parade.

Church bells rang all across the nation at noon on Saturday, August 28, in celebration of women's enfranchisement. Mrs. Catt had instructed the League of Women Voters in every state to arrange a celebration of bells in their communities marking the historic occasion. Church and school bells pealed, factory and train whistles blew, firehouse sirens blared, and car horns were tooted in the state capitals, big cities, and little towns. In Philadelphia, bells were rung on Independence Square. The mayor of Chicago supplemented his order for municipal clamor with a request that at the strike of noon all men doff their hats in honor of the new women citizens.

But the bells and whistles were more muted in Tennessee. Abby Milton's and Catherine Kenny's pleas, on behalf of the Tennessee League of Women Voters, to every mayor in the state, were met with some resistance. In Chattanooga, the mayor instead asked his citizens to bow their heads at noon "in memory of the final passing of the principles for which our forefathers fought, the death of states' rights, and the complete nullification of the Tennessee constitution." The mayor of Tullahoma also balked, saying, "I cannot join with you in this jubilation over the violation of the constitution of Tennessee." Indignation rallies continued to rage across Tennessee just at the hour when the bells were to ring on Saturday.

Even in Nashville, the mayor claimed to be too distracted by the city's streetcar employees' strike, which had turned violent, to issue a proclamation for bells on Saturday. "Local conditions" prevented Nashville from ringing and whistling, the *Tennessean* reported. Those conditions probably had less to do with the streetcar strike than with the inclinations of Davidson County's delegation in the legislature, which had flipped to the Antis and stood solidly against ratification. So Nashville did not take part in the noisy nationwide festivities, and a chagrined Catherine Kenny could only suggest that at noon, when the bells were supposed to ring, local women pause in their work and bow their heads in a moment of silent prayer and thanksgiving.

Carrie Catt and Mollie Hay drove home to Juniper Ledge. Finally at ease in her own house, sitting at her own desk, overlooking her garden, Catt wrote a poignant charge to the women voters of the nation:

The vote is the emblem of your equality, women of America, the guaranty of your liberty. That vote of yours has cost millions of dollars and the lives of thousands of women. Women have suffered agony of soul which you never can comprehend, that you and your daughters might inherit political freedom. That vote has been costly. *Prize it!*

The vote is a power, a weapon of offense and defense, a prayer. Use it intelligently, conscientiously, prayerfully. Progress is calling to you to make no pause. *Act!*

Chapter 23

❖ ❖ ❖

Election Day

O N NOVEMBER 2, 1920, American women did act—they voted. About ten million women went to the polls, just over a third of the eligible female electorate; nationwide, an estimated three women voted for every five voting men. Women voted in every state except Mississippi and Georgia, which, in an effort to prevent black women from participating, refused to extend registration deadlines to allow women enfranchised by the Nineteenth Amendment to cast ballots.

In cities and towns women lined up at their local polling stations, and the mood was festive. Housewives voted on their way to the grocery store, office workers brought their lunch to eat while they waited in line, factory workers joined when they went off shift; rural women in the western states made their way to election sites through fierce snowstorms. Some mothers brought their babies in arms, and obliging policemen held the tots while mom filled out her ballot.

Carrie Catt and Mollie Hay cast their ballots at the polling place near their apartment in Manhattan. (Catt voted for Cox, Hay for Harding.) Alice Paul voted for the first time in her life near her hometown in New Jersey. The Tennessee Suffs voted in their home districts. At Hyde Park, Eleanor Roosevelt also voted for the first time, presumably for her husband and the Cox/FDR Democratic ticket. At the White House, Woodrow and Edith Wilson had already filled out absentee ballots and mailed them to Princeton, New Jersey. Mrs. Wilson amused suffrage veterans with her statement that she was now very pleased to be voting and very proud of her husband's role in getting the Nineteenth Amendment passed. Alva Belmont refused to vote until she could cast a ballot for a woman president.

On Election Day morning, Josephine Pearson went to the Monteagle polling site to distribute Anti literature claiming the Nineteenth Amendment was illegal. The poll watchers were surprised to see her: You're not going to vote, are you? they asked her. You fought it too long and too hard! they said admiringly. She declined to vote, but the men at the polls came up with an ingenious solution: "Tell us what you want voted and we'll vote for you!" In every subsequent election, Josephine Pearson would instruct a friendly Monteagle man on how she wanted to vote so he could cast her ballot for her.

The turnout numbers were disappointing to the suffragists—two out of three women stayed home—and Carrie Catt was called upon to explain. It wasn't due to lack of enthusiasm, she insisted. Registration difficulties in the states—with only ten weeks between ratification and the election—were partly to blame. Also, the act of voting was so new for most women; voting is a learned behavior, and women were only at the very beginning of the learning curve. Catt gave assurance that her League of Women Voters would help to educate and acclimate the female electorate. The Antis crowed that— just as they had always maintained—most women really didn't want the vote.

The women who did vote helped to elect Warren Harding and Calvin Coolidge in a landslide. The weary nation—mired in economic doldrums and labor strikes, frightened by the rise of a radical political ideology in Russia, and shaken by a terrorist bombing in New York City's financial district in September, which killed thirty-eight people on Wall Street—chose a bland president to calm its nerves. Americans eagerly embraced Harding's promise of a "Return to Normalcy" as a retreat from the kinds of liberal policies that had brought disruptive social change. And his campaign platform of "America First" promised a withdrawal from international alliances and entanglements (especially the League of Nations). Fearful that the nation's identity (white and Anglo-Saxon) was being undermined by massive immigration, and anxious that "undesirables" were invading American shores, Congress and the new administration would soon shut the nation's borders to new immigrants. Americans picked a man who promised them strength and security, but whose character was weak and easily manipulated. Harding surrounded himself with cronies and opportunists who used the White House and its agencies to enrich themselves. Harding's short and ignominious term (he died of a heart attack in his third year in office) was defined by scandal.

Governor Albert Roberts was punished at the polls for his efforts to ratify the Nineteenth Amendment. Angry Anti Democrats helped to defeat Roberts as Tennessee broke from the Solid South and, for the first time since Reconstruction, voted Republican. The Tennessee suffragists campaigned hard for Roberts, in gratitude for his help, and were mortified by his defeat.

Carrie Catt wrote a personal note of condolence to Roberts; this was not the electoral "reward" she'd promised to suffrage's brave friends.

The Suffs were also disappointed by the reelection of several congressional antisuffrage stalwarts: Senators Wadsworth of New York, Brandegee of Connecticut, Penrose in Pennsylvania, and Moses in New Hampshire were all returned to their seats, despite the vociferous opposition of woman suffrage veterans. The Antis, grasping their newly endowed ballots, took credit for helping to return these men to office.

Harry Burn was reelected to the Tennessee legislature by the citizens of Niota.

On that same Election Day, American democracy was disgraced by a series of shameful incidents unfolding across the country. In Boston, first-time black women voters received phony notices from a fake state "Election Commission" warning them that they faced fines of $500 and prison if they gave "false statements" when registering to vote. And all through the southern states, black women were intimidated, harassed, or physically barred from registering and voting. In South Carolina, the Ku Klux Klan assisted in keeping black women from the polls, according to reports sent to the National Association for the Advancement of Colored People; accounts from Richmond, Virginia, and other cities told a similar story.

The most horrific incidents played out in Florida. In the town of Lake City, during voter registration, a black Republican club leader, who'd led classes instructing black women in his district how to fill out a ballot, was hauled out of his bed in the middle of the night, a noose tied around his neck. He was driven to the outskirts of town, where his abductors prepared to lynch him. He escaped, but the electoral violence continued. An estimated four thousand black women and men were denied their ballots in Jacksonville, and hostility toward black women voting ran so hot in parts of Florida that state troops were on call to guard polling places. The national secretary of the NAACP, fearful that the all-white state guard would not protect black voters vigorously enough, made a formal request to the U.S. Justice Department to deploy federal troops to dangerous precincts on Election Day. His request was denied.

The worst violence was in Ocoee, near Orlando, where the Ku Klux Klan warned black women, and men, not to attempt to vote. Those who defied the order faced bloody retribution: as many as fifty black men and women died in the spasm of Election Day mob violence, with several men lynched and a woman burned to death as the white mob set fire to twenty-five homes and two churches in the black section of town.

After the election, NAACP officers testified before Congress, bringing documentary evidence of the violent suppression of black women's and men's vote in the southern states. A veteran white suffragist, Mary Ovington, begged her suffrage comrades to help: "We must not rest until we have freed the black as well as white of our sex," she implored. "Will you not show us how to make the 19th Amendment the democratic reality that it purports to be?" It is a race issue, not a woman's issue, insisted Alice Paul in refusing to allow her National Woman's Party to take a stand on black women's disenfranchisement. With rare exceptions, white suffragists, satisfied that they finally possessed the vote, ignored the plight of their black sisters for almost the next half century.

The enforcement provision of the Nineteenth Amendment, which should have protected black women voters, was never used. Neither were the enforcement articles of the Fourteenth Amendment, providing for loss of a state's congressional representation in proportion to the number of citizens denied voting rights. To this day, Congress has never utilized these constitutional powers to punish states for systemic voting rights violations. The federal government averted its eyes from the blatant and violent suppression of black voters for decades; it was not until passage of the Voting Rights Act of 1965 that black citizens had proper recourse for violations of their voting rights through the Department of Justice.

But in a familiar historical dynamic, those voting rights, once considered secure, continue to be threatened and eroded by states' imposition of barriers: restrictive registration requirements, onerous voter ID laws, limitation of flexible early voting opportunities, and inadequate polling place resources in black, Hispanic, and other minority neighborhoods. Pernicious and unfounded allegations of "voter fraud" are used to justify such impediments.

The Voting Rights Act itself was weakened by a 2013 ruling of the U.S. Supreme Court, which overturned the act's most effective enforcement tool, Section 5, requiring jurisdictions with a history of racial discrimination to seek federal approval before making any changes to voting rules. Voter suppression, not only in the southern states, but in districts with minority populations within many other states all around the country, remains a pressing problem. Access to the vote is still manipulated for partisan political advantage, and true universal suffrage remains an elusive goal.

The rallying cries of "states' rights" that sounded through Nashville in the summer of 1920 continued to reverberate throughout the rest of the twentieth century and into the twenty-first. In its basic form, "states' rights" simply reflects the historic conundrum of federalism, the tension between a central authority and a union of autonomous states. But in its most bellicose manifestation, it led to the Civil War, and since then it has been invoked to resist federal involvement in a variety of important and contentious issues, including federal protection of civil rights. The states' rights rationale formed the backbone of southern states' resistance not only to black citizens voting, but also to the desegregation of schools, colleges, and public accommodations in the 1950s and 1960s.

Today, states' rights plays a significant role in policy issues, ranging from gun control to reproductive rights, environmental regulations to gender equality protections, land-use policies to health care to educational standards, as states push back against federal mandates and supervision. Women's health and reproductive rights, once thought secured nationwide at the federal level, are, at this writing, once again being restricted by numerous states.

Although white women completed their quest for the vote in 1920, other Americans would have to wait. Native Americans finally succeeded in convincing Congress to grant them citizenship and suffrage in 1924, yet many Native Americans continued to be barred from voting by state laws until 1957. Asian Americans, even native born, were not permitted to become citizens or vote until the mid-twentieth century: Chinese Americans were not allowed citizenship or suffrage until 1943; for those of Asian Indian descent, these rights were withheld until 1946; and Japanese Americans were forced to wait until 1952. African Americans in southern states, while possessing suffrage on paper, could not freely exercise their franchise until 1965 and still face obstacles.

It is perhaps telling that in a stubborn stance on states' rights, some states that had rejected ratification of the amendment waited decades to finally make a symbolic acceptance: though it had no bearing on (white) women's ability to vote, Maryland did not officially ratify the Nineteenth Amendment until 1958; Mississippi waited until 1984.

By the summer of 1920, twenty-six nations had already granted their women the vote. The postwar surge was due in part to the role women had played in the war (and also the loss of so many men), but it was also thanks in part to Carrie Catt's International Woman Suffrage Alliance, which had nurtured and connected suffrage groups around the world since 1902. With the U.S. campaign completed, Catt redirected funds from the Miriam Leslie bequest to support suffrage campaigns in other lands. Within the next two decades, more than thirty additional nations adopted woman suffrage. The Suffrage Alliance evolved into the International Alliance of Women, which today is based in Geneva and represents fifty human rights organizations, with several hundred thousand members advocating for women's equality and protection around the globe.

Following the 1920 election, the women of the American suffrage movement set off in new directions. While Carrie Catt and Maud Wood Park led the women of NAWSA into its successor, the League of Women Voters (already established earlier in 1920) and its mission of nonpartisan voter education and issue advocacy, Alice Paul's National Woman's Party kept going, with new, ambitious goals. For Paul and her followers, winning suffrage was just the first of many steps toward achieving equal legal, social, and economic rights for women; for them, the fight would go on.

Sue White stayed with the Woman's Party while she joined the staff of Tennessee senator Kenneth McKellar in Washington and realized her dream of becoming a lawyer, obtaining her law degree in 1923. White applied her legal training to help Alice Paul and Woman's Party activist Crystal Eastman draft the Equal Rights Amendment (ERA)—a constitutional amendment guaranteeing equal rights under the law and prohibiting discrimination on account of sex—introduced into Congress in 1923.

The ERA split the women's movement again: it was opposed by labor and social welfare leaders, who feared that even as it guaranteed "equal rights under law," its adoption would erase hard-won protective regulations for women in the workplace. Carrie Catt and the League of Women Voters opposed the ERA, as did, later on, Eleanor Roosevelt and the New Dealers, and without unified support the ERA floundered in Congress even longer than the woman suffrage amendment had: forty-nine years. It was finally passed by Congress in 1972 but met stiff resistance in the states from social and religious conservatives, led by Republican activist Phyllis Schlafly. Schlafly and her allies deployed some of the same arguments that the Antis had used, warning that the ERA would upset traditional gender roles and endanger the home and family, subjecting women to a range of perils. Like Charlotte Rowe six decades before, Schlafly gleefully debated the demerits of the ERA with "women's libbers," and public support for the amendment began to erode.

The ERA has never been ratified. Under public pressure, five states, including Tennessee, actually rescinded their original ratification, and even after a decade of trying, the ERA failed to muster approval of the required number of states. The ERA continues to be reintroduced into each new Congress in hopes of eventual passage and ratification.

There are some who would argue that feminists missed an opportunity to harness the momentum of their suffrage victory by not organizing themselves into a women's political party that could support women candidates and advocate for women's issues. Alva Belmont and others within the Woman's Party urged that it transform itself into a true political party, but the organizational and financial logistics of such an endeavor were too daunting. Instead, Alice Paul dedicated the organization to achieving women's full equality by changing state and national laws.

Carrie Catt never wavered in her insistence that in order to enact broader change, women must not segregate themselves in a single-sex party, but enter the two dominant political parties and push for change from within. She warned that women should not expect to be warmly welcomed into the parties (even if they might enjoy an initial effusive greeting) or expect to be escorted into the inner circles of party power, but they must be persistent, not patient, and demand a role in decision making. Some women did do this and rose in the parties' ranks. But as women failed to coalesce into a unified voting bloc in the first decades after enfranchisement, their power within the parties dissipated. Women candidates were rarely nominated (if they were, it was usually as fodder in a hopeless campaign), and for many years women's issues continued to be given short shrift by both major parties.

In hindsight, some analysts even question the wisdom of channeling women's political energy and expertise into Catt's nonpartisan League of Women Voters. While the LWV grew nationwide in membership and respect, and still plays an important role in educating the voting public on crucial issues and advocating for "good government," it also siphoned off some of the most talented suffrage politicians into the more passive role of political "education" rather than practice.

This is not to say that the suffragists, and their daughters, fell asleep after securing the Nineteenth Amendment, only that they splintered. After the "Votes for Women" umbrella folded, there was nothing to hold together the very broad, diverse coalition that had gathered under it. Suffrage women retreated into their own special interests, organizations, and regional concerns, often taking opposing sides on policy issues. An early attempt to aggregate the new political might of women was the Women's Joint Congressional Committee, formed by suffragists just a few months after ratification in 1920, with the goal of bringing the clout of major women's organizations to bear on social welfare legislation, employing the suffragists' lobbying know-how in the halls of Congress. The experiment lasted just a decade, and by the end of the 1920s Carrie Catt bemoaned the lack of a coordinated women's political movement: the thrill of working for the Cause was gone, the frustration of slow legislative and legal change had set in, and women could not "be joined together for any one purpose," Catt lamented, "because the difference between the reactionary and the progressive is too great to be bridged."

The Suffs' promise of a "women's vote"—a deliverable voting bloc, with the power to reward or punish elected officials and parties for their stance on a range of issues—never materialized, and as politicians came to realize this, their fear of the woman voter subsided and their eagerness to please her evaporated. Women tended to vote for the party of their husbands or fathers, and women's turnout at the polls remained surprisingly—and, to former Suffs, distressingly—low. (To be fair, men's voting participation also lagged.) It was not until the early 1960s that the number of women voting in national elections equaled the number of male voters, and not until 1980 did the percentage of women voters surpass that of men. Since then, women have voted in greater numbers and percentages than men by ever-widening margins, and a politician facing a large "gender gap" in support is often in trouble.

All this was just as the Antis had predicted. Despite their fondness for hyperbole and histrionics, the Antis were actually correct on a number of counts: women did not unite into a cohesive voting coalition; they did not "purify" or elevate politics in any meaningful way or stem the corrupting influence of money and corporate clout; and to Carrie Catt's deep dismay, women did not demand an end to war and a commitment to organizations promoting peaceful conflict resolution.

Ironically, it was the Antis who grew in power and influence over the next decades, their organizations seamlessly evolving from an antisuffrage movement into an antiradical and anti-Communist crusade. Immediately following ratification, national Anti leader Mary Kilbreth and her lieutenants, including several veterans of the Nashville fight, pivoted from fighting the female franchise to battling "Miss Bolsheviki"—the "radical" women they believed were ushering communism into America through advocacy of pacifism and social welfare programs. Once again, their favorite target was Carrie Catt.

Catt's commitment to international peace work proved her intent to weaken America through disarmament and dangerous international alliances, Kilbreth and her *Woman Patriot* comrades maintained; Catt's creation, the National Committee on the Cause and Cure of War, was nothing more than a Commie front, and her League of Women Voters was directed by Moscow, they alleged. Catt joined an ever-expanding list of American women accused of being unpatriotic, even traitorous, including Hull House social reformer and peace advocate Jane Addams and many other highly respected, politically progressive women. In the pages of Kilbreth's *Woman Patriot* publication, now repurposed for the fight against perceived Communists, Catt and Addams were regularly attacked and maligned, and both were featured in the infamous "Spider Web Chart" that drew spurious connections between liberal women activists and Communist operatives. Catt publicly fought back against the "web of lies" and its perpetrators, but the damage was done.

Kilbreth aligned with other conservative women's groups—including the Daughters of the American Revolution, the United Daughters of the Confederacy, and the American Legion Auxiliary—to wage what came to be known as "the Women's Red Scare." They managed to tar what were once considered mainstream groups advocating for mother-and-apple-pie issues, such as maternal and child welfare, an end to child labor, consumer education, and public health programs, as radical plots to secretly install a Communist dictatorship in the United States and destroy the American family. Even the National Parent-Teacher Association was smeared with the *Woman Patriot*'s "radical" brush, and mothers fretted about joining such an "un-American" organization as the PTA.

The women superpatriots, having learned a lesson or two from the Suffs, mastered publicity, lobbying, and public pressure tactics to thwart significant social welfare legislation and initiatives. But they also planted spies in groups they suspected of radical activity, compiled names, created blacklists, made unfounded accusations, and provided unverified information to willing government recipients, including various congressional "un-American activities" investigation committees and J. Edgar Hoover's Federal Bureau of Investigation. Fomenting a culture of paranoia and fear, Kilbreth and her allies built a formidable grassroots movement, trained a cadre of skilled women activists, and developed techniques that would prove useful during the McCarthy-era Communist witch hunts.

Subsequent generations of conservative women inherited this powerful political legacy and used it effectively to marshal resistance to a diverse range of government initiatives and liberal goals. A direct maternal line can be traced from the Antis we met in Tennessee, through Mary Kilbreth and her anti-Communist woman patriots, to the women opponents of the New Deal and the "Minute Women" distaff soldiers of the Cold War and McCarthy era, on to Phyllis Schlafly and her Eagle Forum housewives battling against the ERA as a threat to the American family. And today's outspoken conservative activists—from elected officials such as former governor and vice presidential candidate Sarah Palin and former congresswoman Michele Bachmann, to political commentators Ann Coulter and Laura Ingraham, have proudly assumed this mantle.

Liberal women also continued to excel as activists, playing prominent roles in the labor and civil rights movements, peace and nuclear disarmament efforts, and civil liberties causes; but for the most part, except for the lonely stalwarts of the Woman's Party, they abandoned the banner of women's rights for almost another half century. Not until the reemergence of a feminist political outlook in the 1960s and 1970s, in what was called "the second wave of feminism," did issues of women's rights and roles again become part—a loud part—of the national conversation and enter the political agenda.

This new generation of feminists again demanded a more equitable societal role: not just in the academy and in the workplace, but in their marriages and even in their protest movements (they were still delivering coffee to their male colleagues on the antiwar and civil rights barricades). They demanded control of their sexual lives, their career paths, and their bank accounts (it wasn't until the 1974 Equal Credit Opportunity Act that a woman could obtain a credit card in her own name without a male cosignatory). Though it was a heady time of renewed political activism and "women's liberation," it all sounded depressingly familiar to Alice Paul, who lived to witness the rebirth of the feminist movement but had been fighting for most of those same things since the first decade of the century. It also would have registered as distressingly déjà vu to Elizabeth Stanton and Lucretia Mott, who'd demanded equal pay and full economic and legal parity for women at Seneca Falls.

Quite a number of these issues remain on the table today, almost fifty years since that second wave of feminism crested. But there's been some undeniable progress, though nothing approaching parity: in the most recent Congress, women occupy 20 percent of the seats in both the House and the Senate and three of the nine Supreme Court chairs. In state legislatures, women make up about 25 percent of the delegates, and of the nation's one hundred largest cities, almost 20 percent are run by female mayors. Women presidents lead about 25 percent of American colleges and universities, and women professors hold nearly half of tenure-track faculty positions; nearly half of all medical school students are women, and slightly more women than men are enrolled in law school. But on average, working women still earn 20 percent less than their male counterparts.

The lessons of the woman suffrage struggle deeply influenced later American social justice and advocacy movements. The lobbying, public relations, and grassroots organizing techniques developed by the suffragists, as well as their use of nonviolent protests and civil disobedience, stood as a model for midcentury African American civil rights campaigners, anti–Vietnam War protest groups, and gay rights activists. No doubt the future will bring more causes, more necessary repairs to American democracy, and more need for passionate civic activism.

The League of Women Voters, still active in every state, still educating citizens, and still "making democracy work" as it nears its one hundredth anniversary, is another tangible legacy of the suffragists. Carrie Catt continued as the LWV's honorary president and national board member for the rest of her life. When Catt died in 1947, she was buried beside Mollie Hay, who'd died twenty years before. Their headstone reads:

> Here lie two united in friendship
> for thirty eight years through
> constant service to a great cause

On the ninety-sixth anniversary of the Nineteenth Amendment's entry into the Constitution—August 26, 2016—more than four hundred people gathered in Nashville's Centennial Park for the dedication of the Tennessee

Woman Suffrage Monument. A small group of Tennessee women activists, calling themselves the Perfect 36 Society, had toiled for years on this project: maneuvering around skeptical legislators and hostile bureaucrats, privately raising almost $1 million to commission a statue from a noted sculptor and have it placed in a prominent site.

The bronze monument depicts five heroines of the Nashville ratification battle, striding confidently together toward their mutual goal: four are Tennessee Suffs—Sue White, Anne Dudley, Abby Milton, and Frankie Pierce—and the fifth is Carrie Catt. They're slightly larger than life, dressed in period fashion, draped in sashes, and hoisting banners as if they were setting out on a march. The tableau captures a sense of urgency and agency, of women moving forward, confident of their place.

The morning of the dedication was appropriately hot and steamy; commemorative fans, parasols, and water bottles were favorite accessories. Quite a few women in the audience were dressed in classic suffrage costume—long white dresses, yellow sashes, flower-festooned hats—and a few dapper gents sported seersucker suits and straw boaters. Everyone wore yellow rosebuds. Anne Dudley's grandson and great-grandchildren were there, as were descendants of several other Tennessee suffragists and of Governor Roberts. Nashville mayor Megan Barry, Knoxville mayor Madeline Rogero, and Clarksville mayor Kim McMillan spoke at the ceremonies, as did Beth Harwell, Speaker of the Tennessee House of Representatives. Each offered her own emotional testimony of thanks to the suffrage pioneers, the women they credited with making their own careers in government possible.

When the statue was unveiled, the crowd surged forward to admire and touch it. Mothers brought their daughters to stand at the feet of the activists who'd fought in that last great battle for woman suffrage; smiling groups of Tennesseans, black and white, posed for photos beside their heroic foremothers. Alma Sanford, a Nashville lawyer and civic activist in her spry eighties, dressed in full suffrage-era raiment, rushed to the monument, reaching out to clasp Carrie Catt's bronze hand in her own.

Ten weeks later, on Election Day 2016, in celebration of the possibility that a woman might be elected president of the United States, thousands of women made an emotional pilgrimage: first to their polling place and then to a cemetery. They cast their ballots for Hillary Rodham Clinton, the first woman to run for president as the candidate of a major political party, and then went to visit the graves of some of the suffrage leaders who'd won that ballot for them. In Rochester, New York, almost ten thousand women brought flowers and their "I VOTED" stickers to adorn Susan B. Anthony's headstone; in New York City's Woodlawn Cemetery, women voters decorated the graves of Elizabeth Cady Stanton, Carrie Catt, and Mollie Hay in similar fashion; and in southern New Jersey, Alice Paul's final resting place was festooned with bouquets, stickers, and thank-you notes. In Nashville, the new woman suffrage monument in Centennial Park was decorated with bouquets of yellow roses.

Epilogue

HARRY BURN SERVED in the Tennessee House of Representatives for another term, then in 1923 he returned to McMinn County to practice law. He made an unsuccessful run for governor in 1930; was elected to the Tennessee Senate in 1949; served on the state planning commission for twenty years. He was also a bank president and lawyer for the Southern Railway. Burn died in 1977.

Carrie Catt remained an activist for the rest of her life. Turning her energies to antiwar efforts, she founded the National Committee on the Cause and Cure of War to advocate for peace and disarmament and was monitored by the FBI. Alarmed by Adolf Hitler's rise to power in Germany in 1933, she organized the Protest Committee of Non-Jewish Women Against the Persecution of Jews in Germany and lobbied the U.S. government to ease immigration restrictions for refugees. Catt died of a heart attack in 1947.

James Cox returned to his publishing business in Dayton, expanding it into a media empire. Today, Cox Enterprises is one of the largest media companies in the nation; the Cox family still owns and runs the company.

Anne Dallas Dudley remained active in both the national Democratic Party and Nashville's civic life, establishing the Woman's Civic League to improve municipal government programs. In the 1930s, Dudley led the Maternal Welfare Organization of Tennessee and brought Margaret Sanger to Nashville to raise awareness of the importance of birth control. Dudley died in 1955.

Betty Gram went to Berlin to continue her musical studies and married radio journalist Raymond Swing, who made headlines for his unusual decision to take his wife's name. Betty continued her affiliation with the National Woman's Party, working for passage of the Equal Rights Amendment, and she remained a close friend of Sue White's. She died in 1969.

Joseph Hanover returned to Memphis and with his brother established a thriving law practice, which subsequently grew into one of Memphis's largest law firms. He served as chair of the Shelby County Port Commission, among other posts, and was honored for his community service and philanthropy. Hanover died in 1984.

Warren Harding continued his affair with Nan Britton while in the White House; he died in office in 1923, and his term is remembered chiefly for the Teapot Dome scandal and a generally corrupt administration.

Luke Lea expanded his political influence and business interests, investing in real estate and banking during the 1920s, including some questionable ventures. In 1934, Lea was convicted of violations of banking laws in North Carolina and sent to prison. He was paroled after two years and then pardoned, but by then he had lost the *Nashville Tennessean* and his political clout. Lea died in 1945.

Catherine Talty Kenny served as the second president of the Tennessee League of Women Voters and followed through on her promises to win support for Frankie Pierce's projects to aid black Tennesseans. Kenny also held high posts in the state and national Democratic Party and chaired the Nashville City Hospital Commission for eight years, where she improved working conditions for nurses and brought black nurses onto the staff. Kenny died in 1950.

Abby Crawford Milton led the Tennessee LWV through its first years. She lobbied for legislation and reforms benefiting women and in the late 1930s ran unsuccessfully for a seat in the Tennessee Senate; she also published several volumes of poetry. Abby died in 1991, aged 110 years.

Alice Paul led the National Woman's Party for the rest of her life, working for women's full legal equality. The Woman's Party lobbied in Congress and state legislatures for stronger guarantees of women's rights, most especially for the Equal Rights Amendment to the U.S. Constitution, which was passed by Congress in 1972 but never ratified by the states. Paul died in 1977, and the National Woman's Party ended its political activity in 1997; it is now an educational organization.

Josephine Pearson returned to teaching, mostly at Christian colleges, and continued to be a prolific writer of colorful essays and opinion pieces on political and cultural topics. She died in 1944 and is buried next to her parents in Monteagle Cemetery in Tennessee.

Juno Frankie Pierce continued to advocate for better facilities for Nashville's African American citizens and worked with Catherine Kenny and the League of Women Voters to win legislative approval and funding for the Tennessee Vocational School for Colored Girls; Pierce served as the school's superintendent from its opening in 1923 until her retirement in 1939. She also led Nashville's black club women in a protest march to City Hall, demonstrating against Jim Crow segregation policies decades before such marches became a staple of the modern civil rights era. Pierce died in 1954.

Anita Pollitzer continued working with Alice Paul as an officer of the National Woman's Party for more than fifty years. Pollitzer married, earned a master's degree in international relations, and lobbied strenuously for the ERA. Paul tapped Pollitzer to lead the National Woman's Party as chairwoman in 1945. Pollitzer wrote a memoir of her friendship with Georgia O'Keeffe (*A Woman on Paper*), and their long correspondence was compiled in *Lovingly, Georgia*. Pollitzer died in 1975.

Albert Roberts resumed his law practice in Nashville after losing his bid for reelection as governor. Though he never held office again, Roberts continued his role as a political elder statesman and adviser. He died in 1946.

Eleanor Roosevelt joined the League of Women Voters in late 1920 and became one of Carrie Catt's protégées. Catt brought her onto the LWV board as vice president of legislative affairs, an important step in Eleanor's widening political education. Catt also appointed Eleanor a director of the Leslie Woman Suffrage Commission; the women worked together in peace and justice organizations for years and remained friends. Roosevelt died in 1962.

Harriet Taylor Upton, as vice chair of the RNC Executive Committee, advocated for the appointment of women to government posts. In 1924, at the age of seventy, she made an unsuccessful run for Congress from her home district in Ohio. She died in 1945.

Seth Walker left the Tennessee legislature and resumed his successful private law practice, which included serving as the legal representative of several railroad companies. He ended his career as a district attorney for the Louisville and Nashville Railroad in Nashville. Walker died in 1951.

Sue White put her law degree to good use in helping draft the Equal Rights Amendment and in distinguished government service. She worked closely with Eleanor Roosevelt in Washington to get women involved in the Democratic Party, then joined Franklin Roosevelt's New Deal administration, rising to principal counsel for the newly established Social Security Administration. She died in 1943.

ACKNOWLEDGMENTS

Just as the woman's suffrage movement was powered by extraordinary collaborative effort, the creation of this book has been a joyful joint endeavor.

I have many to thank for their help and support, but my first expression of gratitude must go to my virtuoso literary agent, Dorian Karchmar at William Morris Endeavor, who guided me on this adventure. Dorian lent her perceptive eye and creative vision—and her passionate advocacy—to this book, piloting its progress with her signature sweet moxie. I join the lucky chorus of writers who sing Dorian's praises, offering my own stanzas of esteem and affection.

I also could not have wished for a more delightful co-conspirator than my Viking editor, Wendy Wolf, who brought her keen intellect, lively wit, and whetted pen to this project. Her probing questions and comments made me dive deeper, think harder, write more precisely. Her wise edits—and allergic reaction to dusty metaphors—made this a better book. Both Wendy and Dorian believed in the power of this story, and trusted me to tell it; their confidence gave me courage.

Expanding the circle of publishing professionals who lent their skills to this book are my champions at Viking: I thank president and publisher Brian Tart and editor in chief Andrea Schulz for their spirited support. Georgia Bodnar has been an indefatigable ally. The talented team of Carolyn Coleburn, Lydia Hirt, Alison Klooster, and Brianna Linden have created innovative strategies to bring *The Woman's Hour* to its readers; I thank them all. I've also had the pleasure of working with three of Dorian Karchmar's able literary assistants at WME who've handled the details—and me—with such care: picture hats off to Simone Blaser, Jamie Carr, and Lizzy Weingold. Thanks also to Clare Ferraro for her great early enthusiasm.

Tennesseans are rightly proud of their state's decisive role in securing the vote for American women, and I've benefited enormously from their interest. Tom Vickstrom, historian of the Hermitage Hotel in Nashville, is a devoted steward of its archives and an enthusiastic scholar of its past. Tom is the

Hermitage's controller, but he took time to provide invaluable materials and illuminating tours. I thank him most of all for arranging for me to stay in the room that was Carrie Catt's during her long residence at the hotel in 1920; that was a true thrill.

Paula Casey, a daughter of Nashville and citizen of Memphis, is an organizational dynamo dedicated to telling the story of the "Perfect 36th" state. Her sustained efforts to honor the Tennessee women and men who fought for the vote—making their contributions meaningful to a new generation of civic activists—are impressive and important. Paula is joined in this mission by a committed cadre of women who have organized, fund-raised, and managed to erect suffrage monuments around Tennessee. Compliments also to the Tennessee sculptors who created these suffrage statues: Wanda Stanfill's lovely bust of Sue White in Jackson, and Alan LeQuire's noble monuments in Nashville, Knoxville, and soon, Memphis, which imbue bronze and stone with the spirit of the Suffs. This book is built upon a foundation of documents—thousands of them—and for helping me to find the ones that reside in Tennessee, I'm indebted to Ron Lee, assistant director of research and public services at the Tennessee State Library and Archives in Nashville, who answered my many obscure questions. TSLA archivists Darla Brock and Genny Carter were also very helpful, as was Deborah May at the Nashville Public Library and Eddie Weeks, legislative librarian at the capitol. Jim Havron, oral history projects coordinator at the Albert Gore Research Center at Middle Tennessee State University, provided me with important transcripts. Gundy County historian Jaqueline Layne Partin generously shared her material on the Pearson family. And G. Wayne Dowdy, who presides over the Memphis and Shelby County Room at the Benjamin L. Hooks Central Library in Memphis, and is the biographer of Edward "Boss" Crump, provided excellent insights.

Beyond the Volunteer state, Elizabeth Shortt, head archivist at the Woodrow Wilson Presidential Library in Staunton, Virginia, gave me access to valuable material, and Sherry Hall, manager of the Harding Home presidential site in Marion, Ohio, provided details. The Arthur and Elizabeth Schlesinger Library on the History of Women in America, the jewel of the Radcliffe Institute for Advanced Study at Harvard University, is one of our great national treasures, and I've had the privilege of spending many fruitful hours there. To Ellen Shea, Kathryn Jacob, and the entire research and manuscripts staff, I send deep appreciation. My thanks also to the

manuscript archivists at the New York Public Library and the Library of
Congress, as well as the staff of the Milton S. Eisenhower Library of Johns
Hopkins University.

It is a rare treat, in the course of historical research, to touch your subjects in a more immediate way. I want to thank Dr. Pam Swing, granddaughter of Betty Gram Swing, for providing me with a special connection:
Pam guided me through Betty's papers, which she'd recently donated to the
Schlesinger Library, and offered family memories of her grandmother. Like-
wise, my warm thanks to Edward Kaplan, nephew of Tennessee legislator
Joe Hanover, who spent hours with me—on the telephone, through the
mail, and in person in Memphis—offering a robust and astute portrait of
his colorful uncle. James Jalanek of Memphis, who knew Hanover as a law
partner and friend, also provided me with delicious details, as did Margaret
Jackson Vaughn and Kevin Walsh. It was also exciting to meet the family of
Ann Dallas Dudley: thanks to grandson Guilford Dudley III, granddaughter Trevania Henderson, and great-grandson Chris Dudley for a friendly
chat in Nashville.

In my research travels I was housed, fed, and pampered by kind friends:
Kathy and Rob Jacob in Boston; Betty Marmon in Philadelphia; Jean and
Michael Zinn in New York City; Sam and Natalie Babbitt in New Haven;
Jocelyn Wurzburg and Bobby Bostick in Memphis. As always, my family in
Brooklyn Heights, Babette Krolik and Harry Greenwald, welcomed me
with open arms whenever I knocked on their door.

Back home in Baltimore, the solitude of writing was lightened by many
forgiving friends who cheerfully tolerated a monomaniacal companion while
loyal friends afar gracefully accepted long silences; I treasure the patience
and support of them all. Special thanks to my writing colleague and confi-
dante Jill Jonnes for her generosity, good humor, and expert navigational
advice. Also to fellow scribbler Steve Luxenberg, for many hours of deep
conversation on arcane nineteenth-century topics. Fellow writers of this city,
Rob Kanigel and Ann Finkbeiner, also offered me gracious support. More
heartfelt thanks to that swashbuckling archivist and author Kathy Jacob for
keeping me informed and amused, and to Jean Baker, a great suffrage scholar
and kind, enthusiastic adviser. Sam Babbitt, as ever, listened attentively, read
astutely, and encouraged lovingly.

This is a book about strong women who shaped our nation, and strong
women have also shaped me. In the course of writing this story I lost two of

these special women who've had the most profound influence upon me: I lost my mother just weeks before beginning this book, and I lost my dear friend, my mentor and muse, Natalie Babbitt, just as I completed it. Natalie would say that the wheel has turned as it should, but I just wish they could have held this book in their hands.

My final, and most profound, thanks go to my family: so willing to forgive maternal distraction and domestic malfeasance; so eager to soothe and cheer. My son, Teddy, and daughter, Abby, are adults now: both are attentive and engaged citizens (and voters!) working, in their own fields, to build more just, green, and art-enriched communities. They continue to bring their mom comfort, giggles, and buoyant optimism. My guiding north star—in writing this book, as in all other endeavors—is my husband, Julian Krolik, who brings his scientific rigor, historical knowledge, and demon grammatical skills to his job as my first reader. For more than three decades he has given me firm anchor and allowed me full sail. It is the great pleasure of my life to explore the mysteries of the expanding universe with him.

Notes

Catt Papers (Carrie Chapman Catt Papers)
LoC (Library of Congress)
NWPP (National Woman's Party Papers)
Pearson Papers (Josephine A. Pearson Papers)
TSLA (Tennessee State Library and Archives, Nashville)

Chapter 1: To Nashville

7 **By the time the train:** Catt's arrival in Nashville at 8:30 p.m. on July 17 is mentioned in the Nashville newspapers: "Mrs. Catt will Arrive Tonight," *Nashville Banner,* July 17, 1920. Her travel plan is also discussed in a handwritten annotation to a telegram sent by Marjorie Shuler in Nashville to the National American Suffrage Association headquarters in New York on July 14, in Carrie Chapman Catt Papers, TSLA.

7 **It was Catt's job:** This calculation is recorded in Carrie Chapman Catt and Nettie Shuler, *Woman Suffrage and Politics: The Inner Story of the Suffrage Movement* (New York: C. Scribner's Sons, 1926) and also in the biographical entry on Catt by Van Voris in *American National Biography* (Oxford University Press).

8 **Catt had kicked up her heels:** Catt's dancing response to Senate approval of the 19th Amendment is described by her friend and secretary, Clara Hyde, who was with her at the time: Clara Hyde to Mary Peck, June 5, 1919, NAWSA Papers, LoC, quoted in Jacqueline Van Voris, *Carrie Chapman Catt: A Public Life* (New York: Feminist Press, 1987), 155.

10 **"Our forces are being notified":** Josephine A. Pearson, "My Story: Of How and Why I Became an Antisuffrage Leader," dated April 30, 1939, Josephine A. Pearson Papers, TSLA, Microfilm reel #1.

11 **She knew she was doing:** Pearson describes her mother's attitude toward woman's suffrage in "My Story."

11 **"Daughter, when I'm gone":** This scene is described in Pearson, "My Story."

12 **Even before Josephine made the vow:** Ibid., and Josephine Pearson, "President's Message: Retiring from Antisuffrage Leadership of Tennessee," September 30, 1920, in Marjorie Spruill Wheeler, ed., *Votes for Women!: The Woman Suffrage Movement in Tennessee, the South, and the Nation* (Knoxville: University of Tennessee Press, 1995), 214–23.

13 **Sue White and Alice Paul:** Accounts of White's participation in the Woman's Party confrontation with Gov. Cox in Ohio are found in: "Cox to Receive Women Leaders," *Los Angeles Times,* July 14, 1920; "Cox to Receive Woman's Party Envoys Today," *Chicago Tribune,* July 16, 1920; "Cox Here Tomorrow," *Washington Post,* July 16, 1920; "Militants Plan Raid on Harding," *New York Times,* July 18, 1920; "Militants Send 500 Banners and Regalia For Use in Picketing Harding's Home," *New York Times,* July 20, 1920.

13 **Sue White was by now:** Biographical details from Betty Sparks Huehls and Beverly Greene Bond, "Sue Shelton White: Lady Warrior," in *Tennessee Women: Their Lives and Times,* vol. 1, Sarah Wilkerson Freeman and Beverly Greene Bond, eds. (Athens:

University of Georgia Press, 2009), 140–63; James P. Louis, "Sue Shelton White and the Woman Suffrage Movement in Tennessee, 1913–1920," *Tennessee Historical Quarterly* 22, no. 2 (1963): 170–90; James P. Louis, "Sue Shelton White," in *Notable American Women: A Biographical Dictionary, 1607–1950*, ed. Edward T. James et al. (Cambridge, MA: Harvard University Press), III: 590–2; Marjorie Spruill Wheeler, *New Women of the New South: The Leaders of the Woman Suffrage Movement in the Southern States* (Oxford, UK, and New York: Oxford University Press, 1993); Wheeler, *Votes for Women!* Important details are also found in the Sue Shelton White Papers and the Betty Gram Swing Papers, Schlesinger Library, Radcliffe Institute, Harvard University.

15 **more than twenty nations:** because of the war, national boundaries had changed dramatically—some countries absorbed, others created, so accounting for the exact number of nations offering suffrage to women in 1920 is a bit difficult to pinpoint. Both Catt and Paul claimed twenty-six suffrage nations at this time.

15 **Catt sailed home from Europe:** "Mrs. Catt Back to Help Put Suffrage Over," *New York Tribune,* June 26, 1920.

16 **It was a hornets' nest:** Marjorie Shuler's telegrams from Tennessee are in Catt Papers, TSLA.

16 **"Advise Chief," Shuler wired:** Marjorie Shuler in Nashville to Mrs. Frank Shuler at NAWSA headquarters in New York City, Western Union Telegram, July 10, 1920, Catt Papers, TSLA.

16 **She could still feel the sting:** This incident is recounted in Mary Gray Peck, *Carrie Chapman Catt: A Biography* (New York: H. W. Wilson, 1944), 28, and in Van Voris, *Catt,* 6.

17 **a large "Suffrage Map":** Versions of the suffrage map were published and displayed by both the NAWSA and Woman's Party, and appeared regularly in their publications: the National American Woman Suffrage Association's *The Woman's Journal/The Woman Citizen* and the National Woman's Party's *The Suffragist.*

18 **She was a firm believer in evolution:** Catt's lifelong belief in the concepts of evolution, and her reading of Darwin and Spencer, are described in Van Voris, *Catt,* 9, and Peck, 34.

18 **Union Station was the pride:** Details on the station and Maj. Lewis are in Joe Sherman, *A Thousand Voices: The Story of Nashville's Union Station* (Nashville: Rutledge Hill Press, 1987).

18 **Pearson was born:** Biographical information from Pearson, "My Story"; Anastatia Sims, "Beyond the Ballot: the Radical Vision of the Antisuffragists," in Wheeler, *Votes for Women!,* 105–28; Alice Marie Pettigrew, "Josephine Anderson Pearson: Racism, Class and Gender in the Southern Antisuffrage Movement," honors thesis, Vanderbilt University, 1997.

19 **It had gone rather well:** Gov. Cox's promises to the suffragists are found in "Militants Plan Raid on Harding," *New York Times,* July 18, 1920; "Cox Promises Aid to Suffs," *Baltimore Sun,* July 17, 1920.

19 **She had given Miss Paul her candid assessment:** White's report to Alice Paul, June 29, 1920, in NWPP, LoC, Microfilm reel #79; also in "Suffs Ask for $10,000 for Tennessee Fight," *Baltimore Sun,* July 5, 1920.

20 **an "absolute, united, optimistic front":** Catt to Mrs. Guilford Dudley, Mrs. George Fort Milton, and Mrs. John M. Kenny, July 8, 1920, in Catt Papers, TSLA.

20 **"The Anti-Suffs will flood Tennessee":** Catt to Mrs. John Kenny, June 29, 1920, in Catt Papers, TSLA.

21 **"Whatever you do":** Catt to Dudley, Milton, and Kenny. Catt Papers, TSLA.

21 **"At this time":** Carrie Chapman Catt to Mrs. Guilford Dudley, July 12, 1920, in Catt Papers, TSLA.

21 **When Catt stepped off the train:** Catt's reception upon her arrival in Nashville is described in "Nation Looks to Solons of State For Ratification," *Nashville Tennessean*, July 18, 1920, and "Mrs. Catt Will Arrive Tonight," *Nashville Banner*, July 17, 1920.

21 **"I've come to look over the situation":** "Nation Looks to Solons of State For Ratification," *Nashville Tennessean*, July 18, 1920.

21 **"All the states consider Tennessee":** Ibid.

21 **Miss Pearson sat naked:** Details of Pearson's night in the bathtub appear in her memoir "My Story." Also printed in Wheeler, *Votes for Women!*, 224–42.

Chapter 2: Lay of the Land

23 **The first trip was with Susan Anthony:** Details of this trip are found in Mary Gray Peck, *Carrie Chapman Catt* (New York: H. W. Wilson, 1944), 81–83, and in Jacqueline Van Voris, *Carrie Chapman Catt: A Public Life* (New York: Feminist Press, 1987), 42–43.

23 **Catt returned to Memphis:** Described in A. Elizabeth Taylor, *The Woman Suffrage Movement in Tennessee* (New York: Bookman Associates, 1957), 23, 68.

24 **She knew that if the political men:** Catt to Katherine Burch Warner, July 16, 1920, in Catt Papers, TSLA.

24 **Just a few weeks earlier:** Description in Peck, 348–49.

24 **When her father had discouraged:** Biographical details from Peck; Van Voris; and Robert Booth Fowler, *Carrie Catt: Feminist Politician* (Boston: Northeastern University Press, 1986).

26 **"a team to work for the Cause":** From Carrie Chapman Catt, "A Suffrage Team," *The Woman Citizen*, September 8, 1923, 11–2; and in Van Voris, 20.

27 **They were a formidable pair:** Catt and Hay's relationship is also discussed in Lillian Faderman, *To Believe in Women: What Lesbians Have Done for America* (Boston: Houghton Mifflin, 1999), 61–78.

28 **The reports she'd wired:** Shuler's telegrams are in Catt Papers, TSLA.

28 **And, he had hinted darkly:** Catt to Warner, July 14, 1920, in Catt Papers, TSLA.

28 **During the past few days:** described in Carrie Chapman Catt and Nettie Shuler, *Woman Suffrage and Politics: The Inner Story of the Suffrage Movement* (New York: C. Scribner's Sons, 1926), 432.

28 **"Newspaper attack on chief executive":** Western Union wire, Marjorie Shuler to Mrs. Frank Shuler at NAWSA headquarters, July 14, 1920, Catt Papers, TSLA.

29 **Everyone was away:** Kenny and Catt's frustration with the absence of the other Tennessee suffrage leaders is evident in their letters during early July, contained in Catt Papers, TSLA.

29 **Mrs. Catt insisted she would stay:** Catt's reluctance to travel to Nashville, and her intention to stay only a few days, is documented in her correspondence just prior to her departure from New York City on July 16, especially Catt to Anne Dallas Dudley, July 12, 1920, and Catt to Kenny, July 14, 1920, Catt Papers, TSLA.

30 **These regional differences and animosities:** For an example of careful Grand Division representation at suffrage conferences, see "Tennessee Activities," *The Woman Citizen*, July 19, 1919.

30 **"You know we Tennesseans":** Kenny to Catt, July 11, 1920, Catt Papers, TSLA.

30 **Kenny was in charge:** Kenny's role in the campaign is detailed in Carole Stanford Bucy, "Catherine Kenny: Fighting for the Perfect 36th," in *Ordinary Women, Extraordinary Lives: Women in American History*, ed. Kristie Lindenmeyer (Wilmington, DE: Scholarly Resources Books, 2000), 204–5.

30 **"This [bill] will place":** Taylor, *Woman Suffrage Movement*, 100.

30 **And in a moment:** Seth Walker's conversion is described in the NAWSA publication *The Woman Citizen* (April 26, 1919): 1021.

31 **It would be a "crime and a shame":** Taylor, *Woman Suffrage Movement,* 100.

31 **he signed the bill in the last hour:** Kenny to Nettie Shuler, June 29, 1920, Catt Papers, TSLA.

32 **Suffrage had been Catherine Kenny's ticket:** Biographical details from Bucy, "Catherine Kenny," 197–200; Kenny's obituary in the *New York Times,* July 2, 1950.

32 **"When you hand her the ballot":** Taylor, *Woman Suffrage Movement,* 78.

33 **She'd directed it all:** Bucy, "Catherine Kenny," 199.

33 **"do something else besides fuss":** Kenny to Nettie Shuler, June 29, 1920, Catt Papers, TSLA.

33 **"Get the biggest and most important men":** Catt to Kenny, June 29, 1920, Catt Papers, TSLA.

34 **men who couldn't agree on anything in the world:** The origins of the long-standing animosity between Stahlman and Lea is described in Robert O'Brien, "The U.S. Government's Investigation of E. B. Stahlman as an Enemy Alien: A Case Study of Nativism in Nashville," master's degree thesis, Western Kentucky University, Bowling Green, 1996.

34 **"I don't believe the 'nigger question'":** Kenny to Catt, July 11, 1920, Catt Papers, TSLA.

34 **"The suffragists organized them":** Ibid.

34 **"Our Governor says Woodrow is his Moses":** Kenny to Rose Young, June 21, 1920, Catt Papers, TSLA.

34 **"I conceived the idea":** Ibid.

34 **Catt studied the poll results:** These preliminary polling results of the Tennessee legislature were reported in the *Nashville Tennessean,* July 18, 1920, 12.

35 **They all sang a version:** Catt's visitors' assurances are mentioned in "Mrs Catt Sure Suffrage Will Gain Tennessee," *Nashville Tennessean,* July 19, 1920.

35 **He was the scion:** Biographical details from Lea obituary, *New York Times,* November 19, 1945; and Luke Lea entry in the Tennessee Encyclopedia by Mary Louise Tidwell and "Luke Lea" in the World War I section of "The Volunteer State Goes to War" online exhibit, TSLA, http://sharetngov.tnsosfiles.com/tsla/exhibits/veterans/ww1.htm.

36 **He decided it was simply:** Accounts of Lea's attempt to kidnap the Kaiser include: Theresa Jensen Lacey, *Amazing Tennessee: Fascinating Facts . . . and Historical Oddities about the Volunteer State* (Nashville: Rutledge Hill Press, 2000); *The Hopkinsville Kentuckian,* April 19, 1919; "No Penalty for Trip," *Baltimore Sun,* April 2, 1919; "Rumors of Attempt to Deport Ex-Kaiser," *New York Times,* January 12, 1919; "Ex-Senator Led Party to Kidnap Kaiser," *Washington Times,* April 1, 1919; "Raid on Ex-Kaiser Reported to Baker," *Washington Post,* April 2, 1919; "Had Lea on Carpet for Kaiser Exploit," *New York Times,* April 7, 1919; "Luke Lea, Tried to Kidnap Kaiser," *New York Times,* November 19, 1945.

37 **Lea came home a hero:** Lea's homecoming is described in *The Chattanooga News,* April 1 and April 4, 1919.

37 **But also the news he'd received:** "Death Claims: Wife of Col. Luke Lea Dies Suddenly," *Chattanooga News,* March 10, 1919; "Col Luke Lea Weds," *Washington Post,* May 2, 1920.

Chapter 3: The Feminist Peril

38 **They were horrified:** Pearson, "My Story."

38 **Before he even met her:** A description of the Vertreeses grooming Pearson for leadership of the Antis is in Pearson, "My Story."

38 **Vertrees was a respected attorney:** Biographical details from "John J. Vertrees—October 23, 1931," Memorial Resolution, Nashville Bar Association, https://www.nashvillebar.org/index.cfm?pg=MemorialResolutions#V, and Carole Stanford Bucy, "John Jacob Vertrees," *Tennessee Encyclopedia of History and Culture.*

38 **"modern Eve asks":** J. A. Pearson, letter to editor, *Nashville Banner,* August 5, 1914; Josephine A. Pearson Papers, TSLA.

39 **The Vertreeses organized:** The establishment of the Tennessee chapter of the National Association Opposed to Woman Suffrage is described in Taylor, *The Woman Suffrage Movement in Tennessee,* 80–85.

39 **his 1916 manifesto:** "An Address to the Men of Tennessee on Female Suffrage," by John J. Vertrees, pamphlet (Nashville, 1916) in Abby Crawford Milton Papers, Scrapbooks, TSLA. Also reprinted in Wheeler, *Votes for Women!,* 197–213.

40 **"I do not believe":** Ibid.

41 **giving her strict instructions:** A fine discussion of Vertrees's attempts to control the woman antisuffragists can be found in Anatatia Sims, "The Radical Vision of the Anti-suffragists," in Wheeler, *Votes for Women!,* 111–3.

41 **despite William Jennings Bryan's big pro-suffrage speech:** Taylor, *Woman Suffrage Movement,* 96. Defeat of the partial suffrage bill in the Senate in 1917 is discussed in Carole Stanford Bucy, "Catherine Kenny: Fighting for the Perfect 36th," in *Ordinary Women, Extraordinary Lives: Women in American History,* ed. Kriste Lindenmeyer (Wilmington, DE: Scholarly Resources Books, 2000), 202–4, and in "Senate Deals Blow to Suffrage," unidentified newspaper clipping, January 18, 1917, in Abby Milton Scrapbook, TSLA.

41 **that humiliating defeat:** The Tennessee legislature's consideration of a bill granting women partial suffrage in 1919 is discussed in Taylor, *Woman Suffrage Movement,* 99–103.

41 **Women were at the polls:** Bucy, "Catherine Kenny," 204–5; Anita Shafer Goodstein, "A Rare Alliance: African American and White Women in the Tennessee Elections of 1919 and 1920," *Journal of Southern History* 60, no. 2 (May 1998).

41 **They had their own reasons:** For a succinct discussion of corporate interests opposed to woman suffrage see Sims, "The Radical Vision of the Antisuffragists," 105–28, and Eleanor Flexner and Ellen Fitzpatrick, *Century of Struggle: The Woman's Rights Movement in the United States* (Cambridge, MA: Belknap Press of Harvard University Press, 1996), 286–99. Also see Camhi, *Women Against Women;* Anne Myra Goodman Benjamin, *Women Against Equality: A History of the Anti Suffrage Movement in the United States from 1895 to 1920* (Lewiston, NY: Edwin Mellen Press, 1991).

Chapter 4: The Woman Question

45 **"Many a man who advocated":** Elizabeth Cady Stanton, Susan Bronwell Anthony et al., eds., *History of Woman Suffrage,* vol 1. (New York: Fowler and Wells, 1881), 53.

46 **At Cousin Gerrit's house:** Elizabeth Cady Stanton, *Eighty Years and More.* 1898. (Boston: Northeastern University Press, 1993), 58.

46 **The British Parliament:** Descriptions of the proceedings of the World's Anti-Slavery Conference in London in 1840 may be found in: Kathryn Kish Sklar, "'Women Who Speak for an Entire Nation': American and British women Compared at the World Anti-Slavery Convention, London, 1840," *Pacific Historical Review* (1990), 453–99; Clare Midgley, *Women Against Slavery: The British Campaigns, 1780–1870* (London: Routledge, 1995), chapter 7, "The Woman Question"; Clare Midgley, "Women, Anti-slavery and Internationalism," in *Women and Social Movements International 1840 to Present,* ed. K. K. Sklar and T. Dublin (Alexandria, VA: Alexander Street Press, 2001); and Donald R. Kennon, "An Apple of Discord: The Woman Question at the World's

Anti-Slavery Convention of 1840," *Slavery and Abolition* 5 (1984): 244–66; Stanton and Anthony et al., *History of Woman Suffrage,* 53–62.

47   **"It was really pitiful":** Stanton, *Eighty Years,* 81.

47   **"After battling so many long years":** Ibid.

47   **Their treatment in London:** Stanton and Anthony et al., *History of Woman Suffrage,* 61–62.

48   **In one girlish fit of rage:** Stanton, *Eighty Years,* 31–32.

48   **"My experience at the World's Antislavery Convention":** Theodore Stanton and Harriot Stanton Blatch, eds., *Elizabeth Cady Stanton As Revealed in Her Letters, Diary, and Reminiscences* (New York: Harper and Row, 1922), 141–50.

48   **They swiftly created:** Stanton and Anthony et al., *History of Woman Suffrage,* "Seneca Falls," 67–75; Eleanor Flexner and Ellen Fitzpatrick, *Century of Struggle: The Woman's Rights Movement in the United States* (Cambridge, MA: Belknap Press of Harvard University Press, 1996), 68–69. For an innovative analysis of the suffragists' use of the Seneca Falls event as their origins story, see Lisa Tetrault, *The Myth of Seneca Falls: Memory and the Women's Suffrage Movement, 1848–1898* (Chapel Hill: University of North Carolina Press, 2014).

49   **her own Declaration of Sentiments:** Stanton and Anthony et al., *History of Woman Suffrage,* 70.

49   **Henry was appalled:** Flexner and Fitzpatrick, *Century of Struggle,* 70.

50   **"Lizzie, Thee will make us ridiculous":** Ibid. Also in Sally McMillen, *Seneca Falls and the Origins of the Women's Rights Movement* (Oxford and New York: Oxford University Press, 2008), 93.

50   **unabashed "Woman's Rights Man":** Philip S. Foner, ed., *Frederick Douglass on Women's Rights* (Westport and London: Greenwood Press, 1976), 10–15.

50   **Douglass admired the courage:** Ibid., 10.

51   **"I knew Frederick":** Foner, *Frederick Douglass,* 13, and Faye E. Dudden, *Fighting Chance: The Struggle Over Woman Suffrage and Black Suffrage in Reconstruction America* (Oxford: Oxford University Press), 5.

51   **"In respect to political rights":** Douglass editorial in *The North Star,* July 28, 1848, in Foner, *Frederick Douglass,* 49–51.

51   **Newspapers denounced it:** Stanton and Anthony et al., *History of Woman Suffrage,* 803.

51   **"So pronounced was the popular voice":** Stanton, *Eighty Years,* 148.

52   **"This is just what I wanted":** Elizabeth Stanton to Lucretia Mott, September 30, 1848, in Stanton and Blatch, *Stanton as Revealed,* II: 20–22.

52   **"I expect to plead":** Flexner and Fitzpatrick, *Century of Struggle,* 64.

52   **"I was a woman":** *Woman's Journal,* April 15, 1893, quoted in Carol Lasser, "Stone, Lucy," in *American National Biography Online,* American Council of Learned Societies, Oxford University Press, http://www.anb.org/articles/15/15-00663.html.

53   **"When she once":** Matilda Joclyn Gage to Lydia Becker, August 30, 1878, in Stanton and Blatch, *Stanton as Revealed,* II: 38.

53   **Stanton was "thought":** This description of Stanton and Anthony's relationship as expressed by Stanton's daughter, suffragist Harriot Stanton Blatch, is quoted in Jean H. Baker, *Sisters: The Lives of America's Suffragists* (New York: Hill and Wang, 2005), 89.

53   **"I forged the thunderbolts":** Stanton, *Eighty Years,* 165.

54   **"Here then is work for you":** Henry Stanton to Susan B. Anthony in Wendy Hamand Venet, *Neither Ballots nor Bullets: Women Abolitionists and the Civil War* (Charlottesville: University Press of Virginia, 1991), 101.

54   **Women did not have bullets:** Venet, 94.

54 **With Stanton and Anthony in charge:** Descriptions of the work of the Woman's Loyal League can be found in Flexner and Fitzpatrick, *Century of Struggle*, 103–6; Venet, 94–122; Dudden, *Fighting Chance*, 51–57.

54 **even William Lloyd Garrison protested:** Venet, 108.

Chapter 5: Democracy at Home

57 **The logistics were going to be:** White's report to Alice Paul, June 29, 1920, in NWPP, LoC, microfilm reel #79; also in "Suffs Ask for $10,000 for Tennessee Fight," *Baltimore Sun,* July 5, 1920.

57 **drained its bank account:** The dire financial situation is revealed in numerous documents in NWPP, LoC, during the summer of 1920, including bounced checks (Lexington Hotel to Anita Pollitzer, June 21, 1920) and a July 15 telegram from headquarters to Alice Paul in Ohio, warning her that the Party's bank balance was $130 and unpaid bills totalled about $1,000 (Emma Wold to Alice Paul, July 15, 1920).

58 **Miss Paul was a wizard:** See White's report used in a fundraising appeal, July 3, 1920. NWPP, LoC, reel #80, and "Suffragists Seek Funds for Tennessee," *New York Times,* July 5, 1920.

58 **"Opportunity to win this last state":** An example of this direct appeal is Paul to Mrs. Henry Justice, June 24, 1920, and Paul to a list of possible donors, June 28, 1920, in NWPP, LoC, reel #79.

58 **"To the Suffragists":** On National Woman's Party letterhead, April 2, 1920, in NWPP, LoC, reel #77.

59 **When America entered the war:** White's war work is described in Betty Sparks Huehls and Beverly Greene Bond, "Sue Shelton White: Lady Warrior," in *Tennessee Women: Their Lives and Times,* vol. 1, ed. Sarah Wilkerson Freeman, Beverly Greene Bond, and Laura Helper-Ferris (Athens: University of Georgia Press, 2009), 151–54. White wrote of her efforts to register men and women for war work in Jackson, TN, in the NAWSA publication, *The Woman Citizen,* June 16, 1917 ("Tennessee Women and the Duties of Citizenship"), in Sue Shelton White Papers, Schlesinger Library.

59 **"I see a determination":** Undated MS, possible letter to editor or article for a suffrage publication, signed Sue S. White, Jackson, TN, in White Papers, Schlesinger Library.

60 **"disloyal, pro-German":** Sue White to Carrie Chapman Catt, April 27, 1918, in White Papers, Schlesinger Library, reprinted in Wheeler, *Votes for Women!,* 182–87. White's involvement with the Woman's Party tour of Tennessee and the allegations against her are detailed in Huehls and Bond, "Lady Warrior," 156–59; in Wheeler, *Votes for Women!,* 182–87; and in Reminiscence of Sue White by her friend and suffrage colleague Rebecca Reyher, dated September 26, 1958, in White Papers, Schlesinger Library.

60 **"I saw with my own eyes":** Sue White to Catt, April 27, 1918, in White Papers, Schlesinger Library.

60 **In Jackson, where White lived:** Reminiscence of Sue White by Rebecca Reyher, September 26, 1958, in White Papers, Schlesinger Library.

60 **Her attackers included:** Huehls and Bond, "Lady Warrior," 157.

61 **"I prefer to presume":** White to Catt, April 27, 1918, in White Papers, Schlesinger Library. Also in Wheeler, *Votes for Women!,* 185.

61 **Catt jumped to the conclusion:** Catt made her accusations in a letter to the President of the Tennessee Equal Suffrage Association, Katherine Burch Warner, who relayed the message to White. Catt to Mrs. Leslie Warner, April 24, 1918, quoted in James P. Louis, "Sue Shelton White and the Woman Suffrage Movement in Tennessee, 1913–1920," *Tennessee Historical Quarterly* 22, no. 2 (1963): 179.

61 **her own calmly reasoned letter:** White's correspondence with Carrie Catt is in the Sue Shelton White Papers at Schlesinger Library, and reprinted in "Correspondence Between Sue Shelton White and Carrie Chapman Catt, 1918," in Wheeler, *Votes for Women!,* 181–93.

61 **trying to "wake up":** White to Catt, April 27, 1918, in White Papers, Schlesinger Library.

61 **"Take your stand":** Catt to White, May 6, 1918. Ibid.

61 **"In spite of every effort":** Ibid.

62 **"inclines to hydrophobia":** Sue White to Abby Scott Baker, June 1920, NWPP, LoC, reel #79. See also "Delegation Declines to Hear Militants," *Nashville Tennessean,* June 30, 1920, Abby Milton Papers, TSLA.

63 **already tried, and failed:** White's telegram to Gov. Roberts is quoted in the *Nashville Tennessean,* June 27, 1920, NWPP, LoC.

63 **Roberts really didn't want women:** White to Abby Scott Baker, June 26, 1920, NWPP, LoC.

64 **"I hope never":** Ibid.

64 **"So all the political leaders":** White to Abby Scott Baker, late June 1920, NWPP, LoC.

Chapter 6: The Governor's Quandary

65 **The firefighters in Memphis:** "Arrest Six in Fireman's Strike," *Nashville Tennessean,* July 17, 1920, and "Strikers Jobs Filled by Men of Experience," *Nashville Tennessean,* July 18, 1920.

65 **The labor people:** Gary W. Reichard, "The Defeat of Governor Roberts," *Tennessee Historical Quarterly* 30, no. 1 (1971): 96.

65 **The Memphis mayor:** Western Union Telegram, Mayor Rowlett Paine to Gov. Roberts, July 16, 1920, Gov. Albert H. Roberts papers, TSLA.

65 **Roberts hadn't had it easy:** Biographical details from Roberts Papers, TSLA; Reichard, "Defeat of Governor Roberts," 94–109. Gov. Roberts entry in the *Tennessee Encyclopedia* by Jeanette Keith; Ray Hill, "Governor Roberts," *Knoxville Focus,* April 27, 2014, http://www.knoxfocus.com/2014/04/governor-albert-h-roberts/; National Governor's Association Biographies; Obituary, *New York Times,* June 27, 1946; Kenneth S. Braden, "The Wizard of Overton: Gov. A. H. Roberts," *Tennessee Historical Quarterly* 43, no. 3 (Fall, 1984): 273–94.

67 **this despicable rumor campaign:** These rumors were circulating in June—see Catherine Kenny to Nettie Shuler, June 29, 1920, in Carrie Chapman Catt Papers, TSLA—detailed allegations were published in a letter by E. L. Wirt in the *Putnam County Herald,* July 29, 1920, quoted in Reichard, "Defeat of Governor Roberts," 94–109.

67 **the Tennessee Constitution:** Article III, Section 32: "No convention or general assembly of this State shall act upon any amendment of the Constitution of the United States proposed by Congress to the several States, unless such convention or General Assembly shall have been elected after such amendment is submitted."

67 **As he'd told Mrs. Catt:** A. H. Roberts to Catt, June 13, 1919, Catt Papers, TSLA.

67 **Exactly a year later:** "Hope of Early Extra Session is Doomed," *Nashville Tennessean,* June 22, 1920.

67 **the U.S. Supreme Court pulled:** Hawke v. Smith (253 U.S. 231), argued April 23, 1920, decided June 1, 1920.

68 **"It would be a real service":** Woodrow Wilson to Gov. A. H. Roberts, June 23, 1920, Roberts Papers, TSLA.

68 **Frierson produced an opinion:** Frierson's opinion, contained in a letter to President Wilson, is reprinted in *The Suffragist* 8, no. 6. (July 1920): 121. Also, "Holds Tennessee Can Act At Once," *New York Times,* June 25, 1920.

68 **Tennessee suffragists screamed:** Telegram, Sue White to Roberts, June 28, 1920, Roberts Papers, TSLA. Sue White's plea to Roberts is in "Suffragists Ask Roberts for Extra Session Call," *Nashville Tennessean,* June 20, 1920; White also asked U. S. Sen. Kenneth McKellar to urge Roberts, which he did: McKellar to Sue White, June 2, 1920, NWPP, LoC.

69 **Democrats at their convention:** "National Committee Calls on Governor," *Nashville Tennessean,* June 26, 1920.

69 **He was pelted:** "Heavy Pressure is Brought for Special Session," *Nashville Tennessean,* June 25, 1920. For other sources of pressure on Roberts see "Nation Awaits Action of Tennessee on Suffrage," *New York Tribune,* June 28, 1920, Catt Papers, TSLA.

69 **from his own Tennessee delegation:** See, for example, Abby Milton to Gov. Roberts, Western Union Telegram, June 27, 1920, Roberts Papers, TSLA.

69 **he stalled:** A. H. Roberts to Woodrow Wilson, June 25, 1920, Roberts Papers, TSLA.

69 **ADMINISTRATION AGGRAVATED BY ROBERTS' STAND:** *Nashville Tennessean,* June 26, 1920.

69 **still tied in knots:** Democratic National Committee chairman Homer Cummings telephoned Roberts from the convention in San Francisco. Carol Lynn Yellin, Janann Sherman, and Ilene J. Cornwell, *The Perfect 36: Tennessee Delivers Woman Suffrage* (Memphis: Serviceberry Press, 1998), 83. Other examples include a telegram to Gov. Roberts from the Women Delegates to the Democratic Convention, June 27, 1920, Roberts Papers, TSLA.

70 **"Some Republican state":** Yellin et al., *Perfect 36,* 83.

71 **Roberts finally announced:** "Roberts Tells of Plan to Call Extra Session," *Nashville Tennessean,* July 2, 1920.

71 **if he did not win renomination:** Roberts to Catt, July 10, 1920; Kenny to Catt, July 11, 1920; and Catt to Kate Burch Warner, July 14, 1920. All in Catt Papers, TSLA.

71 **nothing but headaches:** Catt to Roberts, July 14, 1920; Catt to Marjorie Shuler, July 14, 1920. Both in Catt Papers, TSLA.

72 **how can you expect:** Roberts to Catt, July 10, 1920, Catt Papers, TSLA.

72 **Kenny and Milton had already told her:** Kenny to Catt, July 11, 1920, Catt Papers, TSLA.

72 **the more the merrier:** Catt to Kenny, July 14, 1920; Catt to Dudley, Milton, and Kenny, July 8; Catt to Abby Milton, July 12. All in Catt Papers, TSLA.

73 **"Tennessee promising":** Catt to Nettie Shuler, NAWSA New York, July 18, 1920, Catt Papers, TSLA.

Chapter 7: The Blessing

74 **another bad night of nightmares:** Wilson's agitated state at this time is reported in Dr. Cary Grayson's handwritten journal, July–September, 1920. Cary T. Grayson Papers, courtesy of Woodrow Wilson Presidential Library and Museum, Staunton, VA.

74 **They were seeking:** Accounts of this White House meeting are in "Party United, Wilson Says," *New York Times,* July 19, 1920; "Cox Affirms Wilson Pledge," *Baltimore Sun,* July 19, 1920; "Cox is Pleased with Visit," *Washington Post,* July 191, 1920; and "Nominee Accepts Wilson Policy," *Christian Science Monitor,* July 19, 1920.

74 **Wilson didn't want successors:** A. Scott Berg, *Wilson* (New York: G. P. Putnam's Sons, 2013), 688; David Pietrusza, *1920: The Year of the Six Presidents* (New York: Basic Books, 2009), 191, 198–99.

75 **But Wilson insisted:** Berg, 617–18.

75 **Three weeks out:** Berg, 634–38; Phyllis Lee Levin, *Edith and Woodrow: The Wilson White House* (New York: Scribner, 2001), 330–31.

75 **Three nights later:** Berg, 641–42.

75 **Since that night:** Berg, 644–45.

76 **The consulting doctors:** Berg, 643.

76 **She devised a set:** Edith Bolling Wilson, *My Memoir* (New York: Bobbs-Merrill, 1939), 289, 302; Levin, 344.

76 **Edith knew that Woodrow:** Berg, 679–80; Wilson, *My Memoir,* 303; trepidation about Wilson's reaction can be found in Dr. Grayson's Journals, July 1920.

77 COX PROMISES TO HELP: *Chicago Tribune,* July 17, 1920, and *Baltimore Sun,* July 17, 1920.

77 **"I give to you":** *Baltimore Sun,* July 17, 1920.

77 **he was "thoroughly wet":** Pietrusza, 197. As governor of Ohio, Cox did support presidential suffrage. Suffragists' qualms are expressed in letters from Woman's Party headquarters to Ohio contacts, Alice Paul asking for inside information about Cox's character and politics: Headquarters Secretary to Mrs. Cyrus Mead, July 6, 1920, and in a note to NWP Press Secretary Florence Boeckel from a reporter for the *Detroit Journal's* Washington Bureau, claiming Cox was opposed to woman suffrage earlier in his career. Both in NWPP, LoC, reel #80. Antisuffragists also claimed Cox was known in Ohio for his ambivalence, or opposition, to woman suffrage. "Candidates on Suffrage," Letter to the Editor, *New York Times,* July 17, 1920.

77 **"It is true":** "Mrs. Catt Pins Faith to Tennessee Democrats," *Nashville Tennessean,* July 17, 1920.

78 **The way Roosevelt:** Jean Edward Smith, *FDR* (New York: Random House, 2007), 82–83; Joseph Lash, *Eleanor and Franklin* (New York and London: W. W. Norton, 1971), 213.

78 **"I was shocked":** Eleanor Roosevelt, *The Autobiography of Eleanor Roosevelt* (New York: Da Capo Press, 1992), 68, and Blanche Wiesen Cook, *Eleanor Roosevelt, Vol. I: 1884–1933* (New York: Viking, 1992), 195.

78 **"violently opposed":** Eleanor's biographer Joseph Lash writes that she was "violently opposed" to women's enfranchisement (*Eleanor and Franklin,* 159) but her modern biographer, Blanche Wiesen Cook, takes a more nuanced view of her indecision.

78 **as the wife:** Roosevelt, 68; Smith, 83.

78 **Even after New York women:** Lash, 290.

79 **tried to avoid the issue:** An excellent account of Wilson's evolution on the subject of suffrage is Beth Behn, "Woodrow Wilson's Conversion Experience: The President and the Federal Woman Suffrage Amendment," PhD dissertation, University of Massachusetts, Amherst, 2012.

79 **"I must say very frankly":** Woodrow Wilson to Witter Bynner, June 20, 1911, in Arthur S. Link, ed., *The Papers of Woodrow Wilson* (Princeton, NJ: Princeton University Press, 1986), quoted in Behn, "Conversion Experience," 27.

80 **"The suffrage parade was too funny":** Eleanor Roosevelt to Isabella Ferguson, in Cook, 200.

80 **Washington had never seen:** There are many descriptions of the parade, including: "5,000 Women March, Beset by Crowds," *New York Times,* March 4, 1913; "Mobs at Capital Defy Police, Block Suffrage Parade," *Chicago Tribune,* March 4, 1913; "Parade of Suffragettes is Disrupted by Riots," *Los Angeles Times,* March 4, 1913.

80 **Within the next months:** Inez Haynes Irwin, *The Story of Alice Paul and the National Woman's Party* (Fairfax, VA: Denlinger's Publishers, Ltd., 1964), 33–35; Levin, 182; Doris Stevens, *Jailed for Freedom: American Women Win the Vote* (New York: Boni and Liveright, 1920), 37–41.

81 **The Wilsons allowed:** Berg, 168.

81 **"I believe that":** "Wilson Indorses Woman Suffrage," *New York Times,* October 7, 1915; Berg, 376.

81 **"On behalf of a million women":** Catt to President Wilson, October 7, 1915, Woodrow Wilson Papers, LoC, quoted in Behn, "Conversion Experience," 61.

82 **"The joke is":** Cary T. Grayson letter, October 19, 1915, quoted in Berg, 376.

82 **Edith Bolling Galt:** Biographical details from Miller, *Ellen and Edith*; Berg; and Levin.

82 **The day after the wedding:** "Support for Suffrage," *Washington Post,* December 20, 1915.

83 **their split with NAWSA:** During the convention, in a last effort to reconcile the two groups, Catt and Paul met privately, but could not reach agreement. Paul reported that Catt walked out of the meeting after warning: "I will fight you to the last ditch." Zahniser and Fry, *Alice Paul: Claiming Power* (Oxford and New York: Oxford University Press, 2014), 230.

83 **The president was escorted:** Emily Newell Blair and Virginia Jeans Laas, *Bridging Two Eras: The Autobiography of Emily Newell Blair, 1877–1951* (Columbia: University of Missouri Press, 1999), 174–75.

83 **When they began picketing:** Levin, 180.

84 **"What's the use":** Paula Bartley, *Emmeline Pankhurst* (Oxford and New York: Routledge, 2012), 204; and Mary Walton, *A Woman's Crusade: Alice Paul and the Battle for the Ballot* (New York: Macmillan, 2010), 154.

84 **Catt called an emergency meeting:** Jacqueline Van Voris, *Carrie Chapman Catt: A Public Life* (New York: Feminist Press, 1987), 138–39. Catt also reluctantly accepted President Wilson's invitation to serve on the Woman's Committee of the Council of National Defense during the war. Former NAWSA president Anna Howard Shaw was named the committee's chairwoman, and, like Catt, found it to be without sufficient budget or clout, merely the government's attempt to channel and control women's wartime activities.

84 **Catt paid a steep personal price:** Van Voris, 138. Catt's fellow suffragist and pacifist Jane Addams also supported the war and was also ostracized by the Peace Party.

85 **"We have made partners":** Flexner and Fitzpatrick, 302–3; also text of this speech at Woodrow Wilson Presidential Library (www.woodrowwilson.org).

86 **After their hour with the president:** "Text of Statements . . . After Their Conference," *New York Times,* July 19, 1920.

86 **"I found the President":** *Christian Science Monitor,* July 19, 1920.

Chapter 8: On Account of Sex

87 **"Well I have been":** Ida Husted Harper, *The Life and Work of Susan B. Anthony* (Indianapolis and Kansas City: Bowen-Merrill Co., 1889), I: 431–46; Alma Lutz, *Susan B. Anthony: Rebel, Crusader, Humanitarian* (Boston: Beacon Press, 1959), 198–216; Flexner and Fitzpatrick, 158–60; Jean H. Baker, *Sisters: The Lives of America's Suffragists* (New York: Hill and Wang, 2005), 80–84.

88 **And in Battle Creek:** Nell Irvin Painter, *Sojourner Truth: A Life, A Symbol* (New York: W. W. Norton & Co., 1996), 232; Rosalyn Terborg-Penn, *African American Women in the Struggle for the Vote: 1850–1920* (Bloomington: Indiana University Press, 1998), 40.

88 **"Ar'n't I a Woman?":** Truth's modern biographer, Nell Painter, questions whether Truth actually spoke these words, as was reported, and perhaps embroidered, by a writer who witnessed it at the Akron meeting. But Painter agrees that the symbolic power of the phrase was in keeping with Truth's views and other statements and became an important part of her public legacy.

88 **Susan Anthony and her cohorts:** "Trial of Miss Susan B. Anthony for Illegal Voting," *New York Times,* June 18, 1873; Harper, *Susan B. Anthony,* I: 431–46; Lutz, 209–16.

Also, *An Account of the Proceedings on the Trial of Susan B. Anthony on the Charge of Illegal Voting* (Rochester, NY: Daily Democrat and Chronicle Book, 1874).

89 **The court ruled:** Minor v. Happersett, 88 U.S. 162 (1875); Baker, 85; Flexner and Fitzpatrick, 160–63.

90 **They found their champion:** Lutz, 226–30; Flexner and Fitzpatrick, 165–69.

90 **Stanton reported that during her testimony:** Flexner and Fitzpatrick, 166.

91 **at the 1890 National American Suffrage Association convention:** This convention marked the rejoining of the National and American suffrage organizations, which had split in 1869.

91 **Anthony assigned her:** Van Voris, *Catt*, 30.

92 **Everyone knew the vote:** Flexner and Fitzpatrick, 283–84; Carrie Chapman Catt and Nettie Shuler, *Woman Suffrage and Politics: The Inner Story of the Suffrage Movement* (New York: C. Scribner's Sons, 1926), 320–23; Maud Wood Park, *Front Door Lobby* (Boston: Beacon Press, 1960), 137–55.

93 **Her friend Helen Gardener:** Catt's dress is discussed in Park, 149; Van Voris, 149.

93 **When the Senate finally passed:** Van Voris, 155.

93 **They had to sit:** Park, 258–67.

93 **Catt listened quietly:** Hyde to Peck, June 5, 1919, NAWSA papers, LoC, in Van Voris, 155.

93 **She quickly dispatched:** Van Voris, 155.

93 **It was finally time:** Van Voris, 149.

94 **The first votes:** Flexner and Fitzpatrick, 308–13; Catt and Shuler, 343–80 and 387–97.

94 **Ohio suffragists celebrated:** Harriet Upton Taylor to Catt, late June, 1919, quoted in Peck, 315–16.

95 **Governor Ruffin Pleasant:** Catt and Shuler, 353.

95 **"I'd rather see":** Catt and Shuler, 354.

95 **One Oklahoma Suff:** Catt and Shuler, 391; *The Woman Citizen*, February 20, 1920.

96 **"You thought you had":** Catt to Shuler, July 1, 1919, Catt Papers in the Sophia Smith Collection, Smith College; quoted in Flexner and Fitzpatrick, 310.

96 **A high school beau:** Van Voris, 156.

97 **In May 1920:** Catt and Shuler, 400–401.

97 **"lashed to the mast":** Clara Hyde to Catt, July 20, 1920, Catt Papers, LoC, reel #3.

98 **"Things are interesting":** Sue Shelton White to Emma Wold, NWP headquarters, July 20, 1920, NWPP, LoC, reel #80.

98 **During the agonizing Senate delays:** Flexner and Fitzpatrick, 296–97.

98 **"Knowing men pretty well":** Catt to Mrs. George Bass, July 12, 1920, Catt Papers, TSLA.

99 **"We are now so convinced":** Catt to Abby Milton, July 12, 1920. Catt Papers, TSLA.

99 **It was easier:** Catt to Abby Milton, July 12, 1920, and Catt to Bass, July 12, 1920, Catt Papers, TSLA. The Woman's Party expressed similar fears about the parties purposely thwarting ratification, for example see Emma Wold, Headquarters Secretary, to Dr. Gillette Hayden, July 8, 1920, and Wold to Mrs. William Kent, July 16, 1920, in NWPP, LoC. An analysis of the political parties' reluctance is found in "Votes for Women Upset to Campaign Tactics," *Nashville Tennessean*, August 21, 1920.

99 **The chaos of a disputed White House:** Catt and Shuler, 372; *Chicago Daily Tribune*, March 26, 1920.

99 **Catt also heard:** Catt and Shuler, 369–70.

99 **Her demands were polite:** "Democrats Can Win Votes of Women," *Nashville Tennessean*, July 25, 1920.

100 **"Get some kind":** Catt to Esther Ogden, July 19, 1920, Catt Papers, TSLA.

100 **"Nothing can give us":** Catt to Abby Milton, July 12, 1920, Catt Papers, TSLA.

100 **"I am exceedingly glad"**: "Harding Comes Out Flatly on Suffrage Issue," *Nashville Tennessean,* July 22, 1920.

Chapter 9: Front Porch

102 **It sat on a limestone:** Description of Harding's house courtesy of Sherry Hall, site manager of the Harding Home Presidential Site, Marion, Ohio.

102 **A Marion Civic Association:** *Chicago Tribune,* July 21, 1920.

103 **The "militants" had unfurled:** Irwin, *The Story of Alice Paul,* 462.

103 **"I could not":** "Harding Refuses to Urge Suffrage Action," *Baltimore Sun,* June 23, 1920.

103 **"It's the same old bunk":** Ibid. Also, "Harding Holds Out Hope for Suffs," *Washington Post,* June 23, 1920.

103 **He kept promising:** Harding's promises and maneuvers concerning the Vermont and Connecticut governors are extensively discussed in the National Woman's Party correspondence during late June and early July 1920, NWPP, LoC.

104 **"I answer no":** "Harding Bars Advising Holcomb on Suffrage," *New York Times,* July 17, 1920.

104 **Alice Paul loudly announced:** "Militants Plan Raid on Harding," *New York Times,* July 18, 1920; also *New York Times,* July 20, 1920.

104 **Negotiations began:** These negotiations are detailed in Alice Paul's communications with the Woman's Party liaisons to Harding in Ohio. See especially telegram of Gillette Hayden to Alice Paul, July 13, 1920; Alice Paul to Dr. Gillette Hayden, July 13, 1920; and Kenyon Rector to Alice Paul, July 13, 1920. All in NWPP, LoC.

104 **Warren and Florence Harding:** Biographical information on Warren and Florence Harding from: Miller Center of Public Affairs, University of Virginia, American President series, http://millercenter.org/president/harding; National First Ladies Library, Canton, Ohio, http://www.firstladies.org/biographies/firstladies.aspx?biography=30, and David Pietrusza, *1920: The Year of the Six Presidents* (New York: Basic Books, 2009).

105 **The ceremonies began:** Harding's Notification Day is described in: "100,000 to Hear Harding Told He's It," *Chicago Tribune,* July 21, 1920; "Harding Day," *Chicago Tribune,* July 22, 1920; "Harding Pledges Aid for Suffrage Cause," *Baltimore Sun,* July 22, 1920; "Harding Defines His Stand Today," *New York Times,* July 22, 1920; "In Harding's Hometown," *Los Angeles Times,* July 22, 1920; "Grand Old Party Takes Firm Stand," *Los Angeles Times,* July 23, 1920; "30,000 Try To Hear Harding's Speech," *New York Times,* July 23, 1920; "Notification of Mr. Harding Held," *Christian Science Monitor,* July 23, 1920; "Normalcy and Prompt Pledge," *Washington Post,* July 23, 1920. Newsreel of the event can be found at www.loc.gov/item/mp76000342/.

105 **In the doorway:** Albert Lasker was on leave from his Chicago advertising agency, working for the Republican National Committee as director of publicity; see Pietrusza, chapter 19, "Back to Normal," and John A. Morello, *Selling the President, 1920: Albert Lasker, Advertising, and the Election of Warren G. Harding* (Westport, CT: Praeger, 2001).

106 **White's train from Nashville:** Alice Paul to Florence Boeckel, NWP headquarters, Washington, July 21, 1920, NWPP, LoC. Accounts of this meeting in *The Suffragist,* August 1920; Irwin, 465.

106 **Her tiny body:** Descriptions of Alice Paul and her leadership qualities drawn from J. D. Zahniser and Amelia R. Fry, *Alice Paul: Claiming Power* (Oxford and New York: Oxford University Press, 2014); Irwin; and Doris Stevens, *Jailed for Freedom: American Women Win the Vote* (New York: Boni and Liverwright, 1920).

107 **The women, all dressed:** Descriptions and photographs of the "notification" event are in *The Suffragist*, August 1920; LoC newsreel footage, https://www.loc.gov/item/mp7600 0342/, and "Women Displeased by Harding Stand," *New York Times*, July 23, 1920.

109 **Slammed together in a "Black Maria":** Louisine Havemeyer, "Memories of a Militant: The Prison Special," *Scribners*, May 1922.

110 **"Fifty-six years ago":** Ibid.

110 **He folded his arms:** Harding's demeanor while listening is discerned from photographs in *The Suffragist*, August 1920, and LoC newsreel.

111 **When Harding was asked:** Pietrusza, 225.

111 **The baby was safely:** Pietrusza, 79–81.

111 **Harding had not yet bothered:** Pietrusza, 217, quoting Nan Britton, *The President's Daughter* (New York: Elizabeth Ann Guild, Inc., 1927), 134–35.

111 **They'd been carrying on:** Pietrusza, 74–75.

111 **and in the spring:** Harding's replies to Carrie Phillips's threats are among the 240 pieces of correspondence (including Harding's steamy love letters to Phillips) available in the Manuscript Division of the LoC, http://hdl.loc.gov/loc.mss/collmss.ms000023; also discussed in Pietrusza, 88–89; Carl Sferrazza Anthony, *Florence Harding*, 179–84.

111 **she threatened to expose:** Harding discusses these negotiations with Phillips in his letter of July 2, 1920, in the Harding-Phillips correspondence, LoC. Also discussed in Pietrusza, 319–20, and *New York Times*, July 10, 1964.

112 **"To what these ladies":** *The Suffragist*, August 1920.

112 **At two o'clock:** *New York Times*, July 23, 1920; *Washington Post*, July 23, 1920.

112 **Harding wrote the speech:** "Harding Finishes Acceptance Speech," *New York Times*, July 18, 1920.

113 **the inimitable words of journalist H. L. Mencken:** in John W. Dean, *Warren G. Harding* (New York: Macmillan, 2004), 73.

113 **"The womanhood of America":** Text of Harding's acceptance speech in *New York Times*, July 23, 1920.

113 **"If Sen. Harding refuses":** "Women Displeased by Harding's Stand," *New York Times*, July 23, 1920.

113 **Paul threatened to follow:** Ibid.

Chapter 10: Home and Heaven

115 **"They call us":** In "Antis will fight," *Chattanooga Times*, July 18, 1920.

115 **Rowe set off on:** In "South Sees Peril in Suffrage," *The Woman Patriot* 3, no. 21 (September 6, 1919).

116 **"Miss Rowe earned her spurs":** *New York Evening World*, August 9, 1920.

116 **"They Shall Not Pass!":** This phrase was used frequently in antisuffrage literature. For example, in *The Woman Patriot*, May 24, 1919; October 4, 1919; and March 6, April 10, and May 1, 1920.

117 **"Some women have":** Rowe's testimony is in "Extending the Right of Suffrage to Women: Hearings Before the Committee on Woman Suffrage," House of Representatives, Sixty-Fifth Congress, on H. J. Res 200. January 3–7, 1918, 323.

117 **"But if you everlastingly":** Ibid.

118 **"If working girls":** Ibid.

120 **"Feminism is intimately":** "Suffragettes will Ignore Antis," *Tulsa (OK) World*, May 26, 1918.

120 **"Unless America prevents":** Ibid.

121 **"The idea that":** Ida M. Tarbell, *The Business of Being a Woman* (New York: Macmillan Co., 1912), chapter 8.

122 **"There is some limitation":** Addams is quoted in Dr. Paula Treckels, "Ida Tarbell and the Business of Being a Woman," Chautauqua Institute lecture, 1997. Reprinted on the Web site of Tarbell's alma mater, Allegheny College, http://sites.allegheny.edu/tarbell/ida-tarbell-and-the-business-of-being-a-woman. Additional discussion of Tarbell's anti-suffrage views can be found in "Ida Tarbell: The Making of an Anti," in Camhi, *Women Against Women*, and Robert Stinson, "Ida Tarbell and the Ambiguities of Feminism," *Pennsylvania Magazine of History and Biography* 101, no. 2 (April 1977): 217–39.

122 **Meyer was just:** Biographical sketches of Meyer appear in Linda Kerber, "Annie Nathan Meyer," in *Notable American Women: The Modern Period, A Biographical Dictionary*, ed. Barbara Sicherman and Carol Hurd Green (Cambridge, MA: Harvard University Press, 1980), 473-4; also in the biographical sketch accompanying the finding aid for Meyer's papers in the American Jewish Archives, Cincinnati, Ohio; also in Stephen Birmingham, *The Grandees* (New York: Harper and Row, 1971), 310–9, "The Embattled Sisters."

123 **Charlotte Rowe used Meyer's:** Rowe did not employ the arguments of another outspoken antisuffragist, the anarchist Emma Goldman, who believed the franchise was little more than another type of opium for the masses, affording a fake sense of civic power, a distraction from the real work of revolution.

124 **before Rowe's own eyes:** "Antis Will Fight," *Chattanooga Times*, July 18, 1920.

124 **First from the:** Everett P. Wheeler to Gov. Albert Roberts, June 28, 1920, reprinted in *The Woman Patriot*, July 10, 1920.

125 **Adoption of the amendment:** William L. Marbury to Hon. Albert Roberts, July 19, 1920, reprinted in *The Woman Patriot*, July 31, 1920.

125 **"The home loving women":** Mrs. James S. Pinckard to Gov. James Cox, July 26, 1920, reprinted in *The Woman Patriot* 4, no. 31 (July 31, 1920).

126 **"I have ever an ear":** W. G. Harding to Mrs. Horace Brock, July 6, 1920, quoted in "Anti-Suffragists Also Rap Harding," *New York Times*, July 16, 1920.

126 **Harding had no desire:** "Harding Bars Advising Holcombe on Suffrage," *New York Times*, July 17, 1920.

127 **He was caught:** "Democrats Can Win Votes of Women," *Nashville Tennessean*, July 25, 1920. Also in "Anti-Suffragists Also Rap," *New York Times*, July 16, 1920.

127 **"It is my earnest":** "Harding Urges Vote on Suffrage," *New York Times*, July 24, 1920.

128 **"put those frills":** John Vertrees to Josephine Pearson, February 8, 1917, Pearson Papers, TSLA, quoted in Elna C. Green, *Southern Strategies: Southern Women and the Woman Suffrage Question* (Chapel Hill: University of North Carolina Press, 1997), 119. See also Sarah P. Bradford to Miss Pearson, February 6, 1917, Pearson Papers, TSLA, in Green, *Southern Strategies*, 119.

129 **She'd already sent:** in Carol Lynn Yellin et al., *Perfect 36*, 89.

130 **"The fate of white civilization":** Letter to Dear Sir or Madam from Josephine Pearson, President of the Tennessee Division of the Southern Women's League for the Rejection of the Susan B. Anthony Amendment, Nashville, July 9, 1920, Pearson Papers, TSLA.

Chapter 11: The Woman's Hour

131 **Southern women abhor:** "Asks Mrs. Catt to Explain Statement," n.d. (probably *Nashville Banner*, July 24, 1920), in Catt papers, TSLA. Also printed in *The Woman Patriot* 4, no. 31 (July 31, 1920): 2, reprinted as "Questions for Mrs. Catt," published by Southern Women's Rejection League, in Pearson Papers, TSLA.

132 **"Pure buncombe":** Catt uses this phrase in her reply. See "Mrs Catt Answers Charges," *Chattanooga Times,* July 26, 1920.

132 **"The 'nigger question'":** Catt to Catherine Kenny, June 29, 1920, Catt papers, TSLA.

132 **At the close of the Civil War:** For detailed discussion of this period see Faye E. Dudden, *Fighting Chance: The Struggle over Woman Suffrage and Black Suffrage in Reconstruction America* (Oxford: Oxford University Press, 2011), and Brenda Wineapple, *Ecstatic Nation: Confidence, Crisis, and Compromise, 1848–1877* (New York: HarperCollins, 2013), chapter 20, 450–475; also Ellen Carol DuBois, *Feminism and Suffrage* (Ithaca, NY: Cornell University Press, 1978), chapter 2.

133 **"If that word male":** E. C. Stanton to Gerrit Smith, January 1, 1866, quoted in Flexner and Fitzpatrick,137; DuBois, *Feminism and Suffrage,* 61; and in Wineapple, 453.

134 **"I will cut off this right arm":** Philip S. Foner, ed., *Frederick Douglass on Women's Rights* (Westport and London: Greenwood Press, 1976), 33; also in Flexner and Fitzpatrick, 138.

134 **"press in through that constitutional door":** Stanton and Blatch, *Elizabeth Cady Stanton as Revealed in Her Letters, Diary and Reminiscences,* vol. 2. (New York and London: Harper Brothers, 1922), 109.

134 **"It is with us a matter":** Proceedings of the American Equal Rights Association, May 1868, in Foner, *Frederick Douglass,* 84.

134 **"When women . . . because she is black":** Proceedings of the American Equal Rights Association convention, New York City, May 12, 1869, in Foner, *Frederick Douglass,* 87.

135 **Stanton and Anthony descended:** E. C. Stanton editorial, "Women and Black Men," in her newspaper *Revolution,* February 4, 1869, and similar sentiments expressed in other issues, cited in Dudden, *Fighting Chance,* 3; Foner, *Frederick Douglass,* 30–33; and also Flexner and Fitzpatrick, 138.

135 **In a cynical ploy:** Foner, *Frederick Douglass,* 30.

135 **"Think of Patrick":** E. C. Stanton, "Manhood Suffrage," December 24, 1868, in Ann D. Gordon, ed., *The Selected Papers of Elizabeth Cady Stanton and Susan B. Anthony* (New Brunswick, NJ: Rutgers University Press, 2000), II: 196.

135 **George Francis Train:** For an incisive discussion of Train's relationship with Stanton and Anthony see Wineapple, chapter 20, "Deep Water."

135 **"If the Devil steps forward":** Gordon, *Selected Papers,* II: 117; also quoted in Wineapple, 259.

136 **"willing to be part":** Foner, *Frederick Douglass,* 39.

136 **"There are few facts":** F. Douglass, "The Woman's Suffrage Movement," address to the International Council of Women, March 31, 1888, in Foner, *Frederick Douglass,* 113.

136 **"I did not want to subject him":** Ida Wells-Barnett, *Crusade for Justice: The Autobiography of Ida B. Wells-Barnett* (Chicago: University of Chicago Press, 2013), 229–30. Also related in Angela Y. Davis, *Women, Race & Class* (New York: Vintage Books, 1983), 111.

137 **her framed portrait:** Cedar Hill, Douglass's house in Anacostia, D.C., is preserved as a National Park Service Historic Site. The portraits of Anthony and Stanton are displayed as they were during his residence, according to the National Park Service.

137 **Anthony eulogized her friend:** Account of Douglass's funeral, *Rochester Democrat and Chronicle,* February 26, 1895.

137 **"Frederick Douglass is not dead!":** Letter from Elizabeth Cady Stanton, in Helen Douglass, ed., *In Memoriam: Frederick Douglass* (Philadelphia: J. C. Yorston & Co., 1897), 44–45.

137 **"The relation of our leaders":** Carrie Catt to Mrs. Blake, New York, March 7, 1895, Cleveland Historical Society, quoted in Foner, *Frederick Douglass,* 43.

138 **In 1903, when racist southern suffragists:** The racial policies forged at the 1903 New Orleans convention are discussed in Elna C. Green, *Southern Strategies: Southern Women and the Woman Suffrage Question* (Chapel Hill: University of North Carolina Press, 1997), 10–11, and in Marjorie Spruill Wheeler, *New Women of the New South: Leaders of the Woman Suffrage Movement in the Southern States* (Oxford, UK, and New York: Oxford University Press, 1993), 118–19.

138 **It was a matter of simple mathematics:** Suffragists used this census argument for many years, and in attempting to defuse the "boogie" of the Negro Question in the ratification fight in Tennessee, *The Woman Citizen* published the latest available white-black census figures for the state in its July 5, 1920, issue. An example of Alice Paul's use of this tactic can be found in the broadside "Will the Federal Suffrage Amendment Complicate the Race Problem?," published by the Congressional Union, found in Caroline Katzenstein Papers (Record 10442), Historical Society of Pennsylvania.

139 **But Paul refused:** Paula J. Giddings, *Ida, A Sword Among Lions: Ida B. Wells and the Campaign against Lynching* (New York: Amistad, 2008), 5141–9.

139 **"Negro men cannot vote":** Alice Paul's statement is in "Willing to Sacrifice Colored Women," *Baltimore Afro-American,* February 21, 1919, and in Rosalyn Terborg-Penn, *African American Women in the Struggle for the Vote: 1850–1920* (Bloomington: Indiana University Press, 1998), 130. The statement is also quoted in Belinda Southard, "The National Woman's Party's Militant Campaign for Woman Suffrage: Asserting Citizenship Rights through Political Mimesis," PhD dissertation, University of Maryland, 2008, 477–78.

139 **Black suffragists such as Wells:** Wells's impassioned pleas for white suffragists to stand up for black women, including her refutations of Susan B. Anthony's expedient compromises, are chronicled in both Giddings and Terborg-Penn. Church Terrell's distinguished career in civil rights and woman suffrage is described in her autobiography, *Colored Woman in a White World* (Amherst, NY: Humanity Book, 2005); also see Cherisse Jones-Branch, "Mary Church Terrell: Revisiting the Politics of Race, Class, and Gender," in Sara Wilkerson Freeman and Beverly Greene Bond, *Tennessee Women: Their Lives and Times,* vol. 1 (Athens: University of Georgia Press, 2009), 68–92; and in Terborg-Penn. Dr. DuBois's championship of woman suffrage can be found in his speeches and writings, including many editorials in NAACP's *The Crisis.* These are documented in Jean Fagan Yellin, "DuBois' Crisis and Woman's Suffrage," *Massachusetts Review* 14, no. 2 (Spring 1973): 365–75.

139 **Catt refused to endorse:** Catt's hesitancy on the topic of birth control is discussed in Van Voris, *Catt,* 260.

140 **Personally, Catt was offended:** Once suffrage was won, Catt felt freer to express her views on racial issues. For example, in 1921 she denounced vicious accusations made against black U.S. troops stationed in Europe ("The Truth About Black Troops on the Rhine," *The Woman Citizen,* March 5, 1921) and in 1924 she expressed her disgust with segregated hotels in Washington, D.C., which would not lodge black delegates to a peace convention she organized (Van Voris, 201).

140 **"You ask if I":** Catt reply to the *Chattanooga Times,* July 21, 1920, reprinted in the *Nashville Tennessean,* July 26, 1920.

Chapter 12: Cranking the Machine

142 **"I have come to help you":** Catt to Tennessee League of Women Voters, Nashville, July 21, 1920, Catt Papers, TSLA.

142 **"Roll up your sleeves":** Quoted in Gertrude Brown autobiography, unpublished manuscript, Gertrude Brown Papers, Schlesinger Library; also in Van Voris, 129.

143 **"That unheard from number":** Catt to Tennessee League of Women Voters, Nashville, July 21, 1920, Catt Papers, TSLA.

143 **"Please hasten now":** Ibid.

143 **The pledges already in hand:** Catt to Tennessee League of Women Voters, Nashville, July 21, 1920, Catt Papers, TSLA.

144 **Now Ogden offered:** "Mrs. Catt Sends Vote Plea," *New York Times*, July 20, 1920; "Ogden to Bring Message from Cox," *Nashville Tennessean*, n.d. (approx. July 23, 1920).

144 **"We did a whizzing business":** Van Voris, 33–34.

144 **Anthony was so fascinated:** Alma Lutz, *Susan B. Anthony: Rebel, Crusader, Humanitarian* (Boston: Beacon Press, 1959), 262–64.

145 **Cody invited Anthony:** Lutz, 264. Cody's invitation followed Anthony's public defense of his Wild West show performing on Sundays; many clergymen had denounced the Sabbath performances.

145 **"The cartoonists had pictured:"** Van Voris, 33.

145 **the suffragists undertook:** Carrie Chapman Catt and Nettie Shuler, *Woman Suffrage and Politics: The Inner Story of the Suffrage Movement* (New York: C. Scribner's Sons, 1926), 107.

146 **"How long will it delay":** Van Voris, 129.

146 **On election night:** Van Voris, 147.

146 **were roaming the countryside:** Catt and Shuler, 437; Abby Crawford Milton, "Report of the Tennessee League of Women Voters," 1920, Abby Crawford Milton Papers, TSLA, 6–8.

146 **On the second floor:** "Mrs Catt Talks to Kiwanis Club," *Nashville Banner*, July 23, 1920; "Mrs Catt Defends Ratification Plans," *Nashville Tennessean*, July 24, 1920.

147 **Tennessee Bar Association:** "Says Ohio Case Does Not Apply," *Chattanooga Daily Times*, July 22, 1920; Catt and Shuler, 434.

147 **Stahlman had limped:** Biographical details from Stahlman obituaries in *Nashville Banner*, August 12, 1930; *New York Times*, August 13, 1930; "EB Stahlman, A Friend's Appreciation," *Nashville Banner*, August 12, 1930; "A Famous Southerner," *New York Times*, August 14, 1920.

148 **His feud with Luke Lea:** Details from Robert O'Brien, "The U.S. Government's Investigation of E. B. Stahlman as an Enemy Alien: A Case Study of Nativism in Nashville," master's thesis, Western Kentucky University, Bowling Green, 1996.

148 **argue against entry:** One example of Stahlman's resistance to war policy can be found in "Publishers Oppose Espionage Measure," *New York Times*, April 24, 1917.

148 **"a Hun by birth":** *Nashville Tennessean*, May 13, 1918, quoted in O'Brien, 120.

149 **beat the drum for Stahlman:** *Nashville Tennessean*, June 3, 1918, quoted in O'Brien, 4.

149 **Stahlman defended himself:** Stahlman also signed onto the ultra-patriotic "100% American" groups which sprouted during the war. Stahlman joined journalist Ida Tarbell as a director of the American League for National Unity, among other organizations. "War on Hyphenism is Aim of New Body," *Washington Post*, April 20, 1917.

149 **Catt didn't pussyfoot around:** Details of Catt's speech in "Catt Talks to Kiwanis Club," *Nashville Banner*, July 23, 1920, and "Catt Defends Ratification Plans," *Nashville Banner*, July 24, 1920.

150 **"Suffrage is all the rage now":** "Cox Has Won Many Votes in Tn. for Women," *New York Evening World*, July 26, 1920, Catt Papers, TSLA.

151 **It would appear:** Press Release, July 25, Abby Milton Papers, TSLA; "Tennessee Safe for Suffrage Says Mrs. Catt," *Nashville Tennessean*, July 26, 1920; "Poll Suffrage Majority," *Washington Post*, July 26, 1920.

152 **It was the *Banner's* publication:** *Nashville Banner*, July 25, 1920.

Chapter 13: Prison Pin

153 **"It's all bluff":** Sue White to Alice Paul, July 26, 1920, NWPP, LoC.

153 **a whirl of presidential candidates:** "Gov. Cox Will Urge Suff Measure," *Chattanooga News,* July 20, 1920; "Nominees Strive to Win Tennessee," *New York Times,* July 23, 1920; "Militants Counting on Democrats Now," *New York Times,* July 25, 1920.

153 **she found a storefront:** White to Paul, July 24 and July 26, 1920, NWPP, LoC.

154 **Sue White had traveled far:** Sue White's essay, written for the *Nation* magazine, is contained in Elaine Showalter, *These Modern Women: Autobiographical Essays from the Twenties* (New York: Feminist Press, 1989), 51.

154 **As soon as ratification:** "Woman's Party to Meet to Decide Future," *Washington Post,* July 25, 1920.

154 **White wrote directly:** White to Gov. Roberts, July 24, 1920, NWPP, LoC.

155 **"Watchfires of Freedom":** Irwin, *The Story of Alice Paul,* 401–20; J. D. Zahniser and Amelia R. Fry, *Alice Paul: Claiming Power* (New York and Oxford: Oxford University Press, 2014), 311–14; "New Years Day Protest," *The Suffragist,* January 4, 1919; "While Women Go to Jail," *The Suffragist,* January 18, 1919; "The Watchfire Goes On," *The Suffragist,* February 8, 1919; Doris Stevens, *Jailed for Freedom: American Women Win the Vote* (New York: Boni and Liverwright, 1920), chapter 21.

156 **"the most difficult thing":** White to Catt, May 7, 1919, Sue Shelton White Papers, Schlesinger Library.

156 **At four thirty in the afternoon:** Description of the protest from White, "Militant Suffragists and How They Won a Hopeless Cause," written for the *Montgomery (AL) Times,* August 1919, unpublished typescript, White Papers, Schlesinger Library; "The Demonstration of February 9," *The Suffragist,* February 22, 1919; Louisine Havemeyer, "Memories of a Militant: The Prison Special," *Scribners,* May 1922; "Suffragists Burn Wilson in Effigy," *New York Times,* February 10, 1919; Stevens, chapter 22.

157 **"No picketing and no prison":** Havemeyer, "Memories of a Militant."

157 **Havemeyer's heart was beating fast:** Ibid.

158 **"Please, Miss Burns":** Ibid.

159 **"Of course, no one thought":** Ibid.

159 **the grandchildren were crying:** Ibid.

160 **"the I.W.W. of the suffrage movement":** "Suffragists Burn Wilson in Effigy," *New York Times,* February 10, 1919; "Doing Hurt to Cause of Woman Suffrage," *Chattanooga News,* February 10, 1919.

160 **More punishing still:** "Not Connected to Militant Pickets," *Chattanooga News,* February 19, 1919; "Miss Sue White with Suffragists in Washington," *Jackson Daily Democrat,* February 10, 1919, White Papers, Schlesinger Library.

160 **She became the symbol:** Tennessee General Assembly House Journal, April 3, 1919, 921; "Suffrage Bill Passed by Bare Majority," *Nashville Tennessean,* April 15, 1919; "Doing Hurt to Cause," *Chattanooga News,* February 10, 1919.

160 **Her own Aunt Susan had:** "Sue Shelton White," in Showalter.

161 **Anita Pollitzer was only:** Anita Pollitzer's biographical details drawn from: Irwin; Obituary, *New York Times,* July 5, 1975; "Charlestonian Pollitzer a Leader in Suffrage," *Charleston Post and Courier,* March 22, 2013; Mabel Pollitzer interview, June 16, 1974, part of Southern Oral History Program Collection (#4007); "Suffrage Stirs South," *Washington Post,* August 2, 1915; "Handmaidens of History," *Charleston Magazine,* January–February 2005; Clive Giboire, ed., *Lovingly, Georgia: The Complete*

Correspondence of Georgia O'Keeffe and Anita Pollitzer (New York: Simon & Schuster, 1990); and "The Pollitzer Family of South Carolina," Low Country Digital Archive, http://ldhi.library.cofc.edu/exhibits/show/pollitzer_family_sc/.

162 **the "tremendous affair":** Pollitzer to O'Keeffe, letter dated October 1915, in Giboire, 61–2.

163 **He sat Pollitzer down:** Pollitzer describes her visit to Sanders in her report to A. Paul, Monday July 26, 1920, 11 a.m., on the train (handwritten), NWPP, LoC.

163 **"He is a slick":** Pollitzer to Paul, July 28, 1920, NWPP, LoC.

164 **"The papers are full":** Ibid.

164 **"We must not have":** Kenyon Rector to Alice Paul, July 27, 1920, NWPP, LoC.

Chapter 14: Fieldwork

166 **Edward Hull Crump:** Biographical details from G. Wayne Dowdy, *Mayor Crump Don't Like It: Machine Politics in Memphis* (Jackson: University Press of Mississippi, 2006); Ray Hill, "Edward Hull Crump: The Boss, Part 1," *Knoxville News,* March 26, 2012; David Tucker, "Edward Hull 'Boss' Crump," in *Tennessee Encyclopedia of History and Culture.*

167 **Catt enjoyed a warm welcome:** "Mrs Catt Makes Convincing Plea," *Chattanooga News,* July 28, 1920; "Mrs Catt Pleads for Ratification," *Memphis News-Scimitar,* July 26, 1920; Abby Milton, "Report of the Tennessee League of Women Voters, 1920, Abby Crawford Milton Papers, TSLA.

167 **He'd persuaded Thomas Riddick:** "Riddick Will Be Big Help to Suffrage," *Memphis News-Scimitar,* July 27, 1920.

168 **If you support ratification:** Dear Sir or Madam, letter signed by Josephine Pearson on Southern Rejection League stationery, July 9, 1920, Pearson Papers, TSLA.

168 **Building a bigger tent:** "Anti-Suffrage Faction Busy," *Chattanooga Times,* July 30, 1920, Carrie Chapman Catt Papers, TSLA; "To Women Against the Amendment" and "Anti Suffragists to be Well Organized," unidentified news clippings (probably from *Nashville Banner*), late July, 1920, in Pearson Papers, TSLA.

168 **And a delegation:** "Antis of South Appeal to Cox," *Washington Post,* July 29, 1920; "Southern Antis Ask Hearing," *New York Times,* July 29, 1920.

169 **Unless she could:** Pollitzer to Alice Paul, July 29, 1920, NWPP, LoC.

169 **"That is polite":** Pollitzer to Paul, July 29, 1920.

170 **to telephone Burn:** This telephone call is described in Irwin, *The Story of Alice Paul,* 473. Irwin interviewed Pollitzer and other Woman's Party staff working in Tennessee as soon as they returned to headquarters in Washington.

170 **Harry will be all right:** Pollitzer to Paul, July 29, 1920, NWPP, LoC.

170 **in agony whenever she spoke:** In Jessie Haver Butler oral history interview, January 4, 1973. California State University at Long Beach Digital Repository, http://symposia.library.csulb.edu. Butler accompanied Catt on the "Wake Up America" ratification tour in fall 1919 and reported Catt's public speaking anxieties.

171 **In conjunction with Catt's tour:** Milton, "Report of the Tennessee League of Women Voters," Abby Milton Papers, TSLA.

171 **"Are there any":** Catt and Shuler, 436.

171 **a "canny determination":** Ibid.

171 **These suspect lawmakers:** Catt and Shuler, 437.

173 **protect "the letter and spirit":** "League Formed to Fight Ratification," *Nashville Tennessean,* July 30, 1920; "Anti-Suffrage Faction Busy," *Chattanooga Times,* July 30, 1920.

173 **"110 Pounds of Femininity":** Clipping from unidentified Memphis newspaper, August 1 or 2, 1920. Betty Gram Swing Papers, Schlesinger Library, courtesy of Betty Gram's granddaughter, Pam Swing, Concord, MA.

174 **Gram had aspired:** Memoir of Alice Gram (Betty's sister) in Betty Gram Swing Papers, Schlesinger Library.

174 **That month of traveling:** Louisine Havemeyer, "Memories of a Militant: The Prison Special," *Scribners,* May 1922; Sue White, "Militant Suffragists and How they Won," White Papers, Schlesinger Library; Gram to Family, March 10, 1919, Gram Swing Papers, Schlesinger Library.

174 **"Sentiment in favor":** Gram to Paul, August 2, 1920, NWPP, LoC.

175 **Seth Walker was tall:** Biographical information from Tennessee 61st General Assembly member profile, TSLA; and "The Record of Sigma Alpha Epsilon" (vol. 40, no.3), September 1920. Courtesy Sigma Alpha Epsilon Archives, Evanston, IL.

176 **Gram found Walker:** Emma Wold to Sue White, July 20, 1920, NWPP, LoC; Irwin, 468.

176 **they hatched a plan:** Esther Ogden to Catt, July 30, 1920, NAWSA Papers, LoC; Catt to Ogden, July 31, 1920, Catt Papers, TSLA; "Speaker Walker to Support Ratification," unidentified news clipping, July 30, 1920, Catt Papers, TSLA.

176 **White was elated:** "Speaker Walker pledged for," White to Paul, July 28, 1920. "Sue phones me that Seth Walker, Democratic Speaker of House and a strong man is definitely yes," Anita Pollitzer to Paul, July 29, 1920, NWPP, LoC; "Speaker Walker to Support Ratification," unidentified news clipping, July 30, Catt Papers, TSLA.

177 **"I will not perjure":** "Harding Fails to Change Candler's View," *Chattanooga News,* July 28, 1920, Catt Papers, TSLA.

178 **"I fear the Republicans":** Anita Pollitzer to Alice Paul, July 28, 1920, NWPP, LoC.

178 **"It does not look good":** Winfield Jones, Harding-Coolidge Republican League, Washington, D.C., to Hon. Sam Sells and Taylor, July 29, 1920, NWPP, LoC.

178 **"Situation in Tennessee":** Winfield Jones, Harding Coolidge Republican League, to Warren G. Harding, August 3, 1920, NWPP, LoC.

178 **"You can understand":** "Harding Refuses Aid to Suffrage," *New York Times,* August 5, 1920; "Harding Refuses to Aid," *Baltimore Sun,* August 5, 1920; "Both Candidates Renew Pledge to Aid Suffragists," *Christian Science Monitor,* August 7, 1920.

178 **"Tired unto death":** Gram to Sue White, August 4, 1920, NWPP, LoC.

179 **eagerly signed his pledge:** Hanover signed a pledge for Betty Gram. Gram to Paul, August 2, 1920, NWPP, LoC.

179 **"At present I am":** Gram to Paul, August 2, 1920, NWPP, LoC.

179 **Flanagan was a slight woman:** Biographical details from "Hartford Irish Woman was Heroine of Suffrage Drive," *The Shanachie,* newsletter of the Connecticut Irish-American Historical Society, vol. 18, no.1 (Winter 2006): 1. Alice Paul and Lucy Burns supported Ireland's independence from Great Britain, and in gratitude representatives of the Free Ireland movement in America campaigned for ratification in several states, hoping to influence legislators of Irish ancestry. There were plans to send an Irish-American military hero to Tennessee to assist the Woman's Party efforts, though no account of his presence in the state could be found. See Frank P. Walsh to Sue White, July 30, 1920; also Walsh to James O'Mara, American Commission on Irish Independence, July 30, 1920, NWPP, LoC.

180 **"Today I drove":** Flanagan to Alice Paul, handwritten report, August 1, 1920, NWPP, LoC.

180 **Pollitzer took hold:** Irwin, 468.

181 **"We have been able to secure":** "Anti-Suffragists to Open Exhibit Here," *Nashville Banner,* n.d. (early August, 1920), Pearson Papers, TSLA.

183 **"Report 3 Republicans"**: Catt to Will Hays, July 31, 1920, Catt Papers, TSLA.

183 **"Report is of course absolutely false"**: Hays to Catt, August 2, 1920, Catt Papers, TSLA.

183 TENNESSEE DOUBTFUL, POLITICIANS RELIEVED: Newspaper headlines from *Baltimore Sun*, August 3, 1920; *New York Evening World*, August 6, 1920; *Nashville Tennessean*, August 4, 1920.

183 **"I believe liquor"**: Pollitzer to Abby Scott Baker, August 4, 1920, NWPP, LoC; "Harding Stand Alarms Women," *Chattanooga News*, August 5, 1920.

183 **"As to supporting"**: L. M. Whitaker to George White, August 3, 1920, NWPP, LoC.

184 **men were not lining up**: Pollitzer reports White's statement that "Roberts' men are not lining up for us" to Alice Paul in an undated report, probably written August 3, 1920, NWPP, LoC.

184 **she confessed, "worn out"**: White to Kenyon Rector, July 30, 1920, NWPP, LoC.

184 **Abby Milton was awakened**: Carol Sanford Bucy, "The Thrill of History Making: Suffrage Memories of Abby Crawford Milton," *Tennessee Historical Quarterly* 50 (Fall 1996): 231.

Chapter 15: A Real and Threatening Danger

185 **keep "hands off"**: Letter to the presidential candidates in "Nominees Urged to Leave Suffrage Alone," *Nashville Tennessean*, August 6, 1920. Letter to Tennessee Legislators in "Officers Named to Constitution League," *Nashville Tennessean*, August 4, 1920.

186 **"a very real and threatening"**: "Cox and Harding Warned," *Chattanooga News*, August 4, 1920; "Harding Refuses to Aid Suffrage," *New York Times*, August 5, 1920.

187 **"Your telegram received"**: Warren G. Harding to Catt, August 4, 1920, Catt Papers, TSLA.

187 **"I impressed upon him"**: "Harding Refuses to Aid Suffrage," *New York Times*, August 5, 1920; "Harding Stand Alarms Women," *Chattanooga News*, August 5, 1920.

187 **"What will the Negro woman"**: Pierce's speech is in *Nashville Tennessean*, May 19, 1920, p. 8; also quoted in Carol Lynn Yellin et al., 71–3; and Anita Shafer Goodstein, "A Rare Alliance: African American and White Women in the Tennessee Elections of 1919 and 1920," *Journal of Southern History* 64, no. 2 (May 1998): 239.

188 **"We are interested"**: For biographical sketches of Pierce see Carole Bucy, "Juno Frankie Pierce," in the *Tennessee Encyclopedia of History and Culture*, Tennessee Historical Society; Bucy, "Thrill of History," 232; Yellin et al., *Perfect 36*, 71–73; Goodstein, "Rare Alliance," 219–46.

188 **Abby Milton, as the league's**: Bucy, "Thrill of History," 224–39; also Carol Sanford Bucy, "Abby Crawford Milton," *Tennessee Encyclopedia of History and Culture*.

189 **At noon on Wednesday**: "Mrs. Catt is Luncheon Guest," *Chattanooga News*, August 4, 1920.

189 **"Here in Tennessee"**: "Band of New Yorkers Works to Beat Suffrage—Mrs. Catt," *Chattanooga News*, August 4, 1920.

190 **"Can anything more outside"**: Pearson to Gov. Cox, handwritten letter, August 5, 1920, Pearson Papers, TSLA; "Antis Ask Cox Not to Use Party Power," *Nashville Banner*, August 6, 1920, Pearson Papers, TSLA.

191 **She was sending**: Alice Paul to Sue White, August 2, 1920, NWPP, LoC.

191 **"The situation in Tennessee"**: Emma Wold, Headquarters Secretary, to Adeline Atwater, Reno, NV, July 31, 1920, NWPP, LoC.

192 **"Need for money"**: Alice Paul to State Chairwomen, August 6, 1920, NWPP, LoC.

192 **Mrs. Havemeyer sent**: Paul to Havemeyer, August 6, 1920, NWPP, LoC.

192 **Paul pleaded with:** Alice Paul to Elsie Hill, August 2, 1920, NWPP, LoC; Paul to Mrs. Lawrence Lewis, August 11, 1920, NWPP, LoC.

192 **She even asked:** Pollitzer to Paul, August 4, 1920, NWPP, LoC.

192 **down to $10:** Paul to Havemeyer, August 6, 1920, NWPP, LoC.

192 **Paul was a brazen:** Irwin, *The Story of Alice Paul*, 20–1.

193 **"You talk. We act":** Pankhurst quoted in profile of Belmont, National Woman's Party, Belmont-Paul Women's Equality National Monument, http://nationalwomansparty. org/womenwecelebrate/alva-belmont/.

193 **The woman was:** Biographical details from Madeleine B. Stern, *Purple Passage: The Life of Mrs. Frank Leslie* (Norman: University of Oklahoma Press, 1953); Rose Young, "Record of the Leslie Woman Suffrage Commission, Inc. 1917–1929," NAWSA Papers, LoC.

196 **Mrs. Ruffin Pleasant:** Press Release, Tennessee Division of the Southern Women's Rejection League, August 3, 1920, Pearson Papers, TSLA.

196 **"We have no objections":** "Challenge to Mrs Catt," *Chattanooga Times*, August 6, 1920; "Antis Ask Debate," *Nashville Banner*, August 5, 1920.

197 **"I've had two rocky days":** Catt to Hyde, n.d. (probably August 5, 1920), Catt Papers, LoC.

197 **A squad of editors:** "Record Crowd Sees Banner's Bulletins," *Nashville Banner*, August 6, 1920, and photo.

197 **afforded a "slight advantage":** "Roberts and Taylor Win Nominations," *Nashville Tennessean*, August 6, 1920; "Gov. Roberts Ahead," *Baltimore Sun*, August 6, 1920; Sue White to Alice Paul, August 6, 1920, NWPP, LoC.

197 **He formally called:** "Roberts Calls Legislature in Special Session," *Nashville Tennessean*, August 8, 1920; "Called to Ratify Woman Suffrage," *Washington Post*, August 8, 1920; "Tennessee Legislature to Pass on Suffrage," *Chattanooga News*, August 8, 1920.

Chapter 16: War of the Roses

198 **All through the weekend:** "Roberts Calls Extra Session," *Louisville Courier-Journal*, August 8, 1920.

198 **striking a pose:** Photograph in Pearson Papers, TSLA.

199 **"Truth crushed to the Earth":** Pearson annotates the photograph with this caption.

200 **"straighten out" the Republicans:** Catt to Upton, handwritten draft of telegram, n.d. (probably August 6, 1920), Catt Papers, TSLA.

200 **"Who are you?":** *The Woman's Journal*, September 27, 1913; also quoted in Van Voris, 30.

200 **Upton, like Catt:** Alma Lutz, *Susan B. Anthony: Rebel, Crusader, Humanitarian* (Boston: Beacon Press, 1959), 276.

200 **Upton was comfortable:** Biographical details on Upton from Phillip R. Shriver, "Harriet Taylor Upton," in *Notable American Women: A Biographical Dictionary, 1607–1950*, vol. 3, ed. Edward T. James et al. (Cambridge, MA: Harvard University Press, 1971); and Harriet Taylor Upton, *Random Recollections* (manuscript), Alice Marshall Women's History Collection, Pennsylvania State University, Harrisburg.

201 **seated on the stage:** "Normalcy Pledged by Harding," *Washington Post*, July 23, 1920.

201 **"I want to send a message":** "Lady Astor Sends Plea to Tennessee," *Nashville Tennessean*, August 8, 1920; "Lady Astor Appeals to Men of Native State," *Chattanooga News*, August 7, 1920.

202 **The Antis were descending:** "Antis Gather New Strength," *Chattanooga Times*, August 8, 1920; "Anti Suffragists Will be Well Organized," *Nashville Tennessean*, August 8,

1920; "Special Session to Open," news clipping, Catt Papers, TSLA; "Mighty Battle in Prospect," *Nashville Tennessean,* August 8, 1920.

203 **"They are knocking":** "To Arms, To Arms," *Nashville Tennessean,* August 6, 1920.

204 **The book was Stanton's attempt:** Peck, 87–89.

205 **at the next annual convention:** Kathi Kern, *Mrs. Stanton's Bible* (Ithaca, NY: Cornell University Press, 2001), 185; Lutz, 278–80; Peck, 87–89.

205 **She saluted the guests of honor:** Details of the party in "Anti-Suffragists Will be Well Organized," *Nashville Tennessean,* August 8, 1920.

205 **he had a reputation:** McFarland's temper is displayed in "Hot Words Used by Solon," *Nashville Tennessean,* May 8, 1913.

205 **"would trust a woman":** A. Elizabeth Taylor, *The Woman Suffrage Movement in Tennessee* (New York: Bookman Associates, 1957), 101.

206 **"That bunch of fillies":** Carol Lynn Yellin et al., *Perfect 36,* 97.

206 **superintendent of public instruction, Albert Williams:** Transcript of interview with Judge Albert Williams in "Recollections: The Middle Tennessee Voices of their Times Series," Albert Gore Research Center, Middle Tennessee State University, 1980.

207 **had a "change of conviction":** Williams's meeting with Seth Walker is mentioned in the Williams interview, "Recollections," and described in Carol Lynn Yellin et al., 97. The essence of the meeting is agreed upon by all sources, but the timing of when the suffragists learned of Walker's defection is vague and confusing, with contradictory reports. Both Catt and Carol Lynn Yellin et al. relate that the suffragists learned of Walker's change almost immediately, but this is not supported by contemporary press reports nor by private communication between suffragists during the period of Sunday, August 8, and Tuesday, August 10. Based upon all available evidence, there was a delay of at least two days, and I have constructed the most likely time frame for the narrative.

208 **a caravan of forty:** "Mrs. Washington to Entertain Visitors," *Nashville Tennessean,* August 6, 1920; "Woman's Rejection League at Washington Hall," *Nashville Banner,* August 9, 1920.

208 **Clay was the great gardener:** Biographical details from Paul Boyer, "Laura Clay," in *Notable American Women,* ed. James et al., 346–48; Paul E. Fuller, *Laura Clay and the Woman's Rights Movement* (Lexington: University Press of Kentucky, 1975); and Paul E. Fuller, "Suffragist Vanquished: Laura Clay and the 19th Amendment," *Register of the Kentucky Historical Society* 93, no.1 (Winter 1995): 4–24.

208 **Gordon was a New Orleans public health activist:** Biographical details from "Kate and Jean Gordon," in *Encyclopedia of New Orleans,* http://www.knowlouisiana.org/entry/kate-and-jean-gordon; "Kate Gordon's Louisiana," in Elna C. Green, *Southern Strategies: Southern Women and the Woman Suffrage Question* (Chapel Hill: University of North Carolina Press 1997); Kenneth R. Johnson, "Kate Gordon and the Woman Suffrage Movement in the South," *Journal of Southern History* 38 (August 1972): 365–92.

209 **A secret sponsor:** Marjorie Spruill Wheeler, "Woman's Rights and States' Rights," in *New Women of the New South: The Leaders of the Woman Suffrage Movement in the Southern States* (Oxford, UK, and New York: Oxford University Press, 1993), 149.

210 **a family portrait:** Photo in *Nashville Banner,* August 15, 1920.

211 **"Suffrage situation very critical":** Governor A. H. Roberts to Charl Williams, August 8, 1920, A. H. Roberts Papers, TSLA.

212 **"We are ready":** "Woman's Party Worker on Way," *Charlotte* (NC) *Observer,* August 9, 1920.

212 **allusions to "mysterious influences":** "Mighty Battle is in Prospect over Suffrage," *Nashville Tennessean,* August 8, 1920.

212 **"Knowing its personnel":** "Mrs Dudley's Faith in Legislators Strong," *Chattanooga Times,* August 9, 1920.

212 **"We know that pledges":** "Says Fight is for States' Rights," *Nashville Banner,* August 7, 1920, Pearson Papers, TSLA.

213 **"Speakers Walker and Todd":** White to Paul, August 8, 1920, NWPP, LoC.

213 **strange sort of beauty pageant:** "Cry of Liquor," *Chattanooga Times,* August 10, 1920.

214 **"Wish greatly you were here":** White to Paul, August 8, 1920, NWPP, LoC.

Chapter 17: In Justice to Womanhood

215 **"These gentlemen, who do not belong":** "Women Swamp Tennessee Capital," *Charlotte* (NC) *Observer,* August 10, 1920.

215 **Betty Gram puffed:** "Leaders Come Here for Suffrage Fight," *Nashville Tenneseean,* August 7, 1920; "Shelby Solons Leave Sunday for Nashville," *Memphis News-Scimitar,* August 7, 1920.

216 **"I am here to do":** "Gov. Roberts Pleads for Ratification," *Chattanooga News,* August 9, 1920.

216 **porters had been cleaning:** "Capitol is Prepared for Fall of Gavel," *Nashville Tennessean,* August 8, 1920.

216 **decorating the corridors:** "Women Swamp Tennessee Capital," *Charlotte* (NC) *Observer,* August 10, 1920.

216 **Mrs. Edwin Forbes:** Ibid.

216 NATION WATCHES SOLONS: "Nation Watches Solons; Solons Watching Ladies," *Memphis News-Scimitar,* August 9, 1920.

217 **"time of their gay young lives":** Ibid.

217 **"You may say for me":** "Suffrage Battle will Start Today," *New York Times,* August 9, 1920.

217 **"You have heard those in favor":** Account by Mabel Reber in Nashville to Boeckel at NWP headquarters, August 9, 1920, NWPP, LoC.

218 **thirty-four Republicans:** "Suffrage Battle Opens Today," *Nashville Tennessean,* August 10, 1920.

218 **Pollitzer was crestfallen:** Anita Pollitzer to Abby Baker, August 9, 1920, NWPP, LoC; "Gov. Roberts Pleads for Ratification," *Chattanooga News,* August 9, 1920.

218 **"Please come at once":** Mary Winsor to Alice Paul, August 9, 1920, NWPP, LoC.

218 **still at loggerheads:** "We, the undersigned, chairmen of ratification committees desire to say to the public, any statements to the contrary notwithstanding, that we are working and shall continue to work for ratification of the federal suffrage amendment solely and that our ratification committees take no stand on partisan and political differences of opinion," typescript, Catt Papers, TSLA.

218 **They were unwilling:** "Miss Williams Gets Factions Together," *Memphis News-Scimitar,* August 10, 1920.

219 **Shortly past noon:** House Journal of the Extraordinary Session of the Sixty-First General Assembly of the State of Tennessee, Day 1, August 9, 1920, TSLA.

219 **The visitor galleries above:** "Another War of Roses Staged at Capitol," *Chattanooga News,* August 9, 1920; "Women Swamp the State Capital," *Charlotte* (NC) *Observer,* August 10, 1920.

220 **"Tennessee occupies a pivotal position":** "Roberts Urges Ratification," *Nashville Banner,* August 9, 1920.

221 **The delay was blamed:** "Suffrage Resolution Up in Tennessee Today," *Baltimore Sun,* August 10, 1920.

221 **greetings from the Maryland legislature:** Ibid.

221 **"doesn't have a chance":** Ibid.

222 **McKellar made the rounds:** "Miss Williams Gets Factions Together," *Memphis News-Scimitar,* August 10, 1920; "Prospects for Early Ratification Brighter," *Chattanooga News,* August 10, 1920; "Gov. Roberts Adds Pressure in Message," *Chattanooga Times,* August 10, 1920.

222 **"Call Gov. Cox":** Abby Baker to Alice Paul, August 10, 1920, NWWP, LoC. Baker reports that Cox is frustrated by Roberts's not returning his calls.

222 **She handwrote a letter:** Catt to Will Hays, August 9, 1920, Ratification Vertical File, TSLA.

223 **a deputation of Anti women:** "Suffrage Battle Opens Today," *Nashville Tennessean,* August 10, 1920.

223 **The campaign was officially launched:** "Cox Finds Cheer in Roosevelt Tone," *New York Times,* August 10, 1920.

223 **Cox Electric League:** Ibid.

224 **women made their case:** "Anti-Suffragists Fail to Sway Cox," *Nashville Banner,* August 10, 1920; "Cox Finds Cheer in Roosevelt Tone," *New York Times, August 10, 1920.*

224 **That's when he revealed:** Irwin, *The Story of Alice Paul,* 469. There are conflicting accounts of exactly when Walker revealed his intentions to the suffragists in Nashville. This chronology is based upon a careful consideration of contemporary correspondence and news reports. See also "Eyes on Solons," *Memphis News-Scimitar,* August 9, 1920; and "Ratification More Remote," *Chattanooga Times,* August 10, 1920.

225 **"We have long since":** Catt to Kenny, June 29, 1920, Catt Papers, TSLA.

225 **Sue White worked deep:** "Miss Williams Gets Factions Together," *Memphis News-Scimitar,* August 10, 1920. "Gov. Roberts Adds Pressure in Message," *Chattanooga Times,* August 10, 1920.

225 **babysat the joint resolution:** "Ratification More Remote," *Chattanooga Times,* August 11, 1920.

225 **"Republican situation really fearful":** Pollitzer to Abby Baker and to Alice Paul, 4:58 a.m., August 10, 1920, NWPP, LoC.

226 **"go down the line":** "Ratification Seems More Remote," *Chattanooga Times,* August 11, 1920; "Suffrage Resolution to go to Committee," *Nashville Tennessean,* August 11, 1920; "Miss Williams Gets Factions Together," *Memphis News-Scimitar,* August 10, 1920.

226 **"Speculation was rife":** "Move Made to Block Suffrage Vote," *Memphis News-Scimitar,* August 11, 1920; "Suffrage Comes Up in Tennessee Today," *New York Times,* August 11, 1920; "Other Active Members Join in Opposition," *Chattanooga Times,* August 11, 1920; "Tide Ebbs and Flows in Fight for Ratification," *Nashville Tennessean,* August 11, 1920.

226 **received glad tidings:** "North Carolina Likely to Defeat Measure," *New York Times,* August 12, 1920; "North Carolina to Tennessee," *Nashville Banner,* August 12, 1920.

226 **"If we hold Tennessee":** "Outlook Not Encouraging," *Charlotte* (NC) *Observer,* August 11, 1920.

227 **"I'd let the old Capitol":** *Knoxville Journal,* August 11, 1920, quoted in a letter from Mary Winsor to Betty Gram Swing, July 6, 1943, in Betty Gram Swing papers, Schlesinger Library. Gram's encounter with Walker is also related in "Outlook Not Encouraging," *Charlotte* (NC) *Observer,* August 11, 1920; "Speaker Walker to Fight Suffrage Resolution," *Chattanooga Times,* August 11, 1920; "Suffs Turning on Democrats in Tennessee," *Baltimore Sun,* August 11, 1920.

227 **"When I came to Tennessee":** "Move Made to Block Suffrage Vote," *Memphis News-Scimitar,* August 11, 1920.

228 **"In Tennessee whiskey":** Catt and Shuler, 442.

228 **"Don't speak to her":** "Warning," *Nashville Tennessean,* August 10, 1920; "Outlook Not Encouraging," *Charlotte* (NC) *Observer,* August 11, 1920.

229 **accused the "liquor interests":** Flexner and Fitzpatrick, 289–90.

230 **"We find it impossible":** Paul to White, August 10, 1920, NWPP, LoC.

230 **"Her language was offensive":** "Speaker Walker to Fight Suffrage Resolution," *Chattanooga Times*, August 11, 1920.

230 **"We are not":** "Outlook Not Encouraging," *Charlotte* (NC) *Observer*, August 11, 1920.

231 **"began a vigorous opposition":** "Speaker Walker to Fight Suffrage Resolution," *Chattanooga Times*, August 11, 1920.

231 **"It will smoke out":** Recounted in Mary Winsor to Betty Gram Swing, July 6, 1943, in Swing Papers, Schlesinger Library.

231 **"We are losing men":** Headquarters Secretary (Emma Wold) to Mrs. Havemeyer, August 10, 1920, NWPP, LoC.

231 **Riddick told Roberts:** "Gov. Roberts and Alf Taylor Enter Suffrage Fight," *Memphis News-Scimitar*, August 11, 1920.

231 **she soothed them:** "Tide Ebbs and Flows," *Nashville Tennessean*, August 11, 1920.

232 **"I have become convinced":** "Speaker Walker to Fight: Other Members Join in Opposition," *Chattanooga Times*, August 11, 1920.

233 **reference to whispers:** Abby Milton in Bucy, 236.

233 **summoned each man to his room:** "Ratification Seems More Remote," *Chattanooga Times*, August 11, 1920.

233 **"would be constrained":** "Suffrage Comes Up in Tennessee Today," *New York Times*, August 11, 1920.

234 **"Cox appears worried":** Abby Scott Baker to Alice Paul, August 10, 1920, NWPP, LoC.

234 **"The majority for ratification":** "Suffragists Report Desertions," *New York Times*, August 11, 1920; "Washington Rumors Fear for Suffrage," *Nashville Tennessean*, August 12, 1920.

Chapter 18: Terrorizing Tennessee Manhood

235 **He wished to introduce:** House Journal, Third Day, Wednesday, August 11, 1920, 38–9, TSLA.

235 **"Whereas," Bond read:** Accounts in "Defeat Effort to Defer Ratification," *Nashville Banner*, August 11, 1920; "House Beats Motion to Refer Suffrage," *Nashville Tennessean*, August 12, 1920; "Move is Made to Block Suffrage Vote by Postponement," *Memphis News-Scimitar*, August 11, 1920; "Effort to Postpone Action on Suffrage," *Chattanooga News*, August 11, 1920; "Postponement Would Mean Procrastination," *Chattanooga News*, August 11, 1920; and "Suffs Win in Tennessee," *Charlotte* (NC) *Observer*, August 12, 1920.

237 **"Is that an anti-suffrage bomb?":** Carol Lynn Yellin et al., *Perfect 36*, 120, recounting a news account in *Chattanooga Times*, October 21, 1913; biographical details from Carol Lynn Yellin et al., 53–55, adapted from Goodstein, "Anne Dallas Dudley."

238 **Joint Resolution #1:** Senate actions detailed in "Defeat Effort to Defer Ratification," *Nashville Banner*, August 11, 1920.

238 **insulting telegram from Republican chairman Hays:** "Hays Asks Republicans to Insure Ratification," *New York Times*, August 12, 1920; "Hays Strikes Hard for Ratification," *Chattanooga News*, August 11, 1920.

238 **"carries out the spirit":** "Postponement Would Mean Procrastination," *Chattanooga News*, August 11, 1920; "Defeat Effort to Defer Ratification," *Nashville Banner*, August 11, 1920.

239 **Mr. Vertrees had not permitted:** Vertrees's insistence that women not lobby the legislature is discussed in Green, *Southern Strategies*, chapter 5, 119.

239 **She had suffered so long:** Pearson's belief that she'd been punished for her antisuffrage stand is repeated many times in Pearson, "My Story," Pearson Papers, TSLA; and Wheeler, *Votes for Women!*, 224–42.

239 **"CAN ANYBODY TERRORIZE":** Pearson Papers, TSLA.

240 **This resolution was ridiculous:** "Defeat Effort to Defer Ratification," *Nashville Banner,* August 11, 1920.

240 **did a doubletake:** "Ratificationists Score Victories," *Chattanooga News,* August 12, 1920; "Suffragists Win in Test in Tennessee," *Chicago Tribune,* August 12, 1920, Catt Papers, TSLA.

241 **Roberts had finally spoken:** "Cox Encouraged by Gov. Roberts," *New York Times,* August 12, 1920; "Cox Changes Plans," *Washington Post,* August 12, 1920.

241 **causing them to view the governor:** George Milton, Sr., to Gov. Roberts, August 9, 1920, Gov. Albert H. Roberts Papers, TSLA.

241 **they still suspected:** Alice Paul to Abby Baker, August 10, 1920, and memo from Woman's Party to Cox, August 11, 1920, both in NWPP, LoC; "Cox Urged to Go to Nashville," *Chattanooga News,* August 11, 1920.

241 **emphasize the responsibility:** Paul to Reber, August 11, 1920, NWPP, LoC.

241 **make sure they quote us:** Florence Boeckel to Anita Pollitzer, August 10, 1920. NWPP, LoC.

241 **Paul had already purchased:** "I shall probably go to Tennessee tomorrow," Paul to Baker, August 10, 1920, NWPP, LoC.

242 **made that heartrending speech:** Carol Lynn Yellin et al., 94.

242 **"The people of Tennessee":** "Defeat Effort to Defer Ratification," *Nashville Banner,* August 11, 1920.

243 **"do not want suffrage":** Ibid.

244 **this new alliance:** Kenny to Catt, January 5, 1920, Catt Papers, TSLA; Goodstein, "A Rare Alliance," 235–38.

244 **Hays had spent hours:** "Hays Strikes Hard for Ratification," *Nashville Banner,* August 11, 1920; "Hays Asks Republicans," *New York Times,* August 12, 1920.

245 **"The men of Tennessee":** "Defeat Effort to Defer Ratification," *Nashville Banner,* August 11, 1920.

245 **The roll call began:** Ibid.

245 **"call the roll up yonder":** Rep. James H. Galbraith to Tennessee League of Women Voters, June 24, 1920, and August 3, 1920, Catt Papers, TSLA; Abby Milton, "Report of the Tennessee League of Women Voters," 1920, 10, Abby Crawford Milton Papers, TSLA.

245 **four Anti delegates:** "Legislature to Cast Vote," *Nashville Tennessean,* August 12, 1920.

246 **"The fight is won!":** "Suffrage Wins First Test Vote," *New York Evening World,* August 11, 1920.

247 **"Are none sober?":** Catt and Shuler, 442.

247 **"The opposition has yielded":** "Legislature to Cast Vote," *Nashville Tennessean,* August 12, 1920.

247 **"Boys, it looks like":** "Cox Encouraged by Roberts," *New York Times,* August 11, 1920; "Roberts Telephones Suffrage Will Pass," *Nashville Tennessean,* August 12, 1920; *Washington Herald,* August 12.

248 **cool her tapered heels:** "Cox Encouraged by Roberts," *New York Times,* August 11, 1920.

248 **bleary-eyed dawn:** "Suffs Win Again," *Memphis News-Scimitar,* August 12, 1920.

249 **The proceedings moved swiftly:** "Ratificationists Score Two Victories," *Chattanooga News,* August 12, 1920; "Resolution Against Lobbyists Withdrawn," *Nashville*

Tennessean, August 13, 1920; "Ratificationists Win Skirmish in House," *Nashville Banner*, August 12, 1920.

249 **"Just keep it":** Anastatia Sims, "Powers that Pray and Powers that Prey: Tennessee and the Fight for Woman Suffrage," *Tennessee Historical Quarterly* (Winter 1991): 217; Carol Lynn Yellin et al., 98–99.

250 *That Deadly Parallel*: All in Pearson Papers, TSLA.

251 **felt a wave of sadness:** Upton, *Random Recollections;* and Catt, 1921 letter recounting Clay and Gordon not speaking to her in Nashville, Catt Papers, LoC. In some news accounts Jean Gordon accompanied her sister to Nashville, but her participation in anti-ratification activities is not well documented.

251 **"rests as a heavy load":** Headquarters Secretary (Emma Wold) to Anne Calvert Neely, August 12, 1920, NWPP, LoC.

252 **"The women of this country":** Accounts of the debate are in "Debate Suffrage at Joint Hearing," *Nashville Banner*, August 13, 1920; "Ratification is Debated Before Packed Audience," *Nashville Tennessean*, August 13, 1920; "Harding Letter Depresses Suffs," *Memphis News-Scimitar*, August 13, 1920; "Gen. Cates Turns Batteries on Traducers of Tennessee Womanhood," *Chattanooga News*, August 13, 1920; "Candidate Will Not Urge Vote," *Chattanooga Times*, August 13, 1920; and *New York Times*, August 13, 1920.

256 **did not go as smoothly:** "Constitutional Committee Decides," *Chattanooga News*, August 13, 1920; "Harding Letter Depresses Suffs," *Memphis News-Scimitar*, August 13, 1920.

256 **"unless something miraculous":** "Expect Tennessee to Ratify Today," *New York Times*, August 13, 1920.

Chapter 19: Petticoat Government

257 **a "hoodoo" for ratification:** "Story Resolution Meets Defeat," *Chattanooga News*, August 12, 1920; "Friday, 13th, Waterloo for Somebody," *Chattanooga Times*, August 13, 1920.

257 **"clear as mud":** "Roosevelt Attacks Hardings' Record," *Nashville Tennessean*, August 14, 1920.

257 **Tom Riddick's failure:** "Harding Letter Depresses Suffs," *Memphis News-Scimitar*, August 13, 1920.

258 **found a suitable replacement:** Carol Lynn Yellin et al., 102.

258 **Alice Paul was still in D.C.:** Paul had actually purchased a ticket to Nashville, but canceled at the last minute. Her hesitancy is noted in Alice Paul to Mabel Reber, August 12, 1920; Woman's Party secretary Emma Wold to Inez Irwin, August 12, 1920; and Wold wrote to the Pullman Company for a refund on August 12; all in NWPP, LoC.

259 **"If I can get":** Pearson, "My Story," Pearson Papers, TSLA; and reprinted in Wheeler, *Votes for Women!*, 238.

259 **a throng of Suffs and Antis:** Accounts of the debate and passage are in "Senate Ratifies Suffrage Amendment," *Memphis News-Scimitar*, August 13, 1920; "Senate Ratifies Suffrage After Fight," *Nashville Tennessean*, August 14, 1920; "State Senate Ratifies," *Chattanooga News*; "Senate Ratifies by Expected Majority," *Nashville Banner*, August 13, 1920; "Senators Bow Under Lash of Bosses," *Chattanooga Times*, August 14, 1920; "Tennessee Senate Ratifies," *New York Times*, August 14, 1920; "Upper House Votes to Ratify," *Charlotte* (NC) *Observer*, August 14, 1920; and "Candler Hissed by Senators," *Chattanooga News*, August 14, 1920. All descriptions are from these sources unless otherwise noted.

260 **"I have six children!":** Carol Lynn Yellin et al., 100.

261 **"That is the most unfortunate":** "Action Expected on Tuesday," *Harrisburg* (PA) *Evening News,* August 13, 1920.

263 **Senator C. C. Collins, who insisted:** Catt and Shuler, 445.

264 **from the private eye:** Horace E. Parker to Carrie Catt, Catt Papers, TSLA.

264 **beautiful victory brooch:** Van Voris, 158.

264 **"We are waiting":** Emma Wold to Lena Henderson, August 13, 1920, NWPP, LoC.

265 **lifted their skirts:** Carol Lynn Yellin et al., 100.

266 **"an absolute fabrication":** "Wilson Wires to Walker," *Nashville Tennessean,* August 14, 1920.

266 **"been entertained in negro homes":** Catt to Sen. Chrisenen, January 19, 1920, Catt Papers, NYPL.

266 **based his claim:** "Tennessee Senate Ratifies," *New York Times,* August 14, 1920.

267 **"This happened in other":** "Senate Action Does Not Worry Antis," *Nashville Banner,* August 14, 1920.

267 **Joe Hanover took charge:** "Joe Hanover Leads Suffrage Battle," *Chattanooga News,* August 14, 1920; "Wilson Wires to Walker for Aid: Both Suffs and Antis Work Hard for Battle," *Nashville Tennessean,* August 14, 1920.

267 **Finding those delegates:** "House Wishes to Dodge Vote," *Memphis News-Scimitar,* August 14, 1920; "Wilson Wires to Walker for Aid: Both Suffs and Antis Work Hard for Battle," *Nashville Tennessean,* August 14, 1920; "Suffrage for Women Now Depends on House," *Chattanooga News,* August 14, 1920.

267 **Annie Laurie Stahlman:** Carol Lynn Yellin et al., 101.

267 **"cajole and coddle":** Harriet Upton's description of suffragists' tactics is in *Washington Times,* August 27, 1920, also quoted in *The Woman Patriot,* December 4, 1920.

268 **"Automobile rides, hugs, kisses":** "The People Against the Politicians," *The Lookout: A Journal of Southern Society* 25 (August 24, 1920), quoted in Anastatia Sims, "Powers That Pray and Powers That Prey: Tennessee and the Fight for Woman Suffrage," *Tennessee Historical Quarterly* (Winter 1991): 217.

268 **"baptism in righteousness":** "Harding Asks Press to Lead in Morals," *New York Times,* August 14, 1920.

268 **feeling chipper, much improved:** "Wilson Stronger," *New York Times,* August 20, 1920; "Describes What Wilson Does," *Baltimore Sun,* August 20, 1920.

268 **very generous to Tumulty:** Gardener's gifts as well as the tone of her relationship with Tumulty and the Wilsons are described in her correspondence, Papers of Helen Hamilton Gardener, Woman's Rights Collection, Schlesinger Library, Folders 69–72.

269 **"May I not":** "Wilson Wires to Walker for Aid," *Nashville Tennessean,* August 14, 1920.

269 **Tumulty sent a second telegram:** Tumulty to Catt, August 13, 1920, Catt Papers, TSLA.

269 **"The message sent":** "Long Suffrage Fight Won," *Washington Herald,* August 14, 1920.

269 **"I have the profound":** "Can't Vote Contrary to His Conviction," *Chattanooga News,* August 14, 1920; "Tension Relaxes in Suff Battle," *Nashville Tennessean,* August 15, 1920.

269 **"I thank God":** "No Surrender of Convictions," *Nashville Banner,* August 14, 1920; "Speaker Lauded From Many States," *Nashville Banner,* August 16, 1920.

270 **"This is the teaching":** "The Woman's Bible" advertisement in *Nashville Banner,* August 12, 1920.

270 **two dozen men of the cloth:** Bucy, 233; "Antis Take Issue Upon Woman's Bible," *Nashville Tennessean,* August 16, 1920; "Clergymen Petition Against Suffrage," *The Woman Patriot,* August 21, 1920.

270 **"vulgar, igorant, insane":** Van Voris, 160; Catt in *The Woman Citizen,* September 4, 1920.

270 **her phone was being tapped:** Catt in *The Woman Citizen,* September 4, 1920.

270 **opened the door:** Upton, *Random Recollections,* chapter 24, 7.

271 **a civil suit:** "Damage Suits and Fist Fights," *Charlotte* (NC) *Observer,* August 15, 1920.

271 **jostled in the Hermitage elevator:** Harriet Taylor Upton, "Story of the 36th State," Ohio Woman's Suffrage Association Headquarters Bulletin, September 1, 1920.

271 **vile slurs as he walked:** Carol Lynn Yellin et al., 103. These incidents do not appear in newspapers but were probably related to Yellin during her interviews with Hanover.

272 **It was a whiskey bottle:** Carol Lynn Yellin et al., 102.

272 **thriving industry of bribery:** "Both Sides See Victory Loom; Talk of Boodle to Prevent Ratification," *Nashville Tennessean,* August 16, 1920. Allegations of such "middlemen" were given in testimony to a Davidson County grand jury investigating corruption in the ratification process later in August.

273 **Harriet Upton learned:** Upton, *Random Recollections,* chapter 24, 5.

273 **"Sorry, Joe, but I'm going":** Hanover related this anecdote to his nephew, Edward M. Kaplan. Kaplan's letter to the author, February 17, 2015; also in Carol Lynn Yellin et al., 102.

273 **jobs and positions could be offered:** See Abby Milton, "Report of the Tennessee League of Women Voters, 1920," Abby Crawford Milton Papers, TSLA, 10; Bucy, 233; "Tennessee Suffs Raise Fraud Cry," *New York Evening World,* August 16, 1920.

274 **"the Prince of Lobbyists":** Editorial, "The Issue," *Nashville Tennessean,* August 17, 1920.

274 **"look you in the eye":** "House Seeks to Dodge Vote," *Memphis News-Scimitar,* August 14, 1920.

274 **in a searing telegram:** John Houk to Will Hays, August 15, 1920, NWPP, LoC.

274 **"I believe one of the most":** "Big Interests in Plot," *Charlotte* (NC) *Observer,* August 16, 1920; "Declare a Strong Lobby is Working in Tennessee," *Harrisburg* (PA) *Evening News,* August 16, 1920.

274 **In retaliation, White threatened:** "Both Sides See Victory Loom," *Nashville Tennessean,* August 16, 1920.

274 **"Blackmailers!" screamed the Antis:** "Miss Rowe Calls Suffragists' Bluff," unidentified news clipping (probably *Chattanooga Times*), Pearson Papers, TSLA.

275 **articulated this theory:** "Sees Fight on Suffrage," *Washington Post,* August 16, 1920; "Sen. Brandegee's Hand Seen Here in Suff Battle," *Nashville Tennessean,* August 17, 1920.

276 **"Frank Brandegee has no influence":** Abby S. Baker report to A. Paul, handwritten, dated Sunday, August 15, 10 p.m., NWPP, LoC.

276 **things seemed murkier:** "Suffrage Issue Undecided," *Charlotte* (NC) *Observer,* August 16, 1920; "Both Sides See Victory Loom," *Nashville Tennessean,* August 16, 1920; "Expect House Will Ratify," *Washington Post,* August 15, 1920; "Undercurrent of Doubt," *Nashville Banner,* August 16, 1920.

277 **he was "reasonably sure":** "Walker Sure of Rejection," *Chattanooga Times,* August 16, 1920.

277 **"We now have":** Catt to Mary Gray Peck, August 15, 1920, Catt Papers, LoC. Also in Peck, 335.

Chapter 20: Armageddon

278 **"BEWARE!":** Pearson Papers, TSLA.

278 **had been visited:** Catt and Shuler, 447.

279 **began receiving telephone calls:** Carol Lynn Yellin et al., 103.

279 **under police protection:** Ibid.

279 **Catt was appalled:** Catt and Shuler, 447.

279 **their wife was ill:** "Big interests in Plot to Defeat Suffrage," *Charlotte* (NC) *Observer,* August 16, 1920.

279 **that one such legislator:** Upton, *Random Recollections,* chapter 24, 6.

280 **"working in relays":** "Five Members Desert Cause," *Chattanooga Times,* August 17, 1920.

280 **More bad news:** "Five Members from Davidson Desert Cause," *Chattanooga Times,* August 17, 1920; Nashville suffragists also tried to embarrass the delegation by publicizing their previous promises to ratify: "Suffragists Believe Davidson Will Hold," *Nashville Tennessean,* August 17, 1920.

281 **The same band:** "Republicans Refuse to Knife Suffrage, Claim," *Nashville Tennessean,* August 17, 1920.

281 **offered to defend:** "Rowe Calls Suffragists' Bluff," *Nashville Banner,* August 16, 1920; "Threats of Blackmail Called by Miss Rowe," *Chattanooga Times,* August 17, 1920.

281 **When pressed by reporters:** "Harding Fears Trouble Brews Over Suffrage," *Chattanooga Times,* August 17, 1920; "Harding Men Fear Complications," *New York Times,* August 17, 1920.

281 **"I insistently hope":** George White to Gov. Roberts, August 16, 1920, Gov. Albert H. Roberts Papers, TSLA.

281 **"depending upon you":** "Suffrage Vote Taken Today; Cox Final Plea," *Nashville Tennessean,* August 17, 1920.

282 **details of their findings:** White and Pollitzer to James Cox, August 16, 1920, NWPP, LoC.

282 **the alleged conspiracy:** "Suffragists Gain in Tennessee Fight," *New York Times,* August 17, 1920.

282 **"Asinine," a spokesman:** "L&N, Suffrage Foe, Cox is Told," *Louisville Courier-Journal,* August 17, 1920.

282 **At eight p.m.:** Accounts of the committee vote in "Suffrage Vote Will Be Taken Today," *Nashville Tennessean,* August 17, 1920; "Resolution Recommended by Committee," *Chattanooga Times,* August 17, 1920; Carol Lynn Yellin et al., 103; "Suffragists Gain in Tennessee Fight," *New York Times,* August 17, 1920.

282 **"We've got 'em":** Robert B. Jones and Mark E. Byrnes, "The 'Bitterest Fight': The Tennessee General Assembly and the Nineteenth Amendment," *Tennessee Historical Quarterly* 68, no. 3 (Fall 2009): 275, quoting from *Knoxville Journal and Tribune,* August 17, 1920.

283 **"AN APPEAL TO THE CITIZENS":** *Nashville Tennessean,* August 17, 1920.

287 **The luncheon hour:** Louise Graham, "As a Woman Saw the Tennessee Fight," *New York Times,* August 18, 1920.

287 **Brooks read it quickly:** "Loyalty is Shown to Suffrage Cause," *Nashville Tennessean,* August 18, 1920; "Suffragists Get Special Train for Legislator," *Chattanooga Times,* August 18, 1920.

288 **"I cannot pledge myself":** Irwin, *The Story of Alice Paul,* 473–74.

293 **"Opposition only claiming":** Upton to Harding, August 17, 1920, Catt Papers, TSLA.

293 **"Harding's letter to Tillman":** Catt to Will Hays, August 17, 1920, Catt Papers, TSLA.

293 **"Wire me any suggestions":** Hays to Catt, August 17, 1920, Catt Papers, TSLA.

294 **The move to adjourn:** "Adjournment Manuever of Opposition," *Chattanooga Times,* August 18, 1920.

294 **Suddenly a reporter:** "Bedlam Breaks Loose," *Chattanooga Times,* August 18, 1920.

295 **The vote in Raleigh:** "Suffrage Bill is Defeated in North Carolina," *Nashville Tennessean,* August 18, 1920; "Tarheel Coup is Waterloo for Suffrage," *Chattanooga Times,*

August 18, 1920. See also "Anti-Suffragists Seek to Form Alliance," *Charlotte* (NC) *Observer*, August 16, 1920.

295 **Lights burned late:** "Final Action Upon Suffrage Probable Today," *Nashville Tennessean*, August 19, 1920; Catt and Shuler, 445–6; Upton, *Random Recollections*, chapter 24, 9.

296 **"we can pray":** Catt and Shuler, 447; Abby Milton, "Report of the Tennessee League of Women Voters, 1920," 11, Abby Crawford Milton Papers, TSLA.

Chapter 21: The Hour Has Come

297 **with grim resolve:** "Suffrage Amendment Adopted by House," *Nashville Tennessean*, August 19, 1920; "Many Believe Ratification Now Doomed," *Chattanooga Times*, August 18, 1920.

298 **"the mothers of America":** "Cox Is Gratified Over Suffrage," *New York Tribune*, August 19, 1920.

299 **Editorial cartoonists were mining:** All cartoons in Catt Papers, TSLA.

299 **"We really trusted you":** Irwin, *The Story of Alice Paul*, 474.

299 **"The Truth about the Negro Problem":** *Nashville Tennessean*, August 18, 1920.

300 **gaveled the house to order:** Accounts of the vote in "Suffrage Amendment Adopted by House," *Nashville Tennessean*, August 19, 1920; "Tennessee Now Perfect 36," *Chattanooga News*, August 18, 1920; "House Passes Resolution," *Chattanooga Times*, August 19, 1920; "Suffrage Forces Victorious in House," *Nashville Banner*, August 18, 1920; "Tennessee Solons Ratify Suffrage," *Memphis News-Scimitar*, August 18, 1920; "Tennessee Completes Suffrage Victory," *New York Times*, August 19, 1920; "Suffrage Ratification Completed," *New York Tribune*, August 19, 1920; "Tennessee Ratifies," *Washington Post*, August 19, 1920; and "Speaker Walker Changes Vote," *Baltimore Sun*, August 19, 1920.

304 **"Go, get another state":** Van Voris, 117.

305 **"No matter how well":** Catt to Kenny, June 29, 1920, Catt Papers, TSLA.

305 **Certain political leaders:** Irwin, 473.

308 **heart began to pound:** Upton, "Story of the 36th State."

Chapter 22: Liberty Bell

309 **"slipped into the clerk's room":** Eyewitness account of Burn's escape in Louise Davis, "Ladies Had The Last Word," *Nashville Tennessean Magazine*, January 18, 1948.

309 **"The fight is not over":** "Suffrage Amendment Adopted by House," *Nashville Tennessean*, August 19, 1920.

310 **She could, however:** Catt's "ratification dance" is mentioned in Bucy, "Thrill of History."

310 **A jubilant Anne Dudley:** "Mrs. Dudley is Sure House Will Ratify," *Nashville Tennessean*, August 18, 1920; Abby Milton, "Report of the Tennessee League of Women Voters: Containing a Full Account of the Suffrage Ratification Campaign (Tennessee League of Women Voters, 1925)," Abby Crawford Milton Papers, TSLA; "Suffragists All Pleased," *Chattanooga News*, August 19, 1920.

310 **A breathless Sue White:** Congratulatory telegrams in NWPP, LoC.

310 **Some gave full credit:** Congratulations to Catt from Maud Wood Park, August 18, 1920, in Catt Papers, TSLA; to Alice Paul from Rudolph de Zapp, August 18, NWPP, LoC. Congratulations messages can be found in Catt Papers, TSLA; NWPP, LoC; and "Hundreds Wire Congratulations on Suffrage Victory," *Nashville Tennessean*, August 20, 1920.

310 **"The civilization of the world"**: "Ratification Acclaimed by Party Heads," *Nashville Tennessean,* August 18, 1920.

310 **"All along I have"**: Ibid.

311 **"Our mothers began it"**: "Mrs. Catt Tells of Fight," *Baltimore Sun,* August 19, 1920.

311 **Sue White enjoyed:** Congratulatory messages in NWPP, LoC.

311 **"The victory of women today"**: "Colby to Proclaim Suffrage Promptly," *New York Times,* August 19, 1920.

312 **In a series of closed-door meetings:** "Suffrage Ratification Completed," *New York Tribune,* August 19, 1920; "Will Make Protest Against Ratification," *Nashville Banner,* August 19, 1920; "Antis Talking of Sensation to Stir State," *Chattanooga Times,* August 19, 1920.

312 **"he'd been bribed":** Accounts and affadavits in "Burn Deserts Cause of Antis," *Chattanooga Times;* "Promise More in Burn Case," *Nashville Banner,* August 18, 1920; "Bold Attempt to Intimidate Solon Foiled," *Nashville Tennessean,* August 19, 1920; "Was Influenced to Change Vote," *Charlotte* (NC) *News,* August 19, 1920; "Proud of Opportunity," *Chattanooga News,* August 19, 1920; "Tennessee Delays Fight," *Memphis News-Scimitar,* August 19, 1920; "Stories about Bribery," *New York Evening World,* August 19, 1920; "Fraud Charges in Tennessee," *New York Times,* August 20, 1920.

312 **The first thing:** "Mrs. Burn Tells of Son," *Nashville Tennessean,* August 23, 1920; "Word from Mother Won for Suffrage," *Nashville Tennessean,* August 20, 1920; "Mother of Representative Burn," *Chattanooga News,* August 20, 1920; Letter of Phoebe (Febb) Ensminger Burn to Harry Burn, August 17, 1920, in Calvin M. McClung Historical Collection, Knox County Library, Knoxville, TN.

313 **thanks for his "splendid fight":** Alice Paul to A. H. Roberts, August 18, 1920, and Women's Bureau of Democratic National Committee to A. H. Roberts; both telegrams are in Roberts Papers, TSLA.

313 **"The action of Tennessee":** Franklin D. Roosevelt to A. H. Roberts, Roberts Papers, TSLA.

313 **But there were other telegrams:** Men of Fayetville to Gov. A. H. Roberts, August 18, 1920, and W. Lamb to A. H. Roberts, August 18, 1920, in Roberts Papers, TSLA; "Resentment in Lincoln County," *Nashville Banner,* August 19, 1920.

314 **The Hermitage halls:** "Women Watchful," *New York Times,* August 19, 1920; Upton, *Random Recollections,* chapter 24.

314 **Two suffragist legislators:** Catt and Shuler, 450.

314 **"get out of the way":** "Promise More in Burn Case," *Nashville Banner,* August 19, 1920.

314 **blackmail had been foiled:** "Bold Attempt to Intimidate Solon," *Nashville Tennessean,* August 19, 1920.

315 **"I desire to resent":** "Proud of Opportunity to Free Women," *Chattanooga News,* August 19, 1920; "Tennessee Delays Fight," *Memphis News-Scimitar,* August 19, 1920; "Charges of Fraud in Suffrage Fight," *New York Times,* August 20, 1920.

315 **"There never was a finer":** "Candler Says Charges Ridiculous," *Chattanooga News,* August 20, 1920.

315 **"Woman was here to-day":** Catt and Shuler, 266; "Anti Insults Burn's Mother," *Chattanooga News,* August 23, 1920.

316 **"You are blessed":** Catt to Mrs. J. L. Burn, August 19, 1920, Harry T. Burn Papers, McClung Collection, Knox County Library, Knoxville, TN.

316 **The band in the Ryman:** The most detailed account is in "People Protest Suffrage Action," *Nashville Banner,* August 20, 1920; "Claim Enough Votes to Reconsider," *Chattanooga Times,* August 20, 1920; "Antis Hold Mass Meeting," *Nashville Tennessean,* August 20, 1920.

316 **In a hasty conference:** Catt and Shuler, 453; Harriet Taylor Upton, "Story of the 36th State," Ohio Woman's Suffrage Association Headquarters Bulletin, September 1, 1920; Upton, *Random Recollections,* chapter 24. Dodson's child recovered.

317 **The desk of one delegate:** "Antis Ready to Fight," *Chattanooga Times,* August 21, 1920; Sims, "Powers That Pray and Powers That Prey," 219.

317 **Joe Hanover looked haggard:** Carol Lynn Yellin et al., 130.

317 **The Suffs had prevailed:** "Decisive Action," *Nashville Tennessean,* August 21, 1920; "Immortal 49 Stand Like Wall," *Chattanooga News,* August 20, 1920; "House Adjourns Till Saturday," *Nashville Banner,* August 20, 1920; "Suffs Victorious," *Memphis News-Scimitar,* August 20, 1920; Upton, "Story of the 36th State," 3.

317 **Suff women burst into applause:** "Runaway didn't Prevent Victory," *Chattanooga News,* August 21, 1920.

317 **"You are all heroes":** *Nashville Tennessean,* August 21, 1920.

317 **"The victory is complete":** "Suffs Elated," *Nashville Tennessean,* August 21, 1920.

317 **In the middle of the night:** Pearson, "My Story," Pearson Papers, TSLA; also in Wheeler, *Votes for Women!,* 239.

317 **Shielded by darkness:** "Wearing Red Roses on Coats," *Nashville Banner,* August 21, 1920; "Solons Reach Decatur," *Memphis News-Scimitar,* August 21, 1920; "Vote in Tennessee to Clinch . . . Despite Big Bolt," *New York Times,* August 22, 1920.

318 **The rallies debuted:** "How Harry Burns' Home Feels," *Nashville Banner,* August 22, 1920; "Anti Orators to Stump State," *Nashville Banner,* August 23, 1920; "McMinn Folks Hot After Burn," *Chattanooga Times,* August 23, 1920.

319 **One observer at the scene:** Sarah Spence DeBow, *The History of the Case,* privately printed booklet, Tennessee State Library, Nashville, TN.

319 **dissolve the injunction:** Catt and Shuler, 454; "Governor Says He Will Certify," *Nashville Tennessean,* August 23, 1920; "Tennessee Unites Court Knot," *New York Evening World,* August 24, 1920; "Unprecedented Antis Declare," *Nashville Banner,* August 24, 1920.

319 **on Tuesday morning:** "Roberts Certifies," *Nashville Banner,* August 24, 1920; "Roberts Certifies," *New York Times,* August 25, 1920; "Roberts Sends Certificate," *Chattanooga Times,* August 25, 1920; "Suffrage Fight Over," *Nashville Tennessean,* August 25, 1920; "Roberts Certifies," *Memphis News-Scimitar,* August 24, 1920; Photograph of Gov. Roberts's signing in *New York Times,* August 26, 1920; "Governor Forwards Suffrage Certificate," *Chattanooga News,* August 24, 1920; "Suffrage Notice Mailed," *Christian Science Monitor,* August 25, 1920.

319 **During the layover:** Milton to Catt, January 13, 1921, Catt Papers, TSLA.

320 **middle of a suffragist feud:** Secretary of the Navy Josephus Daniels recorded in his diary on August 25, 1920: "Mrs. Helen Gardener [NAWSA Corresponding Secretary] phoned that she had asked Colby not to have any of the Picketting [sic] crowd of women present." E. David Cronon, *The Cabinet Diaries of Josephus Daniels, 1913–1921* (Ann Arbor, MI: University Microfilms International, 1982), 552, quoted in Beth A. Behn, "Woodrow Wilson's Conversion Experience: The President and the Federal Woman Suffrage Amendment," PhD dissertation, University of Massachusetts, Amherst, 2004; "Ratification of Woman Suffrage," *Sausalito News,* September 4, 1920.

320 **Not until 1922:** Leser v. Garnett (1922), U.S. Supreme Court, No. 553.

320 **"tired and heart-sick":** Pearson, "My Story," and in Wheeler, *Votes for Women!,* 241.

321 **to personally thank:** Description from Peck, 339; "Suffrage Tribute to President," *Christian Science Monitor,* August 27, 1920; Helen Gardener to Catt, August 21, 1920, Carrie Chapman Catt Papers, TSLA.

321 **"Woman's Suffrage is now a fact"**: "W.H.A. Moore," *Baltimore Afro-American*, August 27, 1920.

322 **On Friday morning:** Peck, 340–2; "Bringing the Victors Home," *The Woman Citizen*, September 4, 1920.

322 **Hundreds of parading women:** "Suffrage Jubilee in NYC," *Christian Science Monitor*, August 28, 1920; "NY Suffrage Leaders Celebrate," *Nashville Banner*, August 27, 1920; "Tribute is Paid Suff Leader," unidentified news clipping; "Governor Greets Mrs. Catt Here," *New York Times*, August 28, 1920; Gertrude Brown memoir, 200, Gertrude Brown Papers, Schlesinger Library.

323 **Church bells rang:** "Suffragists to Hold Noisy Jubilee," *Baltimore Sun*, August 28, 1920; "Harding Defends Rail Legislation," *New York Times*, August 28, 1920; "Bells Will Ring at Noon," *Wyoming State Tribune* (Cheyenne) August 27, 1920; "Five Minute Din at Noon," unidentified Macon, GA, newsclipping; "Chicago Asked to Doff Hat," *Chicago Tribune*, August 29, 1920.

323 **In Chattanooga, the mayor:** "Bass' Proclamation in Chattanooga," *Nashville Banner*, August 28, 1920; "Suff Celebration Strikes Out," *Nashville Banner*, August 29, 1920; "No Jubilation in Tullahoma," news clipping, Pearson Papers, TSLA.

323 **Even in Nashville:** "Plan to Celebrate Informally," *Nashville Tennessean*, August 28, 1920.

323 **"The vote is the emblem":** Catt in *The Woman Citizen*, September 4, 1920; also in Peck, 342.

Chapter 23: Election Day

325 **About ten million women:** "One in Three Women Vote," *New York Times*, December 19, 1920; The woman's vote in national elections (1927) *Editorial research reports 1927* (vol. II), Washington, D.C.: CQ Press, retrieved from library.cqpress.com/cqre searcher/cqresrre1927053100; Jodie T. Allen, "Reluctant Suffragettes: When Women Questioned Their Right to Vote," Pew Research Reports, March 18, 2009. Women's voting participation also varied from state to state, but only Illinois segregated men's and women's ballots so most counts are estimates.

325 **obliging policemen held the tots:** *Baltimore Sun*, November 3, 1920.

325 **cast their ballots:** Accounts of voting activities found in "Thousands Carry Lunches to Polls," *New York Times*, November 3, 1920; "Cox Hears Returns," *Washington Post*, November 3, 1920; "Large Vote by Women" and "Better Conditions at Polls are Noted," *Christian Science Monitor*, November 3, 1920; "Many Incidents . . . Women at the Polls," *Baltimore Sun*, November 3, 1920; "Cox Smiles Gamely Thru Defeat," *New York Times*, November 3, 1920; "Ballots of President and Mrs. Wilson Cast," *Baltimore Sun*, October 31, 1920.

325 **poll watchers were surprised:** Pearson, "My Story," Pearson Papers, TSLA.

326 **Catt was called upon to explain:** "Mrs. Catt on the Election," *New York Times*, November 21, 1920; "One in Three Women Vote," *New York Times*, December 19, 1920.

326 **The Antis crowed:** *The Woman Patriot*, November 6 and November 13, 1920.

326 **Roberts was punished:** "Tennessee Antis Wage Campaign Against Roberts," *The Woman Patriot*, October 16, 1920; Gary W. Reichard, "The Defeat of Governor Roberts" *Tennessee Historical Quarterly* 30, no. 1 (1971): 94–109.

326 **campaigned hard for Roberts:** Their efforts are found in their correspondence with Catt in September and October 1920; Catt's efforts on behalf of Roberts detailed in her

letter to him on September 7, 1920; Catt's condolence to Roberts on his defeat, November 13, 1920. All in Catt Papers, TSLA.

327 **In Boston, first-time:** Accounts of these incidents are found in the Papers of the NAACP, Administrative Files (subject file: Politics) October 15–December 31, 1920, Manuscript Collection, LoC, reproduced in the ProQuest History Vault, proprietary database accessed through Schlesinger Library, Harvard University.

327 **town of Lake City:** *New York Times,* October 6, 1920. Also referred to in James Weldon Johnson to U.S. Dept. of Justice, October 7, 1920, and in Mary White Ovington, "Free Black as Well as White Women," *The Suffragist,* November 1920.

327 **His request was denied:** James Weldon Johnson to U.S. Department of Justice, October 7, 1920, and R. P. Stewart, Assistant Attorney General, U.S. Department of Justice to James Weldon Johnson, NAACP, October 22, 1920, in NAACP Papers, LoC. See also William Pickens, "The Woman Voter Hits the Color Line," *The Nation,* October 6, 1920.

327 **The worst violence:** "Kill 2 Whites and Six Negroes in Florida Riot," *New York Times,* November 4, 1920; Paul Ortiz, "Remembering the Single Bloodiest Day in Modern Political History," in *Facing South,* the online magazine of the Institute for Southern Studies, May 14, 2010.

328 **NAACP officers testified before Congress:** James Weldon Johnson to Hon. George Tinkham, Rep. from Massachusetts, Washington, D.C., December 6, 1920; "Negro Association to Tell Congress of Voting Frauds," *New York Call,* December 24, 1920. Both clippings in NAACP Papers, Politics file, LoC.

328 **"We must not rest":** Mary White Ovington, "Free Black as Well as White Women," *The Suffragist,* November 1920. Also, handwritten letter to the editor of *The Suffragist* from Ella Rush Murray, November 15, 1920, NAACP Papers, LoC.

328 **It is a race issue:** Freda Kirchwey, "Alice Paul Pulls the Strings," *The Nation,* March 2, 1921; Nancy F. Cott, "Feminist Politics in the 1920s: The National Woman's Party," *The Journal of American History* 71, no. 1 (June 1984): 43–68.

331 **She warned that women:** See Catt, "Political Parties and Women Voters," address to first Congress of League of Women Voters, February 1920, quoted in Flexner and Fitzpatrick, 319.

332 **An early attempt:** For a full chronicle see Jan Doolittle Wilson, *The Women's Joint Congressional Committee and the Politics of Maternalism, 1920–1930* (Urbana: University of Illinois Press, 2007).

332 **could not "be joined together":** Quoted in Kirsten Marie Delegard, *Battling Miss Bolsheviki* (Philadelphia: University of Pennsylvania Press, 2012), 7, from Nancy F. Cott, *The Grounding of Modern Feminism* (New Haven, CT: Yale University Press, 1987), 290.

332 **promise of a "women's vote":** "The Woman's Vote in National Elections," *Congressional Quarterly,* May 31, 1927, CQ Research Archive online, http://library.cqpress.com/cqresearcher/document.php?id=cqresrre1927053100#H2_2.

332 **women have voted:** "Gender Differences in Voter Turnout," Center for American Women and Politics, Eagle Institute of Politics, Rutgers University Fact Sheet, 2015.

333 **pivoted from fighting:** For an excellent account see Delegard, as well as Nick Fischer, *Spider Web: The Birth of American Anticommunism* (Urbana: University of Illinois Press, 2016).

333 **her League of Women Voters:** Delegard, 5.

333 **Even the National Parent-Teacher Association:** Delegard, 11.

334 **direct maternal line:** Delegard, 17.

335 **"Here lie two":** Van Voris, 219.

BIBLIOGRAPHY

Archival Collections

TENNESSEE STATE LIBRARY AND ARCHIVES, NASHVILLE, TN [TSLA]
Carrie Chapman Catt Papers
Josephine A. Pearson Papers
Gov. Albert H. Roberts Papers
Abby Crawford Milton Papers
Vertical Files
Historic Newspaper Collection
Tennessee House and Senate Journals

TENNESSEE STATE MUSEUM, NASHVILLE, TN
Women Suffrage Collection

CALVIN McCLUNG HISTORICAL COLLECTION, KNOXVILLE PUBLIC LIBRARY,
    KNOXVILLE, TN
Lizzie Crozier French Scrapbook
Women's Suffrage Collection

UNIVERSITY OF TENNESSEE KNOXVILLE LIBRARIES, SPECIAL COLLECTIONS
Harry T. Burn Scrapbook

ALBERT GORE RESEARCH CENTER, MIDDLE TENNESSEE UNIVERSITY,
    MURFREESBORO, TN

MEMPHIS PUBLIC LIBRARY, MEMPHIS TN

MEMPHIS AND SHELBY COUNTY HISTORY ROOM

NASHVILLE PUBLIC LIBRARY, NASHVILLE TN
Special Collections

SCHLESINGER LIBRARY, RADCLIFFE INSTITUTE, HARVARD UNIVERSITY,
    CAMBRIDGE, MA
Gertrude Brown Papers
Carrie Chapman Catt Papers
Helen H. Gardener Papers
Mary Garrett Hay Papers
Maud Wood Park Papers
Mary Stephenson Roberts Papers
Edna Lamprey Stantial Papers
Betty Gram Swing Papers
Harriet Taylor Upton Papers
Sue Shelton White Papers
Mary Winsor Papers

LIBRARY OF CONGRESS, MANUSCRIPT DIVISION, WASHINGTON, D.C.
Carrie Chapman Catt Papers

National American Woman Suffrage Association (NAWSA) Papers
National Woman's Party Papers (NWPP)
National Association for the Advancement of Colored People Papers (NAACP)

NEW YORK PUBLIC LIBRARY, MANUSCRIPT DIVISION, NEW YORK, NY
Carrie Catt Papers
Mary Garrett Hay Papers
Everett P. Wheeler Papers
Rossiter and Helen Kendrick Johnson Papers

FIRST LADIES PRESIDENTIAL LIBRARY, CANTON, OH

HISTORICAL SOCIETY OF PENNSYLVANIA, PHILADELPHIA, PA
Caroline Katzenstein Papers
Dora Kelly Lewis Papers

PENNSYLVANIA STATE UNIVERSITY, HARRISBURG, PA
Alice Marshall Women's History Collection

SOUTH CAROLINIANA LIBRARY, UNIVERSITY OF SOUTH CAROLINA, COLUMBIA, SC
Anita Pollitzer Papers

SOUTH CAROLINA HISTORICAL SOCIETY/COLLEGE OF CHARLESTON LIBRARIES, CHARLESTON, SC
Anita Pollitzer and Pollitzer Family Papers

SOUTHERN ORAL HISTORY PROGRAM COLLECTION, UNIVERSITY OF NORTH CAROLINA, CHAPEL HILL, NC
Interview with Mabel Pollitzer

REGIONAL ORAL HISTORY OFFICE, BANCROFT LIBRARY, UNIVERSITY OF CALIFORNIA, BERKELEY, CA
Reminiscences of Alice Paul, 1973

WOODROW WILSON PRESIDENTIAL LIBRARY, STAUNTON, VA
Journals of Dr. Cary Grayson

Newspapers and Periodicals

Baltimore Sun
Brooklyn Daily Eagle
Charleston Magazine
Charleston Post and Courier
Charlotte (N.C.) *News*
Charlotte (N.C.) *Observer*
Chattanooga News
Chattanooga Times
Chicago Tribune
Christian Science Monitor
Cincinnati Enquirer
Harrisburg (PA) *Evening News*
Jackson (TN) *Daily Democrat*
Kingsport (TN) *Times*
Knoxville Journal
Los Angeles Times
Louisville Courier-Journal

Memphis Commercial Appeal
Memphis News-Scimitar
Nashville Banner
Nashville Tennessean
New York Evening World
New York Herald
New York Times
New York Tribune
Pittsburgh Press
The Crisis (Journal of the NAACP)
The Suffragist
The Woman Citizen
The Woman Patriot
The Woman's Journal
The Woman's Remonstrance
Washington (D.C.) *Herald*
Washington Post
Wilmington News-Journal

Books

Anthony, Carl Sferrazza. *Florence Harding: The First Lady, the Jazz Age, and the Death of America's Most Scandalous President.* New York: William Morrow & Co., 1998.

Anthony, Susan B. *An Account of the Proceedings on the Trial of Susan B. Anthony on the Charge of Illegal Voting.* Rochester, NY: Daily Democrat and Chronicle Book, 1874.

Baker, Jean H. *Sisters: The Lives of America's Suffragists.* New York: Hill and Wang, 2005.

Baker, Jean H., ed. *Votes for Women: The Struggle for Suffrage Revisited.* Oxford and New York: Oxford University Press, 2002.

Bartley, Paula. *Emmeline Pankhurst.* Oxford and New York: Routledge, 2012.

Benjamin, Anne Myra Goodman. *Women Against Equality: A History of the Anti Suffrage Movement in the United States from 1895 to 1920.* Lewiston, NY: Edwin Mellen Press, 1991.

Berg, A. Scott, *Wilson.* New York: G. P. Putnam's Sons, 2013.

Birmingham, Stephen. *The Grandees: The Story of America's Sephardic Elite.* New York: Syracuse University Press, 1997.

Blair, Emily Newell, and Virginia Jeans Laas. *Bridging Two Eras: The Autobiography of Emily Newell Blair, 1877–1951.* Columbia: University of Missouri Press, 1999.

Blight, David W. *Frederick Douglass' Civil War: Keeping Faith in Jubilee.* Baton Rouge: Louisiana State University Press, 1989.

Bobo, Jacqueline, Cynthia Hudley, and Claudine Michel, eds. *The Black Studies Reader.* New York: Routledge, 2004.

Bosch, Mineke, ed. *Politics and Friendship: Letters from the International Woman Suffrage Alliance, 1902–1942.* Columbus: Ohio State University Press, 1990.

Britton, Nan. *The President's Daughter.* Bronx, NY: Ishi Press, 2008. Originally published by Elizabeth Britton, Ann Guild, Inc., 1931.

Brown, Nikki. *Private Politics and Public Voices: Black Women's Activism from World War I to the New Deal.* Bloomington: Indiana University Press, 2006.

Buhle, Paul, and Mari Jo Buhle. *The Concise History of Woman Suffrage: Selections from History of Woman Suffrage,* Champagne-Urbana: University of Illinois Press, 2005.

Camhi, Jane Jerome. *Women Against Women: American Anti-Suffragism, 1880–1920.* Brooklyn, NY: Carlson Publishing, 1994.

Catt, Carrie Chapman, and Nettie Shuler. *Woman Suffrage and Politics: The Inner Story of the Suffrage Movement.* New York: C. Scribner's Sons, 1926.

Cook, Blanche Wiesen. *Eleanor Roosevelt, Volume 1: 1884–1933*. New York: Penguin, 1993.

Cooper, John Milton, Jr. *Woodrow Wilson: A Biography*. New York: Vintage Books, 2011.

———. *Reconsidering Woodrow Wilson: Progressivism, Internationalism, War, and Peace*. Baltimore: Johns Hopkins University Press, 2008.

Cott, Nancy F. *The Grounding of Modern Feminism*. New Haven: Yale University Press, 1987.

Cox, James M. *Journey through My Years*. New York: Simon & Schuster, 1946.

Davis, Angela Y. *Women, Race, and Class*. New York: Vintage Books, 1983.

Dean, John W. *Warren G. Harding: The American Presidents Series*. New York: Times Books, Henry Holt and Co., 2004.

DeBow, Sarah Spence. *The History of the Case*. Booklet. Tennessee: n.p., 1920.

Delegard, Kirsten Marie. *Battling Miss Bolsheviki: The Origins of Female Conservatism in the United States*. Philadelphia: University of Pennsylvania Press, Inc., 2012.

Dickinson, W. Calvin, and Eloise R. Hitchcock. *A Bibliography of Tennessee History, 1973–1996*. Knoxville: University of Tennessee Press, 1999.

Douglass, Helen. *In Memoriam: Frederick Douglass*. Philadelphia: J.C. Yorston & Co, 1897.

Dowdy, G. Wayne. *Mayor Crump Don't Like It: Machine Politics in Memphis*. Jackson: University Press of Mississippi, 2008.

Doyle, Don H. *Nashville in the New South 1880–1930*. Knoxville: University of Tennessee Press, 1985.

DuBois, Ellen Carol. *Feminism and Suffrage: The Emergence of an Independent Women's Movement in America, 1848–1869*. Ithaca, NY: Cornell University Press, 1999.

———. *Harriot Stanton Blatch and the Winning of Woman Suffrage*. New Haven, CT: Yale University Press, 1999.

Dudden, Faye E. *Fighting Chance: The Struggle over Woman Suffrage and Black Suffrage in Reconstruction America*. Oxford and New York: Oxford University Press, 2011.

Faderman, Lillian. *To Believe in Women: What Lesbians Have Done for America—A History*. Boston: Houghton Mifflin, 1999.

Farnham, Christie. *Women of the American South: A Multicultural Reader*. New York: New York University Press, 1997.

Farrell, Grace. *Lillie Devereux Blake: Retracing a Life Erased*. Amherst: University of Massachusetts Press, 2009.

Finnegan, Margaret Mary. *Selling Suffrage: Consumer Culture and Votes for Women*. New York: Columbia University Press, 1999.

Fischer, Nick. *Spider Web: The Birth of American Anticommunism*. Champaign: University of Illinois Press, 2016.

Fleming, Thomas. *The Illusion of Victory: America in World War I*. New York: Basic Books, 2008.

Flexner, Eleanor, and Ellen Fitzpatrick. *Century of Struggle: The Woman's Rights Movement in the United States*. Cambridge, MA: Belknap Press of Harvard University Press, 1996.

Foner, Philip S., ed. *Frederick Douglass on Women's Rights*. Westport and London: Greenwood Press, 1976.

Fowler, Robert Booth. *Carrie Catt: Feminist Politician*. Boston: Northeastern University Press, 1986.

Francis, Megan Ming. *Civil Rights and the Making of the Modern American State*. Cambridge and New York: Cambridge University Press, 2014.

Franzen, Trisha. *Anna Howard Shaw: The Work of Woman Suffrage*. Champaign: University of Illinois Press, 2014.

Freeman, Sarah Wilkerson, Beverly G. Bond, and Laura Helper-Ferris. *Tennessee Women: Their Lives and Times*. Vol. 1. Athens: University of Georgia Press, 2009.

Fuller, Paul E. *Laura Clay and the Woman's Rights Movement*. Lexington: University of Kentucky Press, 1975.

Giboire, Clive. *Lovingly, Georgia: The Complete Correspondence of Georgia O'Keeffe and Anita Pollitzer*. New York: Simon & Schuster, 1990.

Giddings, Paula J. *Ida: A Sword Among Lions: Ida B. Wells and the Campaign against Lynching*. New York: Amistad, 2008.

Ginzberg, Lori D. *Elizabeth Cady Stanton: An American Life*. New York: Macmillan, 2010.

Goodier, Susan. *No Votes for Women: The New York State Anti-Suffrage Movement*. Champaign: University of Illinois Press, 2013.

Gordon, Ann D., ed. *The Selected Papers of Elizabeth Cady Stanton and Susan B. Anthony: Against an Aristocracy of Sex, 1866 to 1873*. New Brunswick: Rutgers University Press, 2000.

———. *The Trial of Susan B. Anthony*. Washington, D.C.: Federal Judicial Center, 2005.

Green, Elna C. *Southern Strategies: Southern Women and the Woman Suffrage Question*. Chapel Hill: University of North Carolina Press, 1997.

Gluck, Sherna Berger. *From Parlor to Prison*. New York: Monthly Review Press, 1985.

Hall, Sherry. *Warren G. Harding and the Marion Daily Star: How Newspapering Shaped a President*. Charleston, SC: The History Press, 2014.

Harper, Ida Husted. *History of Woman Suffrage, Volume 6 (1900–1920)*. New York: National American Woman Suffrage Association, 1922.

———. *The Life and Work of Susan B. Anthony*. Indianapolis and Kansas City: Bowen-Merrill Company, 1898.

Irwin, Inez Haynes. *The Story of Alice Paul and the National Woman's Party*. Fairfax, VA: Denlinger's Publishers, Ltd., 1964. Originally published 1921.

Jablonsky, Thomas J. *The Home, Heaven, and Mother Party: Female Anti-Suffragists in the United States, 1868–1920*. Brooklyn, NY: Carlson Publishing, 1994.

James, Edward T., Janet Wilson, and Paul S. Boyer, eds. *Notable American Women: A Biographical Dictionary, 1607–1950*. 3 vols. Cambridge, MA: Harvard University Press, 1971.

Kaplan, Carla. *Miss Anne in Harlem: The White Women of the Black Renaissance*. New York: HarperCollins, 2013.

Katzenstein, Caroline. *Lifting the Curtain: The State and National Woman Suffrage Campaigns in Pennsylvania as I Saw Them*. Philadelphia: Dorrance, 1955.

Keetley, Dawn, and John Pettegrew. *A Documentary History of American Feminism: 1900 to 1960*. Lanham, MD: Rowman & Littlefield, 2005.

Kern, Kathi. *Mrs. Stanton's Bible*. Ithaca, NY: Cornell University Press, 2001.

Keyssar, Alexander. *The Right to Vote: The Contested History of Democracy in the United States*. New York: Basic Books, 2000.

Kraditor, Aileen S. *The Ideas of the Woman Suffrage Movement, 1890–1920*. New York: Norton, 1965.

Kraft, Barbara S. *The Peace Ship: Henry Ford's Pacifist Adventure in the First World War*. New York: Macmillan/McGraw-Hill, 1978.

Lacey, Theresa Jensen. *Amazing Tennessee: Fascinating Facts . . . and Historical Oddities about the Volunteer State*. Nashville: Rutledge Hill Press, 2000.

Lash, Joseph P. *Eleanor and Franklin*. New York: W. W. Norton & Company, 2014.

Lemons, Gary L. *Womanist Forefathers: Frederick Douglass and W. E. B. Du Bois*. Albany: State University of New York Press, 2009.

Levin, Phyllis Lee. *Edith and Woodrow: The Wilson White House*. First edition. New York: Scribner, 2001.

Lindenmeyer, Kriste. *Ordinary Women, Extraordinary Lives: Women in American History*. Lanham, MD: Rowman & Littlefield, 2000.

Lutz, Alma. *Susan B. Anthony: Rebel, Crusader, Humanitarian*. Boston: Beacon Press, 1959.

McMillen, Sally. *Seneca Falls and the Origins of the Women's Rights Movement*. Oxford: Oxford University Press, 2008.

McWhirter, Cameron. *Red Summer: The Summer of 1919 and the Awakening of Black America.* New York: Henry Holt & Company, 2011.

Manning, Beverley. *Index to American Women Speakers, 1828–1978.* New York: Scarecrow Press, 1980.

Marshall, Susan E. *Splintered Sisterhood: Gender and Class in the Campaign against Woman Suffrage.* Madison: University of Wisconsin Press, 1997.

Midgley, Clare. *Women Against Slavery: The British Campaigns, 1780–1870.* London and New York: Routledge, 1995.

Miller, Kristie. *Ellen and Edith: Woodrow Wilson's First Ladies.* Lawrence: University Press of Kansas, 2015.

Milton, Abby Crawford. *Report of the Tennessee League of Women Voters: Containing a Full Account of the Suffrage Ratification Campaign.* Monograph, 1921.

Morello, John A. *Selling the President, 1920: Albert D. Lasker, Advertising, and the Election of Warren G. Harding.* Westport, CT: Praeger, 2001.

Naparsteck, Martin. *The Trial of Susan B. Anthony: An Illegal Vote, a Courtroom Conviction and a Step Toward Women's Suffrage.* Jefferson, NC: McFarland, 2014.

National American Woman Suffrage Association. *Victory: How Women Won It: A Centennial Symposium, 1840–1940.* New York: H. W. Wilson, 1940.

O'Neill, William L. *Everyone Was Brave: The Rise and Fall of Feminism in America.* New York: HarperCollins, 1969.

Painter, Nell Irvin. *Sojourner Truth: A Life, A Symbol.* New York: W. W. Norton & Company, 1997.

Park, Maud Wood. *Front Door Lobby.* Boston: Beacon Press, 1960.

Payne, Phillip G. *Dead Last: The Public Memory of Warren G. Harding's Scandalous Legacy.* Athens: Ohio University Press, 2009.

Peck, Mary Gray. *Carrie Chapman Catt: A Biography.* New York: H. W. Wilson, 1944.

Pietrusza, David. *1920: The Year of the Six Presidents.* New York: Basic Books, 2009.

Pollitzer, Anita. *A Woman on Paper: Georgia O'Keeffe.* New York: Simon & Schuster Books, 1988.

Roosevelt, Eleanor. *The Autobiography of Eleanor Roosevelt.* Boston: Da Capo Press, 1992.

Scott, Anne Firor. *The Southern Lady: From Pedestal to Politics, 1830–1930.* Charlottesville: University of Virginia Press, 1995.

Sicherman, Barbara, and Carol Hurd Green, eds. *Notable American Women: The Modern Period, A Biographical Dictionary.* Cambridge, MA: Harvard University Press, 1980.

Severance, Ben H. *Tennessee's Radical Army: The State Guard and Its Role in Reconstruction.* Knoxville: University of Tennessee Press, 2005.

Shawhan, Dorothy S., and Martha H. Swain. *Lucy Somerville Howorth: New Deal Lawyer, Politician, and Feminist from the South.* Baton Rouge: Louisiana State University Press, 2011.

Sheppard, Alice. *Cartooning for Suffrage.* Alburquerque: University of New Mexico Press, 1994.

Sherman, Joe. *A Thousand Voices: The Story of Nashville's Union Station.* Nashville: Rutledge Hill Press, 1987.

Showalter, Elaine. *These Modern Women: Autobiographical Essays from the Twenties.* New York: Feminist Press. 1989.

Sigerman, Harriet. *Elizabeth Cady Stanton: The Right Is Ours.* Oxford and New York: Oxford University Press, 2001.

Sklar, Kathryn Kish. *Women's Rights Emerges within the Anti-Slavery Movement, 1830–1870: A Brief History with Documents.* Boston: Bedford/St. Martin's, 2000.

Slayden, Ellen Maury. *Washington Wife: Journal of Ellen Maury Slayden from 1897–1919.* New York: Harper & Row, 1963.

Smith, Jean Edward. *FDR.* New York: Random House, 2007.

Sneider, Allison L. *Suffragists in an Imperial Age: U.S. Expansion and the Woman Question, 1870–1929.* Oxford: Oxford University Press, 2008.

Stanton, Elizabeth Cady. *Eighty Years and More (1898).* Boston: Northeastern University Press, 1993.

Stanton, Elizabeth Cady, and Harriot Stanton Blatch. *Elizabeth Cady Stanton as Revealed in Her Letters, Diary and Reminiscences.* New York: Harper & Brothers, 1922.

Stanton, Elizabeth Cady, Susan Brownell Anthony, Matilda Joslyn Gage, and Ida Husted Harper. *History of Woman Suffrage (1848–1861), Vol. 1.* Rochester, NY: Susan B. Anthony, 1887.

Stern, Madeleine B. *Purple Passage: The Life of Mrs. Frank Leslie.* Norman: University of Oklahoma Press, 1953.

Stevens, Doris. *Jailed for Freedom: American Women Win the Vote.* New York: Boni and Liveright, 1920. Rev ed. Edited by Carol O'Hare. Troutdale, OR: New Sage Press, 1995.

Tarbell, Ida M. *The Business of Being a Woman.* New York: MacMillan Co., 1915.

Taylor, A. Elizabeth. *The Woman Suffrage Movement in Tennessee.* New York: Bookman Associates, 1957.

Taylor, Clare. *British and American Abolitionists: An Episode in Transatlantic Understanding.* Edinburgh: Edinburgh University Press, 1974.

Terborg-Penn, Rosalyn. *African American Women in the Struggle for the Vote, 1850–1920.* Bloomington: Indiana University Press, 1998.

Terrell, Mary Church. *A Colored Woman in a White World.* Amherst, NY: Humanity Books, 2005. Originally published 1940.

Tetrault, Lisa. *The Myth of Seneca Falls: Memory and the Women's Suffrage Movement, 1848–1898.* Chapel Hill: University of North Carolina Press, 2014.

Upton, Harriet Taylor. *Random Recollections.* Manuscript, Alice Marshall Collection, Library, The Pennsylvania State University, Harrisburg.

Van Voris, Jacqueline. *Carrie Chapman Catt: A Public Life.* New York: Feminist Press, 1987.

Venet, Wendy Hamand. *Neither Ballots Nor Bullets: Women Abolitionists and the Civil War.* Charlottesville: University of Virginia Press, 1991.

Walton, Mary. *A Woman's Crusade: Alice Paul and the Battle for the Ballot.* New York: Macmillan, 2010.

Ware, Susan. *Beyond Suffrage: Women in the New Deal.* Cambridge, MA: Harvard University Press, 1987.

Wellman, Judith. *The Road to Seneca Falls: Elizabeth Cady Stanton and the First Woman's Rights Convention.* Champaign: University of Illinois Press, 2004.

Wells-Barnett, Ida B. *Crusade for Justice: The Autobiography of Ida B. Wells-Barnett.* Chicago: University of Chicago Press, 2013.

Wheeler, Marjorie Spruill. *Votes for Women!: The Woman Suffrage Movement in Tennessee, the South, and the Nation.* Knoxville: University of Tennessee Press, 1995.

———.*New Women of the New South: The Leaders of the Woman Suffrage Movement in the Southern States.* Oxford, UK, and New York: Oxford University Press, 1993.

Wilson, Edith Bolling Galt. *My Memoir.* Indianapolis: Bobbs-Merrill Company, 1939.

Wilson, Jan Doolittle. *The Women's Joint Congressional Committee and the Politics of Maternalism, 1920–30.* Urbana: University of Illinois Press, 2007.

Wineapple, Brenda. *Ecstatic Nation: Confidence, Crisis, and Compromise, 1848–1877.* New York: Harper Collins, 2013.

Yellin, Carol Lynn, Janann Sherman, and Ilene J Cornwell. *The Perfect 36: Tennessee Delivers Woman Suffrage.* Memphis: Serviceberry Press, 1998.

Zahniser, J. D., and Amelia R. Fry. *Alice Paul: Claiming Power.* New York and Oxford: Oxford University Press, 2014.

Zibart, Carl F. *Yesterday's Nashville.* Miami: E. A. Seemann Pub., 1976.

Journal Articles

Amidon, Kevin S. "Carrie Chapman Catt and the Evolutionary Politics of Sex and Race, 1885–1940," *Journal of the History of Ideas* 68, no. 2 (April 2007).

Behn, Beth A. "Woodrow Wilson's Conversion Experience: The President and the Federal Woman Suffrage Amendment," PhD dissertation, University of Massachusetts, Amherst, 2012.

Braden, Kenneth S. "The Wizard of Overton: Governor A. H. Roberts," *Tennessee Historical Quarterly* 43, no. 3 (Fall 1984): 273–94.

Bucy, Carol Sanford. "The Thrill of History Making: Suffrage Memories of Abby Crawford Milton," *Tennessee Historical Quarterly* 50 (1996).

Clevenger, Ima Fuchs. "Invention and Arrangement in the Public Address of Carrie Chapman Catt," PhD dissertation, University of Oklahoma, Norman, 1955.

Cott, Nancy. "Feminist Politics in the 1920s: The National Woman's Party," *The Journal of American History* 71, no. 1 (June 1984): 43–68.

Dodd, Lynda. "Parades, Pickets, and Prison: Alice Paul and the Virtues of Unruly Constitutional Citizenship," *Journal of Law & Politics* (2008): 339–433.

Eaton, Clement. "Breaking a Path for the Liberation of Women in the South," *The Georgia Review* 28, no. 2 (July 1, 1974): 187–99.

Fuller, Paul E. "Suffragist Vanquished: Laura Clay and the Nineteenth Amendment," *The Register of the Kentucky Historical Society* 93, no. 1 (January 1, 1995): 4–24.

Gilley, B. H. "Kate Gordon and Louisiana Woman Suffrage," *Louisiana History* 24, no. 3 (July 1983): 289–306.

Goodstein, Anita Shafer. "A Rare Alliance: African American and White Women in the Tennessee Elections of 1919 and 1920," *The Journal of Southern History* 64, no. 2 (1998): 219–46.

———. "Anne Dallas Dudley," *Franklin County Historical Review* 23, no. 1 (1992).

Graham, Sally Hunter. "Woodrow Wilson, Alice Paul, and the Woman Suffrage Movement," *Political Science Quarterly* 98, no. 4 (1983).

Green, Elna C. "The Rest of the Story: Kate Gordon and the Opposition to the Nineteenth Amendment in the South." *Louisiana History* 33, no. 2 (April 1, 1992): 171–89.

Hamand, Wendy F. "The Woman's National Loyal League: Feminist Abolitionists and the Civil War," *Civil War History* 35, no. 1 (March 1989): 39–58.

Howard, Jeanne. "Our Own Worst Enemies: Women Opposed To Woman Suffrage," *Journal of Sociology and Social Welfare* 9 (September 1982): 463–72.

Hurwitz, Edith F. "Carrie C. Catt's 'Suffrage Militancy.'" *Signs* 3, no. 3 (April 1, 1978): 739–43.

Kemp, Kathryn W. "Jean and Kate Gordon: New Orleans Social Reformers, 1898–1933," *Louisiana History* 24, no. 4 (Autumn, 1983): 389–401.

Johnson, Kenneth R. "Kate Gordon and the Woman-Suffrage Movement in the South," *The Journal of Southern History* 38, no. 3 (August 1, 1972): 365–92.

———. "White Racial Attitudes as a Factor in the Arguments against the Nineteenth Amendment," *Phylon* (1960–) 31, no. 1 (March 1, 1970): 31–37.

Jones, Robert B., and Mark E. Byrnes. "The 'Bitterest Fight': The Tennessee General Assembly and the Nineteenth Amendment," *Tennessee Historical Quarterly* 68, no. 3 (2009): 270–95.

Kennon, Donald R. "'An Apple of Discord': The Woman Question at the World's Anti-slavery Convention of 1840," *Slavery & Abolition* 5, no. 3 (December 1, 1984): 244–66.

Kirkley, Evelyn A. "'This Work Is God's Cause': Religion in the Southern Woman Suffrage Movement, 1880–1920." *Church History* 59, no. 4 (December 1, 1990): 507–22.

Louis, James. "Sue Shelton White and the Woman Suffrage Movement in Tennessee, 1913–1920," *Tennessee Historical Quarterly* 22, no. 2 (June 1963): 170–90.

Newman, Judith. "Mother Knew Best," *American History* (October 2010).

Pauley, Garth E. "W. E. B. Du Bois on Woman Suffrage: A Critical Analysis of His Crisis Writings," *Journal of Black Studies* 30, no. 3 (January 1, 2000): 383–410.

Quarles, Benjamin. "Frederick Douglass and the Woman's Rights Movement," *The Journal of Negro History* 25, no. 1 (January 1, 1940): 35–44.

Reichard, Gary W. "The Defeat of Governor Roberts," *Tennessee Historical Quarterly* 30 (1971): 94–109.

Russell, Janette C. "The Perfect 36: Tennessee and the Woman Suffrage Movement," *The West Tennessee Historical Society Papers* 49 (1995): 238–42.

Sims, Anastatia. "Powers That Pray and Powers That Prey: Tennessee and the Fight for Woman Suffrage," *Tennessee Historical Quarterly* (Winter 1991): 203–25.

———. "Beyond the Ballot: The Radical Vision of the Antisuffragists," in Wheeler, *Votes for Women!: The Woman Suffrage Movement in Tennessee, the South, and the Nation*. Knoxville: University of Tennessee Press, 1995, 105–28.

Sklar, Kathryn Kish. "Women Who Speak for an Entire Nation: American and British Women Compared at the World Anti-Slavery Convention, London, 1840," *Pacific Historical Review* 59, no. 4 (November 1990): 453–99.

Stinson, Robert. "Ida Tarbell and the Ambiguities of Feminism," *Pennsylvania Magazine of History and Biography* 101, no. 2 (April 1977): 217–39.

Thurner, Manuela. "Better Citizens Without the Ballot: American Anti-Suffrage Women and Their Rationale During the Progressive Era," *Journal of Women's History* 5, no.1 (Spring 1993): 33–60.

Yellin, Carol Lynn. "Countdown in Tennessee, 1920," *American Heritage* 30 (1978): 12–23, 27–35.

Yellin, Jean Fagan. "DuBois' Crisis and Woman's Suffrage," *Massachusetts Review* 14, no. 2 (Spring 1973): 365–75.

INDEX

THE WOMAN'S HOUR

Elaine Weiss

An Introduction to

The Woman's Hour

In the summer of 1920, one of the pivotal political battles in United States history unfolded in Nashville, Tennessee, as the Nineteenth Amendment, granting women the right to vote, was on the cusp of victory—or, possibly, defeat. The enfranchisement of half of the citizens of the nation was at stake, and it all came down to Tennessee. *The Woman's Hour* details the dramatic climax of the suffragists' seven-decade struggle for equal citizenship, bringing into focus the powerful forces arrayed against their cause. Employing all the color and drama of a great political novel, Elaine Weiss shows how the core themes of American history and current-day affairs—race, class, money, gender, states' rights, power, and democracy—all came into play in Nashville, Tennessee, as the Nineteenth Amendment was on the cusp of being ratified. Rich with vivid characters, including appearances by Susan B. Anthony, Woodrow Wilson, Warren Harding, Frederick Douglass, and Eleanor Roosevelt, *The Woman's Hour* reveals what it took for activists to win this crucial battle and how close they came to losing. *The Woman's Hour* is more than just a vivid work of history, it is an inspiration for everyone who continues the fight for justice and equal rights today.

3

A Conversation with
Elaine Weiss

The Woman's Hour *tells a dramatic story of a pivotal event in the twentieth century—one that people know happened but have little idea of how or why. What do you hope the reader will take away from your retelling the story of the suffragists and the Antis?*

The woman suffrage movement really is one of the great civil rights campaigns in our nation's history. It secured the enfranchisement of one-half of the nation's citizens—twenty-seven million women—and yet we know very little about it. It's rarely taught in school (and if it is mentioned, often cartoonishly over-simplified), and it's rarely portrayed in books of popular narrative history.

I hope readers of *The Woman's Hour* will begin to understand what this movement meant—its place in American history and the expansion of democracy, its role in changing attitudes towards women—and gain a deeper appreciation for the women who devoted their lives to what they called "The Cause." Readers will get to know these women in a more intimate way: their ambitions, their fears, their courage, the personal price they often paid for their stance against the status quo. Not just the famous leaders, but the devoted foot soldiers of the movement, in the small cities and towns of Tennessee and across the country. The men—some politicians, some in other professions—who truly believed in a broader democracy, and bravely stood up for women's equal rights. Readers will also come to know the "Antis"— the men, but especially the *women*—who opposed their sisters' holding the ballot. Readers will come away with a visceral sense of what it was like to be in that final confrontation in Nashville: the heat and tension and fear; the political pressures bearing down; the enormous stakes involved. And the real uncertainty of the outcome.

Many have forgotten that it took more than seventy years for women to obtain the right to vote, and far fewer people know that it came down to the six-week battle in one state, Tennessee. In the book you show how all the core elements of American history—race, class, money, gender, states' rights, and power itself—play their roles in the events of August 1920. Could you share some examples of this?

We think we know how women won the vote: A bunch of women met at Seneca Falls in hoop skirts and bonnets, then flash-forward to some marches and a few picturesque picket signs, and *poof*—men decided to give their mothers, wives, and daughters the gift of the vote. That's not how it happened at all. It took seven decades of ceaseless, fearless agitation by three generations of women activists in more than nine-hundred local, state, and national campaigns to win the vote. These women were often ostracized by their families and churches for their suffrage stance; they were pelted with rotten eggs and pilloried in the press; they were imprisoned and force fed and beaten. In the process of challenging political norms and cultural taboos and gender stereotypes, the suffragists became adept politicians and great orators and extraordinary leaders. There are many lessons we can—and should—learn from their courage and political sagacity.

Seventy-two years after Elizabeth Cady Stanton, together with Frederick Douglass at Seneca Falls, demanded that women be allowed to vote, the final battle to ratify the Nineteenth Amendment to the U.S. Constitution was waged in Nashville in the summer of 1920. Because this was the last stand, all the forces—supporting and opposing the federal amendment—gathered in Nashville to slug it out. And, because this last battle was fought in the South, there was tremendous opposition to the Nineteenth Amendment on racist grounds: woman suffrage would allow black women to vote (at least on paper). So all the core elements of American history—race, class, money, gender, states' rights, and even the ghosts of the Civil War— converge and become explosive in Nashville.

How did you come to this story?

I stumbled upon the story of the Tennessee ratification vote while researching something else, deep in the Library of Congress. I was tracing how a large bequest to the suffrage cause, made by a celebrated New York woman publisher, was spent. I found that some of the money was spent in the campaign to ratify the Nineteenth Amendment, and toward funding that last battle in Nashville. So I steered away from the publisher (though she does make an appearance in the book), realizing that the better story was what happened in Tennessee—those wild six weeks—and this would allow me to explore the entire suffrage movement, which, surprisingly, has not received much attention in popular historical writing.

This is not just a book about women's history, but rather a larger look at how we have evolved as a democracy and reacted to those asking for inclusion—a reaction we see playing out again and again. Could you explain further?

At the outset of our democratic experiment, "We the People" really meant "We the White, Wealthy Men"—no one else had a voice, or had a vote. In the almost two-and-a-half centuries since, we've seen great pushes to expand that circle, to extend full rights to all American citizens—civil rights and voting rights—but these efforts have been met with equally strong resistance to such widening.

The vote is power, and those who already have power don't care to share it—it's that simple and stark. Restricting certain groups from voting is a tactic long used for political party advantage. We see it in Nashville in 1920, and it's happening again now. It's a constant struggle.

How did the woman suffrage movement affect later movements, such as Civil Rights, or today's Black Lives Matter and Women's March movements? What precedents, if any, did the suffragists set for political activism?

The campaign for woman suffrage was not only a political movement, though the goal and methods were political. It was also a long-term effort to alter societal norms and cultural customs concerning women's roles.

The genius of the woman suffrage movement—its strategies, lobbying tactics, public education efforts, non-violent protest (demonstrations, marches, picketing, civil disobedience)—would prove to be a valuable template for later civil rights campaigns of the twentieth and twenty-first centuries. The African-American civil rights era, gay rights campaigns, and efforts to secure women's reproductive rights and marriage equality—all took a page from the suffragists, in both their public protests and their political maneuvers.

QUESTIONS FOR DISCUSSION

1. The two branches of the American suffrage movement—the National American Woman Suffrage Association (led by Carrie Catt) and the National Woman's Party (led by Alice Paul)—took different approaches towards their mutual goal of winning the vote. Do you think one group was more effective than the other? Why?

2. If you were a suffragist in 1920, do you think you'd align yourself with the NAWSA or the Woman's Party? (Both women and men were supporters). Why? What attracted women, on the other hand, to the "Antis"? Do you think their fears were unfounded?

3. The suffragists campaigned before there were cell phones; no internet, no social media, not even radio. Can you imagine trying to promote today's causes with these limitations?

4. *The Woman's Hour* describes an important step in our country's evolution as a democracy. What other steps does our democracy still need to take?

5. Although we treasure our self-image as a nation built upon the bedrock of participatory democracy, our history proves we're conflicted about who has the right to participate. Voter suppression is a hot topic today. Do you think we consciously make it harder for some citizens to vote? Is voter suppression a threat to our democracy, or just the usual game political parties play?

6. Hundreds of suffragists were assaulted, attacked, and jailed for demanding the right to vote. Have you ever participated in a protest against government policies? Did you suffer any consequences for your

actions? Would you be willing to go to prison to protest injustice or to promote a cause you think important?

7. Those opposed to woman suffrage often used religious arguments to warn that expanding women's rights, including the vote, violated Biblical teachings and went against "God's Plan" (women belong in the home, not in the public sphere). Do you think religious rationales should be used in forming public policy today?

8. Were the suffragists correct in keeping their eyes on the prize—pursuing the vote for the majority of American women—even if that meant making moral compromises and abandoning some of their own ideals? Can the suffragists' use of racist rationales to win the support of Southern legislators be justified? What are your thoughts on the suffragists' use of racist rationales to win the support of Southern legislators?

9. Some corporations clearly felt threatened by the prospect of women voters, and worked to influence public opinion and legislative action. The suffragists often complained that corporate interests were secretly financing anti-suffrage campaigns around the country. Do you see any similarities in what the suffragists faced then and the modern phenomenon of "dark money" entering political campaigns today?

10. The suffragists touted the benefits of allowing women to vote by maintaining that women would clean up corruption in politics and insist upon better laws protecting families and children. Carrie Catt believed women voters would bring about an end to war. Do you think women voters have improved our political system? In what ways?

11. If the issue of women's political equality—specifically the right to vote—was being decided today, and, as in 1920, only men were given the power to decide, do you think the amendment would pass?

12. Voter participation in the United States is well below other democratic nations. Many Americans, like the suffragists and subsequent civil rights workers, fought long and hard to win the right to vote. Many have died defending our freedoms. Some democracies impose a fine for not voting. Do think voting should be a mandatory responsibility of every eligible U.S. citizen?

13. Do you think the U.S Constitution should be changed in any way? What amendments would you like to see considered?